Peterson's®

MASTER THE™
MILITARY FLIGHT
APTITUDE TESTS

9TH EDITION

Dr. Sonya "Lethal" McMullen—Embry-Riddle Aeronautical University

Dr. Mac "Raven" McMullen—The Pennsylvania State University

About Peterson's

Peterson's®, a Nelnet company, has been your trusted educational publisher for over 50 years. It's a milestone we're quite proud of, as we continue to offer the most accurate, dependable, high-quality educational content in the field, providing you with everything you need to succeed. No matter where you are on your academic or professional path, you can rely on Peterson's for its books, online information, expert test-prep tools, the most up-to-date education exploration data, and the highest quality career success resources—everything you need to achieve your education goals. For our complete line of products, visit www.petersons.com.

For more information about Peterson's range of educational products, contact Peterson's, 3 Columbia Circle, Suite 205, Albany, NY 12203, 800-338-3282 Ext. 54229; or find us online at www.petersons.com.

ISBN-13: 978-0-7689-4113-5

Printed in the United States of America

10 9 8 7 6 5 4 3 2 1   19 18 17

Ninth Edition

Contents

COMMENTS FROM THE AUTHORS

When we designed this book, we had multiple audiences in mind. Some of you may have a very clear idea of your career focus and the path you wish to pursue, others may be exploring all of the possibilities available, and perhaps many of you fall somewhere in between. The purpose of this book is not only to provide you with guidance for taking the various military flight aptitude tests but also to give you more information about service in the various branches of the armed forces, what it means to be an Officer or Warrant Officer, clues about commissioning sources, and long-term expectations for your career beyond aviation duties. Some of the material provided here represents information that our mentors shared with us when we served, or things we wish we had known or considered earlier in our process of becoming active-duty officers. Our intent is not to try to sway your decision making in any particular direction, but only to share information and provide you with questions to seek answers to prior to making any decision about your future career path.

As such, this book has six chapters. The first is an overview of the branches of service, types of service, and commissioning options. Chapter 1 also includes a little insight regarding the long-term expectations for your career and things to plan ahead for in the future. Chapter 2 introduces you to the various service aviation training programs and the requirements of each. Chapter 3 provides a general introduction to the different question types you will encounter on the military flight exams. Chapters 4, 5, and 6 are each devoted to a single assessment exam. Chapter 4 is the Air Force Officer Qualifying Exam Form T and includes information about the exam, how the results are used, and a practice test with some tips for success. Chapter 5 is the Navy ASTB-E and includes a similar discussion of the exam with the practice test and answer key at the end of the chapter. Chapter 6 is the Army SIFT description, practice test, and answer key. Included in the last three chapters are notes that refer you to similar subtests in the book or additional references should you need more practice in specific areas. We certainly encourage you to use all chapters in the book and think about taking all of the tests. Many opportunities await you!

We hope the information in this book serves you well on your journey. A career in the armed forces, whether it be in aviation or in any other specialty, is an honorable calling like no other. In our experience, we met and worked with some amazing people and did some pretty cool things in our combined 29 years of service. We wish only the same for you!

Before You Begin

Congratulations! You have in your hands a powerful tool to ensure your best chances of getting a great score on one of the military flight aptitude tests. By taking time to work on the sample exercises in this book, studying the strategies and techniques for tackling each question type, and taking the full-length practice test and reviewing the answers and explanations, you will gain experience in answering real test questions and give yourself a significant advantage in achieving a top-notch score on your military flight aptitude test.

This book contains information on the following topics:

- Careers in military aviation, including how to qualify, pay and benefits
- Flight training in the Air Force, Army, Navy, Marine Corps, and Coast Guard
- Strategies for tackling multiple-choice test questions
- The Air Force Officer Qualifying Test (AFOQT Form T) and its subtests
- The Navy and Marine Corps Aviation Selection Test Battery (ASTB-E) and its subtests
- The Selection Instrument for Flight Training (SIFT) and its subtests

HOW TO USE THIS BOOK

The book is designed as a self-training course, complete with test-taking tips and strategies, exercises, and three full-length practice tests. Every answer in the book comes with a detailed explanation. You learn immediately why a correct answer is correct and why a wrong answer is wrong. Studying the answer explanations for all the questions in your test—even those you answer correctly—will serve as a course in itself.

- **Chapters 1 and 2** provide an overview of the opportunities and benefits available to military pilots, combat systems officers, and flight officers. Officer rank structure, pay and benefits, and general commissioning requirements are covered in detail. You'll also find information about how to get on the path to a career in military aviation, including available training and programs, for each branch of the Armed Forces.
- **Chapter 3** explains the kinds of questions you can expect on the AFOQT, ASTB-E, and SIFT. We include examples of every question type you are likely to encounter. This section also contains sample questions and practice exercises with detailed answer explanations, as well as strategies for answering multiple-choice questions.

- **Chapters 4, 5, and 6** explain three different military flight aptitude tests: the AFOQT, ASTB-E, and SIFT, respectively. You'll find comprehensive information about each test, including the number of questions you'll encounter and the length of every subtest, followed by full-length AFOQT, ASTB-E, and SIFT practice tests. Each practice test is followed by an answer key with detailed explanations. For the AFOQT, you'll also find 110 sample Self-Description Inventory questions. To accurately measure your performance on these practice tests, be sure to adhere strictly to the stated time limits for each subtest.

SPECIAL STUDY FEATURES

Master the™ Military Flight Aptitude Tests is designed to be as user-friendly as it is complete. To this end, it includes these features to make your preparation more efficient.

Overview

Each chapter begins with a bulleted overview listing the topics covered in the chapter. This allows you to quickly target the areas in which you are most interested.

Summing It Up

Each chapter ends with a point-by-point summary that captures the most important points in the chapter. The summaries offer a convenient way to review key points.

YOU'RE WELL ON YOUR WAY TO SUCCESS

You've made the decision to seek a career in military aviation and have taken a very important step in the process. *Master the™ Military Flight Aptitude Tests* will help you get on the path you need to take to achieve your goal—from scoring high on your exam to becoming a military pilot, combat systems officer, or flight officer in the U.S. Armed Forces.

GIVE US YOUR FEEDBACK

Peterson's publishes a full line of resources to help guide you through the career search process. Peterson's publications can be found at your local bookstore, library, and high school or college guidance office. You can also access us online at **www.petersons.com**. We welcome any comments or suggestions you may have about this publication.

Peterson's Publishing
3 Columbia Circle, Suite 205
Albany, NY 12203
E-mail: custsvc@petersons.com

Becoming an Officer or Warrant Officer in the U.S. Armed Forces

OVERVIEW

- **Branches of Service**
- **Service Types**
- **The Officer Corps**
- **Commissioning Sources**
- **Professional Development**
- **Summing It Up**

Thousands of individuals apply and compete for slots to serve in the armed forces every year. There are tremendous opportunities for those wanting to serve in the military, including those in aviation careers. Each branch of the armed services has some type of aviation capability and a variety of flying missions. To begin the journey of seeking such opportunities, it is important to first understand some of the basics about each branch of the armed services, the types of duty for which you can sign up and be obligated, ways in which to become an officer or warrant officer, and other helpful information about what to expect when you achieve the first milestone. This chapter is designed to give you a broader view of military service and what is needed beyond the basic requirements to earn an opportunity to enter aviation training.

BRANCHES OF SERVICE

The United States Army

The precursor to the United States Army was the Continental Army, founded by the Second Continental Congress in 1775 to protect the thirteen original colonies. The original intent of the Army was to supplement local militia forces. The Army was directed by a board of five civilians and was structured with two types of troops: "Continentals," who were the long-serving enlisted personnel with the most training, and the militia forces, who provided support to the Continentals when needed and returned home after the need for their support ended. Following the American Revolution, all but two regiments of the Army were disbanded in 1783. In 1787, the U.S. Constitution then placed the military forces under the control of the President as the Commander in Chief, and the Department of War was established in 1789 for administration of the armed forces. In 1792, the two remaining regiments of the Continental Army served as the core of the Legion of the United States. The Legion of the United States served as the foundation for the United States Army formed in 1796.

It could be argued that Army aviation dates back to the Civil and Spanish-American Wars and the use of tethered balloons to spy on enemy positions. However, the Army did not have a formal aviation organization until 1907, when the Aeronautical Division of the Signal Corps was established. In 1911, Congress passed appropriations for aeronautics and, in 1914, created the Aviation Section of the Signal Corps. The Army attempted its first use of the airplane in combat operations in Mexico in 1916. When the U.S. entered World War I (WWI), it did so with a single unit, the 1st Aero Squadron. By 1918, aviation was removed from the Signal Corps, and the U.S. Army Air Service was formed through an executive order. Although the Army Air Service was composed of 740 aircraft and 195,000 personnel by the end of WWI, the size was dramatically reduced following combat operations.

In the years between WWI and World War II (WWII), the Army Reorganization Act of 1920 made the Air Service an Army combatant unit. The Air Corps Act of 1926 transformed the Air Service into the Army Air Corps, which trained and provided logistical support for all air units; however, the flying units themselves fell under the command of the various Army units. Entering into WWII, the Army had 24,000 aviation personnel and 1,500 aircraft. Rapid expansion orders increased air forces to 16 units, 243 combat groups, 2.4 million personnel, and approximately 80,000 aircraft for combat operations. Following WWII combat operations, the Army Air Corps was again reduced to approximately 300,000 personnel.

The size of the Army's aviation units was dramatically reduced with the passage of the National Security Act of 1947, which formed the United States Air Force. Today, the U.S. Army operates multiple aircraft platforms, predominately rotorcraft (helicopters) and unmanned aerial systems (UAS). As stated on its web page (**https://www.army.mil/aviation/modern/index.html**), the role of the Army Aviation branch is to "find, fix, and destroy an enemy through fire and maneuver and to provide combat support and combat service support in coordinated operations as an integral member of the combined arms team fully integrated within joint operational framework."

GET THE FACTS

For more information about U.S. Army aviation history, please see the following websites:

- **https://www.army.mil/aviation/**
- **https://www.army.mil/aviation/timeline/index.html**

The United States Navy (USN)

It might be surprising to know that of all of the military services, the U.S. Navy owns and operates the most aircraft! The Navy traces much of its aviation heritage to Glenn Curtiss, an aviation inventor who, in 1911, was permitted to use North Island in San Diego (home to the current Naval Air

Station North Island), where he offered free flight training to the Army and Navy. Among his many accomplishments, Curtiss is created with the development of the seaplane. Curtiss hired Eugene Ely, a test pilot, to take off from the USS *Birmingham*, and in 1911, Ely made the first successful airplane landing on the USS *Pennsylvania*.

Naval aviation has played an important role in the military since its early inception, starting in France in WWI. Lt. Kenneth Whiting led a detachment to France in 1917 and contributed to the antisubmarine warfare. During WWI, the Navy sent 17,524 aviation-related personnel overseas. In addition to antisubmarine and mine patrols, the Navy conducted bombing raids of German submarine bases. The Navy also established the Naval Aircraft Factory to produce aircraft and for research and development.

During the first half of the twentieth century, the Navy was also reliant on lighter-than-air aircraft, or dirigibles, as part of its aviation operations. Dirigibles provided long-duration mission profiles in terms of flight time and distance. Although vulnerable to ground and in-air fire and weather, dirigibles were very successful as ocean patrol craft to aid in spotting enemy vessels. Scout heavier-than-air aircraft were also launched from later models of dirigibles, enhancing their overall capability.

Carrier aircraft played a significant role in the Pacific during WWII and continue to do so today. Fixed-wing and rotorcraft are essential for modern naval operations. The U.S. Navy is also incorporating new UAS capabilities as well.

GET THE FACTS

For more information about U.S. Navy aviation history, visit the Naval History and Heritage Command website:

http://www.history.navy.mil//research/histories/naval-aviation-history.html

The United States Marine Corps (USMC)

Like the Army, the United States Marine Corps (USMC) was founded by the Second Continental Congress in 1775 to protect the thirteen original colonies. The Continental Marines did not have a long history, as they were disbanded with the Navy and its sale of ships at the conclusion of the Revolutionary War. Of important note is the Marine Corps' relationship with the Navy. The Marine Corps operates within the Department of the Navy—it is not a separate service like the Army or Air Force. As such, the Marine Corps is reliant on the Navy for its budget and other purposes. This relationship is also key for training and will be discussed in more detail in later sections.

The USMC was reestablished in July 1798 as part of a small conflict with France. The Marines participated in nearly every conflict through the American Civil War and also saw action overseas at the end of the nineteenth century in the Orient, Caribbean, and the Spanish-American War. They were also deployed in the Philippines and China at the turn of the century.

Marine Corps aviation dates to May 22, 1912, when Marine First Lieutenant Alfred Cunningham reported to Aviation Camp in Annapolis, Maryland, for training as a naval aviator. Cunningham became one of the six aviators (and the first Marine) who comprised the aviator unit between 1912 and 1913. Their first mission with the naval fleet was flying maneuvers over Guantanamo, Cuba, during which they dropped missiles, and took photographs and located submerged submarines without being detected.

In April 1917, the Marine Aeronautic Company was organized at the Philadelphia Navy Yard. The first fully equipped aviation unit ordered to deploy was the First Marine Aeronautic Company, first transferred in 1918. Four Marine Corps aviation squadrons conducted daylight bombing raids in France near the end of WWI.

Between WWI and WWII, Marine Corps aviation units were the only units to see combat. Marine aviation units served in Santo Domingo from 1919 to 1924, Haiti from 1919 to 1934, Nicaragua from 1927 until 1933, and Guam en route to China in 1921. Marine Corps aviation devised dive bombing techniques, air to ground communications, and troop and supply cargo transport by air. As a result of the growing importance of the mission, the Division of Aviation was established in 1936. Marine aviators distinguished themselves in the Pacific theater during WWII, being credited with having shot down 2,355 aircraft and producing 121 aces.

GET THE FACTS

For more information about U.S. Marine Corps aviation history, visit the USMC History and Heritage page:

http://www.marines.com/history-heritage

The United States Coast Guard (USCG)

The U.S. Coast Guard (USCG) is the only branch of the armed forces that operates under the jurisdiction of the Department of Homeland Security. The Coast Guard is actually the amalgam of various federal services: the U.S. Lighthouse Service, formed in 1789; the Revenue Cutter Service, formed in 1790; the U.S Life-Saving Service, formed in 1848; the Bureau of Navigation, formed in 1884; and the Steamship Inspection Service, formed in 1871. With the passing of the Coast Guard Act in January 1915, the Revenue Cutter Service was combined with the Life-Saving Service to form the United States Coast Guard.

U.S. Coast Guard aviation dates to 1915, when Lieutenants Elmer Stone and Norman Hall met with Glenn Curtiss at Newport News, Virginia, to discuss their plans to use aircraft to augment their missions. In 1916, Congress authorized the formation of ten Coast Guard air stations but appropriated no funding for the effort. Nevertheless, Coast Guard aviators did serve with the Navy during WWI. In May 1919, four NC-4 Curtiss Seaplanes began an experimental flight to cross the Atlantic, with Coast Guard Lt. Stone piloting the only aircraft to successfully make the journey.

In 1925, Lt. Commander C. G. Von Paulsen demonstrated the use of an aircraft, a Vought UO-1, to detect smuggling. Due to the interest in the prevention of alcohol smuggling during Prohibition, Congress appropriated $152,000 for five Coast Guard aircraft and created an aviation mission for the service. Then in 1928, an aviation section with the purpose of rescue was established at USCG headquarters with Hall, now a Commander, in charge.

During WWII, the Coast Guard played a key role in national defense, extending its troops all the way to Greenland. Missions included airfield and enemy station surveillance, search and rescue, and U-boat detection. Interest in the development of helicopters for research and rescue operations began in the Coast Guard as early as 1941, but the War delayed progress until 1943, when the Coast Guard trained on Sikorsky HNS-1 and HOS-1 helicopters for antisubmarine warfare missions. The cutter *Cobb* was the first to participate in shipboard helicopter tests. Today the USCG operates 200 aircraft of five aircraft types, and its flying community consists of approximately 800 pilots and 2,500 enlisted support personnel. The aircraft and personnel operate from 24 Air Stations.

GET THE FACTS

For more information about U.S. Coast Guard aviation history, visit these two websites:

- **http://www.uscg.mil/history/aviationindex.asp**
- **http://uscgaviationhistory.aoptero.org/**

The United States Air Force (USAF)

The U.S. Air Force (USAF) traces its history back to the Army Air Corps (see previous section on the U.S. Army). It was established as a separate military service by the National Security Act of 1947. In the modern era, the Air Force has evolved to operate and maintain not only a variety of manned aircraft and unmanned aerial systems (UAS) but space systems as well. The Air Force also has a significant cyberwarfare mission. By far, the largest mission area of the Air Force revolves around the air mission in establishing and maintaining air superiority over a designated region, combat support of ground forces, and the transport of personnel, equipment, and supplies. Air Force Space Command is a force multiplier for these missions by operating and maintaining a network of communications satellites, the Global Positioning System (GPS) satellite network, weather satellites, early warning satellites, and other space-based capabilities.

GET THE FACTS

For more information about U.S. Air Force history, visit these websites:

- **http://www.afhistory.af.mil/AboutUs/FactSheets/tabid/3323/Article/458985/evolution-of-the-department-of-the-air-force.aspx**
- **http://www.afhistory.af.mil/FAQs/FactSheets/tabid/3323/Article/458972/timeline-a-century-of-air-and-space-power-1903-2003.aspx**

The Air Force provides updated data on its current organizational structure by mission type. For the 2012–2019 time period, the Air Force is projecting the following organizational data, as shown in Table 1.1.

Table 1.1

USAF Wing Force Structure (2012)				
Wing Mission Type	**U.S. Based**	**Overseas Based**	**Active Duty**	**Reserve**
Fighter	15	6	16	5
Bomber	6	0	6	0
Airlift	22	2	10	14
Air Refueling	7	1	3	5
Special Operations	6	0	5	1
Reconnaissance	1	0	1	0
Flight Training	5	0	5	0
Flight Test	0	0	0	0
Rescue	1	0	0	1
Space & Missile	4	0	3	1
Composite	11	2	11	2
Other	10	0	7	3
Source: http://www.afhra.af.mil/shared/media/document/AFD-110524-036.pdf				

SERVICE TYPES

At the present time, there are a number of ways in which to serve in the armed forces. These decisions are sometimes based on personal preference, professional goals, and opportunities available through the various services. There are instances throughout history when there were fewer positions available for active duty forces, as the force level numbers (number of personnel serving at any given time or force strength) are determined by Congress and heavily budget-driven. As such, there are times when the active duty force is subject to a drawdown, or a reduction in number; however, the Reserves and Guard may still seek to retain military expertise and hire more personnel. The Reserves are often considered a transition from active duty to the private sector, yet that does not preclude individuals who may not have served on active duty joining the Reserves. It is best to explore all possible options before signing any contracts obligating you to service.

Active Duty

Active duty is a full-time career commitment. In most instances, active duty members live near or on a base and work in a military or government environment. The schedule is dependent on the mission, meaning it is not necessary to work a Monday through Friday 0730 to 1630 job. There might be shift work, weekend shifts, travel, and likely deployments (with and without significant notice). Active duty service members earn 30 days of leave (vacation) per year to travel; however, there are instances in which you must use these days over weekends to account for missed scheduled duty.

Service Commitments

In contrast to how enlisted personnel serve: for specific time frames, such as an enlistment for four years, officer service commitments vary widely. Typically, an officer is committed to four years of active duty service and four years of inactive reserve, during which the member has no duty obligation yet could be recalled to active duty in the event of national security requirements. The four-year commitment might also be dependent on when the service member finished his or her training, not when active duty began, thus extending the time he or she must serve. In other cases, due to its extensive nature and the cost involved, certain training will incur additional service commitments. For example, Air Force flight training incurs a minimum eight-year commitment to begin once the service member is fully mission qualified. A commitment obligation of this type might mean that the individual is not eligible to leave active duty until he or she has served 12 or more years. It is important to ask the various service recruiters about service commitment details as part of the research process.

Active duty service also has limitations relative to job and duty location choices. At various times in your career as you become eligible for reassignment, typically every three years on average, you have an opportunity to fill out a "preference sheet" that rank orders the currently available positions and those you would prefer. Your commanding officer then has the opportunity to comment on these preferences and your next assignment with the personnel center. However, this is no guarantee that you will get any of your desired choices, as the needs of the service come before those of particular service members. In cases in which there is a dire need to move close to one's family because of a serious illness or other circumstances, it is sometimes possible to arrange for humanitarian assignments to allow you to time to help, but these are rare instances and could negatively affect your overall career progression.

That being said, active duty offers the most opportunities for overseas assignments and a broad range of careers, some of which are not available in the Reserves or Guard. Although there are many sacrifices that are made to serve in the active duty ranks, the opportunities are equally amazing. In addition, the current active duty retirement is the only retirement that you will collect immediately upon retirement as well as continued healthcare insurance. Eligibility begins after twenty years of service, regardless of an individual's age at that time. All other retirements are delayed until you reach a particular age. Note that retirement benefits have been the subject of much political debate in recent years. As such, you will need to research the latest developments regarding this topic and ensure you discuss it thoroughly before signing any service agreement.

Reserves

Each branch of the armed forces has a Reserve component to augment its ranks. There are three types of status in the Reserve: Ready Reserve, Standby Reserve, and Retired Reserve. Within the Ready Reserve, there are three additional categories: Selected Reserve, Individual Ready Reserve (IRR), and Inactive National Guard (ING). The ING is a category used only by the Army, but its status is similar to that of the IRR. Individuals with IRR status do not participate in "drill" or annual training for pay or retirement points and cannot be promoted. They are required to present themselves once per year with their unit and can be recalled to service in the event of a mobilization. Those individuals who have completed four years of active duty service will also be assigned to IRR for another four years to complete their service commitment but will not have to report to a unit annually.

The Selected Reserve is composed of the Active Guard and Reserve (AGR), which is a broad category of personnel. AGR personnel serve full-time in administrative or training roles as part of Reserve or Guard units. AGR personnel are also assigned a billet (personnel slot) for mobilization in a one-weekend-a-month and a two-week-per-year position. For the Navy Reserve, the duty time is structured a little differently, as individuals might have to participate in sea duty and will be subject to the schedule of the ship to which they are assigned. The benefit of this career choice is that Selected Reserve members will likely not move as often as an active duty member.

Individual Mobilization Augmentees (IMAs) are personnel who are assigned to support active duty units. IMAs are likely to be called up in the event of combat operations to support their units. IMA duty requires individuals to serve with their unit two weeks per year. IMAs must earn 40 points per year toward retirement, and, in many cases, even though they might be working with their unit, they may not be paid for this investment in time. In some cases, though, IMAs may be able to earn points by taking correspondence courses.

Selective Reserve Units are the most commonly known and understood form of "Reservist" or "Guardsman." Selective Reserve Unit personnel are those who serve one weekend per month and two weeks per year. The benefit here is that on the weekend duty days, you are paid "two for one," meaning you actually earn four days of pay for the two weekend days of duty. A total of 40 "drills" are required per year. Both Reserve and Guard units deploy, so be prepared for that possibility. Before signing up, check the unit drill schedule, as not all activities fall on the weekends. If you are going to school or have another job, you must ensure the schedules do not conflict.

For each of these positions, with the exception of IRR, you must maintain active-duty health and fitness standards as part of this commitment. Reserve members are subject to deployment in support of combat operations around the globe. There are quite a number of variances in assignment selection and overall career progression. A benefit when you sign a contract is that you have more say in your duty assignment. Discuss your options carefully with the various services recruiters. For Guard personnel, each state offers a variety of benefits to its Guardsmen. Check with each state to ascertain specific benefits for service beyond those provided by the Veteran's Administration.

THE OFFICER CORPS

Commissioned Officers

The Officer Corps is the leadership arm of the military. Historically, officers were prominent members of society, aristocrats, or those who held some higher order of social standing. Rulers and government leaders would commission individuals to raise forces to defend a region or deploy at the direction of the ruling class. This was true even through the American Civil War, when plantation owners and other eminent professionals formed and trained militia units to serve either the Union or Confederate Armies. Prior to the advent of public and private universities in the United States, the military academies represented some of the best higher education opportunities possible in the nation, but they were open only to men at the time, and earning an appointment was a highly competitive task.

Today, social status no longer dictates the appointment of officers in the U.S. However, the Officer Corps still represents an elite group of highly trained leaders dedicated to the service of the nation. As such, the expectations for initial health, physical fitness, education, personal character, and leadership skills are of primary importance. Those expectations do not lessen once selected. In fact, the expectations for training performance, maintaining fitness, personal conduct, continued education, and service continue throughout one's career. Only those with the highest levels of personal motivation and discipline to achieve should seek a commission in any branch of the armed services.

Being an officer is not just about your personal performance—you are a leader. You will likely be responsible for others at various points in your career. The performance of your organization and your personnel will reflect upon you as an officer and leader. It is not enough to be a highly skilled specialist in your area of expertise, although this is also expected; you must lead. The well-being of the families of your personnel are also your responsibility. As an officer, in addition to your military service obligations, you are expected to have close ties to the community and volunteer your time in non-work-related base or community service. All of these components make for a well-rounded officer.

There are three tiers of officers:

1. Company Grade officers
2. Field Grade Officers
3. Flag or General officers

The rank structure is shown in Table 1.2. Company Grade officers are the most junior and are grades O-1 through O-3. Field Grade officers are the grades of O-4 through O-6, and Flag or General Officers are O-7 through O-10. Attaining the rank of O-4 and above is an ever-increasing challenge. The current structure of the active duty forces dictates that you must attain the next higher rank within a certain time period in your career, or your career will end, even if you have not yet reached retirement eligibility. This is something to consider as you make decisions about assignments, training and education opportunities, and the overall performance of your duties, as they will affect whether you are able to remain in service until you are eligible for retirement.

Table 1.2

Officer Rank Structure		
Pay Grade	**Army, Marine Corps, & Air Force**	**Navy & Coast Guard**
O-10	General	Admiral
O-9	Lieutenant General	Vice Admiral
O-8	Major General	Rear Admiral Upper Half
O-7	Brigadier General	Rear Admiral Lower Half
O-6	Colonel	Captain
O-5	Lieutenant Colonel	Commander
O-4	Major	Lieutenant Commander
O-3	Captain	Lieutenant
O-2	First Lieutenant	Lieutenant Junior Grade
O-1	Second Lieutenant	Ensign

At the present time, the majority of aviators, especially those who fly the aircraft, are Officers or Warrant Officers. There are a number of aircrew personnel who are enlisted personnel and serve in a variety of non-pilot roles. The additional responsibility of operating some of the most advanced aircraft ever designed in the most adverse of environments only adds to the challenge of the career as a military officer and aviator. The path is not for everyone, so it is recommended that you talk to as many current and former military aviation personnel as possible to learn about the career and all that will be asked of you throughout your service.

Officer Pay

This section will focus on active duty military pay. For for detailed information about Reserve and Guard pay, review their respective websites, as pay is dependent on the number of days served per month, which can vary. Active duty military pay is a little less complex but still has a few components other than basic pay.

Basic Pay

Basic pay is the monthly amount you earn based on your current rank (grade) and years of service. Referring to Table 1.3, you will note that the columns are labeled with the grade that corresponds to one's rank. For grades O-1 through O-3, there are two columns: one with an additional "E" and one without. The "E" denotes prior enlisted service time, which may qualify the individual for higher pay depending on the years of service in the enlisted grade. The column on the far left denotes the years of service. To determine the basic pay earned, find the row with the number of total years of active duty service time and then select the column with the appropriate grade. These charts typically change annually, depending on raises voted by Congress, so you will need to contact your base's finance office or search the Internet (key words: military pay tables year) for the latest information.

Table 1.3

Years of Service	Grade							
	O-1	O-1E	O-2	O-2E	O-3	O-3E	O-4	O-5
2 or less	$2,972.45	$3,793.83	$3,424.56	$4,643.74	$3,963.37	$5,287.22	$4,507.85	$5,224.48
Over 2	$3,093.83	$3,993.83	$3,900.31	$4,739.27	$4,493.03	$5,540.39	$5,218.49	$5,885.62
Over 3	$3,793.83	$4,141.50	$4,492.09	$4,890.29	$4,849.61	$5,818.47	$5,566.56	$6,292.96
Over 4	$3,793.83	$4,292.52	$4,643.74	$5,145.03	$5,287.22	$5,998.49	$5,644.12	$6,369.89
Over 6	$3,793.83	$4,643.74	$4,739.27	$5,341.76	$5,540.39	$6,293.91	$5,967.28	$6,624.00
Over 8	$3,793.83	$4,643.74	$4,739.27	$5,488.37	$5,818.47	$6,543.29	$6,313.77	$6,775.97
Over 10	$3,793.83	$4,643.74	$4,739.27	$5,488.37	$5,998.49	$6,881.58	$6,745.38	$7,110.48
Over 12	$3,793.83	$4,643.74	$4,739.27	$5,488.37	$6,293.91	$6,881.58	$7,081.47	$7,355.76
Over 14	$3,793.83	$4,643.74	$4,739.27	$5,488.37	$6,448.08	$6,881.58	$7,315.09	$7,672.93
Over 16	$3,793.83	$4,643.74	$4,739.27	$5,488.37	$6,448.08	$6,881.58	$7,449.09	$8,388.93
Over 18	$3,793.83	$4,643.74	$4,739.27	$5,488.37	$6,448.08	$6,881.58	$7,526.64	$8,616.88
Over 20	$3,793.83	$4,643.74	$4,739.27	$5,488.37	$6,448.08	$6,881.58	$7,526.64	$8,876.35

Officer Pay Chart Example (2016)

Source: http://www.militaryrates.com/military-pay-charts-o1_o5_2016

Pay Supplements

Basic pay is only one component of your actual monthly paycheck. There are two other components that you will receive and, depending on your assigned duties and career field, you may get additional pay. Also, if you have dependents (spouse and/or children), you may be eligible for additional pay. You can get get information about pay supplement eligibility from the base finance office.

The two primary supplements to your pay are your nontaxable housing allowance, known as the Basic Housing Allowance (BAH), and the Basic Allowance for Subsistence (BAS). The BAH is an allowance provided to help you pay for housing off base. If you live in on-base housing, you will not receive this allowance. This allowance is location dependent and will change based on your location and grade. The BAS is a subsistence allowance calculated by the Department of Agriculture that can help you pay for food. For 2016, the BAS for officers was $253.63 per month. All of this information is also published on your monthly leave and earnings statement, fondly called an LES. You will have access to this information anytime as this data is web-based for your convenience.

GET THE FACTS

To find information on the current BAH and BAS rates, visit the following websites:

- **http://www.militaryrates.com**
- **http://militarybenefits.info/**

Additional information can be found online by searching using the following keywords:

military basic housing allowance rate, military basic allowance for subsistence

There are additional allowances that you may earn during your career. Some of these are due to being separated from your spouse because of a duty assignment location or deployment. You may earn special pay for the duties you perform, such as hazardous duty pay or flight pay. When the services face short-falls in certain career fields and need to retain specific personnel, they sometimes offer bonuses to sign contracts to continue your service. Typically, officers do not re-enlist or sign contracts to continue service beyond their required service commitment. To end their service, they must file separation from service or retirement (if eligible) paperwork to depart the service.

Warrant Officers

Warrant Officers have a long history in the armed forces. Currently, Warrant Officers serve only in the Army, Navy, Marine Corps, and Coast Guard. To be eligible for the Warrant Officer programs in the Navy, Marine Corps, and Coast Guard, an individual typically must have a certain number of enlisted years of service and attain a particular rank (grade). Other qualifications are specific to each branch of service (see Table 1.4). It is not clear how many of the Navy, Marine Corps, and Coast Guard Warrant Officer positions are aviation related. It is recommended that you seek specific information on this topic through the various services' recruiting and personnel centers.

Table 1.4

Warrant Officer Eligibility Requirements for the Navy, Marine Corps, and Coast Guard			
Eligibility Requirements	**Navy**	**Marine Corps**	**Coast Guard**
Years of Service	• At least 12 but not more than 24 years of total qualifying Federal service	No data available	8 years
Grade	• E-7 through E-9 • E-6s selected for E-7	• Most often promoted from Sergeant Major of The Marine Corps • Lower ranks considered	E-6
Degree	Not required but recommended	Bachelor's degree	Not specified
Other	• U.S. citizenship • No court-martial, civil convictions, nonjudicial punishment, or unsatisfactory marks in conduct for 3 years • High school graduate or equivalency	Displays exemplary leadership and technical expertise	• No court-martial, civil convictions, nonjudicial punishment, or unsatisfactory marks in conduct for 3 years • Color vision and no hearing deficiencies

In contrast, the U.S. Army is heavily reliant on Warrant Officers for aviation jobs. Warrant Officers are considered the technical foundation of the Army, yet they compose less than 3 percent of the personnel structure. In 1949, the U.S. Army established the Warrant Officer (WO) Pilot Program, developed with the intent for WOs to fly cargo helicopters. Once selected, Warrant Officers attend the Warrant Officer Candidate School (WOCS), which is similar to Officer Candidate School.

To be eligible for the Army Warrant Officer Candidate program and the Flight Training program, the following requirements must be met:

- U.S. citizenship
- High school diploma
- Minimum 18 years of age and not older than 33 when selected; some age waivers are considered
- Minimum General Technical score of 110 on the Armed Forces Vocational Aptitude Battery (ASVAB)
- Qualifying score achieved on the Selection Instrument for Flight Training (SIFT; see Chapter 6)
- Army height and weight requirements
- Within six months of application, pass the standard three-event Army Physical Fitness Test (APFT). For the standards, see **http://usarmybasic.com/army-physical-fitness/apft-standards** (keywords: Army Physical Fitness Test standards)
- Class 1A Flight Physical Examination within 18 months of application

GET THE FACTS

For additional information on the U.S. Army Flight Training program, visit the following website:

www.goarmy.com.

Additional information can be found online using the following keywords:

Flight Training, Fulfill Your Dream of Becoming a Pilot

Warrant Officer Pay

Similar to officers' pay, Warrant Officers earn basic pay plus a number of allowances. The 2016 Warrant Officer Pay chart is shown in Table 1.5. For more information, see the previous "Officer Pay" section, and note that additional information is available online and through recruiting offices, as well.

Table 1.5

Warrant Officer Pay Chart Example (2016)				
Years of Service	**Grade**			
	WO1	**WO2**	**WO3**	**WO4**	**WO5**
2 or less	$2,905.29	$3,309.79	$3,740.15	$4,096.10	
Over 2	$3,217.73	$3,622.87	$3,896.21	$4,406.02	
Over 3	$3,301.91	$3,719.34	$4,056.06	$4,532.44	
Over 4	$3,479.73	$3,785.55	$4,108.39	$4,656.98	
Over 6	$3,679.30	$4,000.25	$4,276.12	$4,871.05	
Over 8	$3,999.62	$4,333.82	$4,605.90	$5,083.24	
Over 10	$4,144.34	$4,499.02	$4,948.93	$5,297.63	
Over 12	$4,346.11	$4,662.02	$5,121.38	$5,621.10	
Over 14	$4,545.06	$4,860.96	$5,297.31	$5,904.22	
Over 16	$4,701.43	$5,016.40	$5,490.26	$6,173.47	
Over 18	$4,845.52	$5,157.33	$5,836.44	$6,393.85	
Over 20	$5,020.18	$5,325.68	$6,070.37	$6,608.87	$7,282.93

Source: http://www.militaryrates.com/military-pay-charts-w1_w5_2016

COMMISSIONING SOURCES

There are four ways by which to become an officer in the armed forces: through a service academy, Reserve Officer Training Corps (ROTC), Officer Candidate School (OCS), or direct commission. Direct commission is the means in which physicians, lawyers, and chaplains are typically introduced to the active duty ranks. Since their duties are dramatically different from other line officers, their officer training is reduced in scope. Similarly, they do not compete with line officers for promotion. For the purposes of this book, the focus will be on the three primary commissioning programs.

Service Academies

As previously highlighted, the service academies are prestigious education institutions with excellent academic programs. For the government, the cost of this commissioning source is the highest, with figures ranging in the area of $160,000 to $340,000. The four academies are:

1. U.S. Military Academy, West Point, New York:
   http://www.usma.edu/SitePages/Home.aspx
2. U.S. Naval Academy, Annapolis, Maryland:
   http://www.usna.edu/About/index.php
3. U.S. Coast Guard Academy, New London, Connecticut:
   http://www.cga.edu/about/
4. U.S. Air Force Academy, Colorado Springs, Colorado:
   http://www.usafa.af.mil/

Each academy offers a variety of accredited undergraduate degree programs. General information about each academy and the basic admission requirements are outlined in Table 1.6. The admission process to these academies is very competitive, but academy graduates typically are given higher priority than other officers in their year group for assignment selection, including pilot training slots. This is particularly true of the Air Force Academy. In addition, the Air Force Academy offers opportunities for flight training during your college years. Upon completion of the program and graduation with a four-year degree, candidates are commissioned either as a Second Lieutenant in the Army, Air Force, or Marine Corps, or as an Ensign in the Navy or Coast Guard.

Table 1.6

General Information about the Service Academies Admissions and Service Requirements				
	U.S. Military Academy	**U.S. Naval Academy**	**U.S. Coast Guard Academy**	**U.S. Air Force Academy**
Founded	1802	1845	1876	1954
Tuition	No Tuition			
Nomination Requirement	• Congressional or service-connected nomination	• Congressional nomination	• No Congressional nomination	• Congressional nomination
Degree Type	4-year			
Age Limitation	• 17–23	• 17–23	• Not specified	• 17–23
Citizenship	• Required	• No	• Not specified	• Required
Other Specifications	• Not married • Not pregnant • No dependents	• Not married • Not pregnant • No dependents	• Not specified	• Not married • No dependents
Acceptance Rate	• 9.5%	• 7–8%	• 18–20%	• 16.6%
Fitness Test	Yes			
Service Commitment	• 5 years active service	• 5 years active service	• 5 years active service	• 5 years active service (3 years inactive)
Prep School/ Program	• U.S. Military Academy Preparatory School	• Naval Academy Preparatory School	• Academy Introduction Mission • CGA Scholars	• U.S. Air Force Academy Preparatory School

There are several items to note about the military academies. First and foremost, when attending the academies, you will be subject to military law. Although the education is outstanding, the learning environment is intense. You will be required to participate in military drills and organized sports in addition to your academic studies. You will have little control over your schedule to include leave, even during the summer months. However, you will also have a sponsor family in the local area that will offer you support.

Reserve Officer Training Corps (ROTC)

Reserve Officer Training Corps is a program offered at a number of university campuses across the nation. The Army, Navy, and Air Force offer ROTC options for commissioning. Those desiring to become Marine Officers do so through the Navy ROTC program. The program consists of classroom courses, leadership laboratories and, often, mandatory fitness activities and other service. This program is usually completed in either two or four years, with at least one summer of training activity. Some scholarships are available for students and may be dependent on one's major. Cadets (Army and Air Force) or Midshipmen (Navy and Marine Corps) must maintain weight and fitness standards as well as minimum grade point averages to remain in the program, whether on scholarship or not. Upon completion of the program and graduation with a four-year degree, candidates are commissioned as either a Second Lieutenant in the Army, Air Force, or Marine Corps or as an Ensign in the Navy. A four-year active duty commitment is required upon program completion.

There are a number of benefits to the ROTC experience. The first is that you attend a civilian university and experience all that environment has to offer. Cadets and midshipmen also get to experience a little of the military culture through the ROTC experience during the school year, with additional opportunities for summer training and professional development. As a cadet or midshipman, you are not subject to military law as you are not yet an enlisted member of the armed services, which allows for a little more freedom. Depending on your scholarship and/or program completion status, you may also be eligible to leave the program if you decide that the career is not for you. If you have accepted scholarship money or incurred a commitment, that option may not be readily available. It is important to understand the level of commitment as you progress through the program. Last but not least, based on scholarship and program completion, you may be eligible for a monthly stipend and textbook compensation. Some universities also offer funding to bring an ROTC scholarship to their program by offering reduced room and board or other benefits. Carefully research these options as part of the consideration process.

Officer Candidate School (OCS)

Officer Candidate School (OCS) or, in the Air Force, Officer Training School (OTS), is one means to ensure the proper number of officers in the service at a given time. This means of commissioning allows college graduates with no prior military experience or enlisted personnel who have earned their degrees to rapidly transition to the Officer Corps. The training is a very intensive multiweek course. Table 1.7 is a summary of training durations. Note that these training durations are subject to change, so check the respective training website to confirm durations once you have a training date.

Table 1.7

Duration of Officer Candidate/Training Schools by Service				
	Army	Navy	Marine Corps	Air Force	Coast Guard
Training Duration	12 weeks	12 weeks	6–10 weeks (program dependent)	9 weeks	17 weeks

Direct Commission

Direct commission is the means by which individuals with specialized skills, such as physicians, lawyers, and chaplains, are typically introduced to the active duty ranks. While these individuals are required to attend OCS or OTS, since their duties are dramatically different from other line officers, their officer training is reduced in scope. Similarly, they do not compete with line officers for promotion.

Occasionally, opportunities for direct commission of aviators are made available by a particular branch of service.

PROFESSIONAL DEVELOPMENT

As previously mentioned, officer professional development is a career-long process, not one that ends upon commissioning and completion of initial training. There are many expectations of the Officer Corps, and rapidly changing technology in the Information Age only makes continued education more essential. There are many reasons to continue your education throughout your career: the first is to be successful in your military career, and the second is to be able to transition to another career after your military service ends. There are several types of training and education in which you will be expected to participate during your career—some are more obvious than others. You will have duty-specific training related to your position skills, and you will need recurring training to stay proficient in those skills. Periodically, you will attend more formal training to enhance your job skills or become an instructor or take on other responsibilities. There are all types of other training required of every service member that relate to a variety of topics, and your training manager will remind you of these tasks. Finally, there are other courses that you will likely have to seek and track on your own; these relate to your professional military education (PME) and advanced degrees.

Professional Military Education

Each service has some type of professional military education (PME) for officers as well as noncommissioned officers (NCOs). These courses often take two forms: correspondence and in-residence. In many cases, you are required to take the correspondence version of the course before you are eligible to be competitive for the in-residence course. Consult with your commander, mentor, and education office to determine the latest requirements and eligibility for specific courses. For example, Air Force Captains (O-3s) are expected to complete Squadron Officer School (SOS) by correspondence within 18 months of promotion to O-3. In some organizations, eligible officers will not be considered to attend SOS in residence unless they have shown the initiative to complete the correspondence course. When Air Force personnel are promoted to Major, they are expected to complete Air Command and Staff College, and Air War College upon promotion to Lieutenant Colonel. Again, these courses and sequences are service-specific, so consult with your service education office to determine the requirements for your service branch of choice.

Continuing Graduate Education

Some of the services expect officers to earn a graduate degree at some point in their military careers. There are instances in which an advanced degree has been a stated requirement for promotion to Field Grade ranks. The policy on the requirement of advanced degrees among the services tends to shift over time. Education levels can be indicated as part of your personnel record that is viewed by promotion boards. This includes partially completed degrees, such as doctorates. Again, the policies on the use of advance degrees for official promotion selection have shifted historically. Such criteria can be used at lower organizational levels to stratify rankings among promotion recommendations.

The pursuit of an advanced degree, such as a master's degree, may seem like a tremendous challenge and expense. However, the services offer tuition assistance for courses, and there are a growing number of high-quality programs offered through distance-education platforms that can assist active duty service members to earn a degree, even while deployed. Hence, there should be minimal obstacles in meeting this requirement. Some of the PME in-residence courses also offer an option to earn a master's degree upon completion of the course. These programs are very competitive and often are offered after the degree is needed to achieve that particular rank. Do not count on that option to fulfill this requirement.

The Air Force and Navy offer programs for service members to earn advanced degrees during their active duty service, either through a service-connected institution or civilian university.

GET THE FACTS

For more information about obtaining advanced degrees while on active duty, visit the following websites:

- **Air Force Institute of Technology (AFIT): http://www.afit.edu/**
- **Naval Postgraduate School (NPS): http://www.nps.edu/**

Due to the changing nature of the tuition assistance amounts, annual caps, and other details, specifics about tuition assistance (TA) will not be presented here. Check out the various services' websites and visit the education office for the latest information on this topic and the process to apply. Also note that tuition and some expenses, such as books paid out of pocket, may be tax deductible as well.

Post-Military Education Opportunities

In addition to active duty education opportunities, there are a number of federal and state programs available to assist veterans in earning a degree or additional employment education. Such programs change over time, and, therefore, the details will not be presented here. Visit service-specific websites and the Department of Veterans Affairs website (**www.va.gov**) for additional information about these programs. For state programs, you will likely have to conduct a search through each state's veterans' affairs or general government webpage to learn further details.

Military Associations

There are a number of private organizations that support the military in a variety of different ways. Some of these organizations offer professional development opportunities, lobby Congress for veterans' and service members' benefits, offer scholarships to service members and their families, perform base and community outreach, assist veterans with transition and filing of benefits claims, and much more. Many of these organizations are also open to civilians and students, regardless if you have yet served. These organizations are also excellent sources for benefits information, mentorship, and support.

GET THE FACTS

To learn more about military associations, visit the following websites:
- Association of the United States Army (AUSA):
  www.ausa.org
- Association of the United States Navy (AUSN):
  www.ausn.org
- Marine Corps Association Foundation:
  www.mca-marines.org
- Air Force Association (AFA):
  www.afa.org
- Coast Guard Aviation Association:
  https://aoptero.org/
- Reserve Officers Association (ROA):
  https://www.roa.org/membership

SUMMING IT UP

- The various branches of today's military service have a long, rich history, with some dating as far back as the American Revolution.

- Before choosing a branch of the military in which to serve, it is a good idea to research each branch of the service, the history, and missions of interest to you. Know the roles each service plays in national security.

- To find the branch of military service that best suits you, research the types of service available, including the work culture, professional opportunities, and requirements for moves and deployments.

- The four paths to becoming an Officer or Warrant Officer are as follows:
  - Service academy
  - Reserve Officer Training Corps (ROTC)
  - Officer Candidate School (OCS)
  - Direct commission

- Identify the requirements for continued education and training throughout your career. Officer professional development is a career-long process, and each branch of the service offers professional military education for its officers. Some branches require officers to obtain a graduate degree at some point in their military careers.

- Consider reaching out to a professional organization for additional information. Connect with a mentor and become involved.

Becoming a
Military Aviator

Chapter 2

OVERVIEW

- **Training**
- **U.S. Air Force**
- **U.S. Navy/Marines/Coast Guard**
- **U.S. Army**
- **Summing It Up**

TRAINING

Regardless of which branch of service you choose, your career in aviation will start with flight training. Flight training is a serious commitment of time and resources for both the individual and the branch of service involved. The total cost per student to complete advanced pilot training for a USAF, USN, or USMC pilot is approximately $1 million (The time investment is 12 months for the USAF and 18 to 30 months USN/USMC.). The additional cost of qualifying new pilots in their operational aircraft can exceed an additional $9 million. The U.S. Army pilot training cost per student is approximately $200,000 to $270,000 and includes qualifying training in the student's operational platform for a total duration of 12 to 18 months. Upon completion of training, an individual's service commitment varies by the branch of service. These commitments change, but currently they are ten years for the USAF, eight years for the USN/USMC, and five years for the Army, starting at the completion of pilot training. Because requirements do change, be sure to confirm the most current information from a representative of the service branch in which you're interested.

This chapter will acquaint you with the pilot and other aviation career programs within each branch of the military. Its intent is to establish a framework of the general training progression, career track options, and desired outcomes.

U.S. AIR FORCE

Eligibility

Pilots and Combat Systems Officers (CSOs) must meet the same eligibility requirements for admission into flight training, with two exceptions: AFOQT composite scores (to be discussed in Chapter 4), and vision restrictions. Physical requirements that must be met include passing a Class 1 flight physical and having no history of hay fever, asthma, significant allergies, or use of Ritalin. Having a police record (civil involvement) *may* be a disqualifying factor. Corrective eye surgery (not performed by the USAF) *may* also be a disqualifier. Uncorrected vision limits are 20/70 distant and 20/30 near for a pilot, and 20/200 distant and 20/40 near for a CSO. Your undergraduate degree major is not a factor, but the GPA should be 3.4 or above to be competitive. You are competing for candidacy among highly qualified peers, so minimums (class ranking, AFOQT scores, GPA, and Physical Fitness Test) will very likely decrease your chances of being selected. Every eligibility point will matter in all phases of your career, starting with initial eligibility.

Career Categories

Flight career categories include pilot, pilot of remotely piloted aircraft (RPA), and CSOs. Candidates in all three categories first attend Initial Flight Training (IFT), a 40-day program in Pueblo, Colorado, during which the pilot candidates are trained by civilian flight instructors. Upon completion of IFT, pilots (non-RPA) attend either Specialized Undergraduate Pilot Training (SUPT) or Euro-NATO Joint Jet Pilot Training (ENJJPT).

RPA pilots' IFT begins the first part of a nine-month, two-phase pipeline in which these candidates learn to fly a manned trainer airplane, work the flight simulator, and understand the fundamentals of flying in classroom lectures. This phase is split between Pueblo, Colorado, and Randolph Air Force base in Texas. During the second phase, recruits spend three to four months in formal training, where they learn to fly a specific unmanned platform. Figure 2.1 illustrates the training flow for both RPA pilots (commissioned officers) and RPA sensor operators (enlisted personnel).

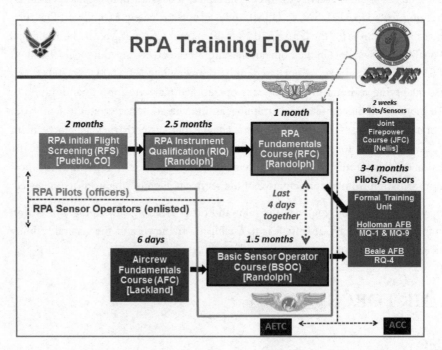

Figure 2.1. RPA Pipeline. New program as depicted by the 558th FTS.

CSOs are trained as mission commanders in multiseat combat aircraft. After completing IFT, the CSO students undergo Undergraduate Combat Systems Officer Training (UCSOT) at NAS Pensacola, Florida. The CSO pipeline includes specialization in combat navigation, electronic warfare, weaponeering and weapons employment, and mission planning. Training includes water survival and one year of operating the T-6A and T-1A. After platform selection (F-15E, B-52, B-1, other), newly winged CSOs qualify in their new aircraft in their formal training unit (approximately six months to a year). Combat survival training can occur before or after formal training. CSO is a combat air forces career and includes career opportunity tours as Joint Terminal Attack Controllers (JTACs) in conducting and managing Close Air Support (CAS), not just from the air but also from the ground embedded with U.S. Army forces (airborne, infantry, and armor) (Figure 2.2).

Figure 2.2. JTAC. CSOs conducting CAS from the ground and air.

Scoring and Selection

Pilot selection used to vary by commission source. For instance, ROTC used an order of merit score to track pilot candidates. Despite changing the means by which to "rack and stack" qualifying officers for pilot board selection, every point still matters. The highest weight of categories is your class ranking. The method used by a commander varies. Other major categories are your GPA and your fitness score (Your medical fitness score is evaluated on a pass fail basis and is not weighted. You are either medically qualified or you are not), and your Pilot Candidate Selection Method (PCSM) score.

The PCSM is a tool used to predict the capability of prospective pilot candidates to complete the first portion of pilot training. Scored on a scale of 1 (lowest) to 99 (highest), the PCSM is composed of three parts:

1. **Test of Basic Aviation Skills (TBAS) test scores.** The TBAS is a computer-based skills test which you will learn more about in Chapter 4.

2. **AFOQT score.** Enlisted members applying for enlisted RPA pilot boards may take the Enlisted Pilot Qualifying Test.

3. **Total number of private/civilian flying hours.**

A candidate's PCSM is just one of the factors taken into consideration by the pilot selection board, but its importance can't be minimized. By using the PCSM to assist in the pilot selection process, the expectation is that more pilot trainees will graduate, making training both more efficient and cost-effective.

Officers who are already active duty can apply through the Air Force Personnel Center (AFPC). The requirements for active duty applications change regularly, but, as with commission source commanders, the squadron commander's recommendation and ranking holds much weight. It is not uncommon for the number of available pilot slots to be split between the Air Force Academy and the ROTC graduates. OTS graduates tend to get a much smaller percentage. Because of the fewer OTS-rated positions available, competition for consideration is high.

Pre-training and screening

Once selected, student pilots (which include pilots, RPA pilots, and CSO candidates) begin their training at the Initial Flight Training (IFT) program in Pueblo, Colorado. This training is designed to introduce the student pilot to the demands of military aviation and training and to gauge a candidate's aptitude for a flight career.

GET THE FACTS

For more information about Air Education and Training Command, visit the following website:

> **http://www.af.mil/AboutUs/FactSheets/Display/tabid/224/Article/104471/air-education-and-training-command.aspx**

Additional information can be found online by searching using the following keywords:

Air Education Training Command, IFT

Initial Flight Training (IFT)

The IFT program lasts for approximately four weeks and includes 25 flight hours in a DA-20 Diamond (Figure 2.3). Week one is characterized by 11 hours of classroom instruction and 1 hour of mandatory physical fitness (PF) per day. A PFT is given at the end of week one, and the following weeks maintain the mandatory 1 hour/day PF. The following weeks prefigure (somewhat) what can be expected in primary and advanced flight training. You will have a formal flight room briefing followed by stand-up emergency procedures (EP). The rest of the day involves briefing and flying. If you are not scheduled to fly (or if flights are cancelled due to weather), trainers/simulators will be used, but the time spent will not count toward the required 25 flight hours. IFT is a high-intensity environment and needs to be given the same respect as the desired training pipeline. After successfully completing IFT, student pilot candidates attend either Euro-NATO Joint Jet Pilot Training (ENJJPT) at Sheppard AFB, Texas, or Specialized Undergraduate Pilot Training (SUPT) at Columbus AFB, Mississippi, Laughlin AFB, Texas, or Vance AFB, Oklahoma.

Figure 2.3. The DA-20 "Diamond" IFT Trainer.

GET THE FACTS

To learn more about IFT, visit the following websites:

- **https://www.baseops.net/militarypilot/usaf_ift.html**
- **http://www.dossaviation.com/usaf-ift**

Additional information can be found online by searching using the following keywords:

baseops, IFT

Euro-NATO Joint Jet Pilot Training

At Euro-NATO Joint Jet Pilot Training (ENJJPT), conducted at Sheppard AFB, Texas, student pilots learn with, and are instructed by, U.S. Air Force officers and officers from various air forces within the NATO alliance. During their 26 weeks of primary aircraft training, student pilots experience approximately 125 hours of flight training instruction. Pilots fly the T-6A Texan II to master contact, instrument, low-level and formation flying. Then they move on to approximately 135 hours of advanced aircraft training in a fighter-trainer, the T-38C Talon, and, over the course of another 26 weeks, continue building the skills necessary to become a fighter pilot. Students will also be trained in water and/or land survival and complete any other required training.

Specialized Undergraduate Pilot Training

Specialized Undergraduate Pilot Training is divided into three phases:

1. **Academic/Pre-Flight Training** is designed to teach the background knowledge and pre-flight instruction vital to becoming a first-class pilot. Instruction includes aerospace physiology, altitude chamber qualification, ejection seat and egress training, parachute landing fall training, and aircraft systems. This phase lasts 6 weeks.

2. **Primary Flying Training** is designed to teach the basic flying fundamentals necessary to safely operate any U.S. Air Force aircraft and to lay the foundation for advanced flying training. Training includes basic flying skills, mission planning, navigation, aviation weather, basic and advanced instrument, low-level navigation, and formation. This phase also provides officer development training to strengthen leadership skills and increase understanding of the role of the military pilot as an officer and supervisor in preparation for future responsibilities as military officers and leaders. Training lasts 22 weeks and includes 90 flight hours in the T-6A Texan II (Figure 2.4) and T-34.

Figure 2.4. The T-6A Texan II, Turboprop.

3. **Advanced Flying Training** is the stage at which student pilots are selected for one of several advanced training tracks (or pipelines) based on their class standing and the needs of the Air Force. Prospective airlift and tanker pilots are assigned to the airlift/tanker track and train in the T-1 Jayhawk. Student pilots headed for bomber or fighter assignments are assigned to the bomber/fighter track and train in the T-38. Both airlift/tanker track and fighter/bomber track training continues at Columbus AFB, Mississippi, Laughlin AFB, Texas, or Vance AFB, Oklahoma. Prospective multi-engine turboprop pilots will train in the T-44 or C-12 turboprop trainer at Naval Air Station Corpus Christi, Texas. Students selected to fly helicopters train in the UH-1 Huey at Fort Rucker, Alabama.

The **Fighter/Bomber track** uses the T-38 (Figure 2.5). Centrifuge training is required to stay within the fighter track. If you do not pass centrifuge training, you will be transferred to one of the other career tracks (typically your next choice). Training lasts 24 weeks and consists of 120 flight hours, with a focus on instruments, formation 2-4 ship, navigation, and low level. Using the same merit system that is used for advanced track selection, including instructor recommendation, graduates become winged pilots and receive follow-on training (water survival, land survival, SERE). For those who are not selected for a fighter, additional follow-on training includes three to six months of introduction to fighter fundamentals (IFF). Those eliminated from training (not including centrifuge training) are removed from flight training and are not considered for another pilot track. The operational platform achieved coming out of advanced training uses a ranking system of top down selection of what is available. Class ranking is blended among other training bases, and platform selection occurs in a trade-off fashion between those of the same ranking among the training bases. Bombers can be chosen for candidates based on instructor assessment. Follow-on platforms include all fighters (e.g. F-35, F-22, and F16) and bombers (B-2, B-1, and B-52). New pilots report to a training command within Air Combat Command (ACC) for their platform for another year (pending platform type) of training. Based on performance and ranking, these new pilots choose their specific platform (if there is one) and desired base (location). Training includes qualification in the aircraft and all the various weapon systems (Figure 2.6).

Figure 2.5. The T-38.

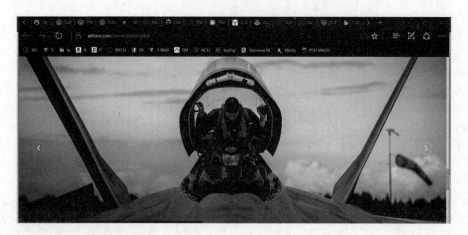

Figure 2.6. The F-22.

The **Airlift and Tanker track** includes the B-52 bomber pilot selection (based on availability and ever-changing policy). Training consists of 105 hours in the T-1 (a Learjet) over 24 weeks (Figure 2.7). Training includes transitions, instruments, navigation, low-level formation, basic airdrop, and refueling training. As with their T-38 brethren, student pilots become winged pilots and proceed to common follow-on survival training. ACC platform training commands follow the same convention as with fighter ACC training. Platforms include the B-52 (Figure 2.8), C-17, C-5, C-130, KC-10, KC-135, E-3, E-8, and MC-12. Teamed with CSOs, pilots who train on B52s must be qualified to handle nuclear weapons and USAF air-to-surface weapons.

Figure 2.7. The T-1A.

Figure 2.8. The B-52H.

Those selecting the **Multi-Engine Prop track** go to NAS Corpus Christi, Texas, within a Navy joint-training pipeline (USAF, USN, USMC, and USCG). Training in the C-12 and T44 includes 114 flight hours over approximately 26 weeks. Training includes transitions (pattern and approach work) instruments, navigation, low-level, formation, and airdrop. Follow-on assignments consist of the C/MC/AC-130, C/MC-12, U-28, and UAVs (Figure 2.9).

Figure 2.9. The KC-10 and B-2s during training.

Those selecting the **Helicopter Training track** go to Fort Rucker, Alabama. Within Army aviation training in the UH-1H Huey, 115 flight hours are attained over 28 weeks. Training includes transitions, instruments, navigation, low-level, formation, remote ops, and night ops with night vision goggles (NVGs). Follow-on assignments include the V-22 Osprey and HH-60 Pave Hawk, within a world that includes special operations command (Figure 2.10).

Figure 2.10. The V-22 Osprey.

RPA Pilot Training

Approximately 160 students per year will be selected for duty flying Remotely Piloted Aircraft. RPA pilot candidates will attend the RPA pilot training program, known as Undergraduate RPA Training or URT, at Joint Base San Antonio-Randolph, Texas. RTA pilot candidates' advanced training begins with the RPA Instrument Qualification course; a simulator-only course based on the T-6. After completion of the qualification course, candidates take a month-long RPA Fundamentals Course designed to give new RPA pilots the tactical grounding experience needed to enter the RPA formal training units.

U.S. NAVY/MARINES/COAST GUARD

Career Categories

United States Navy, Marine, and Coast Guard student naval officers (SNAs) and student naval flight officers (SNFOs) attend Introductory Flight Screening (IFS) and Aviation Preflight Indoctrination (API) at NAS Pensacola, Florida. Upon API graduation, the SNAs and SNFOs move on to separate flight training programs. The USN and USMC do not currently have a student pilot RPA track similar to the USAF.

SNFO primary training continues at NAS Pensacola, Florida. Primary training lasts approximately 15 weeks, during which SNFOs train on the T-6 II Texan and flight simulator to learn aircraft systems and basic flight skills, such as flight rules, navigation, and aerobatics. SNFOs chosen after primary for the maritime pipeline go to NAS Jacksonville, Florida and train with multi-engine aircraft, such as the P-3 Orion. A small number of SNFOs are chosen for strategic communications training at Tinker AFB, Oklahoma. SNFOs chosen for the tactical jet pipeline remain at NAS Pensacola and continue training in the T-6 II Texan and T-1 Jayhawk. Upon completion of the Intermediate phase of training, SNFO's either select the E-2C Hawkeye with follow-on training in Norfolk, Virginia or continue their training in Pensacola.

During advanced training, SNFOs fly the T-39 Sabreliner and the T-45 Goshawk. Students will proceed down either the Strike pipeline to serve as Electronic Countermeasures Officers (ECMO) for the EA-6B Prowler, or the Strike/Fighter pipeline for selection as Weapons Systems Officers for the F/A-18F.

Eligibility

SNAs must be no older than 26 by the projected completion of flight school. For the purpose of determining age cut-off, 18 months is used for the length of flight school (although it is closer to two years). Prior enlisted officers *sometimes* have age waivers extending the upper age to 27 or 28. ASTB-E composite score minimums will be discussed in Chapter 5. These minimum scores will likely not be competitive relative to your peers.

Introductory Flight Screening (IFS)

Introductory Flight Screening (IFS) is the U.S. Navy's version of the U.S. Air Force's FST for both SNAs and SNFOs for all U. S. Navy, Marine, and Coast Guard flight training. Training includes four FAA private pilot tests and 15 flight hours (nine sorties, one checkride (a cross-country flight), and one solo) over 50 days in a Cessna 172. The objective of the program is to decrease pipeline attrition and to reduce the number of candidates waiting for flight training. IFS may be skipped if a candidate already has a private pilot's license.

Aviation Preflight Indoctrination (API)

After completing IFS, SNAs and SNFOs attend Aviation Preflight Indoctrination (API) for 8–16 weeks of classroom instruction, physical training, altitude chamber training, day/night helo dunker training (Figure 2.11), and parachute water landings. Classroom instruction includes advanced aerodynamics, weather, engines, navigation, and flight rules and regulations.

Figure 2.11. The API Helo Dunker.

Primary Flight Training

Upon completion of API, SNAs begin primary training, conducted at NAS Whiting Field in Milton, Florida, and NAS Corpus Christi, Texas, which lasts approximately 22 weeks. It includes ground-based academics, and simulator and flight training in either the T-34 Turbomentor or the T-6A Texan II. Primary training consists of several stages:

- **Familiarization (FAM):** aircraft systems, local course rules, and emergency procedures
- **Basic Instruments:** use of instrumentation (versus visual clues) for maneuvers
- **Precision Aerobatics:** performing maneuvers including the half Cuban eight, barrel rolls, and Split S
- **Formation:** basic section flight, cruise formation flight (sometimes includes a solo sortie)
- **Night FAM:** procedures and best practices specific to night flight
- **Radio Instruments:** intensive simulator and flight sorties

After primary training, SNA pipeline selections are made based on the needs of the service, the SNA's performance, and the SNA's preferences. Based on these factors, when choosing a pipeline, SNAs select from the available slots in Strike (jets), maritime (multi-engine prop), E2/C2, rotary (helos), limited E-6 TACAMO (Take Charge and Move Out) positions, and (for USMC SNAs only) tiltrotor aircraft. Whatever track you select or is selected for you, your professional duty is to dominate whatever route you are on to your utmost ability. Anything outside of that singular focus is a distraction that will likely cost you everything. This is a time for you to be selfish and focus on being the best aviator possible.

Advanced Flight Training

SNAs who enter the Strike (Jet) pipeline complete their training at either NAS Kingsville, Texas, or at NAS Meridian, Mississippi, in the T-45C for up to 27 weeks. Strike training includes instruction in strike tactics, weapons delivery, air combat maneuvering and carrier landing.

Maritime students complete a similar advanced training program at NAS Corpus Christi in the TC-12 or the T-44A/C.

SNAs in the E-2/C-2 pipeline receive multi-engine training as well as carrier landing qualification training. After primary training, they report to NAS Corpus Christi for intermediate training to complete 44 hours of flight training for approximately 17 weeks in the T-44. After intermediate training, E-2/C-2 students report to NAS Kingsville, Texas for advanced training in the T-45. Students complete their training approximately 27 weeks after receiving their carrier landing qualification.

E-6 TACAMO SNAs complete their training in the T-44C at NAS Corpus Christi following the same pipeline as the maritime SNAs.

Student pilots selected for helicopter training report to NAS Whiting Field and complete advanced training in the TH-57 Sea Ranger, where they learn the unique characteristics and tactics of rotary-wing aviation and are instructed on to shipboard landing. USMC SNAs training to pilot the MV-22 (Osprey) will receive instruction from both the helicopter and maritime pipelines. Upon completion of advanced training, naval aviators report to their respective Fleet Replacement Squadrons (FRS) for further training on specific rotorcraft. USMC aviators report to MCAS New River, North Carolina, and U.S. Coast Guard aviators report to the Mobile Coast Guard Aviation Training Center in Mobile, Alabama, for further training.

Training pipelines are continually being changed and improved for efficiency. Ensure you have the most current information to anticipate your path.

U.S. ARMY

Flight Training

Initial entry rotary-wing training is conducted at Fort Rucker, Alabama, and involves flying the TH-67 over 32 weeks, logging 149 flight hours. There are four phases of training. Phase one consists of two weeks of ground school in basic flight, controls, aerodynamics, weather, pre-flight, and start-up procedures. Phase two includes 60 flight hours over ten weeks, learning basic flight fundamentals, approaches, maneuvers, and emergency procedures leading to a solo flight. Phase three consists of 30 flight hours over eight weeks on instrument navigation. Phase four includes combat skills and tactical night and night vision goggles (NVG) operations. Performance in initial training contributes to which career platform track is assigned for advanced graduate flight training (14 to 23 weeks) in either the UH-60A, AH-64D, OH-58D, or CH-47D

SUMMING IT UP

- Knowledge is power. Know what to expect on your chosen training pipeline to identify how you can pre-train to increase your performance outcomes. Keep current on what to expect in your flight training pipeline.

- U.S. Air Force student pilots attend Initial Flight Training (IFT) and then attend either Euro-NATO Joint Jet Pilot Training (ENJJPT) or Specialized Undergraduate Pilot Training (SUPT).

- SUPT is divided into three phases:
  - Academic/ Pre-Flight training
  - Primary Flight Training
  - Advanced Flying Training

- Advanced Flying Training is the phase in which Air Force student pilots are selected for one of the following advanced training tracks: Fighter/Bomber, Airlift and Tanker, Multi-Engine Prop, and Helicopter. Some candidates will be assigned to Remotely Piloted Aircraft (RPA) training.

- United States Navy, Marine, and Coast Guard student naval officers (SNAs) and student naval flight officers (SNFOs) attend Introductory Flight Screening (IFS) and Aviation Preflight Indoctrination (API). Upon API graduation, the SNAs and SNFOs move on to separate flight training programs.

- After primary training, SNFOs are selected for one of several pipelines; maritime, strategic communications, and tactical jet. Those who proceed down the Strike pipeline serve as Electronic Countermeasures Officers (ECMOs); those who proceed down the Strike/Fighter pipeline serve as Weapons Systems Officers.

- Primary Flight training for SNAs consists of several stages:
  - Familiarization (FAM): aircraft systems, local course rules, and emergency procedures
  - Basic Instruments: use of instrumentation (versus visual clues) for maneuvers
  - Precision Aerobatics: performing maneuvers including the half Cuban eight, barrel rolls, and Split S.
  - Formation: basic section flight, cruise formation flight (sometimes includes a solo sortie)
  - Night FAM: procedures and best practices specific to night flight
  - Radio Instruments: intensive simulator and flight sorties

- After primary training, the SNAs either select or are assigned to one of the following pipelines for advanced flight training based on the needs of the service, the SNA's performance, and the SNA's preferences:
    - strike (jets)
    - maritime (multi-engine prop)
    - E2/C2
    - rotary (helicopters)
    - limited E-6 TACAMO (Take Charge and Move Out) positions
    - tiltrotor aircraft (USMC SNAs only)
- U.S. Army student pilots complete a four-phase initial rotary wing training over a 32-week long period:
    - Phase One: ground school in basic flight controls, aerodynamics, weather, pre-flight, and start-up procedures
    - Phase Two: Sixty flight hours, learning basic flight fundamentals, approaches, maneuvers, and emergency procedures leading to a solo flight
    - Phase Three: Thirty flight hours on instrument navigation
    - Phase Four: Combat skills and tactical night and NVG operations.
- Career platform tracks in advanced flight training are determined by a student pilot's performance during initial training.
- Good student aviators often fail because they get distracted by life outside of their training. Plan to be selfish, and focus solely on your flight training.

Question Types You Can Expect on the Test

OVERVIEW

- Synonyms
- Verbal Analogies
- Reading/Paragraph Comprehension
- Arithmetic Reasoning
- Math Knowledge
- Mechanical Comprehension
- Instrument Comprehension
- Block Counting
- Table Reading
- Aviation Information
- Nautical Information
- Physical Science
- Hidden Figures
- Simple Drawings
- Spatial Apperception
- Situational Judgment
- Performance-Based Measurement Battery
- Biographical Inventory and Self-Description Subtests
- Summing It Up

Chapter 3

Each of the military flight aptitude tests (AFOQT, ASTB-E, and SIFT) assesses skills that are geared toward the branch of the military by which it is administered. However, many of the question types you will encounter on these tests, though varied in focus, are similar in nature. This chapter will give you a brief overview of the types of questions found on the tests and some exercises to familiarize you with the question types. Chapters 4, 5, and 6 will go into further detail about each test's specific structure.

SYNONYMS

Synonym test items appear as five-option questions (with answer choices A–E) in the Word Knowledge subtest of the AFOQT. These test items measure breadth of vocabulary or word knowledge. For each word supplied, you must select from the available options the answer choice that is the same or most nearly the same in meaning. Consider all options before answering a synonym test question. Although several options may have some connection with the key word, the word that is closest in meaning to the key word is always the correct answer.

Examples: Synonyms

1. SUCCUMB

   A. aid
   B. be discouraged
   C. check
   D. oppose
   E. yield

2. SUBSUME

   A. belong
   B. cover
   C. include
   D. obliterate
   E. understate

EXERCISES: SYNONYMS

Directions: Each of the following six questions consists of a word in capital letters followed by five suggested meanings of the word. For each question, select the word or phrase that most nearly means the same as the word in capital letters.

1. ANOMALOUS

   A. disgraceful
   B. formless
   C. irregular
   D. threatening
   E. unknown

2. CREDENCE

   A. belief
   B. claim
   C. payment
   D. surprise
   E. understanding

3. FORTUITOUS

   A. accidental
   B. conclusive
   C. courageous
   D. prosperous
   E. severe

4. MALIGN

   A. disturb
   B. mislead
   C. praise
   D. provoke
   E. slander

5. PERMEABLE

   A. flexible
   B. penetrable
   C. soluble
   D. variable
   E. volatile

6. TRANSITORY

   A. significant
   B. obvious
   C. temporary
   D. cumulative
   E. encouraging

ANSWER KEY AND EXPLANATIONS

1. C	2. A	3. A	4. E	5. B	6. C

1. **The correct answer is C.** *Anomalous* means "of uncertain nature; irregular."

2. **The correct answer is A.** *Credence* means "belief."

3. **The correct answer is A.** *Fortuitous* means "occurring by chance; accidental."

4. **The correct answer is E.** *Malign* means "to speak ill of; slander."

5. **The correct answer is B.** *Permeable* means "penetrable."

6. **The correct answer is C.** *Transitory* means "of brief duration; temporary."

VERBAL ANALOGIES

Verbal analogy test items appear as five-option questions in the Verbal Analogies subtest of the AFOQT. Verbal analogy questions test not only your knowledge of word meanings and your vocabulary level, but they also test your ability to reason; that is, to see the relationships between words and the ideas they represent. To determine such relationships, you must know the meaning of each word in the first given pair and determine the precise relationship between the two words. You complete the analogy by selecting the pair of words that best expresses a relationship similar to that expressed by the first two paired words.

Examples: Verbal Analogies

1. You are given the first pair of words and the first word of the second pair. Of the given options, only one best expresses a relationship to the third word that is similar to that expressed between the first two words:

   Man is to **boy** as **woman** is to

   A. baby.

   B. bride.

   C. child.

   D. girl.

   E. lad.

2. Only the first pair of words is provided. Each answer choice consists of a pair of words:

   Man is to **boy** as

   A. adult is to girl.

   B. bride is to groom.

   C. lass is to child.

   D. woman is to youth.

   E. woman is to girl.

Let's analyze the first analogy form.

What is the relationship of the first two paired words?

Man: member of the human race, male, mature

Boy: member of the human race, male, young

Both are male members of the human race. Man is mature; Boy is young.

What is the meaning of the word **Woman** and each of the words appearing in the options?

Woman: member of the human race, female, mature

Baby: member of the human race, either male or female, very young

Bride: member of the human race, female, about to be married or newly married

Child: member of the human race, either male or female, young

Girl: member of the human race, female, young

Lad: member of the human race, male, young

To complete the analogy with **Woman** as the first word, we need a term denoting a young, female member of the human race.

Choice A is incorrect because a **Baby** may be male or female and is very young. Choice B is incorrect because **Bride** is a special kind of female—one about to be married or newly married. If **Groom** had been substituted for **Boy** in the first half of the analogy, then **Bride** would have been the proper choice. Choice C is incorrect because a **Child** may be male or female. Choice E is incorrect because a **Lad** is a male.

Choice D is the correct choice because **Girl** denotes a young, female member of the human race.

Here's a list of relationships commonly encountered in the Verbal Analogies subtests.

Relationship	Example	Relationship	Example
synonyms	ask : inquire	cause : effect	negligence : accident
antonyms	long : short	whole : part	chapter : paragraph
homonyms	mail : male	object : purpose or function	keyboard : type
location	Phoenix : Arizona	object : user	camera : photographer
creator : creation	artist : painting	early stage : later stage	infant : adult
female : male	cow : bull	general : specific	vegetable : broccoli
larger : smaller	lake : pond	more : less (degree)	arid : dry
noun : adjective	texture : coarse	verb : adjective	expand : large

Relationship	Example
distance : mile	measurement (e.g. time, distance, weight)
wood : bench	raw material : finished product
run : ran	verb tense : verb tense
child : children	singular noun : plural noun
he : they	normative pronoun : objective pronoun
she : her	first-person pronoun : third-person pronoun
we : they	first-person pronoun : third-person pronoun
good : better	adjective : comparative adjective
bad : worst	adjective : superlative adjective

Pay careful attention when answering this type of question. The order of the two words in the answer choice must be in the same sequence as the order of words in the question stem. If the sequence of the second pair of words is reversed, the relationship between the two word pairs is not analogous. Here are two examples in which the word pairs are not analogous.

Incorrect: 2 is to **5** as **10** is to **4**.

Correct: 2 is to **5** as **4** is to **10**.

Incorrect: Man is to **Boy** as **Girl** is to **Woman**.

Correct: Man is to **Boy** as **Woman** is to **Girl**.

EXERCISES: VERBAL ANALOGIES

Directions: Each of the following six items consists of an incomplete analogy. Select the answer that best completes the analogy presented in the first two words of each question.

1. **Botany** is to **plants** as **entomology** is to

    A. animals.

    B. climate.

    C. diseases.

    D. languages.

    E. insects.

2. **Epilogue** is to **prologue** as

    A. appendix is to index.

    B. appendix is to preface.

    C. preface is to footnote.

    D. preface is to table of contents.

    E. table of contents is to index.

3. **Octagon** is to **square** as **hexagon** is to

    A. cube.

    B. military.

    C. pyramid.

    D. rectangle.

    E. triangle.

4. **Glow** is to **blaze** as

    A. compact is to sprawling.

    B. eager is to reluctant.

    C. glance is to stare.

    D. hint is to clue.

    E. wicked is to naughty.

5. **Water** is to **thirst** as **food** is to

    A. famine.

    B. grief.

    C. hunger.

    D. indigestion.

    E. scarcity.

6. **Butterfly** is to **cocoon** as

    A. burrow is to rabbit.

    B. web is to spider.

    C. kennel is to dog

    D. kangaroo is to pouch.

    E. bear is to cave.

ANSWER KEY AND EXPLANATIONS

1. E	2. B	3. E	4. C	5. C	6. D

1. **The correct answer is E.** *Botany* is the study of *plants*; *entomology* is the study of *insects*.

2. **The correct answer is B.** *Epilogue* is a speech after the conclusion of a play; *prologue* is an introductory speech to a play. *Appendix* is material added after the end of the book; *preface* is an introductory part of a book.

3. **The correct answer is E.** *Octagon* is an eight-sided figure; *square* is a four-sided figure (one-half of eight). *Hexagon* is a six-sided figure; *triangle* is a three-sided figure (one-half of six).

4. **The correct answer is C.** *Glow* is to burn without any flame; *blaze* is to burn intensely. *Glance* is to look briefly; *stare* is to look intently.

5. **The correct answer is C.** Absence of *water* results in *thirst*; absence of *food* results in *hunger*.

6. **The correct answer is D.** A *butterfly* develops while inside its *cocoon*; a *kangaroo* develops while inside its mother's *pouch*.

READING/PARAGRAPH COMPREHENSION

Reading Comprehension subtests are included on the AFOQT, ASTB-E, and SIFT tests.

- The AFOQT Reading Comprehension subtest presents multi-paragraph passages about which test takers must answer a series of questions.

- The ASTB-E Reading Skills Test presents a short passage about which test takers must answer an inference question based only on the information presented in the passage itself.

- The SIFT Reading Comprehension Test asks the test taker to complete a sentence or answer a question based on the content presented in the passage.

The ability to read and understand written or printed material is an important skill. As mentioned previously, reading comprehension tests present passages that vary in length from one sentence to several paragraphs, followed by one or more questions about the content of each passage. The reading selections are usually samples of the type of material that you would be required to read on the job or at school.

There are five common goals of reading comprehension items:

1. **Finding specific information or directly stated detail in the passage.** Although this type is commonly found in elementary-level tests, it is also found in intermediate-level tests such as the military flight exams. At the intermediate level, the vocabulary is more difficult, the reading passages are of greater complexity, and the questions posed are much more complicated. Here are some examples:

- Helping to prevent accidents is the responsibility of
  - The principal reason for issuing traffic summonses is to
  - The reason for maintaining ongoing safety education is that

2. **Recognizing the central theme, the main idea, or concept expressed in the passage.** Although questions of this type may be phrased differently, they generally require that you summarize or otherwise ascertain the main purpose or idea expressed in the reading passage. In addition to reading and understanding, the ability to analyze and interpret written material is essential. Some questions require the ability to combine separate ideas or concepts found in the reading passage to get the correct answer. Other questions merely require reaching a conclusion that is equivalent to a restatement of the main idea or concept expressed in the passage. Let's review some examples.

   - The best title for this paragraph would be
   - This paragraph is mainly about
   - The passage best supports the statement that
   - The passage means most nearly that

3. **Determining the meaning of certain words as used in context.** The particular meaning of a word as used in the passage requires an understanding of the central or main theme of the reading passage, as well as the idea being conveyed by the sentence containing the word.

   - The word … as used in this passage means
   - The expression … as used in the passage means_____.

4. **Finding implications or drawing inferences from a stated idea.** This type of item requires the ability to understand the stated idea and then to reason by logical thinking to the implied or inferred idea. *Implied* means not exactly stated but simply suggested; *inferred* means derived by reasoning. Although the terms are somewhat similar in meaning, *inferred* implies being further removed from the stated idea. Much greater reasoning ability is required to arrive at the proper inference.

   - Which of the following is implied by the above passage?
   - Of the following, the most valid implication of the above paragraph is
   - The author probably believes that
   - It can be inferred from the above passage that
   - The best of the following inferences that can be made is that

5. **Completing a sentence.** Sentence completion items are considered both vocabulary items and reading comprehension items. They are vocabulary items because they test the ability to understand and use words. However, they also measure an important aspect of reading comprehension: the ability to understand the implications of a sentence or a paragraph.

   Sentence completion items consist of a sentence or paragraph in which a word is missing. The omissions are indicated by a blank underlined space or an ellipsis. You must read and understand the sentence or paragraph as given and then choose the option that best completes the idea in the reading passage. Your choice must also be consistent in style and logic with other elements in the sentence.

Eight General Suggestions for Answering Reading/Paragraph Comprehension Questions:

1. Scan the passage to determine the general intent of the reading selection.

2. Read the passage carefully to understand the main idea and any related ideas. If necessary for comprehension, read the passage again.

3. Read each question carefully and base your answer only on the material in the reading passage. Be careful to base your answer on what is stated or implied. Do not be influenced by your opinions, personal feelings, or any information not expressed or implied in the reading passage.

4. Options that are partly true and partly false are incorrect.

5. Be very observant for such words as *least, greatest, first, not,* and so on, appearing in the preamble of the question.

6. Be suspicious of options containing words such as *all, always, every, forever, never, none, wholly,* and so on.

7. Be sure to consider all answer choices before selecting the one you believe is correct.

8. Speed is an important consideration in answering reading comprehension questions. Try to proceed as rapidly as you can without sacrificing careful thinking or reasoning.

Take a look at the following sample reading comprehension questions. They should familiarize you with just about any question type you will see on the AFOQT Form T, ASTB-E, and SIFT tests. Then try the exercise questions that follow.

Examples: Reading Comprehension

Directions: For each of the following questions, select the choice that best completes the statement or answers the question.

1. The rates of vibration perceived by the ears as musical tones lie between fairly well-defined limits. In the ear, as in the eye, there are individual variations. However, variations are more marked in the ear, since its range of perception is greater.

   The paragraph best supports the statement that the ear

   A. is limited by the nature of its variations.

   B. is the most sensitive of the auditory organs.

   C. differs from the eye in its broader range of perception.

   D. is sensitive to a great range of musical tones.

   E. depends for its sense on the rate of vibration of a limited range of sound waves.

   The correct answer is C. The passage makes the point that individual differences in auditory range are greater than individual differences in visual range because the total range of auditory perception is greater. Although the statements made by choices D and E are both correct, neither expresses the main point of the reading passage.

2. The propaganda of a nation at war is designed to stimulate the energy of its citizens and their will to win, and to imbue them with an overwhelming sense of the justice of their cause. Directed abroad, its purpose is to create precisely contrary effects among citizens of enemy nations and to assure to nationals of allied or subjugated countries full and unwavering assistance.

   The title that best expresses the ideas of this passage is

   A. "Propaganda's Failure."

   B. "Designs for Waging War."

   C. "Influencing Opinion in Wartime."

   D. "The Propaganda of Other Nations."

   E. "Citizens of Enemy Nations and Their Allies."

   The correct answer is C. The theme of this passage is influencing opinion in wartime, both at home and abroad.

Directions: Answer the following two questions on the basis of the information contained in the passage below:

I have heard it suggested that the "upper class" English accent has been of value in maintaining the British Empire and Commonwealth. The argument runs that all manner of folk in distant places, understanding the English language, will catch in this accent the notes of tradition, pride, and authority and so will be suitably impressed. This might have been the case some nine or ten decades ago, but it is certainly not true now. The accent is more likely to be a liability than an asset.

3. The title below that best expresses the ideas of this passage is

    A. Changed Effects of a British Accent.

    B. Prevention of the Spread of Cockney.

    C. The Affected Language of Royalty.

    D. The Decline of the British Empire.

    E. The King's English.

The correct answer is A. The last two sentences of the reading passage indicate that folks in distant places might have been suitably impressed decades ago, but they're not now.

4. According to the author, the "upper class" English accent

    A. has been imitated all over the world.

    B. has been inspired by British royalty.

    C. has brought about the destruction of the British Commonwealth.

    D. may have caused arguments among the folk in distant corners of the Empire.

    E. may have helped to perpetuate the British Empire before 1900.

The correct answer is E. The "upper class" English accent might have been of value in maintaining the British Empire nine or ten decades ago (or before 1900).

Directions: For each of the following questions, select the choice that best completes the statement or answers the question.

5. The view is widely held that butter is more digestible and better absorbed than other fats because of its low melting point. There is little scientific authority for such a view. As margarine is made today, its melting point is close to that of butter, and tests show only the slightest degree of difference in digestibility of fats of equally low melting points.

   The paragraph best supports the statement that

   A. butter is more easily digested than margarine.

   B. the concept that butter has a lower melting point than other fats is a common misconception, disproved by scientists.

   C. there is not much difference in the digestibility of butter and margarine.

   D. most people prefer butter to margarine.

   The correct answer is C. The passage states that the melting points of butter and margarine are similar and that, therefore, they are about equally digestible.

6. We find many instances in early science of "a priori" scientific reasoning. Scientists thought it proper to carry over generalizations from one field to another. It was assumed that the planets revolved in circles because of the geometrical simplicity of the circle. Even Newton assumed that there must be seven primary colors corresponding to the seven tones of the musical scale.

   The paragraph best supports the statement that

   A. Newton sometimes used the "a priori" method of investigation.

   B. scientists no longer consider it proper to uncritically carry over generalizations from one field to another.

   C. the planets revolve about the earth in ellipses rather than in circles.

   D. even great men like Newton sometimes make mistakes.

   The correct answer is B. The tone of the passage and the choice of illustrations showing the fallacy of "a priori" reasoning make it evident that scientists no longer carry generalizations automatically from one field to another. Choices A and D are true statements.

Directions: Answer the following two questions on the basis of the information contained in the passage below:

Science made its first great contribution to war with gunpowder. But since gunpowder can be used effectively only in suitable firearms, science also had to develop the iron and steel that were required to manufacture muskets and cannons on a huge scale. To this day, metallurgy receives much inspiration from war. Bessemer steel was the direct outcome of the deficiencies of artillery as they were revealed by the Crimean War. Concern with the expansion and pressure of gases in guns and combustibility of powder aroused interest in the laws of gases and other matters that seemingly have no relation whatever to war.

7. The title below that best expresses the ideas of this passage is

    A. "Gunpowder, the First Great Invention."

    B. "How War Stimulates Science."

    C. "Improvement of Artillery."

    D. "The Crimean War and Science."

    The correct answer is B. The basic theme of the reading passage is that science contributes to the war effort and that war stimulates science research.

8. An outcome of the Crimean War was the

    A. invention of gunpowder.

    B. origin of metallurgy.

    C. study of the laws of gases.

    D. use of muskets and cannons.

    The correct answer is C. The last sentence in the reading passage indicates that interest in the laws of gases arose as a direct outcome of artillery deficiencies revealed by the Crimean War.

Directions: Questions 9 and 10 consist of sentences containing a blank space indicating that a word has been omitted. Beneath each sentence are four or five choices. Select the choice that, when inserted in the sentence, best fits in with the meaning of the sentence as a whole.

9. If the weather report forecasts fog and smoke, we can anticipate having _____.

   A. rain
   B. sleet
   C. smog
   D. snow
   E. thunder

   The correct answer is C. A mixture of fog and smoke is called smog.

10. Although her argument was logical, her conclusion was _____.

    A. illegible
    B. natural
    C. positive
    D. unreasonable

    The correct answer is D. When a subordinate clause begins with *although*, the thought expressed in the main clause will not be consistent with that contained in the subordinate clause. Since the argument was *logical*, the conclusion would have to be illogical. Of the options given, *unreasonable* is the only opposite to *logical*.

EXERCISES: READING COMPREHENSION

Directions: For each question, select the choice that best completes the statement or answers the question.

1. The mental attitude of the employee toward safety is exceedingly important in preventing accidents. All efforts designed to keep safety on the employee's mind and to keep accident prevention a live subject in the office will help substantially in a safety program. Although it may seem strange, it is common for people to be careless. Therefore, safety education is a continuous process.

   The reason given in the above passage for maintaining ongoing safety education is that

   A. employees must be told to stay alert at all times.

   B. office tasks are often dangerous.

   C. people are often careless.

   D. safety rules change frequently.

   E. safety rules change infrequently.

2. One goal of law enforcement is the reduction of stress between one population group and another. When no stress exists between population groups, law enforcement can deal with other tensions or simply perform traditional police functions. However, when stress between population groups does exist, law enforcement, in its efforts to prevent disruptive behavior, becomes committed to reduce that stress.

   According to the above passage, during times of stress between population groups in the community, it is necessary for law enforcement to attempt to

   A. continue traditional police functions.

   B. eliminate tension resulting from social change.

   C. punish disruptive behavior.

   D. reduce intergroup stress.

   E. warn disruptive individuals.

Directions: Answer questions 3–5 on the basis of the information contained in the following passage.

Microwave ovens use a principle of heating different from that employed by ordinary ovens. The key part of a microwave oven is its magnetron, which generates the microwaves that then go into the oven. Some of these energy waves hit the food directly, while others bounce around the oven until they find their way into the food. Sometimes the microwaves intersect, strengthening their effect. Sometimes they cancel each other out. Parts of the food may be heavily saturated with energy, while other parts may receive very little. In conventional cooking, you select the oven temperature. In microwave cooking, you select the power level. The walls of the microwave oven are made of metal, which helps the microwaves bounce off them. However, this turns to a disadvantage for the cook who uses metal cookware.

3. Based on the information contained in this passage, it is easy to see some advantages and disadvantages of microwave ovens. The greatest disadvantage would probably be

   A. overcooked food.

   B. radioactive food.

   C. unevenly cooked food.

   D. the high cost of preparing food.

   E. cold food.

4. In a conventional oven, the temperature selection would be based upon degrees. In a microwave oven, the power selection would probably be based upon

   A. wattage.

   B. voltage.

   C. lumens.

   D. solar units.

   E. ohms.

5. The source of the microwaves in the oven is

   A. reflected energy.

   B. convection currents.

   C. the magnetron.

   D. short waves and bursts of energy.

   E. the food itself.

Directions: Read the paragraph(s) and select the one lettered choice that best completes the statement or answers the question.

6. Few drivers realize that steel is used to keep the road surface flat in spite of the weight of buses and trucks. Steel bars, deeply embedded in the concrete, are sinews to take the stresses so that the stresses cannot crack the slab or make it wavy.

   The passage best supports the statement that a concrete road

   A. is expensive to build.

   B. usually cracks under heavy weights.

   C. looks like any other road.

   D. is reinforced with other material.

7. Blood pressure, the force that the blood exerts against the walls of the vessels through which it flows, is commonly meant to be the pressure in the arteries. The pressure in the arteries varies with contraction (work period) and relaxation (rest period) of the heart. When the heart contracts, the blood in the arteries is at its greatest, or systolic, pressure. When the heart relaxes, the blood in the arteries is at its lowest, or diastolic, pressure. The difference between the two pressures is called the pulse pressure.

   According to the passage, which one of the following statements is most accurate?

   A. The blood in the arteries is at its greatest pressure during contraction.

   B. Systolic pressure measures the blood in the arteries when the heart is relaxed.

   C. The difference between systolic and diastolic pressure determines the blood pressure.

   D. Pulse pressure is the same as blood pressure.

Questions 8–10 are based on the passage below.

Arsonists are people who set fires deliberately. They don't look like criminals, but they cost the nation millions of dollars in property loss and, sometimes, loss of life. Arsonists set fires for many different reasons. Sometimes a shopkeeper sees no way out of losing his business and sets fire to it to collect the insurance. Another type of arsonist wants revenge and sets fire to the home or shop of someone he feels has treated him unfairly. Some arsonists just like the excitement of seeing the fire burn and watching the firefighters at work; arsonists of this type have been known to help fight the fire.

8. According to the passage above, an arsonist is a person who

    A. intentionally sets a fire.

    B. enjoys watching fires.

    C. wants revenge.

    D. needs money.

9. Arsonists have been known to help fight fires because they

    A. felt guilty.

    B. enjoyed the excitement.

    C. wanted to earn money.

    D. didn't want anyone hurt.

10. According to the passage above, we may conclude that arsonists

    A. would make good firefighters.

    B. are not criminals.

    C. are mentally ill.

    D. are not all alike.

ANSWER KEY AND EXPLANATIONS

1. C	**3.** C	**5.** C	**7.** A	**9.** B
2. D	**4.** A	**6.** D	**8.** A	**10.** D

1. **The correct answer is C.** Safety education must be a continuous process because it is common for people to be careless.

2. **The correct answer is D.** During times of stress, law enforcement becomes committed to reducing that stress between population groups.

3. **The correct answer is C.** The uneven saturation of energy would result in unevenly cooked food.

4. **The correct answer is A.** The watt is a measure of electrical energy. Electrical power in the home is measured in watts or kilowatts.

5. **The correct answer is C.** The magnetron within the microwave oven generates the energy.

6. **The correct answer is D.** The first three choices are not supported by the passage. The second sentence in the passage states that steel bars, deeply embedded in the concrete, are sinews to take the stresses.

7. **The correct answer is A.** The third sentence in the passage states that when the heart contracts, the blood in the arteries is at its greatest pressure.

8. **The correct answer is A.** The first sentence in the passage states that arsonists set fires deliberately or intentionally.

9. **The correct answer is B.** The last sentence in the passage states that some arsonists just like the excitement of seeing the fire burn, and watching the firefighters at work, and even helping fight the fire.

10. **The correct answer is D.** The first three choices are not supported by the passage. Different types of arsonists described in the passage lead to the conclusion that arsonists are not all alike.

ARITHMETIC REASONING

Arithmetic reasoning test items appear as five-option questions in the Arithmetic Reasoning subtest of the AFOQT Form T. Arithmetic reasoning questions also appear as four-option questions in the Math Skills Tests of the ASTB-E and SIFT. Familiarize yourself with the types of questions you may encounter on the tests, and then try the exercise problems that follow.

Examples: Arithmetic Reasoning

1. A mechanic repairs 12 cars per 8-hour work day. Another mechanic in the same shop repairs $1\frac{1}{3}$ times this number in the same period. Theoretically, how long will it take these mechanics, working together, to repair 14 cars in the shop?

   A. $3\frac{1}{2}$ hours

   B. 4 hours

   C. $4\frac{1}{2}$ hours

   D. 5 hours

   E. $5\frac{1}{2}$ hours

   The correct answer is B. The second mechanic repairs $1\frac{1}{3}$ 12, or 16 cars per 8-hour day. On an hourly rate, the first mechanic repairs $1\frac{1}{2}$ cars/hour; the second mechanic repairs 2 cars/hour. Adding both outputs, they repair $3\frac{1}{2}$ cars/hour. To determine the time required to repair 14 cars, divide the 14 cars by the $3\frac{1}{2}$ cars/hour. The answer is 4 hours (choice B).

2. An airplane flying a distance of 625 miles used 50 gallons of gasoline. Under the same conditions, how many gallons will this plane need to travel 2,500 miles?

   A. 120

   B. 140

   C. 165

   D. 180

   E. 200

   The correct answer is E.

   $$\frac{625}{50} = \frac{2,500}{x}$$
   $$625x = 125,000$$
   $$x = 200 \text{ gallons}$$

3. An empty can weighs 6 pounds. When filled with water, it weighs 44 pounds. If one gallon of water weighs 8.32 pounds, the capacity of the can is approximately

   A. 4 gallons.

   B. $4\frac{1}{4}$ gallons.

   C. $4\frac{1}{2}$ gallons.

   D. 5 gallons.

   E. $5\frac{1}{2}$ gallons.

   The correct answer is C. The weight of the filled can (44 pounds) minus the weight of the empty can (6 pounds) equals the weight of the water that can fill the can (44 – 6 = 38 pounds). The number of gallons that will fill the can equals $\frac{38}{8.32}$, which equals 4.57, or approximately $4\frac{1}{2}$.

4. On a scaled drawing of a warehouse, 1 inch represents 8 feet of actual floor dimension. A floor that is actually 20 yards long and 14 yards wide would have which of the following dimensions on the scaled drawing?

   A. 3 inches long and 2 inches wide

   B. 5 inches long and $3\frac{1}{2}$ inches wide

   C. $7\frac{1}{2}$ inches long and $5\frac{1}{4}$ inches wide

   D. 10 inches long and 7 inches wide

   The correct answer is C. First convert actual floor dimensions to feet: 20 yards = 60 feet; 14 yards = 42 feet.

   If 1 inch represents 8 feet, $7\frac{1}{2}$ inches represents 60 feet (length).

   If 1 inch represents 8 feet, $5\frac{1}{4}$ inches represents 42 feet (width).

5. If there are red, green, and yellow marbles in a jar and 40 percent of these marbles are either red or green, what are the chances of blindly picking a yellow marble out of the jar?

   A. 2 out of 3

   B. 3 out of 4

   C. 2 out of 5

   D. 3 out of 5

   The correct answer is D. If 40 percent of the marbles are either red or green, 60 percent of the marbles are yellow. With 60 percent of the marbles being yellow, the probability of selecting a yellow marble is 6 out of 10, or 3 out of 5.

EXERCISES: ARITHMETIC REASONING

Directions: Each of the following five questions consists of an arithmetic problem. Solve each problem and choose the correct answer choice.

1. A rectangular bin 4 feet long, 2 feet wide, and 3 feet high is solidly packed with bricks whose dimensions are 8 inches, 4 inches, and 2 inches. The number of bricks in the bin is

   A. 324

   B. 486

   C. 648

   D. 972

   E. 1,296

2. On a house plan on which 2 inches represents 7 feet, the length of a room measures 5 inches. The actual length of the room is

   A. $14\frac{1}{2}$ feet.

   B. $15\frac{1}{2}$ feet.

   C. $16\frac{1}{2}$ feet.

   D. $17\frac{1}{2}$ feet.

3. A person travels 12 miles at 3 mph, 10 miles at 5 mph, and 10 miles at $2\frac{1}{2}$ mph.

   What is the person's average rate for the complete distance?

   A. 3.2 mph

   B. 3.5 mph

   C. 3.7 mph

   D. 3.9 mph

   E. 4.2 mph

4. A fax machine was listed at $360 and was bought at $288. What was the rate of discount?

   A. 18 percent

   B. 20 percent

   C. 22 percent

   D. 24 percent

5. If shipping charges to a certain point are 75 cents for the first 6 ounces and 10 cents for each additional ounce, the weight of the package for which the charges are $2.35 is

   A. 1 pound, 1 ounce.

   B. 1 pound, 2 ounces.

   C. 1 pound, 3 ounces.

   D. 1 pound, 5 ounces.

   E. 1 pound, 6 ounces.

ANSWER KEY AND EXPLANATIONS

| 1. C | 2. D | 3. A | 4. B | 5. E |

1. **The correct answer is C.**
   Calculate in inches.

   $48 \times 24 \times 36 = 41{,}472 \text{ in}^3$

   (Volume of bin)

   $8 \times 4 \times 2 = 64 \text{ in}^3$

   (Volume of each brick)

   $41{,}472 \div 64 = 648$ bricks

2. **The correct answer is D.**
   Let x = actual length of the room.

   $$2 : 7 = 5 : x$$
   $$2x = 35$$
   $$x = 17\frac{1}{2} \text{ feet}$$

3. **The correct answer is A.**

    4 hours at 3 mph = 12 miles

   $+$ 2 hours at 5 mph = 10 miles

   $+$ 4 hours at $2\frac{1}{2}$ mph = 12 miles

   ———————————————————————

   10 hours for 32 miles = 3.2 mph

4. **The correct answer is B.**
   $360 - $288 = 72 discount.

   $$\frac{72}{360} = \frac{1}{5} = 20\%$$

5. **The correct answer is E.**
   $2.35 - .75 = 1.60$, cost of weight above 6 ounces

   $$\frac{1.60}{.10} = 16 \text{ ounces}$$
   $$6 \text{ ounces} + 16 \text{ ounces} = 22 \text{ ounces}$$
   $$= 1 \text{ pound, } 6 \text{ ounces}$$

MATH KNOWLEDGE

Test items on math knowledge appear as five-option questions in the Math Knowledge subtest of the AFOQT. Math knowledge test items also appear as four-option items in the Math Skills Tests of the ASTB-E and SIFT.

Math knowledge—the ability to use basic mathematical relationships learned in basic courses in mathematics—is one of the important skills for which the military tests. Most of these concepts are included in elementary courses in algebra and geometry.

Examples: Math Knowledge

1. The reciprocal of 4 is

   A. 0.02

   B. 0.25

   C. 0.50

   D. 0.80

   The correct answer is B. If the product of two numbers is 1, either number is called the reciprocal of the other. For example, for $4 \times \frac{1}{4}$, 4 is the reciprocal of $\frac{1}{4}$, and $\frac{1}{4}$ is the reciprocal of 4. $\frac{1}{4}$ is equivalent to 0.25.

2. If a pole 24 feet high casts a shadow 10 feet long, how long a shadow will be cast by a 6-foot person standing next to the pole?

   A. $1\frac{1}{2}$ feet

   B. 2 feet

   C. $2\frac{1}{2}$ feet

   D. 3 feet

   E. $3\frac{1}{2}$ feet

   The correct answer is C. Let x = length of shadow cast by a 6-foot person. Use a simple proportion: $24:10 = 6:x$.

   $$24x = 60$$
   $$x = \frac{60}{24}$$
   $$x = 2\frac{1}{2}$$

3. The numerical value of 5! is

   A. 20

   B. 24

   C. 50

   D. 100

   E. 120

The correct answer is E. The factorial of a natural number is the product of that number and all the natural numbers less than it. $5! = 5 \times 4 \times 3 \times 2 \times 1 = 120$.

4. In the following series of numbers arranged in a logical order, ascertain the pattern or rule for the arrangement and then select the appropriate choice to complete the series.

   1, 2, 4, 7, 11 _____

   A. 14

   B. 15

   C. 16

   D. 17

   E. 18

The correct answer is C. A study of the series of numbers shows a pattern of +1, +2, +3, +4, etc. Inserting 16 in the blank space will conform to this pattern, as 11 + 5 = 16.

5. The square root of 924.16 is

   A. 30.4

   B. 30.6

   C. 31.4

   D. 32.4

The correct answer is A. Starting from the decimal point, separate the number in groups of two going in both directions and then solve with a modified form of long division as shown in the following calculation:

$$
\begin{array}{r}
30.4 \\
\sqrt{9\ 24.16} \\
-9 \\
\hline
60)\ 0\ 24 \\
0 \\
\hline
604)\ 24\ 16 \\
24\ 16 \\
\hline
0
\end{array}
$$

EXERCISES: MATH KNOWLEDGE

Directions: Solve each mathematical problem and indicate which of the given choices is the correct answer.

1. $\dfrac{3}{4} \cdot \dfrac{4}{5} \cdot \dfrac{5}{6} \cdot \dfrac{6}{7} \cdot \dfrac{7}{8} \cdot \dfrac{8}{9} =$

   A. $\dfrac{1}{8}$

   B. $\dfrac{1}{4}$

   C. $\dfrac{1}{3}$

   D. $\dfrac{1}{2}$

2. Of the following, the pair that is NOT a set of equivalents is

   A. 0.18%, 0.0018

   B. $\dfrac{1}{5}$%, 0.002

   C. 3.5%, $\dfrac{7}{200}$

   D. 35%, $\dfrac{35}{100}$

   E. 125%, 0.125

3. $10^4 \times 10^3 \times 10^5 =$

   A. 10^9

   B. 10^{12}

   C. 10^{15}

   D. 10^{60}

4. The hypotenuse of a right triangle whose legs are 6 feet and 8 feet is

   A. 6 feet.

   B. 7 feet.

   C. 9 feet.

   D. 10 feet.

   E. 14 feet.

5. If $a = \dfrac{b}{3}$, then $\dfrac{3}{4}a =$

   A. $\dfrac{3}{3}b$

   B. $\dfrac{4}{3}b$

   C. $3b$

   D. $\dfrac{b}{3}$

   E. $\dfrac{b}{4}$

ANSWER KEY AND EXPLANATIONS

1. C	2. E	3. B	4. D	5. E

1. **The correct answer is C.** The 4s, 5s, 6s, 7s, and 8s cancel out, leaving $\frac{3}{9} = \frac{1}{3}$.

2. **The correct answer is E.** All except choice E are equivalent. 125% = 1.25

3. **The correct answer is B.** When the same bases are multiplied, the exponents are added. $10^4 \times 10^3 \times 10^5 = 10^{(4+3+5)} = 10^{12}$.

4. **The correct answer is D.** The Pythagorean theorem states that for any right triangle, the sum of the squares of the legs is equal to the square of the length of the hypotenuse.

$$6^2 + 8^2 = h^2$$
$$36 + 64 = h^2$$
$$h^2 = 100$$
$$h = 10$$

5. **The correct answer is E.** $a = \frac{b}{3}$;

$$\frac{3}{4}a = \frac{3}{4} \cdot \frac{b}{3} = \frac{b}{4}$$

MECHANICAL COMPREHENSION

Test items on mechanical comprehension are widely used by the military. They appear as the Mechanical Comprehension Tests (MCT) on the ASTB-E and SIFT. On the SIFT, the MCT is computer adaptive, which means that the number of questions you will answer varies based on how accurately you answer the questions. The ASTB-E offers a computer-adaptive version of the MCT as well, but examinees have the option of taking the test on paper. The information below reflects the time limit and number of questions for the ASTB-E paper test.

Tests	Test Time (in Minutes)	Number of Questions	Options/ Questions
SIFT	15	varies	4
ASTB-E	15	30	3

Examples: Mechanical Comprehension

Directions: For each of the following questions, study the diagram carefully and select the choice that best answers the question or completes the statement.

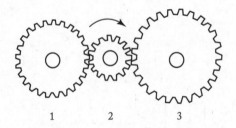

1. Which of the other gears is moving in the same direction as gear 2?

   A. Gear 1

   B. Gear 3

   C. Neither of the gears

   D. Both of the gears

The correct answer is C. The arrow indicates gear 2 is moving clockwise. This would cause both gear 1 and gear 3 to move counterclockwise.

2. The number of threads per inch on the bolt is

   A. 7

   B. 8

   C. 10

The correct answer is B. The bolt thread makes one revolution per eighth of an inch. Accordingly, it has 8 threads in 1 inch.

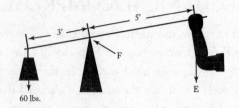

4. What effort must be exerted to lift a 60-pound weight in the figure of a first-class lever shown above (disregard weight of lever)?

    A. 36 pounds

    B. 45 pounds

    C. 48 pounds

    The correct answer is A.

    Let x = effort that must be exerted.

    $$x \cdot 5 = 60 \cdot 3$$
    $$5x = 180$$
    $$x = \frac{180}{5} = 36$$

3. In the figure shown here, the pulley system consists of a fixed block and a movable block. The theoretical mechanical advantage is

    A. 2

    B. 3

    C. 4

    The correct answer is A. The number of parts of the rope going to and from the movable block indicates the mechanical advantage. In this case, it is 2.

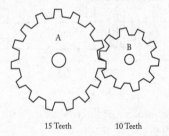

15 Teeth   10 Teeth

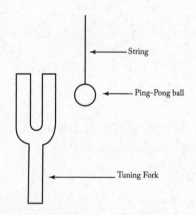

5. In the illustration above, if gear A makes 30 revolutions, gear B will make

    A. 30 revolutions.

    B. 35 revolutions.

    C. 40 revolutions.

    D. 45 revolutions.

    The correct answer is D. For every revolution made by gear A, gear B will make $1\frac{1}{2}$ times as many. If gear A makes 30 revolutions, gear B will make 45.

6. When the Tuning Fork is struck, the Ping-Pong ball will

    A. remain stationary.

    B. bounce up and down.

    C. swing away from the tuning fork.

    The correct answer is C. When a tuning fork vibrates, it moves currents of air. This vibrating air would cause the Ping-Pong ball to be pushed away.

EXERCISES: MECHANICAL COMPREHENSION

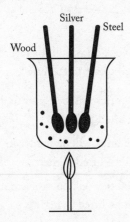

1. Which spoon handle is hottest?

   A. Wood

   B. Silver

   C. Steel

   D. Wood, silver, and steel are all equally hot.

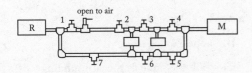

2. In the figure shown above, assume that all valves are closed. For air flow from R through G and then through S to M, open valves

   A. 7, 6, and 5.

   B. 7, 3, and 4.

   C. 7, 6, and 4.

   D. 7, 3, and 5.

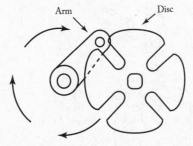

3. The figure above shows a slotted disc turned by a pin on a rotating arm. One revolution of the arm turns the disc

   A. $\frac{1}{8}$ turn.

   B. $\frac{1}{4}$ turn.

   C. $\frac{1}{2}$ turn.

   D. one complete turn.

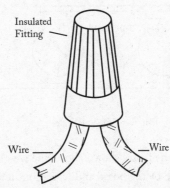

4. Wires are often spliced by the use of a fitting like the one shown above. The use of this fitting does away with the need for

   A. skinning.

   B. soldering.

   C. twisting.

5. The simple machine pictured above is a form of

    A. inclined plane.

    B. torque.

    C. pulley.

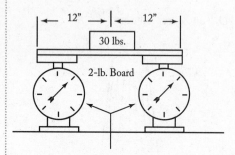

Identical Weighing Scales

6. In the figure shown above, the weight held by the board and placed on the two identical scales will cause each scale to read

    A. 8 pounds

    B. 16 pounds.

    C. 30 pounds

    D. 32 pounds.

7. If the block on which the lever is resting is moved closer to the brick,

    A. the brick will be easier to lift and will be lifted higher.

    B. the brick will be harder to lift and will be lifted higher.

    C. the brick will be easier to lift but will not be lifted as high.

    D. the brick will be harder to lift and will not be lifted as high.

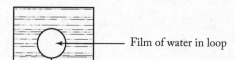

8. The print looked at through the film of water will

    A. be enlarged.

    B. appear smaller.

    C. look the same as the surrounding print.

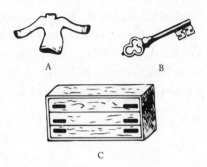

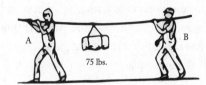

9. If these three items are at the same temperature, and your temperature is higher than the items' temperatures, which one will feel the coldest?

A. A

B. B

C. C

10. The weight is being carried entirely on the shoulders of the two people shown above. Which person bears more weight on his shoulders?

A. Person A

B. Person B

C. Both are carrying the same weight.

ANSWER KEY AND EXPLANATIONS

1. B	3. B	5. A	7. C	9. B
2. D	4. B	6. B	8. A	10. A

1. **The correct answer is B.** Wood is an insulator. Silver is a better conductor than steel.

2. **The correct answer is D.** Only choice D allows air flow through all the valves. Choice A does not permit airflow through G and S, choice B does not permit airflow through S, and choice C does not permit airflow through G.

3. **The correct answer is B.** Each time the rotating arm makes a complete revolution, it moves the slotted disc $\frac{1}{4}$ of a turn.

4. **The correct answer is B.** This is a mechanical or solderless connector. It does away with the need to solder wires and is found in house wiring.

5. **The correct answer is A.** An inclined plane is a sloping, triangular shape, used here as a wedge to force open an axe-cut made in the wood.

6. **The correct answer is B.** The total weight of 32 pounds is balanced equally between the two scales. Each records one half of the total weight or 16 pounds.

7. **The correct answer is C.** If the block is moved toward the brick, the moment for a given force exerted will increase (being farther from the force) making it easier to lift; the height will be made smaller, hardly raising the brick when moved to the limit (directly underneath it).

8. **The correct answer is A.** The film of water inside the loop would form a lens that would enlarge the printing on the page. If you looked through a water-filled globe, objects will also appear larger.

9. **The correct answer is B.** The metal key has the highest conductivity. Metals are the best conductors of heat. Wood can be used as an insulator.

10. **The correct answer is A.** The weight is not centered but is closer to person A. The distance from the center of the load to person A is less than the distance from the center of the load to person B. Therefore, person A would support the greater part of the load.

INSTRUMENT COMPREHENSION

Instrument comprehension test items appear in the Instrument Comprehension subtest of the AFOQT. This subtest is used in calculating the Pilot composite score.

This type of test item measures the test taker's ability to determine the position of an airplane in flight by reading instruments that show its compass heading, amount of climb or dive, and degree of bank to the right or left.

In each question, the left-hand dial is labeled ARTIFICIAL HORIZON. On the artificial horizon, the white area depicts sky, ground is the dark area, and the line between the two is the horizon. The bank scale does include degrees of bank indicators (markings) to the left and right of the pointer (10, 20, 30, 45, 60, and 90 degrees of bank).

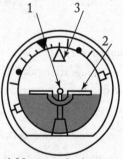

1) Nose on the horizon
2) Wings level
3) No bank

1) Nose slightly above the horizon
2) Right wing down
3) 20 degrees right bank

Let's look at a few examples of the Artificial Horizons dial.

- If the airplane is neither climbing nor diving, the horizon line is directly on the silhouette's fuselage, as in Dial 1.

- If the airplane is climbing, the fuselage silhouette is seen between the horizon line and the pointer, as in Dial 2. The greater the amount of climb, the greater the distance between the horizon line and the fuselage silhouette.

- If the airplane is diving, the horizon line is seen between the fuselage silhouette and the pointer, as in Dial 3. The greater the amount of dive, the greater the distance between the horizon line and the fuselage silhouette.

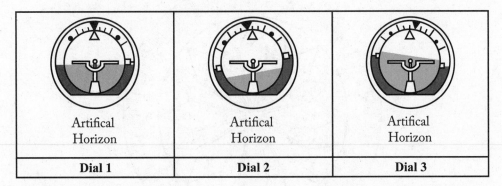

Artifical Horizon	Artifical Horizon	Artifical Horizon
Dial 1	**Dial 2**	**Dial 3**

The HORIZON LINE tilts as the aircraft is banked and is always at right angles to the pointer.

- Dial 1 shows an airplane neither climbing nor diving, with no bank.
- Dial 2 shows an airplane climbing and banking to the left.
- Dial 3 shows an airplane diving and banking to the right.

In each question, the right-hand dial is labeled COMPASS. On this dial, the arrow shows the compass direction in which the airplane is headed at the moment.

Compasses are graduated in degrees clockwise from north. The cardinal points are:

- North 0° or 360°
- East 90°
- South 180°
- West 270°

The intercardinal points are:

- Northeast 45°
- Southeast 135°
- Southwest 225°
- Northwest 315°

The compass card below shows degrees, cardinal points, and intercordinal points

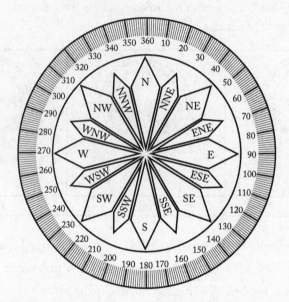

The combination points midway between the cardinal and intercardinal points are:

NNE $22\frac{1}{2}^{\circ}$ SSW $202\frac{1}{2}^{\circ}$

ENE $67\frac{1}{2}^{\circ}$ WSW $247\frac{1}{2}^{\circ}$

ESE $112\frac{1}{2}^{\circ}$ WNW $292\frac{1}{2}^{\circ}$

SSE $157\frac{1}{2}^{\circ}$ NNW $337\frac{1}{2}^{\circ}$

Examples of the compass dial are shown below:

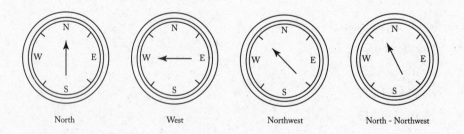

North   West   Northwest   North - Northwest

Each question on instrument comprehension in these tests consists of two dials and four silhouettes of airplanes in flight. Your task is to determine which one of the four airplanes is MOST NEARLY in the position indicated by the two dials. YOU ARE ALWAYS LOOKING NORTH AT THE SAME ALTITUDE AS EACH OF THE PLANES. EAST IS ALWAYS TO YOUR RIGHT AS YOU LOOK AT THE PAGE.

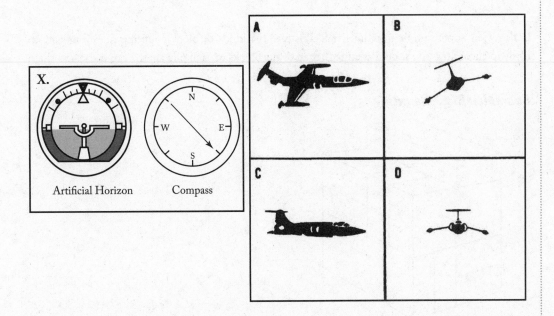

Item X is a sample from the Air Force Officer Qualifying Test. In item X, the dial labeled ARTIFICIAL HORIZON shows that the airplane is NOT banked, and is neither climbing nor diving. The COMPASS shows that it is headed southeast. The only one of the four airplane silhouettes that meets these specifications is in the box lettered C, so the answer to X is C. Note that B is a rear view, while D is a front view. Note also that A is banked to the right and that B is banked to the left.

You will be able to practice with these questions on the AFOQT test (Chapter 4).

BLOCK COUNTING

Block Counting test items constitute a subtest of the AFOQT and are used to assess the test takers ability to determine how many other blocks the numbered block touches. **Blocks are considered touching only if all or part of their faces touch. Blocks that only touch corners do not count. All of the blocks in each pile are the same size and shape.** These questions help determine one's sense of spatial relations. Questions of this type are also used frequently in exams for vocational fields such as architecture, computer technology, design, drafting, engineering, and many military occupational specialties.

Let's review some sample questions that illustrate the kinds of block counting questions you are likely to encounter. You should assume that all of the blocks in each pile are the same size and shape.

Examples: Block Counting

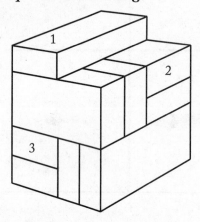

Block	Choices				
	A	B	C	D	E
1	2	3	4	5	6
2	2	3	4	5	6
3	2	3	4	5	6

1. **The correct answer is B.** Box 1 is touched by the three boxes below it, or a total of 3 boxes.

2. **The correct answer is B.** Box 2 is touched by the box below it, the box alongside it, and the box on top, or a total of 3 boxes.

3. **The correct answer is D.** Box 3 is touched by the box below it, the box alongside it, and 3 boxes on top, or a total of 5 boxes.

EXERCISES: BLOCK COUNTING

Directions: Each of the following 5 questions numbered 1–5 are based on the three-dimensional pile of blocks shown below. Determine how many pieces are touched by each numbered block. All of the blocks in the pile are the same size and shape.

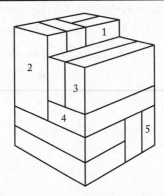

Block	Choices			
	A	B	C	D
1	3	4	5	6
2	4	5	6	7
3	1	2	3	4
4	4	5	6	7
5	4	5	6	7

ANSWER KEY AND EXPLANATIONS

| 1. D | 2. A | 3. B | 4. E | 5. A |

1. **The correct answer is D.** There are 4 alongside and 2 below. 4 + 2 = 6

2. **The correct answer is A.** There are 3 alongside and 1 below. 3 + 1 = 4

3. **The correct answer is B.** There is 1 alongside and 1 below. 1 + 1 = 2

4. **The correct answer is E.** There are 2 above, 3 alongside, and 3 below. 2 + 3 + 3 = 8

5. **The correct answer is A.** There are 3 above and 1 alongside. 3 + 1 = 4

TABLE READING

Table Reading test items constitute a subtest of the AFOQT. They are designed to measure a test taker's ability to read and comprehend tabular material quickly and accurately.

EXERCISES: TABLE READING

Directions: Answer questions 1–3 on the basis of the data in the following table:

Record of Employees				
		Number of Days Absent		
Name of Employee	**Where Assigned**	**Vacation**	**Sick Leave**	**Yearly Salary**
Carty	Laundry	18	4	$19,300
Hart	Laboratory	24	8	17,860
Intersoll	Buildings	20	17	18,580
King	Supply	12	10	17,860
Lopez	Laboratory	17	8	17,500
Martin	Buildings	13	12	17,500
Page	Buildings	5	7	17,500
Quinn	Supply	19	0	17,380
Sage	Buildings	23	10	18,940
Vetter	Laundry	21	2	18,300

1. The only employee who was NOT absent because of illness is

 A. Hart.

 B. Lopez.

 C. Page.

 D. Quinn.

 E. Vetter.

 The correct answer is D. Look down the sick leave column and note that only Quinn had not used any sick leave.

2. The employee with the lowest salary was absent on vacation for

 A. seventeen days.

 B. eighteen days.

 C. nineteen days.

 D. twenty days.

 E. twenty-one days.

 The correct answer is C. Look down the yearly salary column and note that the lowest salary is $17,380. This is the salary received by Quinn who was absent on vacation for nineteen days.

3. Which one of the following was absent on vacation for more than twenty days?

 A. Carty

 B. Ingersoll

 C. Lopez

 D. Quinn

 E. Vetter

 The correct answer is E. Note that there are three employees who were absent on vacation for more than twenty days. However, the only one of the three such employees listed in the choices is Vetter.

EXERCISES: TABLE READING

Directions: Answer questions 1–5 on the basis of the table below. Notice that the X-values are shown at the top of the table and the Y-values are shown on the left of the table. Find the entry that occurs at the intersection of the row and column corresponding to the values given.

X-Value

Y-Value		−3	−2	−1	0	+1	+2	+3
	+3	22	23	25	27	28	29	30
	+2	23	25	27	29	30	31	32
	+1	24	26	28	30	32	33	34
	0	26	27	29	31	33	34	35
	−1	27	29	30	32	34	35	37
	−2	28	30	31	33	35	36	38
	−3	29	31	32	34	36	37	39

	X	Y		A	B	C	D	E
1.	–1	0		29	33	32	35	34
2.	–2	–2		22	29	23	31	30
3.	+2	–1		25	31	35	30	27
4.	0	+3		22	24	25	27	29
5.	+1	–2		36	33	39	35	32

ANSWER KEY AND EXPLANATIONS

1. A	2. E	3. C	4. D	5. D

1. **The correct answer is A.** The entry that occurs at the intersection of an *X*-value of –1 and a *Y*-value of 0 is 29.

2. **The correct answer is E.** The entry that occurs at the intersection of an *X*-value of –2 and a *Y*-value of –2 is 30.

3. **The correct answer is C.** The entry that occurs at the intersection of an *X*-value of +2 and a *Y*-value of –1 is 35.

4. **The correct answer is D.** The entry that occurs at the intersection of an *X*-value of 0 and a *Y*-value of +3 is 27.

5. **The correct answer is D.** The entry that occurs at the intersection of an *X*-value of +1 and a *Y*-value of –2 is 35.

AVIATION INFORMATION

Test items about Aviation Information constitute a subtest of the AFOQT. Aviation Information questions also appear in the Aviation Nautical Information Test (ANIT) of the ASTB-E. The Army Aviation Information Test of the SIFT includes questions that test your general understanding of the principles of helicopter flight.

To further prepare for this subtest, you may want to consult one or more of the many basic books on aviation that have been published. Your local library or bookstore should stock at least a few. More information about these publications can be found in the respective test chapters in this book.

Examples: Aviation Information

Questions 1–8 are based on the following diagram of an airplane:

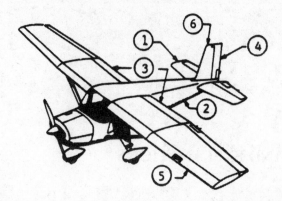

1. The part of the airplane numbered 1 is the

    A. horizontal stabilizer.

    B. left aileron.

    C. left wing.

    D. right aileron.

    E. right wing.

2. The part of the airplane numbered 2 is the

    A. empennage.

    B. flight control and control surfaces.

    C. fuselage.

    D. landing gear.

    E. wing assembly.

3. The parts of the airplane numbered 3 are the

    A. ailerons.

    B. horizontal stabilizers.

    C. landing flaps.

    D. landing wheels.

    E. trim tabs.

4. The part of the airplane numbered 4 is the

    A. elevator.

    B. fuselage.

    C. landing flap.

    D. rudder.

    E. vertical fin.

5. The part of the airplane numbered 5 is the

    A. horizontal stabilizer.

    B. leading edge, left wing.

    C. leading edge, right wing.

    D. trailing edge, left wing.

    E. trailing edge, right wing.

6. The part of the airplane numbered 6 is part of the

    A. empennage.

    B. flight control and control surfaces.

    C. fuselage.

    D. landing gear.

    E. wings.

Answers for questions 1–6 can be found in the diagram below.

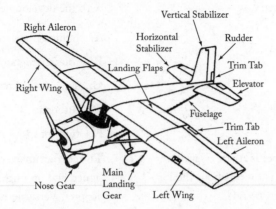

7. The airplane in the diagram above may best be described as

   A. high wing—externally braced; conventional type landing gear.

   B. high wing—externally braced; tricycle type landing gear.

   C. high wing—full cantilever; conventional type landing gear.

   D. high wing—full cantilever; tricycle type landing gear.

   E. mid wing—semi cantilever; tricycle type landing gear.

   The correct answer is B. Note the high wings and external braces, as well as the two main wheels and a steerable nose wheel—the tricycle type.

8. The landing gear on the airplane in the diagram above has a

   A. nose skid.

   B. nose wheel.

   C. tail skid.

   D. tail wheel.

   E. set of parallel skids.

   The correct answer is B. Note the nose wheel. There are no skids.

9. The small hinged section on the elevator of most airplanes is called the

   A. flap.

   B. aileron.

   C. stringer.

   D. trim tab.

   E. vertical fin.

   The correct answer is D. The small hinged section on the elevator is called the trim tab. It helps prevent pilot fatigue by relieving control pressure at any desired flight altitude.

10. The wing shape shown below is best described as

    A. double tapered.

    B. straight leading and trailing edges.

    C. straight leading edge, tapered trailing edge.

    D. tapered leading and trailing edges.

    E. tapered leading edge, straight trailing edge.

    The correct answer is E. Note the tapered leading or forward edge of the wing and the straight trailing or rear edge of the wing.

11. Movement about the longitudinal axis of the aircraft is termed

    A. bank.

    B. pitch.

    C. skid.

    D. slip.

    E. yaw.

    The correct answer is A. In aviation terminology, to *bank* is to roll about the longitudinal axis of the aircraft.

12. Which one of the following does NOT affect density altitude?

    A. Altitude

    B. Atmospheric pressure

    C. Moisture content of air

    D. Temperature

    E. Wind velocity

    The correct answer is E. Density altitude pertains to a theoretical air density that exists under standard conditions at a given altitude. The four factors that affect density altitude are altitude, atmospheric pressure, temperature, and moisture content of the air.

13. The lifting power for dirigibles is now provided by

    A. helium.

    B. hot air.

    C. hydrogen.

    D. nitrogen.

    E. oxygen.

    The correct answer is A. The dirigible, or zeppelin, is lifted by helium. Hydrogen is highly flammable and is no longer used for lifting. Hot air is used to lift balloons.

14. The name Sikorsky is generally associated with the development of

    A. lighter-than-air aircraft.

    B. rotary wing aircraft.

    C. supersonic aircraft.

    D. turbojets.

    E. turboprops.

    The correct answer is B. Igor Sikorsky designed and produced the first practical helicopter. Versatile rotary wing aircraft are now produced in various military and civilian versions.

15. The maneuver in which the helicopter is maintained in nearly motionless flight over a reference point at a constant altitude and a constant heading is termed

    A. autorotation.

    B. feathering action.

    C. hovering.

    D. free wheeling.

    E. torque.

    The correct answer is C. Hovering is the term applied when a helicopter maintains a constant position at a selected point, usually several feet above the ground.

EXERCISES: AVIATION INFORMATION

Directions: Each of the following 25 questions or incomplete statements is followed by five answer choices. Decide which one best answers the question or completes the statement.

1. Most airplanes are designed so that the outer tips of the wing are higher than the wing roots attached to the fuselage in order to

    A. increase the maximum permissible payload.

    B. provide lateral stability.

    C. provide longitudinal stability.

    D. reduce fuel consumption.

    E. streamline the fuselage.

2. If an airfoil moves forward and upward, the relative wind moves

    A. backward and downward.

    B. backward and upward.

    C. forward and downward.

    D. forward and upward.

    E. forward horizontally.

3. Many factors influence lift and drag. If the wing area is doubled,

    A. the lift will be doubled, but the drag will be halved.

    B. the lift will be halved, but the drag will be doubled.

    C. the lift and drag will be doubled.

    D. the lift and drag will be halved.

    E. there is no effect on lift or drag.

4. Tetraethyl lead (TEL) is used principally as an additive that

    A. absorbs moisture in gasoline.

    B. decreases viscosity of gasoline.

    C. has a low antiknock quality.

    D. increases gasoline antiknock quality.

    E. increases volatility of gasoline.

5. Standard weights have been established for numerous items used in weight and balance computations. The standard weight for gasoline used in an airplane is

    A. 6 lbs./U.S. gal.

    B. 7.5 lbs./U.S. gal.

    C. 8.35 lbs./U.S. gal.

    D. 10 lbs./U.S. gal.

    E. 15 lbs./U.S. gal.

6. The internal pressure of a fluid decreases at points where the speed of the fluid increases. This statement, which partially explains how an airplane wing produces lift, is called

    A. Archimedes' Principle.

    B. Bernoulli's Principle.

    C. Kepler's Law.

    D. Newton's Law.

    E. Pascal's Principle.

7. The rearward force acting on an airplane during flight is termed

    A. drag.

    B. gravity.

    C. lift.

    D. thrust.

    E. weight.

8. The acute angle between the chord line of the wing and the direction of the relative wind is the

    A. angle of attack.

    B. angle of incidence.

    C. axis of rotation.

    D. lift vector.

    E. pitch angle.

9. Which of the following statements is true regarding lift and drag?

    A. As the air density increases, lift and drag decrease.

    B. As the air density increases, lift increases but drag decreases.

    C. As the air density increases, lift decreases but drag increases.

    D. As the air density increases, lift and drag increase.

    E. Lift varies inversely with the density of air.

10. The aft end of the airfoil where the airflow over the upper surface meets the airflow from the lower surface is called the

    A. camber.

    B. chord.

    C. leading edge.

    D. relative wind.

    E. trailing edge.

11. The empennage of an airplane is the

    A. fuselage.

    B. landing gear.

    C. power plant.

    D. tail section.

    E. wing assembly.

12. The primary use of the ailerons is to

    A. bank the airplane.

    B. control the direction of yaw.

    C. control the pitch attitude.

    D. permit a lower landing speed.

    E. provide a steeper climb path.

13. The pitot is an important component in measuring

    A. airspeed.

    B. altitude.

    C. direction.

    D. fuel pressure.

    E. oil pressure.

14. Applying forward pressure on the control causes the elevator surfaces to move downward. This

    A. pushes the airplane's tail downward and the nose downward.

    B. pushes the airplane's tail downward and the nose upward.

    C. pushes the airplane's tail upward and the nose downward.

    D. pushes the airplane's tail upward and the nose upward.

    E. yaws the nose in the desired direction.

15. Runways are assigned numbers that are determined by the magnetic direction of the runway. The runway's magnetic direction is rounded off to the closest 10 degrees and the last 0 is omitted. If a runway is numbered 3 at one end of the runway strip, what would it be numbered at the other end?

    A. 3
    B. 12
    C. 15
    D. 21
    E. 33

16. At a controlled airport, the light signal used by the tower to warn an aircraft in flight that the airport is unsafe and not to land is a(n)

    A. alternating red and green.
    B. flashing green.
    C. flashing red.
    D. steady green.
    E. steady red.

17. Airport runway lights used to illuminate the runway are

    A. blue.
    B. green.
    C. red.
    D. white.
    E. yellow.

18. The illustration shown below is a ground view of a weathervane, looking up from the street below. The wind is coming from the

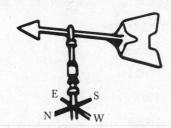

    A. NE
    B. SE
    C. SW
    D. NW
    E. SSE

19. The time 2:00 p.m. is expressed in the 24-hour system as

    A. zero two zero zero.
    B. zero four zero zero.
    C. one four.
    D. one four zero zero.
    E. two zero zero.

20. In the figure below, the pilot has banked the airplane

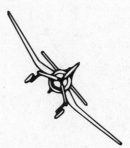

    A. 30 degrees to the right.
    B. 45 degrees to the right.
    C. 60 degrees to the right.
    D. 45 degrees to the left.
    E. 30 degrees to the left.

Questions 21–25 pertain to helicopter operations.

21. Which of the following is used by the helicopter pilot to increase or decrease tail-rotor thrust, as needed, to counteract torque effect?

    A. Clutch

    B. Collective

    C. Throttle control

    D. Pedals

    E. Free wheeling unit

22. Limiting airspeeds are shown on an airspeed indicator by a color coding. The radial line placed on the airspeed indicator to show the airspeed limit beyond that operation is dangerous is colored

    A. blue.

    B. brown.

    C. green.

    D. red.

    E. yellow.

23. If engine failure is experienced while hovering below 10 feet, the pilot should cushion the landing by applying the

    A. clutch.

    B. collective.

    C. cyclic.

    D. pedals.

    E. throttle.

24. Weight and balance limitations must be met before takeoff. Which of the following is NOT part of the useful load (payload)?

    A. Baggage

    B. Oil

    C. Passengers

    D. Pilot

    E. Usable fuel

25. A basic principle of helicopter performance states that for any given gross weight,

    A. the higher the density altitude, the lesser the rate of climb.

    B. the higher the density altitude, the greater the rate of climb.

    C. the lower the density altitude, the lesser the rate of climb.

    D. the density altitude and rate of climb are directly proportional.

    E. There is no relationship between density altitude and rate of climb.

ANSWER KEY AND EXPLANATIONS

1. B	6. B	11. D	16. C	21. D
2. A	7. A	12. A	17. D	22. D
3. C	8. A	13. A	18. A	23. B
4. D	9. D	14. C	19. D	24. B
5. A	10. E	15. D	20. D	25. A

1. **The correct answer is B.** The upward angle formed by the wings, called *dihedral,* counteracts any balance upset caused by a gust of wind and returns the airplane to a wing-level attitude.

2. **The correct answer is A.** The flight path and relative wind are parallel but travel in opposite directions. If an airfoil moves forward and upward, the relative wind moves backward and downward.

3. **The correct answer is C.** The lift and drag acting on a wing are proportional to the wing area. If the wing area is doubled and the other variables remain the same, the lift and drag created by the wing will be doubled.

4. **The correct answer is D.** Tetraethyl lead is the best available knock inhibitor. It is added to improve the antiknock quality of a fuel.

5. **The correct answer is A.** The standard weight for gasoline is 6 lbs./U.S. gal., that for oil is 7.5 lbs./U.S. gal., and that for water is 8.35 lbs./U.S. gal.

6. **The correct answer is B.** Bernoulli's principle and Newton's third law of motion are the basis for explaining how an airplane wing produces lift.

7. **The correct answer is A.** The rearward or retarding force acting on an airplane during flight is called drag.

8. **The correct answer is A.** The angle of attack is the angle between the chord line of the airfoil and the direction of the relative wind.

9. **The correct answer is D.** Lift varies directly with the density of air. As the density of air increases, lift and drag increase.

10. **The correct answer is E.** The trailing edge of the airfoil or wing is the aft end of the airfoil, where the airflow over the upper surface meets the airflow from the lower surface.

11. **The correct answer is D.** The empennage is the tail section and generally consists of a vertical stabilizer, a horizontal stabilizer, a movable rudder, and a movable elevator.

12. **The correct answer is A.** The ailerons, located on the rear edge of the wings near the outer tips, are used to bank or roll the airplane around its longitudinal axis.

13. **The correct answer is A.** The pitot is used to ascertain the impact pressure of the air as the airplane moves forward.

14. **The correct answer is C.** Applying forward pressure on the control causes the elevator surfaces to move downward. The flow of air striking the deflected surfaces exerts an upward force, pushing the airplane's tail upward and the nose downward.

15. **The correct answer is D.** Runway numbers are different at each end of the runway strip because the magnetic directions are 180 degrees apart. The approximate magnetic direction for runway numbered 3 is 30 degrees. The other end would be numbered 21 as it has a magnetic direction of 210 degrees.

16. **The correct answer is C.** The tower operator uses a flashing red signal to instruct pilots not to land because the airport is unsafe.

17. **The correct answer is D.** White lights are used to illuminate airport runways.

18. **The correct answer is A.** The arrow of the weathervane points into the wind midway between north and east, or northeast.

19. **The correct answer is D.** The 24-hour system consists of a four-digit number with 0000 as midnight to 2400 the following midnight. The time 2:00 p.m. would be expressed as 1400 hours in the 24-hour system.

20. **The correct answer is D.** Note the tail assembly on the airplane. The pilot has banked the airplane 45 degrees to the left.

21. **The correct answer is D.** Foot pedals in the cockpit permit the helicopter to increase or decrease tail-rotor thrust, as needed, to neutralize torque effect.

22. **The correct answer is D.** A red radial line is placed on the airspeed indicator to show the airspeed limit beyond that operation is dangerous.

23. **The correct answer is B.** In the event of engine failure while hovering or on takeoff below 10 feet, apply collective pitch as necessary to cushion the landing.

24. **The correct answer is B.** The useful load (payload) is the weight of the pilot, passengers, baggage, removable ballast, and usable fuel. Oil is considered to be part of the empty weight.

25. **The correct answer is A.** For any given gross weight, the higher the density altitude, the less the rate of climb for any helicopter.

NAUTICAL INFORMATION

Questions on nautical information appear in the Aviation/Nautical Information Test of the ASTB-E.

Examples: Nautical Information

1. To go in the direction of the ship's bow is to go

   A. aft.

   B. below.

   C. forward.

   D. outboard.

   E. topside.

   The correct answer is C. The bow is the forward part of a ship. To go in that direction is to go forward.

2. In marine navigation, speed is measured in

   A. knots.

   B. miles.

   C. nautical miles.

   D. range.

   E. standard miles.

   The correct answer is A. Speed is measured in knots, a term meaning nautical miles per hour.

3. The ratio of the international nautical mile to the statute mile is most nearly

   A. $\frac{3}{4}$

   B. $\frac{7}{8}$

   C. $\frac{1}{1}$

   D. $\frac{8}{7}$

   E. $\frac{4}{3}$

4. On the compass, which is used to determine direction, EAST is indicated at a reading of

   A. 000 degrees.

   B. 090 degrees.

   C. 180 degrees.

   D. 270 degrees.

   E. 360 degrees.

   The correct answer is B. All directions are measured from north on a 360-degree system. East is 090 degrees; south is 180 degrees; west is 270 degrees; north is 000 or 360 degrees.

5. Compass north is generally not the same as magnetic north because of

   A. diurnal change.

   B. gyrocompass error.

   C. parallax.

   D. the influence of local magnetic forces.

   E. vessel speed, heading, and latitude.

   The correct answer is D. The influence of local magnetic forces, such as iron, near the compass causes deviation from magnetic north.

The correct answer is D. The international nautical mile is most nearly 6,078 feet; the statute mile is 5,280 feet. The ratio is approximately $\frac{8}{7}$.

6. Using the 24-hour basis in navigation, 8:45 a.m. would be written as

   A. 845

   B. 0845

   C. 08.45

   D. 2045

   E. 20.45

   The correct answer is B. The 24-hour clock uses four digits. Hours and minutes less than 10 are preceded by a zero.

7. Delicate, feather-like, white clouds occurring at very high altitude are termed

   A. altostratus clouds.

   B. cirrocumulus clouds.

   C. cirrus clouds.

   D. cumulus clouds.

   E. nimbostratus clouds.

   The correct answer is C. Cirrus clouds are high-altitude, delicate white clouds with little shading.

8. The formation of fog may be predicted by determining the

   A. atmospheric pressure.

   B. changes in atmospheric pressure.

   C. color of the sky.

   D. difference between the wet-and-dry bulb temperatures.

   E. wind speed.

   The correct answer is D. The formation of fog may be predicted by using the wet-and-dry bulb. Fog usually forms when the wet-bulb depression is less than 4 degrees.

9. Icebreakers are operated by the

   A. U.S. Army.

   B. U.S. Coast Guard.

   C. U.S. Department of Commerce.

   D. U.S. Department of the Interior.

   E. U.S. Navy.

   The correct answer is B. The U.S. Coast Guard is responsible for national icebreaking missions.

10. A ship, at a latitude of 35°N and a longitude of 30°E, is in the

    A. Bering Sea.

    B. Caribbean Sea.

    C. Mediterranean Sea.

    D. North Sea.

    E. Sea of Japan.

    The correct answer is C. The coordinates given indicate a position in the Mediterranean Sea.

EXERCISES: NAUTICAL INFORMATION

Directions: Each of the following 25 questions or incomplete statements is followed by five answer choices. Decide which one best answers the question or completes the statement.

1. "Zulu Time" used in ship communication is

   A. Daylight Savings Time.

   B. Local Mean Time.

   C. Greenwich Mean Time.

   D. Standard Time.

   E. Zone Time.

2. Which of the following is a common type of visual communication used shipboard?

   A. Facsimile

   B. Foghorn

   C. Radiotelegraph

   D. Satellite

   E. Semiphore

3. The plane perpendicular to the Earth's axis and midway between the two poles divides the Earth into the

   A. eastern and western hemispheres.

   B. north and south poles.

   C. northern and southern hemispheres.

   D. parallels and meridians.

   E. upper meridian and lower meridian.

4. Which of the following types of rope is strongest?

   A. Cotton

   B. Hemp

   C. Manila

   D. Nylon

   E. Sisal

5. Greenwich, at prime meridian, is at a latitude of approximately 50°N. Which of the following cities is closest to Greenwich?

   A. Amsterdam—52°22′N 4°53′E

   B. Athens—37°58′N 23°43′E

   C. Copenhagen—55°40′N 12°54′E

   D. Oslo—50°57′N 10°42′E

   E. Stockholm—59°17′N 18°3′E

6. A latitude of 21°N and longitude of 159°W is in the vicinity of

   A. Cuba.

   B. the Falkland Islands.

   C. Hawaii.

   D. the Philippines.

   E. Samoa.

7. An unlighted buoy, used to mark the left side of a channel when facing inland, is called a

   A. bell buoy.

   B. can buoy.

   C. nun buoy.

   D. spar buoy.

   E. whistle buoy.

8. If the clock shows the time to be 1400 aboard a ship sailing in time zone +3, what would be the time in the Greenwich zone?

   A. 0800

   B. 1100

   C. 1400

   D. 1700

   E. 2000

9. The navigation light associated with "port" is colored

   A. green.

   B. red.

   C. white.

   D. yellow.

   E. None of the above

10. To go in the direction of the ship's stern is to go

   A. aft.

   B. below.

   C. forward.

   D. inboard.

   E. topside.

11. The vertical distance from the waterline to the lowest part of the ship's bottom is the

   A. draft.

   B. freeboard.

   C. list.

   D. sounding.

   E. trim.

12. The forward part of the main deck of a ship is generally called the

   A. fantail.

   B. forecastle.

   C. quarterdeck.

   D. superstructure.

   E. topside.

13. The International Date Line is located at

   A. the 0 meridian.

   B. the 180th meridian.

   C. the celestial meridian.

   D. Greenwich, England.

   E. the prime meridian.

14. Compass error in a magnetic compass caused by change in the magnetic field of the Earth from place to place is termed

   A. bearing.

   B. deviation.

   C. reckoning.

   D. sighting.

   E. variation.

15. The lubber's line used in ascertaining the ship's heading indicates

   A. compass error.

   B. the direction of the ship's bow.

   C. the ship's heading.

   D. magnetic north.

   E. true north.

16. A tide falling after high tide is

   A. breaking.

   B. bulging.

   C. ebbing.

   D. flooding.

   E. slacking.

17. Low even clouds that form just above the Earth and give the sky a hazy appearance are termed

   A. altocumulus clouds.

   B. altostratus clouds.

   C. cirrocumulus clouds.

   D. cirrus clouds.

   E. stratus clouds.

18. The Beaufort scale is generally used at sea in estimating

   A. wind direction.

   B. wind speed.

   C. atmospheric pressure.

   D. relative humidity.

   E. water depth.

19. The instrument used in celestial navigation to measure angles in degrees, minutes, and seconds is called a(n)

   A. azimuth.

   B. compass.

   C. protractor.

   D. sextant.

   E. transit.

20. When a person is reported overboard, the action to take first is to

   A. bring the ship to a halt.

   B. track the person with a pair of binoculars.

   C. throw life buoys over at once.

   D. turn the ship around 180 degrees.

   E. reduce the ship's speed.

21. A fathometer is generally used to

   A. determine direction.

   B. determine Greenwich mean time.

   C. make deep-sea soundings.

   D. make shallow water soundings.

   E. measure distance in nautical miles.

22. 6:00 p.m. is written in the 24-hour system as

   A. 0600

   B. 0900

   C. 1200

   D. 1500

   E. 1800

23. In marine navigation, which of the following is NOT a method of determining position?

   A. Celestial navigation

   B. Dead reckoning

   C. Electronic navigation

   D. Piloting

   E. Ranging

24. The intersection of the ship's main deck with the side plating is termed the

   A. bilge.

   B. fantail.

   C. gunwale.

   D. platform.

   E. stanchion.

25. The docking structure built at right angles to the shore is called a(n)

    A. abutment.

    B. mooring.

    C. pier.

    D. slip.

    E. wharf.

Questions 26–30 deal with boat rudder operations on a single-screw boat with a right-hand propeller. **These questions are three-choice items.**

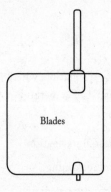

26. A balanced rudder (shown above) has about $\frac{1}{5}$ of the total rudder area projecting ahead of the rudder stock. An unbalanced rudder has the rudder stock attached to the edge of the blade. Which one of the following statements is characteristic of the balanced rudder but NOT of the unbalanced rudder?

    A. It makes steering easier.

    B. It makes steering more difficult.

    C. It exerts considerable effect in increasing the strain on the steering gear.

27.

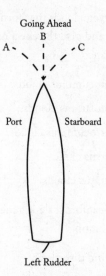

The figure above shows a boat that has left rudder and is going ahead. The bow of the boat would proceed in direction

    A. A

    B. B

    C. C

28.

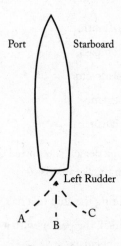

The figure above shows a boat that has left rudder and is going astern. The stem of the boat would proceed in direction

    A. A

    B. B

    C. C

29.

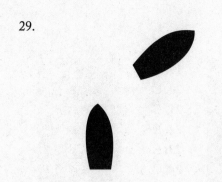

In the figure above, for the boat to swing from position 1 to position 2, she should proceed with

A. left rudder.

B. right rudder.

C. rudder amidship.

30.

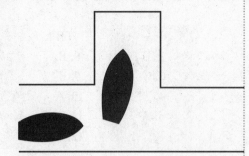

In the figure above, for the boat to back out from position 1 in a slip to position 2 into the channel, she should back out with

A. left rudder.

B. right rudder.

C. rudder amidship.

ANSWER KEY AND EXPLANATIONS

1. C	**7.** B	**13.** B	**19.** D	**25.** C
2. E	**8.** B	**14.** E	**20.** C	**26.** A
3. C	**9.** B	**15.** B	**21.** C	**27.** A
4. D	**10.** A	**16.** C	**22.** E	**28.** A
5. A	**11.** A	**17.** E	**23.** E	**29.** B
6. C	**12.** B	**18.** B	**24.** C	**30.** A

1. **The correct answer is C.** "Zulu time" or Greenwich mean time is used in communications between ships in different time zones.

2. **The correct answer is E.** The foghorn is a type of *sound* communication; facsimile, radiotelegraph, and satellite are types of *electronic* communication; and semiphore is a type of *visual* communication using hand flags.

3. **The correct answer is C.** The plane intersects the earth's surface at the equator and divides the earth into the northern and southern hemispheres.

4. **The correct answer is D.** Nylon is a synthetic fiber of great strength and is much stronger than manila rope.

5. **The correct answer is A.** Amsterdam, with coordinates of 52°22 N and 4°53 E, is closest to Greenwich.

6. **The correct answer is C.** Hawaii is located at a latitude of 21°N and longitude of 159°W.

7. **The correct answer is B.** If unlighted, a green channel marker is can-shaped.

8. **The correct answer is B.** It would be 1400 − 3, or 1100 Greenwich mean time.

9. **The correct answer is B.** *Red* is for port; *green* is starboard. *White* navigation lights inform an observer in which direction a vessel is going. *Yellow* is for special circumstances.

10. **The correct answer is A.** The stern is the after part of the ship. To go in that direction is to go *aft*.

11. **The correct answer is A.** *Draft* is the vertical distance from the waterline to the lowest part of the ship's bottom. *Freeboard* is the vertical distance from the waterline to the edge of the lowest outside deck.

12. **The correct answer is B.** The forward part of the main deck is generally the *forecastle*. The after part is the *fantail*.

13. **The correct answer is B.** The 180th meridian is also known as the International Date Line. Greenwich, England, is located at 0 meridian, or prime meridian.

14. **The correct answer is E.** The magnetic north pole and true north are not at the same location. The magnetic compass does not usually point directly north in most places. This compass error is termed *variation*.

15. **The correct answer is B.** The lubber's line indicates the fore-and-aft line of the ship.

16. **The correct answer is C.** When the tide is falling after high tide, it is called ebb tide.

17. **The correct answer is E.** Stratus clouds are gray clouds found at low altitude and consist of a uniform layer of water droplets.

18. **The correct answer is B.** The Beaufort scale of wind force is useful in estimating wind speed.

19. **The correct answer is D.** The sextant is a precision instrument used in celestial navigation to measure angles.

20. **The correct answer is C.** Life buoys should be thrown over immediately.

21. **The correct answer is C.** A fathometer is an electronic device used in making deep-sea soundings.

22. **The correct answer is E.** 12:00 noon would be written as 1200; 6:00 p.m. would be written as 1800.

23. **The correct answer is E.** In marine navigation, the four methods of determining position are piloting, dead reckoning, celestial navigation, and electronic navigation.

24. **The correct answer is C.** The gunwale is the deck edge, the intersection of the main deck with the shell or side plating.

25. **The correct answer is C.** A *pier* is built at right angle to the shore; a *wharf* is parallel. The space between adjacent piers is called a *slip*.

26. **The correct answer is A.** A balanced rudder with part of the area of the blade surface projected ahead of the rudder stock has a great effect in reducing the strain on the steering gear and in making steering easier.

27. **The correct answer is A.** With left rudder (to port), water flowing past the hull hits the rudder at the port side forcing the stern to starboard, and the boat's bow swings to port.

28. **The correct answer is A.** With left rudder (to port) and going astern, the stern swings to port.

29. **The correct answer is B.** With right rudder (to starboard), water flowing past the hull hits the rudder at the starboard side forcing the stern to port, and the boat's bow swings to starboard.

30. **The correct answer is A.** With left rudder (to port) and going astern, the stem swings to port.

PHYSICAL SCIENCE

Test items in the Physical Science subtest of the AFOQT are five-option questions. The questions assess the test taker's familiarity with physical science concepts. Physical science items pertain to elementary chemistry and physics, astronomy, and the earth sciences.

Examples: Physical Science

1. What temperature is shown on a Fahrenheit thermometer when the centigrade thermometer reads 0°?

   A. −40°

   B. −32°

   C. 0°

   D. +32°

   E. +40°

   The correct answer is D. Water freezes at 0° on the centigrade or Celsius thermometer. Water freezes at 32° Fahrenheit.

2. The bending of waves as they pass from one medium into another is known as

   A. deflection.

   B. diffraction.

   C. displacement.

   D. reflection.

   E. refraction.

   The correct answer is E. Refraction is the bending of a wave's path as it passes from one medium to another.

3. In 4 hours, the earth rotates

   A. 20 degrees.

   B. 30 degrees.

   C. 40 degrees.

   D. 60 degrees.

   E. 90 degrees.

   The correct answer is D. The earth rotates 360 degrees in 24 hours. Four hours is $\frac{1}{6}$ of 24 hours; $\frac{1}{6}$ of 360° is 60°.

4. The moon is a

   A. meteor.

   B. planet.

   C. planetoid.

   D. satellite.

   E. star.

   The correct answer is D. The moon is a satellite of the earth.

5. The capability to hold an electric charge is called

   A. current.

   B. capacitance.

   C. resistance.

   D. wattage.

   E. voltage.

   The correct answer is B. The capability to hold an electric charge is called capacitance.

EXERCISES: PHYSICAL SCIENCE

Directions: Each of the following five questions or incomplete statements is followed by five answer choices. Decide which one of the choices best answers the question or completes the statement.

1. "Shooting stars" are

   A. exploding stars.

   B. cosmic rays.

   C. meteors.

   D. planetoids.

   E. X-rays.

2. The energy of motion is called

   A. chemical energy.

   B. potential energy.

   C. kinetic energy.

   D. mechanical energy.

   E. static energy.

3. When two or more elements combine to form a substance that has properties different from those of the component elements, the new substance is known as a(n)

   A. alloy.

   B. compound.

   C. mixture.

   D. solution.

   E. suspension.

4. If a $33\frac{1}{3}$ rpm phonograph record is played at a speed of 45 rpm, it will

   A. give no sound.

   B. play louder.

   C. play softer.

   D. sound higher-pitched.

   E. sound lower-pitched.

5. Which one of the following gases is necessary for burning?

   A. Argon

   B. Carbon dioxide

   C. Hydrogen

   D. Nitrogen

   E. Oxygen

ANSWER KEY AND EXPLANATIONS

| 1. C | 2. C | 3. B | 4. D | 5. E |

1. **The correct answer is C.** Meteors, or "shooting stars," come into the earth's atmosphere from outer space with high velocity. The resistance offered by the earth's atmosphere makes these meteors incandescent in flight.

2. **The correct answer is C.** Kinetic energy is the energy of motion.

3. **The correct answer is B.** Substances are classified as elements or compounds. A compound is a substance composed of the atoms of two or more different elements.

4. **The correct answer is D.** The greater the number of vibrations per second produced by the sounding object, the higher will be the pitch produced. Playing a $33\frac{1}{3}$ rpm phonograph record at a faster speed (45 rpm) will produce a higher-pitched sound.

5. **The correct answer is E.** Combustion cannot occur in the absence of oxygen.

HIDDEN FIGURES

Questions on hidden figures appear in the Hidden Figures subtest of the SIFT. They are designed to measure your ability to see simple figures in complex drawings. Although these figures are fairly well camouflaged, proper visualization should enable you to discern them without too much difficulty.

At the top of each section of this subtest are five figures lettered A, B, C, D, and E. Below these on each page are several numbered drawings. You must determine which lettered figure is contained in each of the numbered drawings.

The lettered figures are shown below:

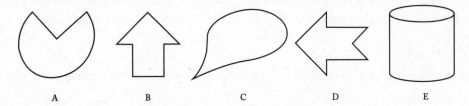

As an example, look at drawing X below:

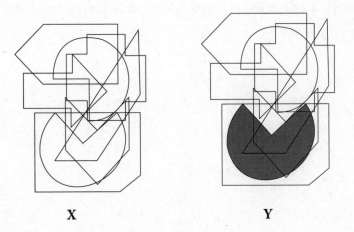

Which one of the five figures is contained in drawing X? Now look at drawing Y, which is exactly like drawing X except that the outline of figure A has been shaded to show where to look for it. Thus, A is the answer to sample item X.

Each numbered drawing contains only *one* of the lettered figures. The correct figure in each drawing will always be of the same size and in the same position as it appears at the top of the page. Therefore, you will not need to rotate the page in order to find it. For more practice with hidden figure questions, go to Chapter 6, "Army Selection Instrument for Flight Training (SIFT)."

SIMPLE DRAWINGS

The Simple Drawings subtest is part of the SIFT. It's a test of speed and accuracy when identifying one shape that is different within a group of five shapes. This test goes quite quickly—you have only two minutes to complete 100 items!

Take a look at this group of five shapes. Identify which figure is not the same as the others.

The correct answer here is D. Figure D is different because it is solid. This is an example of an easier item, bur the questions can increase in difficulty as the differences become more subtle.

In this question, the correct answer is E. The beveled edges on Figure E make it different. For more practice with simple drawings, go to Chapter 6, "Army Selection Instrument for Flight Training (SIFT)."

SPATIAL APPERCEPTION

Questions in the Spatial Apperception Test of the SIFT measure your ability to determine the position or attitude of an airplane in flight by viewing through the windshield of the cockpit the natural horizon and terrain. You must determine whether the airplane is flying straight and level, or climbing, diving, banking to the right or left, or any combination of these maneuvers. You must also determine the general direction of flight of the plane.

Sketches of the view of the horizon and terrain from an airplane in various attitudes are shown below.

View of Horizon and Terrain from Airplanes in Various Altitudes

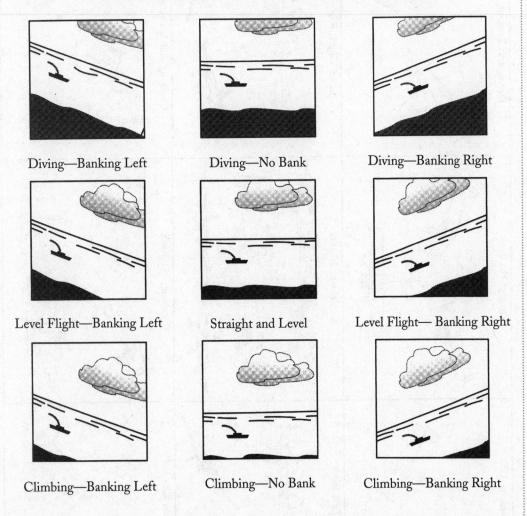

| Diving—Banking Left | Diving—No Bank | Diving—Banking Right |

| Level Flight—Banking Left | Straight and Level | Level Flight— Banking Right |

| Climbing—Banking Left | Climbing—No Bank | Climbing—Banking Right |

Notice that the view is out to sea. The land is darkened, the coastline separates the land from the sea, and the horizon is shown where the sea meets the sky. The direction of flight can be determined by looking at the coastline. In all views shown, the planes are flying out to sea.

Note that when the airplane is flying straight and level, the horizon is horizontal and is in the middle of the pictured view. When in a level flight but banking to the left, the horizon appears tilted to the right, with the center point of the horizon still at the middle of the pictured view. When the plane is in level flight but banking to the right, the horizon appears tilted to the left, with the center point of the horizon still at the middle of the pictured view.

Airplanes in Various Altitudes

Sketches of airplanes in various altitudes are shown below. Note that when the airplane is banked left or right, this means it is banked to the left or right of the pilot seated in the cockpit and looking directly forward, not as viewed from outside the airplane.

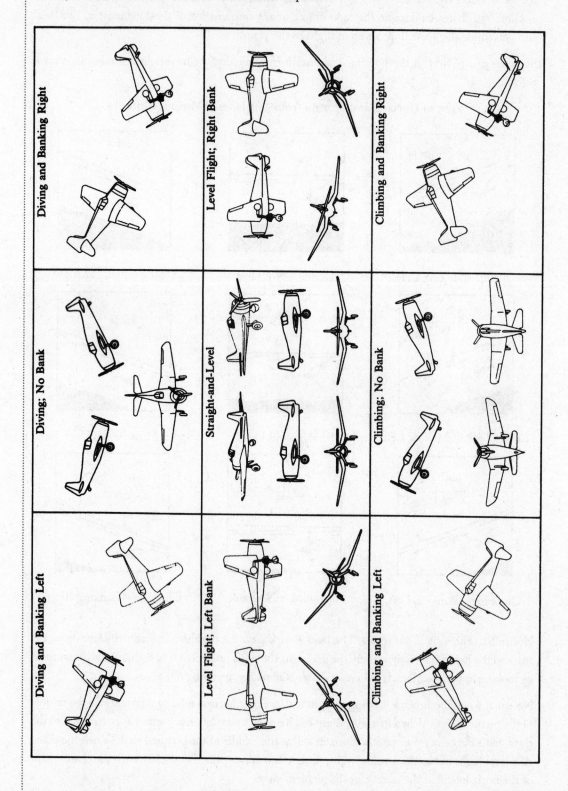

When the airplane is nose-down (diving) but not banking left or right, the horizon appears horizontal and in the upper half of the pictured view. When the plane is nose-down and banking to the left, the horizon appears tilted to the right, with the center point of the horizon in the upper half of the pictured view. When the plane is nose-down and banking to the right, the horizon appears tilted to the left, with the center point of the horizon in the upper half of the pictured view.

When the airplane is nose-up (climbing) but not banking left or right, the horizon is horizontal and is in the lower half of the pictured view. When the plane is nose-up and banking to the left, the horizon appears tilted to the right, with the center point of the horizon in the lower half of the pictured view. When the plane is nose-up and banking to the right, the horizon appears tilted to the left, with the center point of the horizon in the lower half of the pictured view. Note that when the horizon is tilted, the coastline also appears tilted.

Examples: Spatial Apperception

1.

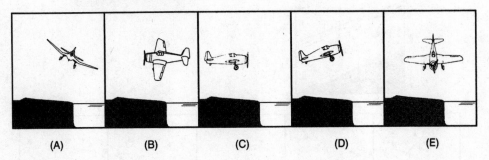

   (A)   (B)   (C)   (D)   (E)

The correct answer is C. Choice A shows a plane banking to the right; choice B shows one banking to the left; choice D shows a plane climbing; and choice E shows a plane diving. Choice C shows a plane in straight-and-level flight heading out to sea.

2.

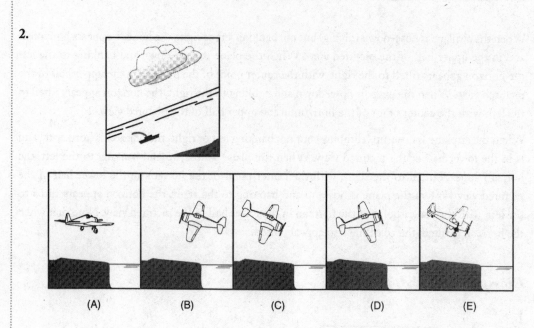

The correct answer is D. Choice A shows a plane in straight-and-level flight; choice B shows one climbing and banking left; choice C shows a plane diving and banking right; and choice E shows a plane diving and banking left. Choice D shows a plane climbing and banking right heading out to sea.

3.

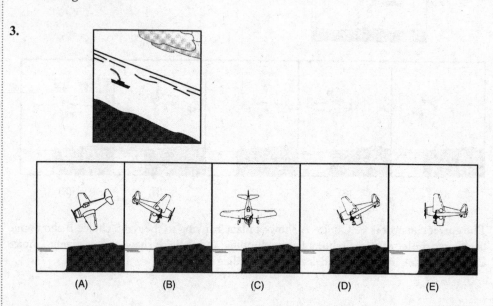

The correct answer is A. Choice B shows a plane diving and banking to the left heading toward land; choice C shows one diving but not banking; choice D shows a plane diving and banking to the right; and choice E shows a plane banking to the right. Choice A shows a plane diving and banking to the left heading out to sea.

Note that in examples 1 and 2, the sea is to the right of the coastline. In example 3, the sea is to the left of the coastline. The sea may be above or below the coastline or be in any other position, depending on how the coastline is drawn.

EXERCISES: SPATIAL APPERCEPTION

Directions: In each of the following five questions, the view at the upper left represents what a pilot sees looking straight ahead through the windshield. Five sketches labeled A, B, C, D, and E are shown below. Each lettered sketch shows a plane in a different altitude and in a different direction of flight. From the aerial view shown, determine which of the sketches most nearly represents the altitude of the plane and the direction of flight from which the view would be seen by the pilot.

1.

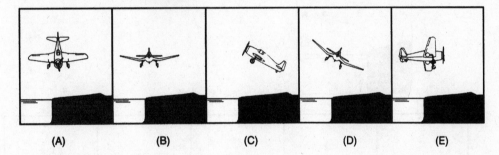

(A)	(B)	(C)	(D)	(E)

2.

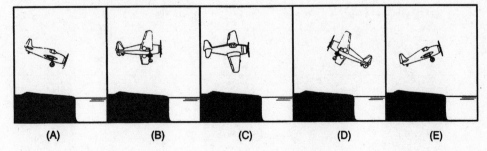

(A)	(B)	(C)	(D)	(E)

3.

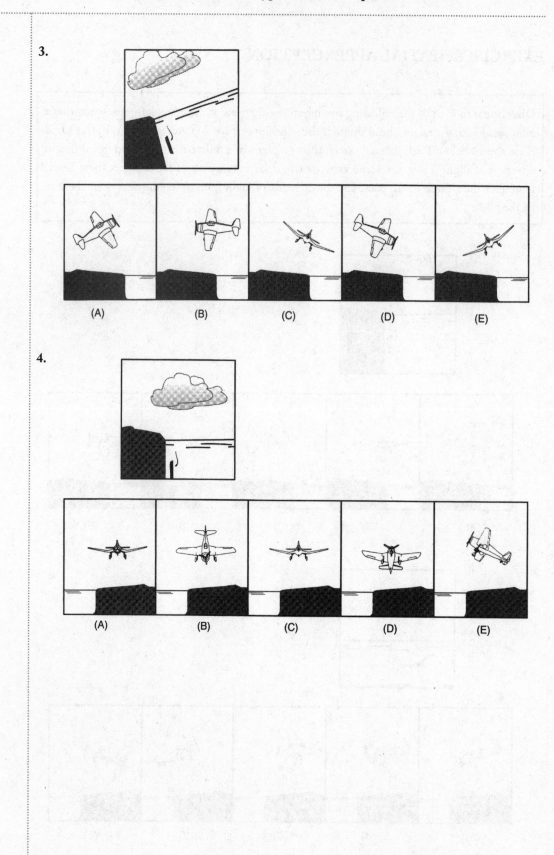

4.

5.

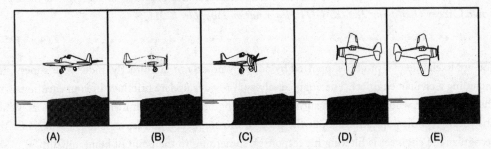

(A) (B) (C) (D) (E)

ANSWER KEY AND EXPLANATIONS

1. B   2. E   3. C   4. D   5. A

1. **The correct answer is B.** Straight-and-level flight along the coastline.

2. **The correct answer is E.** Climbing; no bank; flying out to sea.

3. **The correct answer is C.** Level flight; right bank; flying up the coastline.

4. **The correct answer is D.** Climbing, no bank; flying down the coastline. (Note that the sea is left of the coastline in the lettered choices but right of the coastline in the aerial view.)

5. **The correct answer is A.** Straight-and-level flight heading 45 degrees left of coastline.

SITUATIONAL JUDGMENT

The Situational Judgment subtest on the AFQOT measures judgment and decision-making in responding to the types of interpersonal situations often encountered by junior U.S. Air Force officers. The questions on this portion of the test are based on actual situations encountered by junior officers. These scenarios require application of the core competencies of Integrity and Professionalism, Leadership, Resource Management, Communication, Innovation, and Mentoring.

The following is an example of a situation judgment scenario provided in the United States Air Force Officer *Qualifying Test (AFOQT) Information Pamphlet (2015)*:

You are in charge of a project supported by people who do not fall directly under your supervision, including a civilian engineer. The engineer always provides update briefings in your meetings with the commander, who is superior in authority to the engineer and your immediate supervisors. When answering technical questions about the project, the engineer often leaves out relevant facts. You recognize the engineer is filtering his responses, sometimes to the point of being untruthful.

Possible actions:

A. Speak up during the meeting to present the full, unfiltered information yourself.

B. Immediately after the meeting, discuss your concerns privately with the engineer.

C. Immediately after the meeting, notify the engineer's supervisor of your concerns.

D. Immediately after the meeting, notify your supervisor of your concerns to seek advice.

E. Immediately after the meeting, meet privately with the commander to present the full, unfiltered information.

1. Select the MOST EFFECTIVE action (A-E) in response to the situation.
2. Select the LEAST EFFECTIVE action (A-E) in response to the situation.

ANSWER KEY AND EXPLANATIONS

1. **The correct answer (MOST EFFECTIVE action) is E.** Going directly to the commander shows a lack of respect for the chain of command. Bypassing your superiors with information that they may not be aware of can potentially reflect poorly on them, and your motives could come under scrutiny. By neglecting to engage the engineer to determine the reasons for his information filtering, you miss an opportunity to improve communication and help the engineer become a better team member.

2. **The correct answer (LEAST EFFECTIVE action) is B.** Speaking privately with the engineer allows him to explain his reasons for his approach to information dissemination without publicly challenging his findings and his honesty, therefore respecting his dignity, which is a display of both good communication and professionalism. Informing the engineer that you are aware of his actions and that deception is unacceptable serves as an admonition to the engineer to adjust his presentation technique before any further action needs to be taken. These actions display integrity and mentoring skills.

PERFORMANCE-BASED MEASUREMENT BATTERY

The Performance Based Measurement Battery on the ASTB-E assesses manual dexterity, processing speed, and multi-tasking capability, giving you a real-time, hands-on flight simulation experience. You will be tested on your dichotic listening and spatial orientation skills while using a mock-up throttle, headset, and joystick. The test is composed of seven subtests, some of which are combinations of the other subtests:

1. Unmanned Aerial Vehicle Test
2. Dichotic Listening Test
3. Airplane Tracking Test
4. Vertical Tracking Test
5. Airplane Tracking and Horizontal Tracking Test
6. Airplane Tracking, Vertical Tracking, and Dichotic Listening Test
7. Emergency Scenario Test

Detailed information about each of these subtests is covered in Chapter 5.

BIOGRAPHICAL INFORMATION AND SELF-DESCRIPTION SUBTESTS

Some sections you will encounter on the ASTB-E and AFOQT do not assess specific skills; rather they are designed to assess a candidate's suitability as a military officer and more specifically, a career in aviation. The ASTB-E contains two: the Naval Aviation Trait Facet Inventory (NAFTI) and the Biographical Inventory with Response Validation (BI-RV). The AFOQT contains the Self-Description Inventory. Biographical or personal background inventories such as the BI-BV have been proven fairly good predictors of success in technical, professional, and executive training. Personality test such as the NAFTI and the Self-Description Inventory help identify candidates who are truly motivated to become pilots and who have a good attitude about their work.

Because biographical and personality test questions have no right or wrong answers, it is difficult to prepare for taking such a test. Here are a few guidelines you can follow, however, that can improve your chances of doing well on a personality subtest. Keep the following three tips in mind when answering questions:

- **Always tell the truth.** Personality tests are designed in part to identify people who are not being candid. One of the main reasons some people do poorly on personality tests is because they answer questions in a way that they think makes them look perfect. This is a big mistake: No one is perfect.

- **Go with your first thought.** Because personality test questions have no right or wrong answers, it's easy to read too much into them. The questions are usually straightforward and should be answered as such. Don't try to second-guess the intent of the questions or look for hidden meanings; doing so will certainly lower your performance.

- **Don't be afraid to say how you feel.** The answers to many questions on personality tests are stated in terms of the extent to which you agree or disagree with a particular statement.

For example, on the AFOQT Self-Description Inventory, your answer choices are: A Strongly Disagree; B Moderately Disagree; C Neither Agree nor Disagree; D Moderately Agree; E Strongly Agree. If you feel strongly about a particular statement, don't be afraid to answer with an A or E. It's usually not wise to respond with answer choice C too often, unless you're really not certain of how you feel.

More information and about these tests and sample questions will be presented in Chapters 4 and 5.

SUMMING IT UP

- Synonym questions appear in the Word Knowledge subtest of the AFOQT.

- Verbal analogy questions appear in the Verbal Analogies subtest of the AFOQT; they test your knowledge of word meanings, your vocabulary level, and your ability to reason.

- The Reading Comprehension subtest is part of the AFOQT. Sentence comprehension questions also appear in the Reading Skills Test of the ASTB-E.

- Arithmetic reasoning questions appear in the Arithmetic Reasoning subtest of the AFOQT. This type of test item also appears in the Math Skills Test of the ASTB-E.

- Math Knowledge questions appear in the AFOQT. These questions also appear in the Math Skills Test of the ASTB-E.

- Questions on mechanical comprehension are presented in the Mechanical Comprehension subtests of the ASTB-E and the SIFT. Both of these tests are computer-adaptive, but the ASTB-E also administers this test on paper.

- Instrument Comprehension subtests of the AFOQT measure your ability to determine the position of an airplane in flight.

- The questions in the Block Counting subtest of the AFOQT items are designed to assess your ability to "see into" a three-dimensional group of blocks.

- The Table Reading subtest of the AFOQT measures your ability to read tabular material quickly and accurately.

- The Aviation Information subtest of the AFOQT measures aviation knowledge. A similar section, the Aviation and Nautical Information Test, which assesses both aviation and nautical knowledge, also appears on the ASTB-E.

- The Physical Science subtest of the AFOQT assesses your knowledge of physical science, which includes chemistry, physics, and astronomy/earth science.

- The Hidden Figures subtest of the AFOQT measures your ability to see simple figures in complex drawings.

- The Naval Aviation Trait Facet Inventory subtest on the ASTB-E and the Self-Description Inventory subtest of the AFOQT contain questions about one's background, interests, likes and dislikes, personality traits, opinions, and attitudes.

Air Force Officer Qualifying Test (AFOQT Form T)

Chapter 4

OVERVIEW

- AFOQT Form T Overview
- Test of Basic Aviation Skills (TBAS)
- Composite Scoring
- Test Section Descriptions and Strategies
- AFOQT Answer Sheet
- AFOQT Practice Test
- AFOQT Answer Keys and Explanations
- Summing It Up

AFOQT FORM T OVERVIEW

As of January 2016, the AFOQT Form T is the only test version used for officer selection and career field selection; it replaced the previous AFOQT Form S in August 2014. Avoid using any non-Form T version of the AFOQT in your preparation. Changes include certain test sections having been removed, new sections added, and new questions drafted among new categories within test sections. In addition, the composites of what test sections are used in calculated career field scores has also been modified. Sections not included in composite scores, which will be discussed later in this chapter, may still be relevant in officer candidacy selection and for aviation career field consideration. Effective test preparation requires a thorough review and understanding of material in this chapter before taking the practice test within this chapter. Our discussion of the test sections may include a recommendation to take a similar test section within this book (Chapter 5 for the ASTB-E or Chapter 6 for the SIFT) as a practice before taking the AFOQT Form T practice test. When taking the tests in this book, attempt to adhere to the provided timelines for the test section. Review the answers for understanding and as a means to identify areas to further research and expand your knowledge or skill base. In some cases, wrong answer options may be identified within the test answer discussion as important knowledge areas that you should also understand. Take the test again as needed, but be aware of your test-taking bias (familiarity with the test) that will skew your time and result in a more favorable outcome.

Similar to other armed services exams, this test can be taken only a limited number of times. After taking the test, the AFOQT can be taken only once more in your lifetime after a minimum of six months between the test dates. Scores are valid for life and are first used in officer candidate selection and then later for career field selection. It is not uncommon for those having achieved officer candidate selection to take the test a second time to improve their scores prior to career field selection. However, all results from the second test replace results from the first, even if the result is a less desirable score. A waiver process, through an officer recruiting office, can be used to adjust testing time limits or scores; however, extensive factual reasoning is required and approval is unlikely. For instance, if a person has a disability or condition that requires a test adjustment, then that disability or condition may eliminate the candidate from officer candidacy consideration. Obtaining a waiver to reduce the retest wait period *might* be more likely if an extreme situation interrupted the taking of the initial test (e.g. fire, emergency, power failure). Plan on performing your very best on the test the first time, and take it again later as an officer candidate *only* if you are certain you can improve the scores.

TEST OF BASIC AVIATION SKILLS (TBAS)

The Test of Basic Aviation Skills (TBAS) is a computer-based test battery that measures psychomotor skills, spatial ability, and multitasking aptitude. The test consists of nine subtests and takes approximately 1 hour and 15 minutes to complete. The TBAS is used as a tool for the selection of U. S. Air Force pilot and RPA pilot candidates. TBAS scores are combined with the candidate's AFOQT Pilot composite scores and flying hours to produce a Pilot Candidate Selection Method (PCSM) score.

You can schedule the TBAS either before or after taking the AFOQT. If you take the TBAS after you have taken the AFOQT, your PCSM score should be available 1 to 2 days after your TBAS has been submitted to a central scoring facility.

The TBAS is very similar to the Performance-Based Measures Battery (PBM) used on the ASTB-E by the U. S. Navy, Marine Corps, and Coast Guard. The primary difference between the two tests is the use of a rudder pedal on the Test of Basic Aviation Skills (TBAS) for horizon tracking. The PBM uses a throttle for vertical tracking. You might want to read the description and strategies of the PBM in Chapter 5, as they directly apply. For more information about the TBAS, visit the U. S. Air Force Personnel Center (AFPC) website: (**http://access.afpc.af.mil/pcsmdmz/TBASInfo. html**). Use this same link to access your TBAS/PCSM results once they are available.

COMPOSITE SCORING

The AFOQT Form T is composed of 12 subtests. No overall composite score is calculated for the entirety of the 12 tests. Instead, various sections are used to calculate seven composite scores (Table 4.1). A score is generated for a subtest based on correct answers. Scores are then statistically calculated relative to a normal distribution of test results among all those competing for limited officer candidate positions and then later for limited career field positions. This translates to determining not just how well a person performed on the test but rather how well he or she did relative to their peers. For example, a score of 90 means that you did better than 90 percent of others who took that part of the test and that 10 percent scored higher than you. In addition to other factors included in officer candidacy and career selection (discussed in Chapters 1 and 2), selection comes down to ranking those wanting limited jobs relative to the number of those jobs available for a given time period.

Table 4

AFOQT Form T Schedule and Composites									
			Composite Scores						
Subtest or *(activity)*	Questions	Time (Min.)	Pilot	CSO	ABM	Academic	Verbal	Quantitative	Situational Judgment
(Pretest admin)		(10)							
Verbal Analogies	25	8			X	X	X		
Arithmetic Reasoning	25	29				X		X	
Word Knowledge	25	5		X		X	X		
Math Knowledge	25	22	X	X	X	X		X	
Reading Comprehension	25	38				X		X	
(Break)		(10)							
Situational Judgment	50	35							X
Self-Description Inventory	240	45							
(Answer sheet preparation)		(15)							
(Break)		(15)							
(Pretest admin)		(3)							
Physical Science	20	10							
Table Reading	40	7	X	X	X				
Instrument Comprehension	25	5	X		X				
Block Counting	30	4.5		X	X				
Aviation Information	20	8	X		X				
(Collect Materials)		(2)							

Note: Testing time does not include time for the proctor to read subtest instructions and examples.

The officer candidate selection board uses the AFOQT academic, verbal, and quantitative composite scores as a component of the selection process. Following officer candidacy selection, rated officer (Pilot, Combat Systems Operator, and Air Battle Manager) career field selection is more complex, with each career field's Order of Merit (OM) score including one of the three AFOQT-rated composite scores. Minimum scores may be required in categories other than pilot, CSO, and ABM composites and may be identified by the detachment proctoring the test. For example, minimum composite scores of 15 verbal and 10 quantitative are required in order to qualify to apply for pilot candidacy. In addition, pilots must have a combined Pilot and CSO score of 50 as well as a minimum of 25 in Pilot and 10 in CSO. CSOs require a combined 50 and 25 in CSO and 10 in Pilot. These scores represent the *minimum* needed to qualify for those rated positions; keep in mind that selections are based on a ranked order of candidates against the available positions (also known as slots).

A subtest that is not identified as part of a composite does not mean it is not taken into consideration. Subtests are used to help predict success as an officer and within various Air Force training programs. For instance, the physical science subtest is not aligned with composites, yet it could be relevant for a specific desired career field selection. Situational judgment composite score and self-description inventory (a personality test) are also not listed as used for officer candidacy, career field, nor rated aviation selection; however, they *may* be used as additional measures for consideration.

The time listed for each test in Table 4.1 does not include additional time used by the proctor to read instructions and examples for each subtest. The AFOQT Form T is administered over 4 hours, 47 minutes, and 30 seconds, within which (minus breaks and administrative time) 3 hours, 36 minutes, and 30 seconds are devoted to taking the 12 subtests. You will likely have more than enough time to answer all the questions on most of the subtests. However, you may not be able to complete several of the subtests in the alloted time period. Don't worry if this happens; many people do not finish these subtests. Even if you are unsure of the answer to a question, make a selection anyway, even if you have to guess. Your score on the AFOQT will be based on the number of correct answers you select. You will not lose points or be penalized for guessing. With the exception of the personality test, results of how you did on the test and your scored averages relative to your peers are eventually provided to you through your officer recruiting organization.

TEST SECTION DESCRIPTIONS AND STRATEGIES

Verbal Analogies

The Verbal Analogies test is a measure of reasoning in identifying associations among five different relationship categories: synonyms/definitions, antonyms, function/relationship, classification, and part-to-whole. Such assessments are common on standardized tests and are also often used in employment screening. The function of the assessment is to determine verbal acuity and relative quickness of thinking. These skills are essential for aviators as well as in a variety of other military jobs.

Arithmetic Reasoning

Arithmetic Reasoning is a test of rationally used math for real-world problem resolution, and it is comparable to SAT® and ACT® testing. Again, such skills are not only of value to military aviators but also to many other military jobs.

Word Knowledge

The Word Knowledge test is an evaluation of your overall vocabulary. The purpose of this assessment is to determine either specific word knowledge or one's general vocabulary level. In addition, vocabulary is indicative of someone's ability to communicate efficiently and effectively, which is imperative for a sucessful career as an officer. To succeed in this section, the best strategy is to enhance one's vocabulary through extensive reading and proper use of language, rather than attempting to study multiple words in isolation and memorize their meanings.

Math Knowledge

The Math Knowledge test is an evaluation of college-level mathematical terms and principles.

Reading Comprehension

The Reading Comprehension test is an evaluation of one's reading level and vocabulary relative to comprehending technical writing, also known as academic writing, which requires a high reading level. No knowledge of the subject matter is needed to answer five questions relative to each of the five passages. Common question types include the following:

- Identification of the primary purpose of the passage
- Memory recall of the applied meaning of a term or phrase within the passage
- Determination of whether the author would or would not agree to a statement about the passage
- Identification of an item as belonging or not belonging to a list of items (or concepts) from the passage
- Potential inquiry if the author makes use of supported/unsupported statements to persuade or inform

Your reading comprehension was most likely tested when you took the SAT® or ACT®. To improve your reading comprehension, try reading the various journal and research articles online through Google Scholar (**https://scholar.google.com**).

While reviewing the articles, avoid reading the abstract, recommendations, and summary sections. Instead try to identify the main purpose, and determine if the author(s) would agree or disagree with your thoughts on the study. Use the abstract, recommendation, and summary sections to compare with your understanding of the main purpose and support your assumptions about with what the author(s) would or would not agree. Identify terms and phrases within the abstract and summary, and recall their meaning or implied meaning relative to the article. Validate your understanding of those terms by reviewing how the author(s) defined them within the document. Look for items and concepts distributed throughout the passage to recognize them as those supported (or not supported) by the author. Be sure to eliminate distractions as you develop your comprehension and information recollection skills when reading lengthier journal articles. Reading comprehension is an invaluable skill. With time always being your most limited resource, the ability to absorb and process relevant aspects of massive amounts of information efficiently will serve you well throughout your professional career.

Situational Judgment Test

This new section of the AFOQT Form T is a character assessment similar to the self-description inventory (a personality test). A brief situation is presented, followed by five response choices marked A through E. Two questions are tied to each of the 25 situational statements. One question asks you to select the most effective action, and the other question has you select the least effective action. Subtest validity is assessed relative to the situations having occurred, response outcomes relative to the officer, and as a consensus among officer peers. Correct responses are based on USAF competencies: integrity, professionalism, leadership, resource management, communication, innovation, and mentoring. Instead of thinking of actions relative to the most or least effective, consider thinking of them as the most or least "appropriate" action relative to the core competencies. The "most correct" action is the one that optimizes one or more of the competencies relative to other choices. The "most incorrect" action is the one that violates one or more of the competencies relative to other bad actions. Selection of a bad action does not mean that other bad actions are acceptable, but rather that this particular bad action is simply much more severe than the others. Preparation for this subtest requires memorizing and understanding each of the USAF core competencies so you can apply them in addressing the most and least effective actions per scenario.

Self-Description Inventory

AFOQT scores are categorically assessed, meaning that each category has an individual score, and no composite score of all sections is generated. The self-description inventory (a personality assessment known as the NEO Personality Inventory—Revised, or NEO PI-R) is similar to the situational judgment section, in that it is a separately assessed category. However, unlike other subtests and categories, the output generates an array of information, none of which is shared with you. The USAF conducted longitudinal tests of the NEO PI-R (also known generally as "The Big Five") between 1994 and 2011, which resulted in the inclusion of the personality measure in the 2014 AFOQT revision. Results from NEO PI-R Air Force research trials indicated statistically significant personality trait differences between military officers and military aviators relative to the general population.

Component AFOQT subtests are based on historic success measures as an officer and for specific aviation career selection. While traditional categories are still used in officer candidacy and rated career selection, the NEO PI-R *can* be used as an additional *consideration* for both. Because you are providing information that *may* be used in your selection, it is important for you to understand the assessment. In addition, exploratory studies have been conducted relative to personality differences between a general population of junior officers and senior command track officers. The future potential use of information you provide *may* have long-term implications not currently incorporated in career progression considerations.

The NEO PI-R is a psychological assessment that measures the five major personality domains: Neuroticism, Extraversion, Openness to Experience, Agreeableness and Conscientiousness. The five categories are higher order constructs (personality domains). Each domain is further defined by six facets. Each facet is measured from an assortment of questions, totaling 240, using a 5-point Likert scale ranging from "Strongly Agree" to "Strongly Disagree". Even though the Likert scale is categorical, it is treated as continuous for inferential statistical analysis (Figure 4.1).

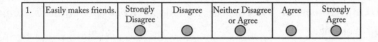

Figure 4.1. Likert Scale Example. Figure depicts the type of question used in personality assessments.

The USAF study results indicated that pilots have dramatically higher Extraversion, Openness to Experience, and Conscientiousness, and lower Neuroticism and Agreeableness than the general population. Female pilots scored even higher on Extraversion and Openness to Experience relative to women in the general population. Table 4.2 indicates these differences with each personality factor and subgroup as greater than the national norm (+), less than the norm (–), or not greatly different from the norm (0). The USAF study also identified the differences within career categories as limited to comparisons within those groups only due to the homogeneity of each group. The objective of another 2015 research study was to enhance the use of the NEO PI-R to augment airframe selections to reduce training time and associated costs. This additional PI trend found differences between fighter and bomber pilots and airlift and tanker pilots that *may* be used for additional track selection considerations.

Table 4.2

USAF Findings of Pilots versus the General U.S. Population				
Neuroticism (–)	**Extraversion (+)**	**Openness to Experience (+)**	**Agreeableness (–)**	**Conscientiousness (+)**
Anxiety (–)	Warmth (+)	Fantasy (+)	Trust (0)	Competence (+)
Angry Hostility (–)	Gregariousness (+)	Aesthetics (-)	Straightforwardness (–)	Order (0)
Depression (–)	Assertiveness (+)	Feelings (0)	Altruism (0)	Dutifulness (+)
Self-Consciousness (–)	Activity (+)	Action (0)	Compliance (+)	Achievement Striving (+)
Impulsiveness (–)	Excitement-Seeking (+)	Ideas (+)	Modesty (–)	Self-Discipline (+)
Vulnerability (–)	Positive Emotions (–)	Values (–)	Tender-Mindedness (–)	Deliberation (0)

Note: Symbols indicates USAF pilots scored (–) less than, (+) more than, (0) about the same as the general U.S. population.

Each personality factor and subgroup are described as follows:

Neuroticism is the degree to which a person wants to experience emotionally unstable behavior such as anger, sorrow, and fear.

- **Anxiety:** The propensity to not control nervousness, apprehension, and dread.
- **Angry Hostility:** The inclination to project frustration, hatred, and bitterness.
- **Depression:** The predisposition to feelings of gloominess, misery, and desolation.
- **Self-Consciousness:** The degree of unassertiveness, timidity, reluctance, and group avoidance.
- **Impulsiveness:** A tendency for reckless behavior, carelessness, and thoughtlessness.
- **Vulnerability:** The degree of susceptibility to the effects of stress.

Extraversion is the extent of social situational enjoyment, excitement, and self-stimulation.

- **Warmth:** Cordiality and kindness toward others.
- **Gregariousness:** The acceptability of companionship, fellowship, and comradeship.
- **Assertiveness:** The extent of resoluteness, decisiveness, and desire for purpose of action.
- **Activity:** The degree to which a person pursues liveliness and hustle in their life.
- **Excitement Seeking:** The extent a person is motivated by a sense of adventure and environmental engagement.
- **Positive Emotions:** A propensity for hopefulness, liveliness, cheerfulness, and joy.

Openness to Experience is the degree of willingness to explore new innovative ideas or differing values.

- **Fantasy:** The extent of broad-mindedness towards inventiveness, creativity, and ingenuity.
- **Aesthesis:** The appreciation of beauty, art, and detail.
- **Feelings:** The degree of emotional intelligence, or receptiveness, in recognizing feelings and emotions.
- **Actions:** A willingness for new experiences and responsibility.
- **Ideas:** The degree of creative, rational, and scholarly interest.
- **Values:** An ability to synthesize and formulate constructive criticism.

Agreeableness is a measure of the degree of sympathy toward others.

- **Trust:** The extent of confidence in the sincere intentions of others.
- **Straightforwardness:** To what extent a person is outspoken and impartial.
- **Altruism:** The propensity to selflessness and benevolence for the welfare of others.
- **Compliance:** A behavior associated with an ability to conform to communal order.
- **Modesty:** A humility and unpretentiousness of achievement.
- **Tender-mindedness:** The degree of compassion and empathy for others.

Conscientiousness is the degree of behavioral tendency to plan and organize; also associated with self-discipline.

- **Competence:** The extent a person facilitates his or her own aptitude and effectiveness.
- **Order:** A behavior associated with a need to organize and plan outcomes.
- **Dutifulness:** The extent of self-accountability of obligations.
- **Achievement Striving:** The degree that a person exhibits a personal drive for personal accomplishment.
- **Self-Discipline:** The tendency to self-organize and complete a responsibility despite environmental distractions or boredom.
- **Deliberation:** A behavior of desiring planned outcomes.

Although a shorter section with questions similar to the NEO PI-R is included in the AFOQT practice test, the actual NEO PI-R test is copyrighted and controlled, inclusive of a USAF contract for use and application. The Pennsylvania State University (PSU) Department of Psychology has a free online test that is similar to the NEO PI-R and includes an informed consent form and an option to provide an unofficial name to promote privacy. The questions are not the same copyrighted material used in the NEO PI-R; however, they are very close and are used to assess the same personality subgroups and domains. Instead of 240 questions, the long test uses 300 questions, and the short version has 60 questions. If you want more practice taking a personality survey, take the PSU test to familiarize yourself with the types of questions you will see in the AFOQT Personality Inventory and how your responses score. A WORD OF CAUTION: The use of the Myers-Briggs Type Indicator (MBTI®) Test to assess your personality in preparation for NEO PI-R is NOT recommended, as it is geared more toward civilian careers than military officer placement.

GET THE FACTS

To learn more about the free PSU online test, visit the following website:

http://www.personal.psu.edu/~j5j/IPIP/

Physical Science

This section is a measure of your knowledge in the categories of astronomy, chemistry, geology/geophysics, physics/general science, math/statistics, and meteorology. An understanding of all of the choices to questions in the practice subtest will be beneficial. Some practice questions are designed to facilitate a more thorough understanding of underlying concepts that may exceed the complexity of the actual test. The purpose of this added layer of complexity is to help you identify categories that you may need to improve your knowledge base. Upon completing the practice subtest, group questions missed by one of the six categories. Self-learn what you can relative to those categories. Cover all the basic concepts and terminologies first, and then tackle the more complex ones.

Table Reading

You will be required to make sense of numerous tables, charts, and diagrams during training in any career field that includes rated pilots, CSOs, and ABMs. During pilot training, expect to quickly calculate weight and balance, takeoff and landing speeds/distances for wet and dry runways, various weather charts, and, later, weaponeering and ballistics. Both accuracy and speed are required to navigate through tables as presented in the sample questions. If necessary, use your answer sheet as a straight edge.

Instrument Comprehension

This is a test of your ability to interpret aircraft orientation (bank and pitch) relative to an artificial horizon (attitude indicator) and aircraft heading relative to a generic heading indicator (not to be confused with a RMI or vertical card compass). Once you mentally orient yourself relative to the instruments, you then choose one of four aircraft pictures that best represents the instrumentation. **Images of an aircraft are depicted as if the top of the page is always north (left side of the page is west), and you are always viewing the aircraft at the same altitude that it is flying.** Understanding basic instrumentation is vital as a professional aviator.

A valuable resource to augment your understanding of aircraft instrumentation is the FAA publication, the *Pilot's Handbook of Aeronautical Knowledge*, downloadable as a PDF in its entirety or as individual chapters.

Within the online handbook, select the "Chapter 8 Flight Instruments" PDF. While familiarizing yourself with the material, for the purpose of this AFOQT subtest, focus your review on the altitude indicator relative to pitch and bank.

GET THE FACTS

To access the *Pilot's Handbook of Aeronautical Handbook*, visit the following website:

https://www.faa.gov/regulations_policies/handbooks_manuals/aviation/phak/

Note that the altitude indicator used on the test does not include indications for degrees of pitch. Pitch interpretations are made relative to the artificial horizon and the depicted wings and nose on the instrument. On the artificial horizon, the white area depicts sky, ground is the dark area, and the line between the two is the horizon. The bank scale does include degrees of bank indicators (markings) to the left and right of the pointer (10, 20, 30, 45, 60, and 90 degrees of bank).

A modified *out-of-control flight* recovery technique is presented as a technique to consistently and precisely tackle each question. Be consistent in whatever technique you use when scanning your instruments (in this case just the available two gauges). FIRST, what is your pitch orientation relative to the horizon (slightly/very/extremely above/below the horizon)? SECOND, what is your bank relative to the wing to horizon orientation (left/right wing above/below the horizon)? THIRD, what is your bank angle (difference between the white and dark triangles)? FOURTH (for the purpose of the test), what is your direction of flight as a general cardinal heading (north, northwest, north-northwest)? The second and third steps can be combined; however, some student military pilots find viewing both the relative wing position and bank indicator helps to overcome disorientation (something that you might experience as you go through the subtest). Figure 4.2 is a depiction of this technique. Note that you may not be familiar with the heading indicator that is used in the test. The top of the compass card always points north, not relative to the aircraft heading; instead, a moving arrow needle is used to indicate aircraft heading (Figure 4.3). Answers to the subtest are presented using the same easy technique but in combine steps two and three. Practice questions on this subtest may be more extreme than your official test; however, mastering the provided subtest should make the actual subtest appear less complex. Also, aerobatic maneuvers and extreme out-of-control recoveries (to include instrument-only recoveries) are performed during pilot training.

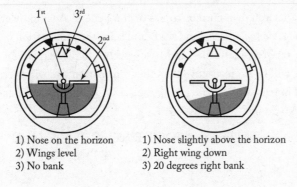

1) Nose on the horizon
2) Wings level
3) No bank

1) Nose slightly above the horizon
2) Right wing down
3) 20 degrees right bank

Figure 4.2. Artificial Horizon used on test. An aircraft orientation technique is depicted.

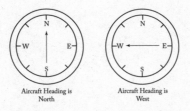

Aircraft Heading is
North

Aircraft Heading is
West

Figure 4.3. Compass Indicator used on test. The left and right compass
instruments indicate aircraft heading relative to needle direction.

Block Counting

This test is another measure of spatial orientation (similar to instrument comprehension) and also the ability to think in three dimensions. Real-world examples of this ability include memorizing battlespace environments and the mental mapping of how various aircraft systems interact. The test is a visual pile of blocks having equal dimensions (similar to a Jenga® game) with an isometric perspective (viewed from a corner with a top down vantage point). Some of the blocks are numbered, and you are asked to determine how many flat surfaces (NOT edges) are in direct contact with other blocks. For the purpose of the test, do not assume blocks exist unless part of the block is visible.

Using the fact that all blocks have the same size and shape, you will need to estimate block dimensions for relative length to determine if unseen sections of blocks are touching.

Aviation Information

This test is a general measure of your knowledge inclusive of aerodynamics, aerodrome operation, aircraft instrumentation, airspace, meteorology, and human factors. Material in basic flight and for instrument ground school can be expected in this subtest. Despite a myth that it is best to know nothing going into military pilot training, the more you know beforehand will most certainly enhance your performance on this test. You will have very limited time to absorb the material during flight school, should that be the first time you are exposed to it.

We also recommend that you own current copies of the Federal Aviation Regulations (FAR) and *Aeronautical Information Manual* (AIM), and study and learn the information contained within these guides. Even though service-, platform-, and base-specific flight regulations will be increasingly more restrictive, none will be *less* restrictive than the information you will encounter. Students who apply themselves and prepare well before taking the AFOQT will have the advantage during pilot training over those who do not.

On the following pages, you will find an AFOQT Practice Test. Good luck!

AFOQT ANSWER SHEET

Part 1: Verbal Analogies

1. Ⓐ Ⓑ Ⓒ Ⓓ Ⓔ   6. Ⓐ Ⓑ Ⓒ Ⓓ Ⓔ   11. Ⓐ Ⓑ Ⓒ Ⓓ Ⓔ   16. Ⓐ Ⓑ Ⓒ Ⓓ Ⓔ   21. Ⓐ Ⓑ Ⓒ Ⓓ Ⓔ
2. Ⓐ Ⓑ Ⓒ Ⓓ Ⓔ   7. Ⓐ Ⓑ Ⓒ Ⓓ Ⓔ   12. Ⓐ Ⓑ Ⓒ Ⓓ Ⓔ   17. Ⓐ Ⓑ Ⓒ Ⓓ Ⓔ   22. Ⓐ Ⓑ Ⓒ Ⓓ Ⓔ
3. Ⓐ Ⓑ Ⓒ Ⓓ Ⓔ   8. Ⓐ Ⓑ Ⓒ Ⓓ Ⓔ   13. Ⓐ Ⓑ Ⓒ Ⓓ Ⓔ   18. Ⓐ Ⓑ Ⓒ Ⓓ Ⓔ   23. Ⓐ Ⓑ Ⓒ Ⓓ Ⓔ
4. Ⓐ Ⓑ Ⓒ Ⓓ Ⓔ   9. Ⓐ Ⓑ Ⓒ Ⓓ Ⓔ   14. Ⓐ Ⓑ Ⓒ Ⓓ Ⓔ   19. Ⓐ Ⓑ Ⓒ Ⓓ Ⓔ   24. Ⓐ Ⓑ Ⓒ Ⓓ Ⓔ
5. Ⓐ Ⓑ Ⓒ Ⓓ Ⓔ   10. Ⓐ Ⓑ Ⓒ Ⓓ Ⓔ   15. Ⓐ Ⓑ Ⓒ Ⓓ Ⓔ   20. Ⓐ Ⓑ Ⓒ Ⓓ Ⓔ   25. Ⓐ Ⓑ Ⓒ Ⓓ Ⓔ

Part 2: Arithmetic Reasoning

1. Ⓐ Ⓑ Ⓒ Ⓓ Ⓔ   6. Ⓐ Ⓑ Ⓒ Ⓓ Ⓔ   11. Ⓐ Ⓑ Ⓒ Ⓓ Ⓔ   16. Ⓐ Ⓑ Ⓒ Ⓓ Ⓔ   21. Ⓐ Ⓑ Ⓒ Ⓓ Ⓔ
2. Ⓐ Ⓑ Ⓒ Ⓓ Ⓔ   7. Ⓐ Ⓑ Ⓒ Ⓓ Ⓔ   12. Ⓐ Ⓑ Ⓒ Ⓓ Ⓔ   17. Ⓐ Ⓑ Ⓒ Ⓓ Ⓔ   22. Ⓐ Ⓑ Ⓒ Ⓓ Ⓔ
3. Ⓐ Ⓑ Ⓒ Ⓓ Ⓔ   8. Ⓐ Ⓑ Ⓒ Ⓓ Ⓔ   13. Ⓐ Ⓑ Ⓒ Ⓓ Ⓔ   18. Ⓐ Ⓑ Ⓒ Ⓓ Ⓔ   23. Ⓐ Ⓑ Ⓒ Ⓓ Ⓔ
4. Ⓐ Ⓑ Ⓒ Ⓓ Ⓔ   9. Ⓐ Ⓑ Ⓒ Ⓓ Ⓔ   14. Ⓐ Ⓑ Ⓒ Ⓓ Ⓔ   19. Ⓐ Ⓑ Ⓒ Ⓓ Ⓔ   24. Ⓐ Ⓑ Ⓒ Ⓓ Ⓔ
5. Ⓐ Ⓑ Ⓒ Ⓓ Ⓔ   10. Ⓐ Ⓑ Ⓒ Ⓓ Ⓔ   15. Ⓐ Ⓑ Ⓒ Ⓓ Ⓔ   20. Ⓐ Ⓑ Ⓒ Ⓓ Ⓔ   25. Ⓐ Ⓑ Ⓒ Ⓓ Ⓔ

Part 3: Word Knowledge

1. Ⓐ Ⓑ Ⓒ Ⓓ Ⓔ   6. Ⓐ Ⓑ Ⓒ Ⓓ Ⓔ   11. Ⓐ Ⓑ Ⓒ Ⓓ Ⓔ   16. Ⓐ Ⓑ Ⓒ Ⓓ Ⓔ   21. Ⓐ Ⓑ Ⓒ Ⓓ Ⓔ
2. Ⓐ Ⓑ Ⓒ Ⓓ Ⓔ   7. Ⓐ Ⓑ Ⓒ Ⓓ Ⓔ   12. Ⓐ Ⓑ Ⓒ Ⓓ Ⓔ   17. Ⓐ Ⓑ Ⓒ Ⓓ Ⓔ   22. Ⓐ Ⓑ Ⓒ Ⓓ Ⓔ
3. Ⓐ Ⓑ Ⓒ Ⓓ Ⓔ   8. Ⓐ Ⓑ Ⓒ Ⓓ Ⓔ   13. Ⓐ Ⓑ Ⓒ Ⓓ Ⓔ   18. Ⓐ Ⓑ Ⓒ Ⓓ Ⓔ   23. Ⓐ Ⓑ Ⓒ Ⓓ Ⓔ
4. Ⓐ Ⓑ Ⓒ Ⓓ Ⓔ   9. Ⓐ Ⓑ Ⓒ Ⓓ Ⓔ   14. Ⓐ Ⓑ Ⓒ Ⓓ Ⓔ   19. Ⓐ Ⓑ Ⓒ Ⓓ Ⓔ   24. Ⓐ Ⓑ Ⓒ Ⓓ Ⓔ
5. Ⓐ Ⓑ Ⓒ Ⓓ Ⓔ   10. Ⓐ Ⓑ Ⓒ Ⓓ Ⓔ   15. Ⓐ Ⓑ Ⓒ Ⓓ Ⓔ   20. Ⓐ Ⓑ Ⓒ Ⓓ Ⓔ   25. Ⓐ Ⓑ Ⓒ Ⓓ Ⓔ

Part 4: Math Knowledge

1. Ⓐ Ⓑ Ⓒ Ⓓ Ⓔ   6. Ⓐ Ⓑ Ⓒ Ⓓ Ⓔ   11. Ⓐ Ⓑ Ⓒ Ⓓ Ⓔ   16. Ⓐ Ⓑ Ⓒ Ⓓ Ⓔ   21. Ⓐ Ⓑ Ⓒ Ⓓ Ⓔ
2. Ⓐ Ⓑ Ⓒ Ⓓ Ⓔ   7. Ⓐ Ⓑ Ⓒ Ⓓ Ⓔ   12. Ⓐ Ⓑ Ⓒ Ⓓ Ⓔ   17. Ⓐ Ⓑ Ⓒ Ⓓ Ⓔ   22. Ⓐ Ⓑ Ⓒ Ⓓ Ⓔ
3. Ⓐ Ⓑ Ⓒ Ⓓ Ⓔ   8. Ⓐ Ⓑ Ⓒ Ⓓ Ⓔ   13. Ⓐ Ⓑ Ⓒ Ⓓ Ⓔ   18. Ⓐ Ⓑ Ⓒ Ⓓ Ⓔ   23. Ⓐ Ⓑ Ⓒ Ⓓ Ⓔ
4. Ⓐ Ⓑ Ⓒ Ⓓ Ⓔ   9. Ⓐ Ⓑ Ⓒ Ⓓ Ⓔ   14. Ⓐ Ⓑ Ⓒ Ⓓ Ⓔ   19. Ⓐ Ⓑ Ⓒ Ⓓ Ⓔ   24. Ⓐ Ⓑ Ⓒ Ⓓ Ⓔ
5. Ⓐ Ⓑ Ⓒ Ⓓ Ⓔ   10. Ⓐ Ⓑ Ⓒ Ⓓ Ⓔ   15. Ⓐ Ⓑ Ⓒ Ⓓ Ⓔ   20. Ⓐ Ⓑ Ⓒ Ⓓ Ⓔ   25. Ⓐ Ⓑ Ⓒ Ⓓ Ⓔ

answer sheet

Part 5: Reading Comprehension

1. Ⓐ Ⓑ Ⓒ Ⓓ Ⓔ   6. Ⓐ Ⓑ Ⓒ Ⓓ Ⓔ   11. Ⓐ Ⓑ Ⓒ Ⓓ Ⓔ   16. Ⓐ Ⓑ Ⓒ Ⓓ Ⓔ   21. Ⓐ Ⓑ Ⓒ Ⓓ Ⓔ

2. Ⓐ Ⓑ Ⓒ Ⓓ Ⓔ   7. Ⓐ Ⓑ Ⓒ Ⓓ Ⓔ   12. Ⓐ Ⓑ Ⓒ Ⓓ Ⓔ   17. Ⓐ Ⓑ Ⓒ Ⓓ Ⓔ   22. Ⓐ Ⓑ Ⓒ Ⓓ Ⓔ

3. Ⓐ Ⓑ Ⓒ Ⓓ Ⓔ   8. Ⓐ Ⓑ Ⓒ Ⓓ Ⓔ   13. Ⓐ Ⓑ Ⓒ Ⓓ Ⓔ   18. Ⓐ Ⓑ Ⓒ Ⓓ Ⓔ   23. Ⓐ Ⓑ Ⓒ Ⓓ Ⓔ

4. Ⓐ Ⓑ Ⓒ Ⓓ Ⓔ   9. Ⓐ Ⓑ Ⓒ Ⓓ Ⓔ   14. Ⓐ Ⓑ Ⓒ Ⓓ Ⓔ   19. Ⓐ Ⓑ Ⓒ Ⓓ Ⓔ   24. Ⓐ Ⓑ Ⓒ Ⓓ Ⓔ

5. Ⓐ Ⓑ Ⓒ Ⓓ Ⓔ   10. Ⓐ Ⓑ Ⓒ Ⓓ Ⓔ   15. Ⓐ Ⓑ Ⓒ Ⓓ Ⓔ   20. Ⓐ Ⓑ Ⓒ Ⓓ Ⓔ   25. Ⓐ Ⓑ Ⓒ Ⓓ Ⓔ

Part 6: Situational Judgment

1. Ⓐ Ⓑ Ⓒ Ⓓ Ⓔ   11. Ⓐ Ⓑ Ⓒ Ⓓ Ⓔ   21. Ⓐ Ⓑ Ⓒ Ⓓ Ⓔ   31. Ⓐ Ⓑ Ⓒ Ⓓ Ⓔ   41. Ⓐ Ⓑ Ⓒ Ⓓ Ⓔ

2. Ⓐ Ⓑ Ⓒ Ⓓ Ⓔ   12. Ⓐ Ⓑ Ⓒ Ⓓ Ⓔ   22. Ⓐ Ⓑ Ⓒ Ⓓ Ⓔ   32. Ⓐ Ⓑ Ⓒ Ⓓ Ⓔ   42. Ⓐ Ⓑ Ⓒ Ⓓ Ⓔ

3. Ⓐ Ⓑ Ⓒ Ⓓ Ⓔ   13. Ⓐ Ⓑ Ⓒ Ⓓ Ⓔ   23. Ⓐ Ⓑ Ⓒ Ⓓ Ⓔ   33. Ⓐ Ⓑ Ⓒ Ⓓ Ⓔ   43. Ⓐ Ⓑ Ⓒ Ⓓ Ⓔ

4. Ⓐ Ⓑ Ⓒ Ⓓ Ⓔ   14. Ⓐ Ⓑ Ⓒ Ⓓ Ⓔ   24. Ⓐ Ⓑ Ⓒ Ⓓ Ⓔ   34. Ⓐ Ⓑ Ⓒ Ⓓ Ⓔ   44. Ⓐ Ⓑ Ⓒ Ⓓ Ⓔ

5. Ⓐ Ⓑ Ⓒ Ⓓ Ⓔ   15. Ⓐ Ⓑ Ⓒ Ⓓ Ⓔ   25. Ⓐ Ⓑ Ⓒ Ⓓ Ⓔ   35. Ⓐ Ⓑ Ⓒ Ⓓ Ⓔ   45. Ⓐ Ⓑ Ⓒ Ⓓ Ⓔ

6. Ⓐ Ⓑ Ⓒ Ⓓ Ⓔ   16. Ⓐ Ⓑ Ⓒ Ⓓ Ⓔ   26. Ⓐ Ⓑ Ⓒ Ⓓ Ⓔ   36. Ⓐ Ⓑ Ⓒ Ⓓ Ⓔ   46. Ⓐ Ⓑ Ⓒ Ⓓ Ⓔ

7. Ⓐ Ⓑ Ⓒ Ⓓ Ⓔ   17. Ⓐ Ⓑ Ⓒ Ⓓ Ⓔ   27. Ⓐ Ⓑ Ⓒ Ⓓ Ⓔ   37. Ⓐ Ⓑ Ⓒ Ⓓ Ⓔ   47. Ⓐ Ⓑ Ⓒ Ⓓ Ⓔ

8. Ⓐ Ⓑ Ⓒ Ⓓ Ⓔ   18. Ⓐ Ⓑ Ⓒ Ⓓ Ⓔ   28. Ⓐ Ⓑ Ⓒ Ⓓ Ⓔ   38. Ⓐ Ⓑ Ⓒ Ⓓ Ⓔ   48. Ⓐ Ⓑ Ⓒ Ⓓ Ⓔ

9. Ⓐ Ⓑ Ⓒ Ⓓ Ⓔ   19. Ⓐ Ⓑ Ⓒ Ⓓ Ⓔ   29. Ⓐ Ⓑ Ⓒ Ⓓ Ⓔ   39. Ⓐ Ⓑ Ⓒ Ⓓ Ⓔ   49. Ⓐ Ⓑ Ⓒ Ⓓ Ⓔ

10. Ⓐ Ⓑ Ⓒ Ⓓ Ⓔ   20. Ⓐ Ⓑ Ⓒ Ⓓ Ⓔ   30. Ⓐ Ⓑ Ⓒ Ⓓ Ⓔ   40. Ⓐ Ⓑ Ⓒ Ⓓ Ⓔ   50. Ⓐ Ⓑ Ⓒ Ⓓ Ⓔ

Part 7: Self-Description Inventory

1. Ⓐ Ⓑ Ⓒ Ⓓ Ⓔ	23. Ⓐ Ⓑ Ⓒ Ⓓ Ⓔ	45. Ⓐ Ⓑ Ⓒ Ⓓ Ⓔ	67. Ⓐ Ⓑ Ⓒ Ⓓ Ⓔ	90. Ⓐ Ⓑ Ⓒ Ⓓ Ⓔ
2. Ⓐ Ⓑ Ⓒ Ⓓ Ⓔ	24. Ⓐ Ⓑ Ⓒ Ⓓ Ⓔ	46. Ⓐ Ⓑ Ⓒ Ⓓ Ⓔ	68. Ⓐ Ⓑ Ⓒ Ⓓ Ⓔ	91. Ⓐ Ⓑ Ⓒ Ⓓ Ⓔ
3. Ⓐ Ⓑ Ⓒ Ⓓ Ⓔ	25. Ⓐ Ⓑ Ⓒ Ⓓ Ⓔ	47. Ⓐ Ⓑ Ⓒ Ⓓ Ⓔ	69. Ⓐ Ⓑ Ⓒ Ⓓ Ⓔ	92. Ⓐ Ⓑ Ⓒ Ⓓ Ⓔ
4. Ⓐ Ⓑ Ⓒ Ⓓ Ⓔ	26. Ⓐ Ⓑ Ⓒ Ⓓ Ⓔ	48. Ⓐ Ⓑ Ⓒ Ⓓ Ⓔ	70. Ⓐ Ⓑ Ⓒ Ⓓ Ⓔ	93. Ⓐ Ⓑ Ⓒ Ⓓ Ⓔ
5. Ⓐ Ⓑ Ⓒ Ⓓ Ⓔ	27. Ⓐ Ⓑ Ⓒ Ⓓ Ⓔ	49. Ⓐ Ⓑ Ⓒ Ⓓ Ⓔ	71. Ⓐ Ⓑ Ⓒ Ⓓ Ⓔ	94. Ⓐ Ⓑ Ⓒ Ⓓ Ⓔ
6. Ⓐ Ⓑ Ⓒ Ⓓ Ⓔ	28. Ⓐ Ⓑ Ⓒ Ⓓ Ⓔ	50. Ⓐ Ⓑ Ⓒ Ⓓ Ⓔ	73. Ⓐ Ⓑ Ⓒ Ⓓ Ⓔ	95. Ⓐ Ⓑ Ⓒ Ⓓ Ⓔ
7. Ⓐ Ⓑ Ⓒ Ⓓ Ⓔ	29. Ⓐ Ⓑ Ⓒ Ⓓ Ⓔ	51. Ⓐ Ⓑ Ⓒ Ⓓ Ⓔ	74. Ⓐ Ⓑ Ⓒ Ⓓ Ⓔ	96. Ⓐ Ⓑ Ⓒ Ⓓ Ⓔ
8. Ⓐ Ⓑ Ⓒ Ⓓ Ⓔ	30. Ⓐ Ⓑ Ⓒ Ⓓ Ⓔ	52. Ⓐ Ⓑ Ⓒ Ⓓ Ⓔ	75. Ⓐ Ⓑ Ⓒ Ⓓ Ⓔ	97. Ⓐ Ⓑ Ⓒ Ⓓ Ⓔ
9. Ⓐ Ⓑ Ⓒ Ⓓ Ⓔ	31. Ⓐ Ⓑ Ⓒ Ⓓ Ⓔ	53. Ⓐ Ⓑ Ⓒ Ⓓ Ⓔ	76. Ⓐ Ⓑ Ⓒ Ⓓ Ⓔ	98. Ⓐ Ⓑ Ⓒ Ⓓ Ⓔ
10. Ⓐ Ⓑ Ⓒ Ⓓ Ⓔ	32. Ⓐ Ⓑ Ⓒ Ⓓ Ⓔ	54. Ⓐ Ⓑ Ⓒ Ⓓ Ⓔ	77. Ⓐ Ⓑ Ⓒ Ⓓ Ⓔ	99. Ⓐ Ⓑ Ⓒ Ⓓ Ⓔ
11. Ⓐ Ⓑ Ⓒ Ⓓ Ⓔ	33. Ⓐ Ⓑ Ⓒ Ⓓ Ⓔ	55. Ⓐ Ⓑ Ⓒ Ⓓ Ⓔ	78. Ⓐ Ⓑ Ⓒ Ⓓ Ⓔ	100. Ⓐ Ⓑ Ⓒ Ⓓ Ⓔ
12. Ⓐ Ⓑ Ⓒ Ⓓ Ⓔ	34. Ⓐ Ⓑ Ⓒ Ⓓ Ⓔ	56. Ⓐ Ⓑ Ⓒ Ⓓ Ⓔ	79. Ⓐ Ⓑ Ⓒ Ⓓ Ⓔ	101. Ⓐ Ⓑ Ⓒ Ⓓ Ⓔ
13. Ⓐ Ⓑ Ⓒ Ⓓ Ⓔ	35. Ⓐ Ⓑ Ⓒ Ⓓ Ⓔ	57. Ⓐ Ⓑ Ⓒ Ⓓ Ⓔ	80. Ⓐ Ⓑ Ⓒ Ⓓ Ⓔ	102. Ⓐ Ⓑ Ⓒ Ⓓ Ⓔ
14. Ⓐ Ⓑ Ⓒ Ⓓ Ⓔ	36. Ⓐ Ⓑ Ⓒ Ⓓ Ⓔ	58. Ⓐ Ⓑ Ⓒ Ⓓ Ⓔ	81. Ⓐ Ⓑ Ⓒ Ⓓ Ⓔ	103. Ⓐ Ⓑ Ⓒ Ⓓ Ⓔ
15. Ⓐ Ⓑ Ⓒ Ⓓ Ⓔ	37. Ⓐ Ⓑ Ⓒ Ⓓ Ⓔ	59. Ⓐ Ⓑ Ⓒ Ⓓ Ⓔ	82. Ⓐ Ⓑ Ⓒ Ⓓ Ⓔ	104. Ⓐ Ⓑ Ⓒ Ⓓ Ⓔ
16. Ⓐ Ⓑ Ⓒ Ⓓ Ⓔ	38. Ⓐ Ⓑ Ⓒ Ⓓ Ⓔ	60. Ⓐ Ⓑ Ⓒ Ⓓ Ⓔ	83. Ⓐ Ⓑ Ⓒ Ⓓ Ⓔ	105. Ⓐ Ⓑ Ⓒ Ⓓ Ⓔ
17. Ⓐ Ⓑ Ⓒ Ⓓ Ⓔ	39. Ⓐ Ⓑ Ⓒ Ⓓ Ⓔ	61. Ⓐ Ⓑ Ⓒ Ⓓ Ⓔ	84. Ⓐ Ⓑ Ⓒ Ⓓ Ⓔ	106. Ⓐ Ⓑ Ⓒ Ⓓ Ⓔ
18. Ⓐ Ⓑ Ⓒ Ⓓ Ⓔ	40. Ⓐ Ⓑ Ⓒ Ⓓ Ⓔ	62. Ⓐ Ⓑ Ⓒ Ⓓ Ⓔ	85. Ⓐ Ⓑ Ⓒ Ⓓ Ⓔ	107. Ⓐ Ⓑ Ⓒ Ⓓ Ⓔ
19. Ⓐ Ⓑ Ⓒ Ⓓ Ⓔ	41. Ⓐ Ⓑ Ⓒ Ⓓ Ⓔ	63. Ⓐ Ⓑ Ⓒ Ⓓ Ⓔ	86. Ⓐ Ⓑ Ⓒ Ⓓ Ⓔ	108. Ⓐ Ⓑ Ⓒ Ⓓ Ⓔ
20. Ⓐ Ⓑ Ⓒ Ⓓ Ⓔ	42. Ⓐ Ⓑ Ⓒ Ⓓ Ⓔ	64. Ⓐ Ⓑ Ⓒ Ⓓ Ⓔ	87. Ⓐ Ⓑ Ⓒ Ⓓ Ⓔ	109. Ⓐ Ⓑ Ⓒ Ⓓ Ⓔ
21. Ⓐ Ⓑ Ⓒ Ⓓ Ⓔ	43. Ⓐ Ⓑ Ⓒ Ⓓ Ⓔ	65. Ⓐ Ⓑ Ⓒ Ⓓ Ⓔ	88. Ⓐ Ⓑ Ⓒ Ⓓ Ⓔ	110. Ⓐ Ⓑ Ⓒ Ⓓ Ⓔ

Part 8: Physical Science

1. Ⓐ Ⓑ Ⓒ Ⓓ Ⓔ	5. Ⓐ Ⓑ Ⓒ Ⓓ Ⓔ	9. Ⓐ Ⓑ Ⓒ Ⓓ Ⓔ	13. Ⓐ Ⓑ Ⓒ Ⓓ Ⓔ	17. Ⓐ Ⓑ Ⓒ Ⓓ Ⓔ
2. Ⓐ Ⓑ Ⓒ Ⓓ Ⓔ	6. Ⓐ Ⓑ Ⓒ Ⓓ Ⓔ	10. Ⓐ Ⓑ Ⓒ Ⓓ Ⓔ	14. Ⓐ Ⓑ Ⓒ Ⓓ Ⓔ	18. Ⓐ Ⓑ Ⓒ Ⓓ Ⓔ
3. Ⓐ Ⓑ Ⓒ Ⓓ Ⓔ	7. Ⓐ Ⓑ Ⓒ Ⓓ Ⓔ	11. Ⓐ Ⓑ Ⓒ Ⓓ Ⓔ	15. Ⓐ Ⓑ Ⓒ Ⓓ Ⓔ	19. Ⓐ Ⓑ Ⓒ Ⓓ Ⓔ
4. Ⓐ Ⓑ Ⓒ Ⓓ Ⓔ	8. Ⓐ Ⓑ Ⓒ Ⓓ Ⓔ	12. Ⓐ Ⓑ Ⓒ Ⓓ Ⓔ	16. Ⓐ Ⓑ Ⓒ Ⓓ Ⓔ	20. Ⓐ Ⓑ Ⓒ Ⓓ Ⓔ

answer sheet

Part 9: Table Reading

1. Ⓐ Ⓑ Ⓒ Ⓓ Ⓔ	9. Ⓐ Ⓑ Ⓒ Ⓓ Ⓔ	17. Ⓐ Ⓑ Ⓒ Ⓓ Ⓔ	25. Ⓐ Ⓑ Ⓒ Ⓓ Ⓔ	33. Ⓐ Ⓑ Ⓒ Ⓓ Ⓔ
2. Ⓐ Ⓑ Ⓒ Ⓓ Ⓔ	10. Ⓐ Ⓑ Ⓒ Ⓓ Ⓔ	18. Ⓐ Ⓑ Ⓒ Ⓓ Ⓔ	26. Ⓐ Ⓑ Ⓒ Ⓓ Ⓔ	34. Ⓐ Ⓑ Ⓒ Ⓓ Ⓔ
3. Ⓐ Ⓑ Ⓒ Ⓓ Ⓔ	11. Ⓐ Ⓑ Ⓒ Ⓓ Ⓔ	19. Ⓐ Ⓑ Ⓒ Ⓓ Ⓔ	27. Ⓐ Ⓑ Ⓒ Ⓓ Ⓔ	35. Ⓐ Ⓑ Ⓒ Ⓓ Ⓔ
4. Ⓐ Ⓑ Ⓒ Ⓓ Ⓔ	12. Ⓐ Ⓑ Ⓒ Ⓓ Ⓔ	20. Ⓐ Ⓑ Ⓒ Ⓓ Ⓔ	28. Ⓐ Ⓑ Ⓒ Ⓓ Ⓔ	36. Ⓐ Ⓑ Ⓒ Ⓓ Ⓔ
5. Ⓐ Ⓑ Ⓒ Ⓓ Ⓔ	13. Ⓐ Ⓑ Ⓒ Ⓓ Ⓔ	21. Ⓐ Ⓑ Ⓒ Ⓓ Ⓔ	29. Ⓐ Ⓑ Ⓒ Ⓓ Ⓔ	37. Ⓐ Ⓑ Ⓒ Ⓓ Ⓔ
6. Ⓐ Ⓑ Ⓒ Ⓓ Ⓔ	14. Ⓐ Ⓑ Ⓒ Ⓓ Ⓔ	22. Ⓐ Ⓑ Ⓒ Ⓓ Ⓔ	30. Ⓐ Ⓑ Ⓒ Ⓓ Ⓔ	38. Ⓐ Ⓑ Ⓒ Ⓓ Ⓔ
7. Ⓐ Ⓑ Ⓒ Ⓓ Ⓔ	15. Ⓐ Ⓑ Ⓒ Ⓓ Ⓔ	23. Ⓐ Ⓑ Ⓒ Ⓓ Ⓔ	31. Ⓐ Ⓑ Ⓒ Ⓓ Ⓔ	39. Ⓐ Ⓑ Ⓒ Ⓓ Ⓔ
8. Ⓐ Ⓑ Ⓒ Ⓓ Ⓔ	16. Ⓐ Ⓑ Ⓒ Ⓓ Ⓔ	24. Ⓐ Ⓑ Ⓒ Ⓓ Ⓔ	32. Ⓐ Ⓑ Ⓒ Ⓓ Ⓔ	40. Ⓐ Ⓑ Ⓒ Ⓓ Ⓔ

Part 10: Instrument Comprehension

1. Ⓐ Ⓑ Ⓒ Ⓓ Ⓔ	6. Ⓐ Ⓑ Ⓒ Ⓓ Ⓔ	11. Ⓐ Ⓑ Ⓒ Ⓓ Ⓔ	16. Ⓐ Ⓑ Ⓒ Ⓓ Ⓔ	21. Ⓐ Ⓑ Ⓒ Ⓓ Ⓔ
2. Ⓐ Ⓑ Ⓒ Ⓓ Ⓔ	7. Ⓐ Ⓑ Ⓒ Ⓓ Ⓔ	12. Ⓐ Ⓑ Ⓒ Ⓓ Ⓔ	17. Ⓐ Ⓑ Ⓒ Ⓓ Ⓔ	22. Ⓐ Ⓑ Ⓒ Ⓓ Ⓔ
3. Ⓐ Ⓑ Ⓒ Ⓓ Ⓔ	8. Ⓐ Ⓑ Ⓒ Ⓓ Ⓔ	13. Ⓐ Ⓑ Ⓒ Ⓓ Ⓔ	18. Ⓐ Ⓑ Ⓒ Ⓓ Ⓔ	23. Ⓐ Ⓑ Ⓒ Ⓓ Ⓔ
4. Ⓐ Ⓑ Ⓒ Ⓓ Ⓔ	9. Ⓐ Ⓑ Ⓒ Ⓓ Ⓔ	14. Ⓐ Ⓑ Ⓒ Ⓓ Ⓔ	19. Ⓐ Ⓑ Ⓒ Ⓓ Ⓔ	24. Ⓐ Ⓑ Ⓒ Ⓓ Ⓔ
5. Ⓐ Ⓑ Ⓒ Ⓓ Ⓔ	10. Ⓐ Ⓑ Ⓒ Ⓓ Ⓔ	15. Ⓐ Ⓑ Ⓒ Ⓓ Ⓔ	20. Ⓐ Ⓑ Ⓒ Ⓓ Ⓔ	25. Ⓐ Ⓑ Ⓒ Ⓓ Ⓔ

Part 11: Block Counting

1. Ⓐ Ⓑ Ⓒ Ⓓ Ⓔ   7. Ⓐ Ⓑ Ⓒ Ⓓ Ⓔ   13. Ⓐ Ⓑ Ⓒ Ⓓ Ⓔ   19. Ⓐ Ⓑ Ⓒ Ⓓ Ⓔ   25. Ⓐ Ⓑ Ⓒ Ⓓ Ⓔ

2. Ⓐ Ⓑ Ⓒ Ⓓ Ⓔ   8. Ⓐ Ⓑ Ⓒ Ⓓ Ⓔ   14. Ⓐ Ⓑ Ⓒ Ⓓ Ⓔ   20. Ⓐ Ⓑ Ⓒ Ⓓ Ⓔ   26. Ⓐ Ⓑ Ⓒ Ⓓ Ⓔ

3. Ⓐ Ⓑ Ⓒ Ⓓ Ⓔ   9. Ⓐ Ⓑ Ⓒ Ⓓ Ⓔ   15. Ⓐ Ⓑ Ⓒ Ⓓ Ⓔ   21. Ⓐ Ⓑ Ⓒ Ⓓ Ⓔ   27. Ⓐ Ⓑ Ⓒ Ⓓ Ⓔ

4. Ⓐ Ⓑ Ⓒ Ⓓ Ⓔ   10. Ⓐ Ⓑ Ⓒ Ⓓ Ⓔ   16. Ⓐ Ⓑ Ⓒ Ⓓ Ⓔ   22. Ⓐ Ⓑ Ⓒ Ⓓ Ⓔ   28. Ⓐ Ⓑ Ⓒ Ⓓ Ⓔ

5. Ⓐ Ⓑ Ⓒ Ⓓ Ⓔ   11. Ⓐ Ⓑ Ⓒ Ⓓ Ⓔ   17. Ⓐ Ⓑ Ⓒ Ⓓ Ⓔ   23. Ⓐ Ⓑ Ⓒ Ⓓ Ⓔ   29. Ⓐ Ⓑ Ⓒ Ⓓ Ⓔ

6. Ⓐ Ⓑ Ⓒ Ⓓ Ⓔ   12. Ⓐ Ⓑ Ⓒ Ⓓ Ⓔ   18. Ⓐ Ⓑ Ⓒ Ⓓ Ⓔ   24. Ⓐ Ⓑ Ⓒ Ⓓ Ⓔ   30. Ⓐ Ⓑ Ⓒ Ⓓ Ⓔ

Part 12: Aviation Information

1. Ⓐ Ⓑ Ⓒ Ⓓ Ⓔ   5. Ⓐ Ⓑ Ⓒ Ⓓ Ⓔ   9. Ⓐ Ⓑ Ⓒ Ⓓ Ⓔ   13. Ⓐ Ⓑ Ⓒ Ⓓ Ⓔ   17. Ⓐ Ⓑ Ⓒ Ⓓ Ⓔ

2. Ⓐ Ⓑ Ⓒ Ⓓ Ⓔ   6. Ⓐ Ⓑ Ⓒ Ⓓ Ⓔ   10. Ⓐ Ⓑ Ⓒ Ⓓ Ⓔ   14. Ⓐ Ⓑ Ⓒ Ⓓ Ⓔ   18. Ⓐ Ⓑ Ⓒ Ⓓ Ⓔ

3. Ⓐ Ⓑ Ⓒ Ⓓ Ⓔ   7. Ⓐ Ⓑ Ⓒ Ⓓ Ⓔ   11. Ⓐ Ⓑ Ⓒ Ⓓ Ⓔ   15. Ⓐ Ⓑ Ⓒ Ⓓ Ⓔ   19. Ⓐ Ⓑ Ⓒ Ⓓ Ⓔ

4. Ⓐ Ⓑ Ⓒ Ⓓ Ⓔ   8. Ⓐ Ⓑ Ⓒ Ⓓ Ⓔ   12. Ⓐ Ⓑ Ⓒ Ⓓ Ⓔ   16. Ⓐ Ⓑ Ⓒ Ⓓ Ⓔ   20. Ⓐ Ⓑ Ⓒ Ⓓ Ⓔ

answer sheet

AFOQT PRACTICE TEST

Part 1: Verbal Analogies

Directions: This part of the test has 25 questions designed to measure your ability to reason and see relationships between words. Each question begins with a comparison of two words. You are to choose the choice that best completes the analogy developed at the beginning of each question. That is, select the choice that shows a relationship similar to the one shown by the original pair of words. Then, mark the space on your answer form that has the same number and letter as your choice.

Now look at the two sample questions below:

1. **Finger** is to **hand** as tooth is to

    A. tongue.

    B. lips.

    C. nose.

    D. mouth.

    E. molar.

The correct answer is D. A *finger* is part of the *hand*; a *tooth* is part of the *mouth*.

2. **Racquet** is to **court** as

    A. tractor is to field.

    B. blossom is to bloom.

    C. stalk is to prey.

    D. plan is to strategy.

    E. moon is to planet.

The correct answer is A. A *racquet* is used (by a tennis player) on the *court*; a *tractor* is used (by a farmer) on the *field*.

Your score on this test will be based on the number of questions you answer correctly. You should try to answer every question. You will not lose points or be penalized for guessing. Do not spend too much time on any one question.

When you begin, be sure to start with question number 1 of Part 1 on your answer sheet.

Part 1: Verbal Analogies

25 Questions • 8 Minutes

1. **Book** is to **chapter** as **building** is to
   A. elevator.
   B. lobby.
   C. roof.
   D. story.
   E. wing.

2. **Musician** is to **stage** as **physician** is to
   A. nurse.
   B. hospital.
   C. patient.
   D. treatment.
   E. medicine.

3. **Carrot** is to **vegetable** as
   A. dogwood is to oak.
   B. foot is to paw.
   C. pepper is to spice.
   D. sheep is to lamb.
   E. veal is to beef.

4. **Alpha** is to **omega** as
   A. appendix is to preface.
   B. head is to body.
   C. intermission is to finale.
   D. beginning is to end.
   E. prelude is to intermission.

5. **Concave** is to **convex** as
   A. cavity is to mound.
   B. hill is to hole.
   C. oval is to oblong.
   D. round is to pointed.
   E. square is to round.

6. **Micrometer** is to **machinist** as
   A. trowel is to mason.
   B. vise is to electrician.
   C. cutter is to blacksmith.
   D. anvil to a pressman.
   E. die to welder.

7. **Gown** is to **garment** as
   A. coolant is to freon.
   B. gasoline is to fuel.
   C. grease is to lubricant.
   D. lubricant is to oil.
   E. oil is to energy.

8. **Conductor** is to **orchestra** as
   A. quarterback is to football.
   B. president is to congress.
   C. coach is to team.
   D. driver is to vehicle.
   E. sergeant is to platoon.

9. **Hyper-** is to **hypo-** as
   A. actual is to theoretical.
   B. diastolic is to systolic.
   C. over is to under.
   D. small is to large.
   E. stale is to fresh.

10. **Hypothesis** is to **premise** as
    A. explore is to study.
    B. corroborate is to collaborate.
    C. authenticate is to abrogate.
    D. challenge is to veto.
    E. negate is to sanction.

11. **Dachshund** is to **dog** as

A. lion is to pride.

B. bengal is to cat.

C. animal is to zoo.

D. bengal is to tiger.

E. tiger is to jungle.

12. **Kilometer** is to **meter** as

A. century is to decade.

B. century is to year.

C. decade is to month.

D. millennium is to century.

E. millennium is to year.

13. **Trickle** is to **gush** as

A. tepid is to hot.

B. trepid is to fear.

C. water is to steam.

D. tap is to hose.

E. apathy is to attentive.

14. **Altimeter** is to **pressure** as

A. stethoscope is to heartrate.

B. timer is to microwave.

C. sphygmomanometer is to oxygen.

D. binoculars is to distance.

E. spectrometer is to frequency.

15. **Node** is to **network** as

A. computer is to Internet.

B. star is to constellation.

C. planet is to galaxy.

D. person is to city.

E. link is to chain.

16. **Vector** is to **velocity** as

A. course is to sailing.

B. compass is to direction.

C. decibel is to sound.

D. navigation is to plotting.

E. casting is to manufacturing.

17. **Piston** is to **engine** as

A. shoe is to box.

B. book is to shelf.

C. planet is to star.

D. tire is to road.

E. chip is to computer.

18. **Unit** is to dozen as

A. day is to week.

B. hour is to day.

C. minute is to hour.

D. month is to year.

E. week is to month.

19. **Sheep** is to **lamb** as

A. lion is to pride.

B. doe is to horse.

C. horse is to colt.

D. mule is to ox.

E. pack is to cub.

20. **Pathology** is to **disease** as

A. forensics is to crime.

B. geophysics is to earth.

C. autopsy is to body.

D. investigation is to accident.

E. surgery is to operation.

practice test—AFOQT (Form T)

21. Ignore is to **disregard** as

    A. agree is to consent.

    B. attach is to separate.

    C. climb is to walk.

    D. dull is to sharpen.

    E. learn is to remember.

22. Corona is to **nimbus** as

    A. cask is to barrel.

    B. agave is to root.

    C. peat is to charcoal.

    D. bark is to oak.

    E. lime is to rind.

23. Frequently is to **seldom** as

    A. always is to never.

    B. everybody is to everyone.

    C. generally is to usually.

    D. continually is to constantly.

    E. sorrow is to sympathy.

24. Vehicle is to **bus** as

    A. football is to handball.

    B. game is to baseball.

    C. hunting is to fishing.

    D. play is to sport.

    E. sport is to recreation.

25. Jubilant is to **apathetic** as **delighted** is to

    A. fervent.

    B. indifferent.

    C. discord.

    D. irritation.

    E. hassle.

STOP! DO NOT GO ON UNTIL TIME IS UP.

Part 2: Arithmetic Reasoning

Directions: This part of the test has 25 questions that measure mathematical reasoning and your ability to arrive at solutions to problems. Each problem is followed by five possible answers. Decide which one of the five choices is most nearly correct. Then, mark the space on your answer form that has the same number and letter as your choice. Use the scratch paper that has been given to you to do any figuring.

Now look at the two sample problems below.

1. A field with an area of 560 square yards is twice as large in area as a second field. If the second field is 20 yards long, how wide is it?

   A. 7 yards
   B. 14 yards
   C. 28 yards
   D. 56 yards
   E. 90 yards

The correct answer is B. The second field has an area of 280 square yards. If one side is 20 yards, the other side must be 14 yards ($20 \times 14 = 280$).

2. An applicant took three typing tests. The average typing speed on these three tests was 46 words per minute. If the applicant's speed on two of these tests was 49 words per minute, what was the applicant's speed on the third test?

   A. 46 words per minute
   B. 44 words per minute
   C. 42 words per minute
   D. 40 words per minute
   E. 38 words per minute

The correct answer is D. The formula for finding an average is as follows:

$$average = \frac{sum\ of\ terms}{numbers\ of\ terms}$$

In this case, the problem provides the average (46), two of the terms (49 + 49), and the number of terms (3). Substitute this information into the formula for average and then solve for x (the missing term).

$$46 = \frac{49 + 49 + x}{3}$$
$$46 \times 3 = 98 + x$$
$$138 = 98 + x$$
$$40 = x$$

Your score on this test will be based on the number of questions you answer correctly. You should try to answer every question. You will not lose points or be penalized for guessing. Do not spend too much time on any one question.

When you begin, be sure to start with question number 1 of Part 2 on your answer sheet.

Part 2: Arithmetic Reasoning

25 Questions • 29 Minutes

1. An athlete jogs 15 laps around a circular track. If the total distance jogged is 3 kilometers, what is the distance around the track?

    A. 0.2 meters

    B. 2 meters

    C. 20 meters

    D. 200 meters

    E. 2,000 meters

2. The floor area in an Air Force warehouse measures 200 feet × 200 feet. What is the maximum safe floor load if the maximum weight the floor area can hold is 4,000 tons?

    A. 100 pounds per square foot

    B. 120 pounds per square foot

    C. 140 pounds per square foot

    D. 160 pounds per square foot

    E. 200 pounds per square foot

3. A crate containing a tool weighs 13 pounds. If the tool weighs 9 pounds, 9 ounces, how much does the crate weigh?

    A. 2 pounds, 7 ounces

    B. 2 pounds, 9 ounces

    C. 3 pounds, 3 ounces

    D. 3 pounds, 7 ounces

    E. 3 pounds, 9 ounces

4. Assume that the U.S. Mint produces one million nickels a month. The total value of the nickels produced during a year is

    A. $50,000

    B. $60,000

    C. $250,000

    D. $500,000

    E. $600,000

5. In order to check on a shipment of 500 articles, a sampling of 50 articles was carefully inspected. Of the sample, 4 articles were found to be defective. On this basis, what is the probable percentage of defective articles in the original shipment?

    A. 8 percent

    B. 4 percent

    C. 0.8 percent

    D. 0.4 percent

    E. 0.04 percent

6. There are 20 cigarettes in one pack and 10 packs of cigarettes in a carton. A certain brand of cigarette contains 12 mg of tar per cigarette. How many grams of tar are contained in one carton of these cigarettes? (1 gram = 1,000 milligrams)

    A. 0.024 grams

    B. 0.24 grams

    C. 2.4 grams

    D. 24 grams

    E. 240 grams

7. Assume that it takes an average of 3 man-hours to stack 1 ton of a particular item. In order to stack 36 tons in 6 hours, the number of people required is

A. 9

B. 12

C. 15

D. 18

E. 21

8. Two office workers have been assigned to address 750 envelopes. One addresses twice as many envelopes per hour as the other. If it takes 5 hours for them to complete the job, what was the rate of the slower worker?

A. 50 envelopes per hour

B. 75 envelopes per hour

C. 100 envelopes per hour

D. 125 envelopes per hour

E. 150 envelopes per hour

9. A room measuring 15 feet wide, 25 feet long, and 12 feet high is scheduled to be painted shortly. If there are two windows in the room, each 7 feet by 5 feet, and a glass door, 6 feet by 4 feet, then the area of wall space to be painted measures

A. 842 square feet.

B. 866 square feet.

C. 901 square feet.

D. 925 square feet.

E. 4,406 square feet.

10. A pound carton of margarine contains four equal sticks of margarine. The wrapper of each stick has markings that indicate how to divide the stick into eight sections, with each section measuring one tablespoon. If a recipe calls for four tablespoons of margarine, the amount to use is

A. $\frac{1}{16}$ lb.

B. $\frac{1}{8}$ lb.

C. $\frac{1}{4}$ lb.

D. $\frac{1}{2}$ lb.

E. $\frac{3}{4}$ lb.

11. The price of a $100 item after successive discounts of 10 percent and 15 percent is

A. $75.00

B. $75.50

C. $76.00

D. $76.50

E. $77.00

12. A certain governmental agency had a budget last year of $1,100,500. Its budget this year was 7 percent higher than that of last year. The budget for next year is 8 percent higher than this year's budget. Which one of the following is the agency's approximate budget for next year?

A. $1,117,600

B. $1,161,600

C. $1,261,700

D. $1,265,600

E. $1,271,700

13. The length of a rectangle is 4 times its width. If the area of the rectangle is 324 square feet, the dimensions of the rectangle are

   A. 8 feet × 32 feet

   B. 8 feet × 33 feet

   C. 9 feet × 36 feet

   D. 9 feet × 40 feet

   E. 9 feet × 46 feet

14. On a scaled drawing of an office building floor, 0.5 inch represents 3 feet of actual floor dimension. A floor that is actually 75 feet wide and 132 feet long would have which of the following dimensions on the scaled drawing?

   A. 12.5 inches wide and 22 inches long

   B. 17 inches wide and 32 inches long

   C. 25 inches wide and 44 inches long

   D. 29.5 inches wide and 52 inches long

   E. none of these

15. If the weight of water is 62.4 pounds per cubic foot, the weight of the water that fills a rectangular container 6 inches by 6 inches by 1 foot is

   A. 3.9 pounds.

   B. 7.8 pounds.

   C. 15.6 pounds.

   D. 31.2 pounds.

   E. 62.4 pounds.

16. If there are red, green, and yellow marbles in a jar, and 20 percent of these marbles are either red or green, what are the chances of blindly picking a yellow marble out of the jar?

   A. 1 out of 3

   B. 1 out of 5

   C. 2 out of 3

   D. 2 out of 5

   E. 4 out of 5

17. An Air Force recruiting station enlisted 560 people. Of these, 25 percent were under 20 years old and 35 percent were 20–22 years old. How many of the recruits were over 22 years old?

   A. 196

   B. 224

   C. 244

   D. 280

   E. 336

18. A passenger plane can carry two tons of cargo. A freight plane can carry six tons of cargo. If an equal number of both kinds of planes are used to ship 160 tons of cargo, and each plane carries its maximum cargo load, how many tons of cargo are shipped on the passenger planes?

   A. 40 tons

   B. 60 tons

   C. 80 tons

   D. 100 tons

   E. 120 tons

19. The area of a square is 36 square inches. If the side of this square is doubled, the area of the new square will be

    A. 72 square inches.
    B. 108 square inches.
    C. 216 square inches.
    D. 244 square inches.
    E. none of these.

20. When 550 gallons of oil are added to an oil tank that is $\frac{1}{8}$ full, the tank becomes $\frac{1}{2}$ full. The capacity of the oil tank is most nearly

    A. 1,350 gallons.
    B. 1,390 gallons.
    C. 1,430 gallons.
    D. 1,470 gallons.
    E. 1,510 gallons.

21. If an aircraft is traveling at 630 miles per hour, how many miles does it cover in 1,200 seconds?

    A. 180 miles
    B. 210 miles
    C. 240 miles
    D. 280 miles
    E. 310 miles

22. If your watch gains 20 minutes per day and you set it to the correct time at 7:00 a.m., the correct time when the watch indicates 1:00 p.m. is

    A. 12:45 p.m.
    B. 12:50 p.m.
    C. 12:55 p.m.
    D. 1:05 p.m.
    E. 1:10 p.m.

23. It takes a runner 9 seconds to run a distance of 132 feet. What is the runner's speed in miles per hour? (5,280 feet = 1 mile)

    A. 5
    B. 10
    C. 12
    D. 15
    E. 16

24. The arithmetic mean of the salaries paid to five employees earning $18,400; $19,300; $18,450, $18,550 and $17,600, respectively, is

    A. $18,450
    B. $18,460
    C. $18,470
    D. $18,475
    E. $18,500

25. How many meters will a point on the rim of a wheel travel if the wheel makes 35 rotations and its radius is one meter?

    A. 110
    B. 120
    C. 210
    D. 220
    E. 240

STOP! DO NOT GO ON UNTIL TIME IS UP.

practice test—AFOQT (Form T)

Part 3: Word Knowledge

> **Directions:** This part of the test has 25 questions designed to measure verbal comprehension involving your ability to understand written language. For each question, you are to select the option that means the same or most nearly the same as the capitalized word. Then mark the space on your answer form that has the same number and letter as your choice.

Here are two sample questions:

1. CRIMSON:

    A. Bluish

    B. Colorful

    C. Crisp

    D. Lively

    E. Reddish

The correct answer is E. *Crimson* means "a deep purple red." Choice E has almost the same meaning. None of the other options has the same or a similar meaning.

2. CEASE:

    A. Continue

    B. Fold

    C. Start

    D. Stop

    E. Transform

The correct answer is D. *Cease* means "to stop." Choice D is the only option with the same meaning.

Your score on this test will be based on the number of questions you answer correctly. You should try to answer every question. You will not lose points or be penalized for guessing. Do not spend too much time on any one question.

When you begin, be sure to start with question number 1 of Part 3 on your answer sheet.

Part 3: Word Knowledge

25 Questions • 5 Minutes

1. ADAMANT

   A. Belligerent

   B. Cowardly

   C. Inflexible

   D. Justified

   E. Petty

2. ALTERCATION

   A. Controversy

   B. Defeat

   C. Irritation

   D. Substitution

   E. Vexation

3. ASSENT

   A. Acquire

   B. Climb

   C. Consent

   D. Emphasize

   E. Participate

4. ATTRITION

   A. Expanding

   B. Surrendering

   C. Purifying

   D. Solving

   E. Wearing down

5. AUTHENTIC

   A. Detailed

   B. Genuine

   C. Literary

   D. Practical

   E. Precious

6. CONDUCIVE

   A. Confusing

   B. Participative

   C. Energetic

   D. Helpful

   E. Respectful

7. COUNTERACT

   A. Criticize

   B. Conserve

   C. Erode

   D. Neutralize

   E. Retreat

8. DELETERIOUS

   A. Delightful

   B. Frail

   C. Harmful

   D. Late

   E. Tasteful

9. DILATED

   A. Cleared

   B. Clouded

   C. Decreased

   D. Enlarged

   E. Tightened

10. FLEXIBLE

    A. flammable

    B. Fragile

    C. Pliable

    D. Rigid

    E. Separable

11. FORTNIGHT

    A. Two days

    B. One week

    C. Two weeks

    D. One month

    E. Two months

12. IMPARTIAL

    A. Complete

    B. Fair

    C. Incomplete

    D. Sincere

    E. Watchful

13. INCIDENTAL

    A. Minor

    B. Eventful

    C. Infrequent

    D. Unexpected

    E. Unnecessary

14. INDOLENT

    A. Hopeless

    B. Lazy

    C. Lenient

    D. Rude

    E. Selfish

15. NOTORIOUS

    A. Annoying

    B. Condemned

    C. Ill-mannered

    D. Official

    E. Well known

16. REBUFF

    A. Forget

    B. Ignore

    C. Recover

    D. Polish

    E. Snub

17. SPURIOUS

    A. False

    B. Maddening

    C. Obvious

    D. Odd

    E. Stimulating

18. SUCCINCT

    A. Concise

    B. Helpful

    C. Important

    D. Misleading

    E. Sweet

19. SULLEN

    A. Angrily silent

    B. Grayish yellow

    C. Mildly nauseated

    D. Soaking wet

    E. Very dirty

20. SYMPTOM

    A. Cure

    B. Disease

    C. Mistake

    D. Sign

    E. Test

21. TEDIOUS

    A. Demanding

    B. Dull

    C. Hard

    D. Simple

    E. Surprising

22. TERSE

    A. Faulty

    B. Lengthy

    C. Oral

    D. Pointed

    E. Written

23. TRIVIAL

    A. distressing

    B. enjoyable

    C. exciting

    D. important

    E. negligible

24. VERIFY

    A. alarm

    B. confirm

    C. explain

    D. guarantee

    E. question

25. VIGILANT

    A. cross

    B. patient

    C. suspicious

    D. understanding

    E. watchful

STOP! DO NOT GO ON UNTIL TIME IS UP.

practice test—AFOQT (Form T)

Part 4: Math Knowledge

> **Directions:** This part of the test has 25 questions designed to measure your ability to use learned mathematical relationships. Each problem is followed by five possible answers. Decide which one of the five choices is most nearly correct. Then, mark the space on your answer form that has the same number and letter as your choice. Use scratch paper to do any figuring.

Here are three sample questions:

1. The reciprocal of 10 is

    A. 0.1

    B. 0.2

    C. 0.5

    D. 1.0

    E. 2.0

The correct answer is A. The reciprocal of 10 is $\frac{1}{10}$ or 0.1.

2. The expression "4 factorial" equals

    A. $\frac{1}{16}$

    B. $\frac{1}{4}$

    C. 16

    D. 24

    E. 64

The correct answer is D. "4 factorial" or 4! equals $4 \times 3 \times 2 \times 1 = 24$.

3. The logarithm to the base 10 of 100 is

    A. 1

    B. 1.6

    C. 2

    D. 2.7

    E. 3

The correct answer is C. $10 \times 10 = 100$. The logarithm of 100 is the exponent 2 to which the base 10 must be raised.

Your score on this test will be based on the number of questions you answer correctly. You should try to answer every question. You will not lose points or be penalized for guessing. Do not spend too much time on any one question.

When you begin, be sure to start with question number 1 of Part 4 on your answer sheet.

Part 4: Math Knowledge

25 Questions • 22 Minutes

1. Which of the following integers is NOT a prime number?

   A. 3
   B. 5
   C. 7
   D. 9
   E. 11

2. What is the distance in miles around a circular course with a radius of 35 miles? (Use pi = $\frac{22}{7}$)

   A. 110 miles.
   B. 156 miles.
   C. 220 miles.
   D. 440 miles.
   E. 880 miles.

3. If $5x + 3y = 29$ and $x - y = 1$, then $x =$

   A. 1
   B. 2
   C. 3
   D. 4
   E. 5

4. Which value of x is a solution to $\frac{2x}{7} = 2x^2$?

   A. $\frac{1}{7}$
   B. $\frac{2}{7}$
   C. 2
   D. 7
   E. 14

5. If x is an odd integer, which one of the following is an even integer?

   A. $2x + 1$
   B. $2x - 1$
   C. $x^2 - x$
   D. $x^2 + x - 1$
   E. none of these

6. $\frac{x - 2}{x^2 - 6x + 8}$ can be reduced to

   A. $\frac{1}{x - 4}$
   B. $\frac{1}{x - 2}$
   C. $\frac{x - 2}{x + 2}$
   D. $\frac{1}{x + 2}$
   E. $\frac{1}{x + 4}$

7. 10^x divided by 10^y equals

   A. $10^{x/y}$
   B. 10^{xy}
   C. 10^{x+y}
   D. 10^{x-y}
   E. none of these

8. $(-3)^3$ is equal to

   A. 9
   B. -9
   C. 27
   D. -27
   E. none of these

9. One million may be represented as:

    A. 10^4

    B. 10^5

    C. 10^6

    D. 10^7

    E. 10^8

10. $\left(\frac{2}{5}\right)^2$ equals:

    A. $\frac{4}{5}$

    B. $\frac{2}{10}$

    C. $\frac{4}{10}$

    D. $\frac{2}{25}$

    E. $\frac{4}{25}$

11. If $3^n = 9$, what is the value of 4^{n+1}?

    A. 24

    B. 48

    C. 64

    D. 108

    E. None of the above

12. 10^{-2} is equal to:

    A. 0.001

    B. 0.01

    C. 0.1

    D. 1.0

    E. 100.0

13. The expression $\sqrt{28} - \sqrt{7}$ reduces to:

    A. $\sqrt{4}$

    B. $\sqrt{7}$

    C. $3\sqrt{7}$

    D. $\sqrt{21}$

    E. $-\sqrt{35}$

14. The hypotenuse of a right triangle whose legs are 5 inches and 12 inches is

    A. 7 inches

    B. 13 inches

    C. 14 inches

    D. 17 inches

    E. none of these

15. The sum of the angle measures of a hexagon is

    A. 360°.

    B. 540°.

    C. 720°.

    D. 900°.

    E. 1,180°.

16. If the ratio of $3x$ to $5y$ is 1:2, what is the ratio of x to y?

    A. $\frac{1}{2}$

    B. $\frac{2}{3}$

    C. $\frac{3}{4}$

    D. $\frac{4}{5}$

    E. $\frac{5}{6}$

17. A scale of $\frac{1}{24,000}$ is the same as a scale of:

   A. $\frac{1}{32}$ inch $\cong$ 1 yard

   B. 1 inch $\cong$ 2,000 feet

   C. 1 foot $\cong$ $\frac{1}{2}$ mile

   D. 1 yard $\cong$ 2 miles

   E. none of these

18. The distance between two points on a graph whose rectangular coordinates are (2, 4) and (5, 8) is most nearly:

   A. 4.7

   B. 4.8

   C. 4.9

   D. 5.0

   E. 5.1

19. The volume of a cylinder with a radius of r and a height of h is:

   A. $\pi r h$

   B. $2\pi r h$

   C. $2\pi r^2 h$

   D. $4\pi r^2 h$

   E. none of these

20. Which of the following lengths of a side of an equilateral triangle would produce a triangle that has a perimeter divisible by both 3 and 5?

   A. 3

   B. 4

   C. 5

   D. 6

   E. 7

21. The numerical value of $\frac{4!}{5!}$ is:

   A. 0.75

   B. 1

   C. 1.25

   D. 1.33

   E. 4

22. The cube root of 729 is equal to the square of

   A. 11

   B. 9

   C. 7

   D. 5

   E. 3

23. If the log of x is 2.5464, the number of digits in x to the left of the decimal point is:

   A. 0

   B. 1

   C. 2

   D. 3

   E. 4

24. What is the appropriate number that would follow the last number in the following series of numbers arranged in a logical order?

   2, 4, 12, 48, __

   A. 96

   B. 144

   C. 192

   D. 204

   E. 240

25. What is the appropriate option for the next two letters in the following series of letters that follow some definite pattern?

A R C S E T G __ __

A. U H
B. H I
C. U I
D. I U
E. I H

STOP! DO NOT GO ON UNTIL TIME IS UP.

Part 5: Reading Comprehension

Directions: This section contains five (5) passages with five (5) questions for each situation. You are to read each passage and select which option you think best answers the question. Then mark the space on the answer form that has the same number and letter as your choice.

Example Passage 1:

The retirement of the Space Shuttle created a gap in the nation's ability to launch humans and other payloads to space. At the *Line* same time private companies have emerged 5 to play a larger role in developing and providing space transportation services in the U.S. Some of these efforts have been supported by government contracts to provide services for NASA, the Department 10 of Defense, and other government agencies. New commercial space ventures have surfaced, challenging the traditional roles of actors in space and questioning the legal ramifications of the Outer Space Treaty of 15 1967.

The high cost of space systems, both the launch vehicles and spacecraft (e.g. satellites and space stations) have historically limited such activities to the purview of 20 state actors, most notably American, Russian, and Soviet national space programs such as NASA. The Cold War era and nuclear weapons build up concerned other nations that space might be become the new "high 25 ground" for military deployment. Further concerns related to the potential colonization of space for the exclusive use of those initial space fairing countries, barring nations that did not have the resources to 30 keep up with development. As such, the Outer Space Treaty of 1967 was devised and signed by the United States.

The Outer Space Treaty of 1967 specifies that space and celestial bodies cannot be 35 appropriated by state entities by claim of

sovereignty; however, all space systems remain the property of the launching nation. The exploration of outer space must not be hindered by other actors and astronauts are 40 envoys of mankind. All activities conducted in space must be for the benefit of all mankind. As such, weapons (particularly nuclear weapons), weapons testing, and military bases in outer space are prohibited. Military 45 personnel may conduct research in space. Nations are liable for damages caused by their space activities.

Commercial telecommunications activities in space date back to the passage of the 50 Communications Satellite Act of 1962, which formed the Comsat Corporation, a quasi-public corporation to provide space-based communications services from geostationary orbiting satellites. By 1969, the 55 multi-national corporation, Intelsat, achieved global communications coverage with three geostationary satellites. Although satellite communications has been a successful space business venture, space transportation has 60 been less so due to the high cost of launch services and employment of single-use vehicles to carry spacecraft to orbit.

The development of new launch systems to dramatically reduce the cost to 65 orbit has prompted fresh commercial space-based ventures. These emerging businesses include space tourism, private space stations orbiting the Earth, settlements on the Moon and Mars, and asteroid mining. The 70 proposed activities raise questions as to the legality under the Outer Space Treaty, particularly with regard to the provision of "benefit to all mankind" and property ownership of resources such as minerals and the 75 locations in which bases and stations are positioned in orbit and on celestial bodies. Several articles have been published by legal experts as to the potential legal challenges that could be posed to these new ventures 80 under the Outer Space Treaty. Other research indicates that the space transportation industry does not view this provision as a threat to industry growth.

With the emerging U.S. commercial 85 space activities, the Federal Aviation Administration (FAA) has implemented procedures to ensure the public safety and the intent of certain provisions of the Outer Space Treaty. For example, space launch 90 licensing requirements ensure corporations follow practices to minimize the risk to the public and property, and that insurance is procured to cover liability that would otherwise fall to the U.S. government under the 95 treaty. Further, corporations are actively lobbying Congress and the FAA for revised legislation to ensure protection against international interference that could affect their investment.

Example Questions:

1. The primary purpose of this passage is to

   A. discuss the history of the U.S. space program.

   B. present the roles of government agencies in space.

   C. highlight emerging commercial space business ventures.

   D. analyze various aspects of the Outer Space Treaty of 1967.

   E. advocate for military operations in space.

The correct answer is D. Each of the paragraphs in the passage refers to the Outer Space Treaty of 1967, making that the predominate theme.

2. Which of the following statements is supported by the passage?

   A. Military personnel cannot conduct activities in outer space.

   B. Commercial communications space ventures can be successful.

   C. Appropriation of outer space by the various nations is inevitable.

   D. The U.S. government takes no responsibility for the conduct of private space activities.

   E. Since the retirement of the space shuttle, there is no interest in space exploration by the U.S.

The correct answer is B. By discussing the growth of the telecommunications sector, the author indicates that commercial space ventures could be successful and profitable.

3. In line 48, *commercial* most likely means

A. advertise.

B. for profit.

C. promotion.

D. government endorsed.

E. supplied in bulk.

The correct answer is B. The term *commercial* in this passage is used to refer to organizations that are conducting space activities for the ultimate purpose of generating profit. This is indicated by references to space tourism and asteroid mining predominately.

4. Which one of the following claims would the author most likely agree?

A. The Outer Space Treaty has no potential influence on the operations of state actors or corporations in future space activities.

B. The Outer Space Treaty will prevent commercial space activities from being successful in the near- and long-term future.

C. U.S. corporations have no interest in pursuing space ventures due to the high costs and challenges presented by the Outer Space Treaty.

D. The U.S. government has no interest in supporting commercial space ventures either through policy or financial support in the near- or long-term future.

E. There is significant potential for a variety of successful commercial space businesses in the future even with potential uncertainty relating to the Outer Space Treaty.

The correct answer is E. By discussing the number of proposed space ventures currently in development in the United States and highlighting the previous success of the telecommunications sector, the author indicates that commercial space ventures could be successful and profitable.

practice test—AFOQT (Form T)

5. Which one of the following is an accurate and descriptive title of the passage?

   A. The History of Commercial Telecommunications Space Ventures in the United States

   B. The Retirement of the Space Shuttle and future of the U.S. National Space Program

   C. Analysis of the Outer Space Treaty of 1967 and the Potential Influences on Future Commercial Space Ventures

   D. How the Outer Space Treaty of 1967 Guided the Activities of State-Sponsored Space Activities

   E. Evolving Roles of State Actors and Commercial Ventures in Outer Space

The correct answer is C. The last sentence of the first paragraph and paragraphs four and five provide support for the selected title.

Your score on this test will be based on the number of questions you answer correctly. You should try to answer every question. You will not lose points or be penalized for guessing. Do not spend too much time on any one question.

When you begin this section of the test, be sure to start with number 1 of Part 5 on your answer sheet.

Part 5: Reading Comprehension

25 Questions • 38 Minutes

Passage 1:

The Department of Defense (DoD) budget declined from 4.2% in 2008 to 3.3% in 2015 and is projected to shrink as low as *Line* 2.3% over 10 years. National budgetary 5 fluctuation is a contributing factor effecting defense budget outcomes. National concern about economic stability and marketplace job creation, byproducts associated with small business entrepreneurial (SBE) perfor- 10 mance, were emphasized with an economic recession beginning in 2007 and a resulting 4% gross domestic product (GDP) decline, causing immediate federal, state, and city budget deficits. In alignment with a decrease 15 in federal revenue, the Department of Defense budget was affected by sequestration in 2013, with 10% across-the-board cuts.

Public opinion ranked unemployment/ 20 jobs and the economy within the top three national concerns, along with congressional dissatisfaction, from September 2013 to May 2014, relative to other categories (healthcare, education, poverty, immigration, 25 environment, racism, federal deficit, ethics, and the shrinking middle class). A positive correlation between GDP and unemployment describes 8.2 million workers reduced to part-time employment and 12.8 million 30 who are unemployed. Not federally counted as unemployed were 2.8 million discouraged workers and 656,000 homeless citizens. Excluding discouraged workers and those wanting to work full time, national unem- 35 ployment is approximately 5.8%; however, when including those demographics, actual unemployment is approximately 13%.

Capitalism within the U.S. consists of approximately 29.1 million enterprises 40 comprising 23 million small non-employer establishments, 5.8 million small employer firms, and 170,654 large firms. Increases or decreases in the survival rates for small businesses affects national GDP and employment. 45 The societal effect of small business entrepreneurs' performance (farm and non-farm small businesses) includes the generation of approximately 47% of the 2014 U.S. $17.4 trillion GDP; the generation of 48.5% of 50 the national jobs for 58.5% of the U.S. total population who want to work (152,867,000 total labor force); generation of 37% of all skilled technical labor jobs; and it accounted for 98% of all national exporters.

55 National emphasis has been placed on the importance of small business owner performance within the United States. In alignment with public opinion, the Small Business Jobs Act of 2010 distributed $1.5 60 billion among individual state programs to facilitate $15 billion in small business loans. The U.S. Small Business Administration (SBA) commanded a 2015 budget of $710 million with the objective of creating jobs 65 by facilitating SBE performance using public training programs and $36 billion in small business loan guarantees.

SBE performance in the U.S. is a social concern for the enhancement of national 70 prosperity and indirectly to mitigate defense budget pressures. Assuming a linear relationship, a 1% change in the annual national SBE success-to-failure rate equates to an increase or decrease of $8.18 billion in GDP

75 and 74,000 jobs. The SBE population remains approximately stable with 10% closing annually and an equal number attempting to start a business. While there are fewer business start-ups during a reces-

80 sion, SBE survival rates are reasonably consistent despite economic swings. Assuming 2.9 million start-ups over one year, 1 million will survive five years, and, of those, less than half a million will remain

85 in business when confronted with initial marketplace changes.

SBEs typically do not use business plans to manage their businesses, yet are more likely to fail without them. Project,

90 Program, and Portfolio Management (P3M) has been identified in research as a collection of valuable business planning and management processes that SBEs should understand; however, the researched value of P3M to

95 SBE success was not fully identified until a 2015 national research study. Research findings included an average performance efficiency of 59% among U.S. SMEs. P3M was identified as detailed planning and

100 management processes with a 0.308 total effect on national SBE performance. A 1% improved adaptation of P3M managerial knowledge area processes predicted 18.17% SBE performance improvement.

1. The primary purpose of the passage is to

   A. describe the effect of the recession on the United States.

   B. compare and contrast unemployment levels to small business performance.

   C. identify implications of improved small business entrepreneurial performance and the indirect benefit to the Department of Defense budget.

   D. provide a comprehensive historical account of the Department of Defense budget since the recession.

   E. summarize the contribution of small business owners relative to national employment levels.

2. In line 68, *performance* most nearly means

   A. ranking.

   B. persistence.

   C. success.

   D. employment.

   E. determination.

3. As inferred from the passage, which of the following factors contributes to small businesses' instability?

   A. Unemployment levels

   B. Defense spending cuts

   C. Recession

   D. National economic stability

   E. Lack of planning

4. The national unemployment rates are discussed primarily to

   A. illustrate the threat of an increase in unemployment with an increase in small business failure.

   B. suggest that small business owners could have prevented the recession.

   C. contrast Department of Defense budget changes with unemployment levels.

   D. demonstrate that unemployment rates are typical of GDP.

   E. show that unemployment rates are atypical of GDP.

5. With which one of the following claims about small business performance would the author most likely agree?

   A. Budget cuts are sufficient to overcome economic instabilities.

   B. Increases in Small Business Administration loans are needed to improve small business performance, reduce unemployment, and mitigate Department of Defense cuts.

   C. Policy makers exaggerate the consequences of recessions.

   D. Department of Defense budgets should not be tied with GDP.

   E. Adaptation of project management planning and management techniques can strengthen national prosperity.

Passage 2:

Aviation accidents tend to be dramatic events, whether they involve military or civilian aircraft. Paradoxically, as aircraft
Line become more technologically complex, they
5 are substantially more reliable, resulting in fewer accidents than previous aircraft models. Modern aircraft accidents are now predominately 70% to 80% the result of human error. Rarely do single errors result
10 in catastrophic aviation accidents or are catastrophic aviation accidents solely caused by the actions or inactions of the aircrew. Accidents are more likely the result of a series of multiple errors made over time that
15 cascade into a tragic result. Accident investigators seek to determine all of the errors made that led to a particular accident and make recommendations relating to equipment design, operations and maintenances
20 procedures, and regulatory oversight.

Several models have been devised to describe the errors that culminate in aviation accidents. These models represent different perspectives to assess the source of error in
25 accidents. A few examples are cognitive, decision-making, ergonomic, behavioral, aeromedical, psychosocial, and organizational. The cognitive model focuses on human information processes to evaluate
30 human performance. The ergonomic approach uses the SHEL model to describe the human interactions with various system components. The components of the SHEL model are software (S), hardware (H), envi-
35 ronment (E), and liveware (L). Liveware represents the human in the human-machine system. With the exception of the SHEL model, the limitation with such techniques is the usability for end-to-end
40 accident data analysis or use as an investigative guide.

A commonly employed framework used by the U.S. military and other organizations in accident investigation, and originally
45 developed for the U.S. Navy and Marine Corps, is the Human Factors Analysis and

Classification System (HFACS). HFACS is an expansion of Reason's "Swiss Cheese" model of accident causation and could be
50 employed for accident causation analysis. Reason's model is composed of four layers: organizational influences, unsafe supervision, preconditions for unsafe acts, and unsafe acts. Failed or absent defenses in the layers
55 are represented as "holes" that, should they all be present for a particular flight (but not necessarily occur on a specific day), will result in an accident or incident. Although Reason's model integrates key factors not
60 considered by other models, it does not characterize the nature of the "holes" to effectively provide insight for future intervention.

Reason's model is descriptive, not
65 analytical, by its nature. The notions presented in Reason's model do not provide the means for the characterization to allow for the development of defenses and corrective measures. For example, the HFACS
70 taxonomy describes unsafe acts by aircrews as either an error or violation. An error can be either skill-based, decision-based, or perception-based. Violations are either routine or exceptional. Preconditions for
75 unsafe acts include environmental factors, the condition of operators, and personnel factors. Unsafe supervision can involve inadequate supervision, planned inappropriate operations, supervisory violations, or the
80 failure to correct a problem. Organizational influences are also branded as either resource management, organizational climate, or organizational process issues. The specific classification of such error types drives
85 differing interventions post-incident or accident.

Human error is inevitable, but understanding the sources of error can add in the design of systems, processes, and training
90 to mitigate errors. Human error is well understood and has a level of predictability. This is key because aviation accidents, particularly in commercial aviation, are not tolerated by the public at large, regardless
95 of how few occur. The perception of safety and human error in aviation is a driving factor of public perception about the industry. Therefore, implementation of efforts to reduce error and accident rates is
100 a goal of aircraft manufacturers, maintainers, and operators.

6. The primary purpose of this passage is to

    A. present the accident rates of U.S. airline operators.

    B. discuss the roles of aviation investigators.

    C. highlight how commercial aviation operators implement safety programs.

    D. identify methods and models to assess human error in aviation accidents.

    E. advocate for more automation in aircraft cockpits to enhance safety.

7. Which of the following statements is supported by the passage?

    A. Pilots are typically solely responsible for aviation accidents.

    B. The complexity of aircraft technology makes aviation less safe.

    C. Any of the presented models can be effectively used to investigate and analyze all accident causes.

    D. There is no means to accurately assess the complex human causes of aviation accidents.

    E. The HFACS model is the more commonly employed model to describe accident causes.

8. In line 89, *processes* most likely means

   A. production.

   B. treatment.

   C. operational procedures.

   D. material handling.

   E. proceedings.

9. With which one of the following claims would the author most likely disagree?

   A. Once the actions of the pilot or aircrew have been assessed with regard to the accident, no further investigation is required.

   B. Accident investigators have the responsibility to classify errors to aid in corrective measures.

   C. The results of accident investigations can affect key changes to aircraft design, procedures, training, and regulations.

   D. The HFACS framework is a comprehensive aviation accident analysis and investigation tool.

   E. The SHEL model is not suitable as an aviation accident analysis tool or investigation guide.

10. Which one of the following is an accurate and descriptive title of the passage?

   A. Aircraft Complexity as the Cause of Military and Commercial Aviation Accidents

   B. Primary Causes of Aviation Accidents and the Analysis Models Used to Assess Human Error

   C. Public Perception of Aviation Safety and the Need for Investigation and Analysis

   D. Effectiveness of Various Human Error Assessment Models for Aircraft Accident Investigation

   E. Use of Human Factors Assessment Models to Enhance Public Perception of Safety

Passage 3:

Air-to-air and air-to-ground combat training traditionally took place with adversary squadrons on a common flying range.
Line As a case study, a Mobile Training Team
5 (MTT), as a new concept, was created to export large-scale air-to-air and air-to-ground combat training to other military base training ranges. Project outcomes from the $2.6 million proof-of-concept included
10 a disparity of objectives between the training squadrons and those of the base receiving the training, resulting in tense relations and negative training outcomes. Communication shortfalls internal to the MTT resulted in
15 a loss of synergy among component aggressor fighter, cyber-warfare, counter-intelligence, and integrated air defense training squadrons.

Post-project assessment included risk
20 management not having been developed to identify and manage uncertainties during the project's lifecycle. Research survey findings indicated 70% of organizational leaders identified risk management as
25 important to success; however, fewer than 50% identified as using or integrating any risk management strategies. Risk management begins with defining objectives and scope. Risks to project success include unresolved assumptions, ineffective

30 communication, scope creep, network power concentrations, and personality conflict. Research suggests that poor planning and ill-defined objectives are causal with project outcome disillusionment. Not separating 35 assumptions from facts during planning decreases desired outcomes and increases risk.

Transformational leaders readily capitalize on opportunities in risk management, 40 whereas transactional managers focus only on controlling negative outcomes. Human behavioral studies suggest a tendency of people to focus on threats rather than opportunity. Ineffective managers associate 45 opportunity as only a lack of a project threat occurring and fail to separate opportunity management as being a component of risk management. Effective managers forecast negative threats and positive opportunities 50 while taking proactive shaping action. The inclusion of both project threats and opportunities optimize organizational Darwinism, also referred to as design thinking, by holistically adapting to both threats and 55 opportunities within dynamic evolving environments for successful outcomes.

Risk response planning aligns avoidance, transfer, mitigation, or acceptance strategies based on the associated implementation 60 cost. Threat avoidance techniques include removing or bypassing risk triggers. Transferring a threat means distributing the effect among an alliance or directing it to 65 another better equipped group to deal with it. Teaming arrangements, or strategic joint ventures, create contractual relationships in sharing profits with a shift in risks to one member or another. Mitigating strategies 70 target a threat's severity or likelihood of occurrence. A last strategic resort is simply accepting the possibility of a threat by either making contingency plans or doing nothing

other than monitoring for an increase in 75 threat severity.

Management of project opportunities complements those of threats throughout the fluid process of defining, identifying, analyzing, responding, and controlling 80 uncertainties. The defining phase creates a plan that governs all aspects of the risk management process focused on organizational and project objectives. Strategies to identify opportunities includes qualitative 85 or sequential mixed-methods research for analysis of interactive relationships within the modeled project. Response-planning establishes actionable strategies to manipulate an uncertainty's cause and/or effect in 90 order to shape the desired outcome. Controlling strategies consist of the timely execution of planned responses in the management of new and evolving uncertainty events.

95 Integrated risk management facilitates timely and effective managerial decision-making. A risk management challenge is in communicating opportunity versus threat management for upper-management deci-100 sion-making from their vantage point. A common risk process facilitates effective organizational management integration and communication. Communication is more effective when it's not ambiguous, by using 105 commonly understood terminology in the expansion of risk to include both threats and opportunities. It is a project manager's responsibility to ensure top organizational support via effective and robust communica-110 tion skills to mitigate surprises. Effective organizational and cross-organizational project communication is required to plan, anticipate, and manipulate outcomes.

11. The primary purpose of the passage is to

    A. describe the effect of inadequate planning on MTT training programs.

    B. compare and contrast risk and opportunity management.

    C. provide a broad account of a failed training project.

    D. summarize threat management components.

    E. identify how risk management could have been useful in the MTT project.

12. In the sixth paragraph, *risk* most nearly means

    A. things not going as planned.

    B. bankruptcy.

    C. poorly defined objectives.

    D. opportunities.

    E. dangers and prospects.

13. According to the passage, which of the following factors is a primary cause of project training failure?

    A. Inadequate communication

    B. Undocumented intentions

    C. Not using risk management

    D. Nonexistent project preparation

    E. Confirmation bias

14. Communication management is discussed primarily to

    A. clarify the cyclic relationship between communication and risk management.

    B. advocate opportunity management as the result of good communication.

    C. associate communication as a threat management tool.

    D. demonstrate why the training program underperformed.

    E. identify good communication as a result of effect risk management.

15. With which one of the following claims about training projects would the author most likely agree?

    A. Threat identification results in lost opportunity management.

    B. Risk management may enhance successful training outcomes.

    C. Transactional leadership improves project success.

    D. Communication is not a threat to project success.

    E. Mobile training is needed for combat air force synergy.

Passage 4:

The events of September 11, 2001, illustrated the vulnerability of the commercial aviation industry to attack. Commercial
Line aviation as a target to terrorists is certainly
5 not a new concept in the twenty-first century. However, previous attacks on aviation were typically characterized by the hijacking of an airliner and a variety of demands prior to the release of the aircraft,
10 aircrew, and passengers. A few other attacks involved bombings by terrorists, such as Pan Am flight 103 that exploded over Lockerbie, Scotland, killing all passengers, crew, and several on the ground. With enhanced
15 physical security of airports and aircraft as well as awareness by passengers to stay vigilant in detecting threats, extremists must seek new and creative means to target aviation. In fact, the nature of attacks by
20 terror and criminal groups has taken a new

approach to target computer networks to bring havoc to a variety of organizations and individuals.

Even under the threat of terrorism, the aviation industry is growing globally. New technologies such as unmanned aerial systems are creating a strain on an already overcrowded airspace, particularly in the United States and Europe. In the U.S. national airspace, 7,000 aircraft operate on average at any given time. The most modern air traffic control infrastructure in the United States, prior to the upgrades under the Next Generation Air Transportation System, known as NextGen, is 43 years old. The aging system causes annual delays that cost the industry approximately 1 million hours at a cost in excess of $1 billion and the use of an additional 38 million gallons of fuel daily. The demands placed on the aging air traffic control infrastructure in the U.S. is driving new concepts in air traffic control, such as NextGen, to relieve the burden.

Modern air traffic control networks seek to evolve from ground-based sensor systems to space-based sensor networks that provide more rapid information. Instead of a reliance on ground radars, the Global Positioning System (GPS) is used to pinpoint the location of aircraft in 4D. Additional data is shared via an Internet-based data network to air traffic controllers and between aircraft to ensure inter-aircraft spacing in a dynamic and congested airspace. New aircraft, such as the Boeing 787, are "e-enabled," meaning they provide sensing, computing, communications, and networking capabilities to the air traffic control network; they do not just fly through the airspace as a passive sensed target.

Reliance on computer technology and networks presents challenges for security, especially with the global nature of aviation and the communications and data required to sustain such operations. Reliance on computing technology and the dangers of "outages" have been illustrated on multiple occasions in recent years, with airlines grounded due to problems with computer-based scheduling and reservation systems. Cyberattacks on airlines and the aviation industry do not necessarily have to involve the catastrophic loss of an airplane. Attacks resulting in even minor delays affecting airline and cargo carrier performance can cause lost revenue, customer dissatisfaction, and far-reaching economic damage. Such attacks may also be more difficult to detect and correct, making them more effective.

Although terrorism is typically thought of as dramatic events involving the loss of life and the hijacking or loss of an aircraft, less overt attacks on industries may be equally effective. The disruption of services or even slight delays can cost the aviation industry millions in revenue and profit. Further, delays in flight operations likely also result in burned fuel and higher emissions polluting the environment. The transformation of the air traffic control network, although much needed, creates new challenges for security in the modern era. Networked systems must be designed, operated, and maintained with an awareness of cybersecurity threats and potential consequences.

16. The primary purpose of this passage is to

- **A.** discuss the modern air traffic control network and potential threats.

- **B.** share the history of how terrorism has affected the commercial aviation industry.

- **C.** highlight air traffic control security practices in the United States.

- **D.** identify the efficiencies created by the NextGen air traffic control network.

- **E.** advocate for a less complex air traffic control network to ensure security.

17. Which of the following statements is NOT supported by the passage?

- **A.** The implementation of NextGen will result in a safer aviation industry and operational environment.

- **B.** NextGen offers new efficiencies for aviation for fuel and cost savings and reduced emissions.

- **C.** Terrorist threats to aviation can take a variety of forms, not just physical harm to aircraft, aircrew, and passengers.

- **D.** The complexity and use of space-based sensors by NextGen makes the system immune to terror attacks.

- **E.** The aviation industry has been evolving to become more reliant on networks for operational efficiencies.

18. In the third paragraph, *networks* most likely means

- **A.** passages.

- **B.** associations.

- **C.** communications.

- **D.** television stations.

- **E.** veins.

19. Which one of the following claims would the author most likely AGREE?

- **A.** With the implementation of NextGen, aviation security concerns are dramatically reduced.

- **B.** With the implementation of NextGen, aviation safety concerns are dramatically reduced.

- **C.** The current air traffic control network does not require dramatic upgrades with the potential cybersecurity risks associated with implementation.

- **D.** Although NextGen offers the potential for aviation safety in operations, system security is an ongoing concern for all users.

- **E.** The efficiencies promised by the implementation of NextGen do not warrant the cost or potential risk.

practice test—AFOQT (Form T)

20. Which one of the following is an accurate and descriptive title of the passage?

A. History of Terrorist Threats to the Commercial Aviation Industry in the United States

B. Development and Implementation Processes for the Next Generation Air Transportation System

C. Public Perception of Terrorist Threats to the Commercial Aviation Industry and Security

D. New Capabilities for the Commercial Aviation Industry With NextGen Implementation

E. Evolving Threat Considerations for the Aviation Industry With the Implementation of NextGen

Passage 5:

The Chairman of the Joint Chiefs of Staff advised national leaders in 2005 of a need to increase joint service integration for
Line synergistic battlefield lethality. Resulting
5 increases in close air support (CAS) fratricide facilitated Congressional pressure for a new Joint Fires Center of Excellence (JFCOE) to halt internal joint and multinational air and land force casualties.
10 Existing training integration processes for small scale exercises achieved 0% integration of 20,412 work hours among 21 U.S. Air Force JTAC (Joint Terminal Attack Controller) personnel and a loss of $120,000
15 in flight hours among 13 supporting sorties. Large exercises achieved 2% integration and a loss of $6.4 million in flight hours among 346 sorties.

Adult learning principles were used in
20 designing teamed solutions. Institutional bias, of both learner and facilitator, can effect adult learning. Understanding organizational dynamics is key to facilitating successful new knowledge integration. Adult
25 learners have a tendency to resist new information if they do not know why it is relevant or if it is forced. New information is retained if it is associated with existing learner experiences. New capabilities are adopted by a
30 learner if found to be useful in solving real-world needs. While adult learners are motivated to some degree by external factors, such as survival, intrinsic factors of team contribution have a higher effect.

35 Using adult learning principles, observers of Army planning processes identified a disconnect in Air Force Liaisons forcing assets instead of generating solutions of which Army planners could incorporate
40 airpower capabilities. A solution resulted in a training program for land force personnel to learn how to pull airpower capabilities in planning, communicating, and coordinating with non-collocated JTACs for lethal
45 or non-lethal problem solutions. A new

program was embedded with land force training programs consisting of four phases:

1. Academics for land force personnel on how to use and integrate airpower

50 2. Virtual combat simulations to prosecute targets through a non-collocated JTAC

3. Practical application field scenarios with JTACs, land forces, and fighter aircraft

4. Large-scale dynamic field exercises 55 using simulated aircraft and Hollywood effects

Social learning concepts were incorporated through academic material that addressed real-world collective learner needs. 60 Virtual training allowed teams to learn from each other through social learning by observing and imitating successful behavior. Virtual environments were used for teamed problem solving in using CAS-amplified 65 learning. Findings from a 1972 Scarborough experiment identified combined audio and visual data with improved immediate short-term memory, but it was less effective in sustained long-term memory. Long-term 70 memory requires operant conditioning schedules of reinforcement achieved in phases three and four. From this, a person develops a cognitive map of the sought environment as well as its spatial operation 75 and a prioritization of items within it.

Project training efficiency requires environmental factor considerations, repetitive learning efficiency, focused task specialization, improved production procedures, 80 innovative equipment utilization, automation labor substitution, comparative knowledge transfer, improved performance innovations, and learner incentives. Positive behavior reinforcement increases a subject's 85 attention, learning rate, and performance. For example, instant learner feedback in the practical application of CAS integration contributed to an increase in the learning curve relative to initial academic 90 environments.

Increased initial training costs, in terms of time to train, decrease with each advanced training phase as changes in a learning curve can be non-linear from one training phase 95 to another. The validity of forecasting training-time effectiveness is positively correlated with a longitudinal increase in representative data. The resulting learning curve rate is a unit of measure for efficiency 100 over time. As learning improves, the magnitude for additional learning diminishes toward 100% on the curve. A training phase having a steeper learning slope equates to more optimized and rapid learning events. 105 With regard to CAS-integration changes, the pre-JFCOE learning curve averaged 2%. Changes in the learning process improved the overall learning curve to 100%, and combat CAS fratricide among trained units 110 ceased.

21. The primary purpose of the passage is to

   A. describe difficulties in joint and multi-national operations.

   B. compare and contrast different learning styles.

   C. identify problems with adult learning.

   D. provide a historical account of how to build a training program.

   E. summarize a resolution methodology to avoid Close Air Support fratricide events.

22. In line 94, *non-linear* most nearly means

   A. continuous.

   B. different.

   C. straightaway.

   D. decreasing.

   E. flat.

23. As inferred from the passage, which of the following factors does NOT contribute to successful learning?

- **A.** Audio and visual data
- **B.** Behavior reinforcement
- **C.** Social learning
- **D.** Pperant conditioning
- **E.** Institutional bias

24. Operant conditioning (line 70) is discussed primarily to

- **A.** identify stair-stepped training phases as a repetitively process of improving long-term knowledge retention.
- **B.** suggest that academic environments need to threatening for successful training outcomes.
- **C.** contrast forced versus pulled outcomes.
- **D.** identify self-actualization as critical to learning.
- **E.** show that airpower is needed for land force success.

25. With which one of the following claims about integrated close air support training would the author most likely agree?

- **A.** Academic and simulator training was more effective for long-term knowledge retention.
- **B.** Airpower assets are best integrated when incorporated by a user, not when forced upon him or her.
- **C.** Low learning outcomes are associated with high learning curves.
- **D.** Learning curves tend to get smaller over time with repetitive learning.
- **E.** Congressional objectives were for increased battlespace lethality.

STOP! DO NOT GO ON UNTIL TIME IS UP.

Part 6: Situational Judgment

> **Directions:** This section contains 25 situations with two questions for each situation. You are to review the situation and select which option you think it the MOST EFFECTIVE given the information provided and the LEAST EFFECTIVE option. Then mark the space on the answer form that has the same number and letter as your choice.

Here's a sample situation:

• •

Example Situation: You have noticed that the junior officer that works for you has been very flirtatious with members of the opposite gender, both senior ranking officers and enlisted personnel. You note that other individuals in the organization have witnessed this conduct, and their demeanor toward the junior officer is rapidly deteriorating. You have not yet mentioned your observation to your junior officer.

Possible actions:

A. Meet with the junior officer to describe the flirtatious behavior as being inappropriate and likely to affect other office relationships.

B. The next time you witness the behavior, publicly correct the junior officer.

C. Report the inappropriate conduct of the junior officer to the commanding officer.

D. Ignore the situation as interpersonal relationships in the organization are not your concern.

E. Ask a friend of the junior officer to confront the officer in an attempt to correct the behavior.

1. Select the MOST EFFECTIVE action (A–E) in response to the situation.

2. Select the LEAST EFFECTIVE action (A–E) in response to the situation. Select the LEAST EFFECTIVE action in response to the situation.

1. **The correct answer is A.** A positive leader and effective mentor would meet with the junior officer and kindly discuss the behavior of the junior officer and the potential perception by other personnel in the organization when a less than professional behavior is displayed. A careful reminder that perception is often viewed as reality could create hardships in that officer's working relationship with other personnel.

2. **The correct answer is D.** Ignoring the problem will likely create hardship for the junior officer and not reflect well on your leadership by the other personnel in the organization for not identifying and attempting to correct the behavior.

• •

Your score on this test will be based on the number of questions you answer correctly. You should try to answer every question. You will not lose points or be penalized for guessing. Do not spend too much time on any one question.

When you begin this section of the test, be sure to start with number 1 of Part 6 on your answer sheet.

Part 6: Situational Judgment

50 Questions • 35 Minutes

Situation I: You are an instructor who teaches training courses, which are required monthly, to all aircrew on the base. Recently, an exercise was conducted in which only a portion of the requirements of the monthly training was presented to the aircrews. A senior officer comes to you and asks you to generate a training completion document indicating that the aircrews received the monthly training requirement. You verify in the training requirement directives that the exercise scenario is not sufficient to meet the monthly training requirement.

Possible actions:

A. Prepare the paperwork as the senior officer asked. The request was probably meant as a direct order and should be followed.

B. Inform the senior officer that the exercise scenario does not meet the training requirements, so any crew that did not attend the monthly training will be delinquent for the month.

C. Prepare the paperwork as the senior officer asked. Tell him that you will only fulfill the request on this one occasion.

D. Immediately report the senior officer's request to your supervisor.

E. Tell the senior officer that you will need to contact higher headquarters authorities to get clarification before you can process the request.

1. Select the MOST EFFECTIVE action (A–E) in response to the situation.

2. Select the LEAST EFFECTIVE action (A–E) in response to the situation.

Situation II: You are a missile combat crew commander with an annual simulator evaluation scheduled for this month. These evaluations are very challenging, and failure will mean that your upgrade to an instructor will be cancelled. A fellow crew member in your squadron recently took the evaluation and sent you information about the simulation script that includes classified information to your personal e-mail account.

Possible actions:

A. Delete the message from your e-mail and forget the incident.

B. Immediately report the incident to the security officer, supervisor, and commanding officer, and seek guidance to resolve the situation.

C. Use the information to prepare for the evaluation and delete the message from your e-mail account.

D. Use the information to prepare for the evaluation and share it with other individuals who are also scheduled for the evaluation.

E. Call the person who sent the e-mail and have him or her report the incident to the security office and the commanding officer for resolution.

3. Select the MOST EFFECTIVE action (A–E) in response to the situation.

4. Select the LEAST EFFECTIVE action (A–E) in response to the situation.

Situation III: You are a nuclear command and control instructor who develops training and actual mission documentation for bomber aircrews. You typically coordinate with your counterparts at the other bomber and missile bases to share training scenarios to better prepare your crews for any operational contingencies and use a SECRET network to share data up to the SECRET data classification level. A recent revision to procedures changed the classification of some of the training characters, but you missed the change and sent TOP SECRET (a higher classification of information) data over the SECRET system. After sending the data, you realize your error.

Possible actions:

A. Do nothing. Perhaps the recipients of the message did not note the classification change.

B. Delete the message from your sent mail and attempt to recall the message before it is read.

C. Inform the recipients of the classification breach and have them delete the message immediately without following up with a formal report.

D. Inform the security officer and seek guidance in resolving the situation.

E. Immediately report the incident to the security officer, supervisor, commanding officer, and recipients of the message of your error, and seek guidance to resolve the situation.

5. Select the MOST EFFECTIVE action (A–E) in response to the situation.

6. Select the LEAST EFFECTIVE action (A–E) in response to the situation.

Situation IV: You have a junior officer in your charge who is a very hard worker and has taken on a number of projects that benefit the organization. However, his additional projects are likely resulting in lower performance in his primary duties and preventing him from being considered for upgrade in his job because his proficiency is not up to the highest standard. The junior officer has expressed frustration to you that he is not advancing as fast as he'd hoped and that he is not being considered for other important duties.

Possible actions:

A. Meet with the junior officer to discuss his overall performance in the primary and additional duties, describe the areas that need improvement, and suggest methods for primary duty enhancement.

B. Take no immediate action but downgrade the officer on his annual performance report based on his primary duty proficiency.

C. Reprimand the officer for his primary duty proficiency level and poor attitude.

D. Ignore the situation to see if the junior officer can determine what he is doing wrong and can correct the behavior on his own.

E. Reassign the junior officer's additional duties until he raises his proficiency levels to the expected standard.

7. Select the MOST EFFECTIVE action (A–E) in response to the situation.

8. Select the LEAST EFFECTIVE action (A–E) in response to the situation.

practice test—AFOQT (Form T)

Situation V: You are a junior officer and in your first year as part of a new organization. A colleague and fellow officer comes to you and confides that she has been sexually assaulted by someone in your unit while both were on duty a few days prior. The individual that she named is a more senior officer and very well respected among the other officers and enlisted personnel in the organization. She is asking for you to help her to decide how to handle the incident.

Possible actions:

A. Because the individual involved is senior and well respected, it is better to not report the incident as it will only create backlash for both the victim and yourself.

B. Both you and the victim immediately report the incident to the commanding officer. Stay with your friend to serve as her advocate.

C. Both you and the victim immediately report the incident to the local police.

D. You confront the accused individual, ask the senior officer if the claim of rape is true, and tell him to turn himself in to Security Forces (military police).

E. You tell your friend to wait to report the incident while you ask others in the organization if they have heard anything about this individual conducting himself in this way in the past.

9. Select the MOST EFFECTIVE action (A–E) in response to the situation.

10. Select the LEAST EFFECTIVE action (A–E) in response to the situation.

Situation VI: A new junior officer has just reported to your organization, and you are her supervisor. Upon reporting in, you note quite a few ribbons on her uniform that are unlikely to have been earned by such a junior officer. There are a number of enlisted personnel that the junior officer will be directing that are also in the office when you note the possible discrepancy.

Possible actions:

A. Take mental note of the ribbons on the officer's uniform, and confirm the decorations through her personnel record prior to meeting with the officer privately.

B. Confront the junior officer privately about the ribbons without reviewing the individual's service record.

C. Immediately report the individual to the commander for the improper wear of military decorations.

D. Confront the junior officer and ask about the origin of all of the ribbons on her uniform in front of everyone in the office.

E. Discredit the junior officer by mentioning the various ribbons to other personnel in the unit.

11. Select the MOST EFFECTIVE action (A–E) in response to the situation.

12. Select the LEAST EFFECTIVE action (A–E) in response to the situation.

practice test—AFOQT (Form T)

Situation VII: You and your deputy crew commander arrive at a control center to take over the watch of the nuclear weapons for the next 24 hours. As you walk up to the blast door, you note that the crew did not follow procedure and extend the pins to secure the door. This is both a procedural violation and one that could result in serious harm to the crew inside in certain emergency situations. You are the supervisor of the current crew on duty.

Possible actions:

    A. Take mental note of the blast door pins, report the crew to the unit commanding officer, and recommend they be relieved of duty.

    B. Refuse to take over the shift as you and your deputy assume they have not properly handled the other responsibilities during their shift.

    C. Once inside the Launch Control Center, ask the current commander of the facility why the pins were not extended when your crew arrived at the door.

    D. Verbally reprimand the on-duty commander and deputy in their failure to follow procedure, and follow up with formal documentation after your shift.

    E. Say nothing about the status of the door pins. It is likely the crew just retracted the pins in preparation for your arrival.

13. Select the MOST EFFECTIVE action (A–E) in response to the situation.

14. Select the LEAST EFFECTIVE action (A–E) in response to the situation.

Situation VIII: You are responsible for overseeing an important communications test involving multiple aircraft and crews. The crews fly the mission and are trained to document the communications received during a nuclear test window and bring the data back to you for review before it is sent to higher headquarters. One crew brings back incomplete documentation, and you report the discrepancy to their commander—who is not your supervisor—who tells you the crew was busy dealing with weather and to just do the paperwork for the crew.

Possible actions:

    A. Without alteration, submit the documentation submitted by the crew to higher headquarters for analysis, and report the senior officer's request to your supervisor.

    B. Inform the senior officer that there is no way you can fill in the missing data because you would have needed to be on the aircraft during the exercise.

    C. Prepare the paperwork as the senior officer asked by inputting guessed but inaccurate data.

    D. Immediately report the senior officer's request to your supervisor.

    E. Ask the aircrew to fill in the missing data after the exercise, using their best guess.

15. Select the MOST EFFECTIVE action (A–E) in response to the situation.

16. Select the LEAST EFFECTIVE action (A–E) in response to the situation.

Situation IX: Your annual performance evaluation is coming due. In the past, your supervisors have asked you to put together a list of accomplishments and activities as inputs for the evaluation and have used that data and their own observations of your performance to develop the formal report in accordance with official directives. This year, you are in a new unit and have a new supervisor, and, instead of asking you for the expected list of inputs, the officer asks you to write the evaluation and submit it to him for signature.

Possible actions:

A. Immediately report the request to your commanding officer.

B. Without consulting the commanding officer, file a formal complaint with the base inspector general office.

C. Ask the other junior officers supervised by this officer to determine if this is a common practice in the unit.

D. Inform your supervisor that you would be happy to provide inputs but that you are uncomfortable writing the formal evaluation.

E. Fearing a negative evaluation, you comply with your supervisor's request even though it violates personnel procedures.

17. Select the MOST EFFECTIVE action (A–E) in response to the situation.

18. Select the LEAST EFFECTIVE action (A–E) in response to the situation.

Situation X: You and your colleagues are attending a formal military ball in which you all wear your medals on your uniforms. You note that one of the junior officers in your charge is wearing a medal that is not included in his formal military record. Concerned about other senior officers taking note, what action do you take?

Possible actions:

A. Take no action. It is the junior officer's responsibility to present their decorations accurately and appropriately.

B. In private, confront the junior officer discrepancy and have them make the necessary change to the medals on the spot before returning to the event.

C. Immediately report the individual to the commander for the improper wear of military decorations.

D. You confront the junior officer and ask about the origin of all of the ribbons on their uniform in front of everyone at the event.

E. Take no action at the event, but counsel the junior officer at a later time regarding the proper wear of military decorations.

19. Select the MOST EFFECTIVE action (A–E) in response to the situation.

20. Select the LEAST EFFECTIVE action (A–E) in response to the situation.

Situation XI: You are the supervisor of a junior officer who has an annual evaluation due in the next month. This officer is a good performer with no disciplinary issues, but not outstanding as compared to other individuals in your charge or compared to their peers. You are torn as to how to evaluate this officer because this individual's mother is a general officer with potential influence over your next duty assignment.

Possible actions:

A. Fearing a less than desirable future duty assignment, you give this officer a high rating on the performance report.

B. You schedule a meeting with the unit commander to discuss your concerns and a course of action for writing the evaluation, as the commander must also approve the final product.

C. You write an evaluation that is an accurate representation of the junior officer's performance.

D. You schedule a meeting with the junior officer to discuss the proposed content of the performance evaluation.

E. You ask the junior officer to write an evaluation of their performance based on what they think is appropriate.

21   Select the MOST EFFECTIVE action (A–E) in response to the situation.

22. Select the LEAST EFFECTIVE action (A–E) in response to the situation.

Situation XII: You are the supervisor of a junior officer who routinely must pull duty shifts in remote locations with various members of the organization. Recently this officer has informed you that he does not feel comfortable pulling duty with members of the opposite gender for religious reasons and requests that he not be scheduled with female crew members. Due to the strained nature of the duty schedule, this request will create significant challenges for all members of the organization to fill the shifts, get the required training, and schedule medical appointments and leave.

Possible actions:

    A. Because this request is for a religious accommodation, you work with the scheduler to fulfill the request regardless of the disruption to others in the organization.

    B. Schedule a meeting with the unit commander to discuss this request and get instructions for a course of action.

    C. Deny the request and report the individual to the equal opportunity office on base for discrimination.

    D. Immediately deny the request and do not report the conversation to the commanding officer.

    E. Schedule a meeting with the unit Chaplain to discuss this request to see if the request has any religious foundation.

23. Select the MOST EFFECTIVE action (A–E) in response to the situation.

24. Select the LEAST EFFECTIVE action (A–E) in response to the situation.

Situation XIII: As a flight commander, you returned to your stateside flight having been on deployment for half the year. You are approached by a junior officer under your charge, and he informs you that your assistant flight commander, in your absence, allowed the flight to lapse on flight hours and currencies by scheduling a majority of sorties for him and his crew. Looking through the records, you verify that was what occurred and that the morale of other crews is very low.

Possible actions:

    A. Identify the officer's actions to your squadron commander and ask to have him replaced.

    B. Take full control over flight scheduling and deprioritize him and his crew for all future flight opportunities.

    C. Harshly council the officer in public and downgrade his performance report for that period.

    D. Schedule all future *good deal* flights for yourself and your crew.

    E. Meet in private with the officer, identify currency and perceived morale problems, and have the officer and his crew fly and train with other crews to gain proficiency on the rest of the flights.

25. Select the MOST EFFECTIVE action (A–E) in response to the situation.

26. Select the LEAST EFFECTIVE action (A–E) in response to the situation.

Situation XIV: While deployed, you are performing your flight and weapons safety collateral duty. In doing so, you observe ground crews wrongly installing arming pins on the 2,000 lb. GPS-guided bombs. The crews inform you that is how the ground weapons officer, a senior officer, instructed them.

Possible actions:

A. You inform the weapons officer of the procedural deviation observed with the ground crews and relay what happened to others pulling flight safety duty.

B. You report the problem to your squadron commander and leave it for the senior commanders to resolve the issue.

C. Ignore the situation because there must be a reason for the procedural difference.

D. Ask the ground crew to bring up the issue with their supervisor for resolution.

E. Direct the ground crews to correctly install the arming pins for the sorties before notifying both the weapons officer and your squadron commander of the observed deviation and corrective action taken.

27. Select the MOST EFFECTIVE action (A–E) in response to the situation.

28. Select the LEAST EFFECTIVE action (A–E) in response to the situation.

Situation XV: You are responsible for writing performance reports for junior officers under your charge. However, you have never written a performance report and are task-saturated with flying, new weapon qualification needs, and upcoming exercise preparations.

Possible actions:

A. Have the officers write their own performance report and submit them to you.

B. Inform your commander that you don't have time to do the performance reports and inquire as to what to do.

C. Let the performance reports' due dates lapse, as doing the job is more important than paperwork.

D. Deprioritize the reports and throw something together when you can get around to it.

E. Learn from Air Force instructions on performance reports and solicit advice from peers who are already skilled in writing them.

29. Select the MOST EFFECTIVE action (A–E) in response to the situation.

30. Select the LEAST EFFECTIVE action (A–E) in response to the situation.

practice test—AFOQT (Form T)

Situation XVI: A new weapons delivery procedure initiated by your organization resulted in the death of fellow service members. Your Commander adamantly orders everyone to not cooperate with an investigating team. As an example, you are told that should they ask for a technical document that happens to be on your desk, you are directed to feign ignorance.

Possible actions:

    A. Confront the commander and identify pros and cons over the directive.

    B. Do as ordered and hamper the investigation.

    C. Do as directed but discredit the officer among peers.

    D. Meet with the investigative team and inform them of the directive.

    E. Ignore the directive and answer any questions truthfully and without bias.

31. Select the MOST EFFECTIVE action (A–E) in response to the situation.

32. Select the LEAST EFFECTIVE action (A–E) in response to the situation.

Situation XVII: Your fellow flight commanders ask you to be less productive because you are making them look bad. You designed new processes for managing flight tasks and needs that seem to be working effectively. The other commanders are swamped with late reports, flight scheduling problems, exercise demands, maintaining their own flight currencies, and family stressors.

Possible actions:

    A. Ignore their request and continue to take care of your flight.

    B. Contact your squadron commander about being asked to be less effective.

    C. Do slightly less by not completing some tasks early.

    D. Inform the other flight commanders that they need to do more.

    E. Partner with the other flight commanders in coming up with unified ways to help each other with workloads.

33. Select the MOST EFFECTIVE action (A–E) in response to the situation.

34. Select the LEAST EFFECTIVE action (A–E) in response to the situation.

Situation XVIII: Your operations office is stressed due to a shortage of people able to fill the flight schedule. You show up ready to brief and fly but are starting to feel significant sinus congestion. If you do fly, you might have a sinus block, and if you don't your squadron will be very upset with you. You don't look sick, and going to the flight doctor would take all day.

Possible actions:

A. Fly but make sure you have a bottle of nasal congestion spray with you just in case, so you won't have to declare an inflight emergency or rupture your sinuses.

B. Take yourself off flight status and take the heat for leaving a hole in the flight schedule.

C. Complain to the operations officer that you are feeling pressured to fly.

D. Find someone who can take your flight, even from outside the squadron, and provide that solution to the operations officer.

E. Feign being more ill than you feel and take yourself off flight status.

35. Select the MOST EFFECTIVE action (A–E) in response to the situation.

36. Select the LEAST EFFECTIVE action (A–E) in response to the situation.

Situation XIX: You are incredibly efficient, having worked hard to finish your squadron collateral duties early in the day. You are not scheduled to fly nor have any simulators for the rest of the day.

Possible actions:

A. Take some down time while you can and leave work early.

B. Pretend to be busy by toying with e-mail or surfing the Web until the normal duty day ends.

C. Tell your flight commander or assistant flight commander that you are ahead of things and would like to head out early.

D. Get to know others around the squadron by socializing.

E. Find out what others are doing and what you can do to help.

37. Select the MOST EFFECTIVE action (A–E) in response to the situation.

38. Select the LEAST EFFECTIVE action (A–E) in response to the situation.

Situation XX: A peer in the instructor shop tells you of a new junior officer being perceived as either lazy, indifferent, or incompetent during flight missions. You do not know the officer nor do you know anything about this person. The new flight officer is in another flight and is not making a good first impression.

Possible actions:

A. Counsel the new officer and ask what is happening in his or her private life that might be affecting their performance.

B. Ensure that neither you nor those in your flight crew are scheduled to fly with the new person.

C. Acknowledge your peer's concern, ignore the comments, and do not repeat them to others.

D. Ask the instructor to fly you with the new person for a few sorties to see if a fresh perspective might help.

E. Let the new officer know that he or she will likely lose their wings if things don't improve.

39. Select the MOST EFFECTIVE action (A–E) in response to the situation.

40. Select the LEAST EFFECTIVE action (A–E) in response to the situation.

Situation XXI: You have your commission and your shiny wings, and you are assigned to your first squadron. In addition to flying, your assigned squadron job is something called SnackO (snack officer). You are tasked with the menial duty of keeping the squadron fridge stocked, having coffee at the ready, and managing the snack fund.

Possible actions:

A. Blow off the duty and focus on flying.

B. Do what you need to do grudgingly until the duty is passed on the next new officer.

C. Look around for other jobs you would like, and ask to be reassigned to them instead.

D. Do the job enthusiastically and efficiently, and look for ways to improve this assignment.

E. Tell your supervisor that you are capable of doing more responsible jobs than SnackO.

41. Select the MOST EFFECTIVE action (A–E) in response to the situation.

42. Select the LEAST EFFECTIVE action (A–E) in response to the situation.

Situation XXII: You are working a pre-combat exercise to help the combat readiness of others before they deploy. Your team is very understaffed, and the team's senior commander doesn't show for the start of the exercise. Later that day he is reached briefly and explains that he gave himself personal leave for most of the exercise in order to attend the Pope's visit to a nearby city.

Possible actions:

A. Immediately go up the chain of command and inform them of the behavior.

B. Respect his religious convictions and accept degraded training.

C. Do not cover for him, and let his duties go unfilled even if the training suffers.

D. Identify what needs to be accomplished, perform prioritized tasks, and inform the officer what was and was not accomplished during his absence.

E. Ensure that those in the exercise know you are understaffed and that your team's senior commander took personal time off.

43. Select the MOST EFFECTIVE action (A–E) in response to the situation.

44. Select the LEAST EFFECTIVE action (A–E) in response to the situation.

Situation XXIII: Your remote unit commander wants to include the release of live weapons from Air Force jets near Army soldiers undergoing training. You suspect he is under pressure for his upcoming performance report and from the local army commander. In discovering that the regulations for both services prohibit his proposed activity, your commander decides to label all such events as a *proof of principle* to bypass directives. According to him, any loss of life will be the fault of the Army and not him. You are ordered to make the new range capability happen, and your request for guidance from higher headquarters is denied.

Possible actions:

A. Refuse the order.

B. Set up the live weapon range and ignore regulations.

C. Develop and execute a plan that is in adherence to both sets of regulations.

D. Take your concerns to the media in pressuring safety compliance.

E. Go immediately up the chain of command about the project.

45. Select the MOST EFFECTIVE action (A–E) in response to the situation.

46. Select the LEAST EFFECTIVE action (A–E) in response to the situation.

Situation XXIV: A subordinate requests an official meeting with you and informs you that his wife is having an affair with a senior officer on the base but outside of the command. He presents no evidence to support his statement and is emotionally charged.

Possible actions:

    A. Contact the senior officer and inform him of the charge being made against him.

    B. Meet with your subordinate and his wife and gather more information as to the validity of the charge.

    C. Sympathize with the junior officer and then say and do nothing.

    D. Schedule a meeting between the junior officer and your commanding officer over the presented charges.

    E. Direct the junior officer to consult the area defense council (base lawyers) and to follow their guidance.

47. Select the MOST EFFECTIVE action (A–E) in response to the situation.

48. Select the LEAST EFFECTIVE action (A–E) in response to the situation.

Situation XXV: A troops-in-contact event occurs (troops in a firefight) while you are flying a close air support (CAS) patrol in the area. You are asked over comms how soon you can get to them. If it takes you too long another asset might get the mission.

Possible actions:

    A. Tell the controller that you will get there as soon as possible.

    B. Pad the time it will take in order to give yourself a margin of error.

    C. Give a vague reply.

    D. Give a rounded down estimate to better ensure you get the mission, and try to make up the time difference.

    E. Point the aircraft toward the need while giving the actual time to the target.

49. Select the MOST EFFECTIVE action (A–E) in response to the situation.

50. Select the LEAST EFFECTIVE action (A–E) in response to the situation.

STOP! DO NOT GO ON UNTIL TIME IS UP.

Part 7: Self-Description Inventory

The AFOQT 240-question, 45-minute long self-description personality inventory test is copyrighted, and result interpretation requires software analysis of your responses. This shortened version has been created for the practice test so that you can become familiar with the format.

Despite there being no right or wrong answers, results *may* be used as an additional consideration in your selection as an officer candidate, your aviation career field selection, and potentially for future unknown applications.

> **Directions:** This inventory measures personal traits and attitudes. The inventory consists of a list of statements. The task is to read each statement carefully and decide how well each one describes you.

Look at the sample statement below:

1. I enjoy reading poetry.

Decide whether statement 1 is characteristic of you and indicate your agreement using the scale below.

A	B	C	D	E
Strongly Disagree	Moderately Disagree	Neither Agree nor Disagree	Moderately Agree	Strongly Agree

If you <u>strongly agree</u> that the statement describes you, select E on your answer sheet next to the statement number. If you <u>strongly disagree</u>, select A on your answer sheet. You would mark B, C, or D to indicate other levels of agreement.

You should work quickly but reply to all statements. Give your first impression about how well each statement describes you by comparing yourself to people in your same sex and age group. Don't spend a long time deciding what your answer should be. There is no right or wrong answer to each statement. Answer all statements, even if you're not sure of your answer.

When you begin, be sure to start with question 1 of Part 7 on your answer sheet. If you complete all of the statements before the allotted time has elapsed, you may return to this section to review.

110 Questions • 20 Minutes

(Note: On the AFOQT, you will have 45 minutes to answer 240 questions.)

A	B	C	D	E
Strongly Disagree	Moderately Disagree	Neither Agree nor Disagree	Moderately Agree	Strongly Agree

TIP

You can take a self-description personality inventory test similar to the NEO PI-R test used on the AFOQT by going to the following site: http://www.personal.psu.edu/~j5j/IPIP/. You can choose to take either the 300- or 120-question test to familiarize yourself with the types of questions you will encounter.

1. I try to find a balance between my work and personal interests.

2. I am very comfortable supervising others.

3. I get annoyed when friends drop by unexpectedly.

4. I like being involved in group activities.

5. I always set high work standards for myself.

6. I am quiet and reserved.

7. I enjoy being the center of attention.

8. I like to have a daily routine.

9. I always think hard before making decisions.

10. I am easily hurt.

11. I am quite talkative.

12. I worry more about pleasing others than myself.

13. I do things at my own pace.

14. I am more stressed than relaxed.

15. I am extremely organized.

16. I keep my emotions under control.

17. I dislike large parties.

18. I worry about things.

19. I make friends easily.

20. I have a vivid imagination.

21. I trust others.

22. I complete tasks successfully.

23. I get angry easily.

24. I believe in the importance of art.

25. I use others for my own ends.

26. I like to tidy up.

27. I often feel blue.

28. I tend to take charge.

29. I experience my emotions intensely.

30. I love helping others.

31. I keep my promises.

32. I find it difficult to approach others.

33. I'm always busy.

34. I prefer variety to routine.

35. I love a good fight.

36. I work hard.

37. I occasionally go on binges.

38. I love excitement.

39. I love reading challenging material.

40. I believe that I am better than others.

41. I'm always prepared.

42. I panic easily.

43. I radiate joy.

44. I tend to vote for liberal political candidates.

45. I sympathize with the homeless.

46. I tend to jump into things without thinking.

47. I often fear for the worst.

48. I put little time and effort into my work.

49. I enjoy wild flights of fantasy.

50. I generally believe that others have good intentions.

51. I excel in what I do.

52. I am easily irritated.

53. I talk to a lot of different people when I'm at a party.

54. I like to see beauty in things that others might not notice.

55. I would cheat to get ahead.

56. I often forget to put things back in their

proper place.

57. I tend to waste my time.

58. I try to lead others.

59. I feel others' emotions.

60. I generally tell the truth.

61. I am concerned about others.

62. I'm afraid to draw attention to myself.

63. I'm always on the go.

64. I prefer to stick with what I know.

65. I tend to yell at people.

66. I often do more than what's expected of me.

67. I rarely overindulge.

68. I seek adventure.

69. I avoid philosophical discussions.

70. I think highly of myself.

71. I carry out my plans.

72. I sometimes become overwhelmed by events.

73. I like to have a lot of fun.

74. I believe that there is no absolute right or wrong.

75. I sympathize with those who are worse off than me.

76. I tend to make rash decisions.

77. I'm afraid of many things.

78. I avoid contacts with others.

79. I love to daydream.

80. I trust what people say.

81. I usually handle tasks smoothly.

82. I tend to lose my temper.

83. I prefer to be alone.

84. I do not like poetry.

85. I take advantage of others.

86. I leave a mess in my room.

87. I'm often down in the dumps.

88. I take control of things.

89. I rarely notice my emotional reactions.

90. I'm indifferent to the feelings of others.

91. I break rules.

92. I only feel comfortable with friends.

93. I do a lot in my spare time.

94. I dislike changes.

95. I insult people.

96. I do just enough work to get by.

97. I can easily resist temptations.

98. I enjoy being reckless.

99. I have trouble understanding abstract ideas.

100. I love life.

101. I'm able to control my cravings.

102. I act wild and crazy.

103. I'm not interested in theoretical discussions.

104. I boast about my virtues.

105. I have difficulty starting tasks.

106. I remain calm under pressure.

107. I look at the bright side of life.

108. I believe that we should be tough on crime.

109. I try not to think about the needy.

110. I act without thinking.

STOP! DO NOT GO ON UNTIL TIME IS UP.

Part 8: Physical Science

Directions: This section contains 20 questions relating to astronomy, chemistry, geology, geophysics, physics, and meteorology. You are to review each question and select the best response given the information provided. Then mark the space on the answer form that has the same number and letter as your choice.

Example Questions:

1. An eclipse of the sun throws the shadow of the

    A. moon on the sun.

    B. earth on the sun.

    C. sun on the earth.

    D. earth on the moon.

    E. moon on the earth

The correct answer is E. An eclipse of the sun, or solar eclipse, occurs when the moon passes in front of the sun, resulting in the earth falling into the moon's shadow.

2. The rate of flow of electrons through a substance is measured in

    A. currents.

    B. ohms.

    C. watts.

    D. amperes.

    E. volts.

The correct answer is D. Amperes are used to measure the rate of flow of electrons through a substance.

3. The center layer of the earth is the

    A. crust.

    B. inner core.

    C. magma core.

    D. mantle.

    E. outer core.

The correct answer is B. The inner core, made up mostly of iron and nickel, is the center layer of the earth.

Your score on this test will be based on the number of questions you answer correctly. You should try to answer every question. You will not lose points or be penalized for guessing. Do not spend too much time on any one question. When you begin this section of the test, be sure to start with number 1 of Part 8 on your answer sheet.

Part 8: Physical Science

20 Questions • 10 Minutes

1. Charged particles erupting from the surface of the sun are

   A. solar flares.

   B. sun spots.

   C. coronal mass ejections.

   D. galactic cosmic rays.

   E. solar wind.

2. The positively charged particles that compose an atom are called

   A. electrons.

   B. isotopes.

   C. neutrons.

   D. protons.

   E. quarks.

3. What is the primary cause of the earth's magnetic field?

   A. Metals in the earth's crust

   B. No scientific consensus about this

   C. Convection and coriolis force of the earth's liquid iron core

   D. Earth's semi-solid iron core

   E. Electromagnetic energy from the sun

4. What constitutes a scientific theory?

   A. Ability to reject it conflicts with opinions or beliefs

   B. Empirically testable using hypothesis

   C. An idea or hunch

   D. Not supported by facts or data

   E. Explanations of observations using nonrepeatable processes

5. A statistical significance is used to

   A. identify the probability of a result occurring randomly.

   B. measure construct validity.

   C. determine if the effect is important.

   D. identify a range of scores within a population.

   E. prove a hypothesis.

6. The layer of the atmosphere closest to the surface of the earth is

   A. stratosphere.

   B. thermosphere.

   C. tropopause.

   D. mesosphere.

   E. troposphere.

7. The time required for light of a solar flare to reach the earth is

   A. 4–5 minutes.

   B. 5–6 minutes.

   C. 7–8 minutes.

   D. 9–10 minutes.

   E. 11–12 minutes.

8. Which of following primarily protects the earth from the most harmful space radiation?

   A. Earth's troposphere

   B. Earth's magnetosphere

   C. Solar wind

   D. Van Allen belt

   E. Asteroid belt

9. In a system with no external forces present, every force has an equal and opposite reactive force, is

     A. Newton's Second Law.

     B. Kepler's First Law.

     C. Bernoulli's Principle.

     D. Newton's Third Law.

     E. Boyle's Law.

10. All of the following will stop beta radiation EXCEPT:

     A. Paper

     B. Wood

     C. Aluminum

     D. Steel

     E. Lead

11. Which of the following is NOT considered a Greenhouse gas?

     A. Water vapor

     B. Carbon dioxide (CO_2)

     C. Methane

     D. Carbon monoxide (CO)

     E. Chlorofluorocarbons (CFCs)

12. Which planet in the solar system has one or more moons that may support life due to the presence of ice?

     A. Saturn

     B. Mercury

     C. Uranus

     D. Mars

     E. Jupiter

13. Which gas is the most prevalent in the earth's atmosphere?

     A. Nitrogen

     B. Oxygen

     C. Carbon dioxide

     D. Helium

     E. Hydrogen

14. Which of the following CANNOT be determined from a histogram?

     A. Response counts

     B. Distribution of the data

     C. Mode

     D. Median

     E. Percentiles

15. Which of the following is NOT a force acting on an object in flight?

     A. Lift

     B. Drag

     C. Thrust

     D. Weight

     E. Roll

16. A material that is made out of two or more physically and chemically different materials is best described as a(n)

     A. alloy.

     B. composite.

     C. homogeneous mixture.

     D. heterogeneous mixture.

     E. substance.

17. A lunar eclipse occurs when the

    A. earth's shadow blocks the sun.

    B. moon's shadow blocks the sun.

    C. sun blocks the moon.

    D. earth's shadow blocks the moon.

    E. moon's shadow blocks the earth.

18. All of the following are effects of soil erosion EXCEPT:

    A. Pesticide retention

    B. Loss of natural nutrients

    C. Seed distribution

    D. Soil holding capacity

    E. Soil quality

19. Air pressure at higher altitudes is reduced primarily because of what factor?

    A. No gravity acting on the molecules

    B. Lower temperatures at higher altitude

    C. Higher temperatures at higher altitude

    D. Greater dispersion of the molecules/ lower density

    E. Changes in the earth's magnetic field

20. The type of energy that is relative to the state of other objects in the immediate proximity is

    A. electromagnetic.

    B. kinetic.

    C. potential.

    D. atomic.

    E. thermal.

STOP! DO NOT GO ON UNTIL TIME IS UP.

Part 9: Table Reading

> **Directions:** This part of the test has 40 questions designed to test your ability to read tables quickly and accurately.

Look at the following sample items based on the tabulation of turnstile readings shown below:

Tabulation Of Turnstile Readings

Turnstile Number	Turnstile Readings At					
	5:30 a.m.	6:00 a.m.	7:00 a.m.	8:00 a.m.	9:00 a.m.	9:30 a.m.
1	79078	79090	79225	79590	79860	79914
2	24915	24930	25010	25441	25996	26055
3	39509	39530	39736	40533	41448	41515
4	58270	58291	58396	58958	59729	59807
5	43371	43378	43516	43888	44151	44217

For each question, determine the turnstile reading for the turnstile number and time given. Choose as your answer the letter of the column in which the correct reading is found.

	Turnstile Number	Time	A	B	C	D	E
1.	1	8:00 a.m.	25441	25996	79225	79590	79860
2.	2	6:00 a.m.	24915	24930	25010	39530	79090
3.	4	9:30 a.m.	41515	44217	44151	59729	59807
4.	5	7:00 a.m.	39530	39736	43516	58291	58396
5.	3	5:30 a.m.	39509	39530	39736	58270	58291

1.   **The correct answer is D.** The reading for Turnstile 1 at 8:00 a.m. is 79590.

2.   **The correct answer is B.** At 6:00 a.m., the reading for Turnstile 2 is 24930.

3.   **The correct answer is E.** The 9:30 a.m. reading for Turnstile 4 is 59807.

4.   **The correct answer is C.** At 7:00 a.m., Turnstile 5's reading is 43516.

5.   **The correct answer is A.** Turnstile 3's reading at 5:30 a.m. is 39509.

Your score on this test is based on the number of questions you answer correctly. You should try to answer every question. You will not lose points or be penalized for guessing. Do not spend too much time on any one question.

When you begin, be sure to start with question number 1 of Part 9 on your answer sheet.

Part 9: Table Reading

40 Questions • 7 Minutes

Questions 1–5 are based on the table below. Note that the *X*-values are shown at the top of the table and the *Y*-values are shown on the left side of the table. Find the entry that occurs at the intersection of the row and the column corresponding to the values given.

				X-Value			
		–3	–2	–1	0	+1	+2	+3
Y-Value	+3	22	23	25	27	28	29	30
	+2	23	25	27	29	30	31	32
	+1	24	26	28	30	32	33	34
	0	26	27	29	31	33	34	35
	–1	27	29	30	32	34	35	37
	–2	28	30	31	33	35	36	38
	–3	29	31	32	34	36	37	39

	X	Y	A	B	C	D	E
1.	0	–1	29	33	32	35	34
2.	–3	–3	22	29	23	31	28
3.	–1	+2	25	31	29	30	27
4.	+3	0	30	34	35	37	39
5.	–2	+1	26	23	29	25	22

Questions 6–10 are based on the following table showing height-weight standards used by the Air Force in its commissioning program.

Commission Height-Weight Standards						
Men				Women		
Height Inches	Weight			Height Inches	Weight	
	Min.	Max.			Min.	Max.
60	100	153		60	92	130
61	102	155		61	95	132
62	103	158		62	97	134
63	105	164		63	100	136
64	105	169		64	103	139
65	106	169		65	106	144
66	107	174		66	108	148
67	111	179		67	111	152
68	115	184		68	114	156
69	119	189		69	117	161
70	123	194		70	119	165
71	127	199		71	122	169
72	131	205		72	125	174
73	135	211		73	128	179
74	139	218		74	130	185
75	143	224		75	133	190
76	147	230		76	136	196
77	151	236		77	139	201
78	153	242		78	141	206
79	157	248		79	144	211
80	161	254		80	147	216

		A	B	C	D	E
6.	The maximum weight for 66" women is	152	148	169	144	174
7.	The minimum weight for 72" men is	128	125	127	231	131
8.	The maximum weight for 68" men is	189	156	179	184	161
9.	The minimum weight for 62" women is	100	97	95	92	103
10.	The maximum weight for 75" men is	224	190	236	196	230

Questions 11–15 are based on the table below showing the blood alcohol content in relation to body weight and the number of drinks consumed during a 2-hour period. For each question, ascertain the blood alcohol content-percent.

Blood Alcohol Content (Bac)—Percent								
No. of Drinks* **(2-hour period)**	**Body Weight (in pounds)**							
	100	**120**	**140**	**160**	**180**	**200**	**220**	**240**
12	0.33	0.25	0.21	0.19	0.17	0.16	0.15	0.14
11	0.29	0.23	0.19	0.18	0.16	0.15	0.14	0.14
10	0.26	0.21	0.18	0.17	0.15	0.14	0.13	0.13
9	0.23	0.19	0.16	0.15	0.14	0.13	0.12	0.12
8	0.20	0.17	0.15	0.14	0.13	0.12	0.11	0.11
7	0.17	0.15	0.14	0.13	0.12	0.11	0.10	0.10
6	0.15	0.13	0.12	0.11	0.11	0.10	0.09	0.08
5	0.13	0.11	0.10	0.10	0.09	0.08	0.08	0.07
4	0.10	0.09	0.08	0.08	0.07	0.06	0.06	0.06
3	0.08	0.07	0.06	0.05	0.05	0.04	0.04	0.04
2	0.05	0.04	0.04	0.03	0.03	0.03	0.02	0.02
1	0.03	0.02	0.02	0.02	0.01	0.01	0.01	0.01

* One drink is equivalent to $1\frac{1}{2}$ oz. 85-proof liquor, 6 oz. wine, or 12 oz. beer.

		A	**B**	**C**	**D**	**E**
11.	A 160-pound person—2 drinks	0.01	0.02	0.03	0.04	0.05
12.	A 200-pound person—3 drinks	0.01	0.02	0.03	0.04	0.05
13.	A 180-pound person—4 drinks	0.06	0.07	0.08	0.09	0.10
14.	A 100-pound person—2 drinks	0.01	0.02	0.03	0.04	0.05
15.	A 240-pound person—3 drinks	0.04	0.05	0.06	0.07	0.08

Questions 16–20 are based on the weekly train schedule given below for the Dumont Line:

	Eastbound			Magic Mall		Westbound		
Train #	Harvard Square Leave	Pleasure Plaza Leave	Harding Street Leave	Arrive	Leave	Harding Street Leave	Pleasure Plaza Leave	Harvard Square Leave
69	7:48	7:51	7:56	8:00	8:06	8:10	8:15	8:18
70	7:54	7:57	8:02	8:06	8:12	8:16	8:21	8:24
71	8:00	8:03	8:08	8:12	8:18	8:22	8:27	8:30
72	8:04	8:07	8:13	8:17	8:22	8:26	8:31	8:34
73	8:08	8:11	8:17	8:21	8:26	8:30	8:35	8:38
74	8:12	8:15	8:20	8:24	8:30	8:34	8:39	8:42
75	8:16	8:19	8:24	8:28	8:34	8:38	8:43	8:46
69	8:20	8:23	8:28	8:32	8:38	8:42	8:47	8:50
70	8:26	8:29	8:34	8:38	8:44	8:48	8:53	8:56

The table title: **Weekday Train Line Schedule—Dumont Line**

16. Train #73 is scheduled to arrive at Magic Mall at

- **A.** 8:26
- **B.** 8:21
- **C.** 8:22
- **D.** 8:17
- **E.** 8:24

17. Train #75 is scheduled to leave Harvard Square at

- **A.** 8:20
- **B.** 8:12
- **C.** 8:15
- **D.** 8:19
- **E.** 8:16

18. Train #70 is scheduled to leave Pleasure Plaza on its second westbound trip to Harvard Square at

- **A.** 8:48
- **B.** 8:21
- **C.** 8:53
- **D.** 8:24
- **E.** 8:56

19. Going toward Harvard Square, Train #71 is scheduled to leave Pleasure Plaza at

- **A.** 8:27
- **B.** 8:03
- **C.** 8:22
- **D.** 8:08
- **E.** 8:18

20. Passengers boarding at Harding Street and wishing to get to Harvard Square by 8:42 would have to board a train that is scheduled to leave Magic Mall no later than

- **A.** 8:34
- **B.** 8:24
- **C.** 8:39
- **D.** 8:30
- **E.** 8:28

practice test—AFOQT (Form T)

Questions 21–30 are based on the mileage between the two cities:

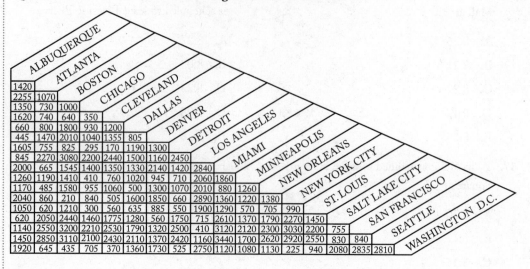

		A	B	C	D	E
21.	Chicago to Dallas	1,040	930	1,200	1,355	825
22.	New Orleans to Miami	1,360	1,260	570	880	715
23.	Albuquerque to Denver	660	845	825	755	445
24.	Washington, D.C. to Seattle	2,835	2,080	2,200	2,810	2,250
25.	Atlanta to Salt Lake City	2,050	2,850	1,920	2,440	2,210
26.	San Francisco to Boston	3,200	3,110	2,850	2,440	2,530
27.	Cleveland to Minneapolis	410	1,060	1,020	760	1,350
28.	St. Louis to Detroit	660	550	560	885	715
29.	Los Angeles to Detroit	2,010	2,060	2,840	2,140	2,450
30.	New York City to Dallas	1,300	1,850	1,600	1,060	1,280

Questions 31–40 are based on the table below. Note that the X-values are shown at the top of the table and the Y-values are shown on the left of the table. Find the entry that occurs at the intersection of the row and the column corresponding to the values given.

X-Value											
	−5	**−4**	**−3**	**−2**	**−1**	**0**	**+1**	**+2**	**+3**	**+4**	**+5**
+5	32	30	29	28	27	25	23	22	21	19	17
+4	34	32	31	30	29	27	25	23	22	20	18
+3	36	34	33	32	30	28	26	24	23	21	19
+2	37	35	34	33	31	29	27	26	25	23	21
+1	39	37	35	34	32	30	29	27	26	24	22
0	40	38	36	35	33	31	30	28	27	25	23
−1	41	39	37	36	34	32	31	29	28	26	25
−2	43	41	39	38	36	34	33	31	30	28	26
−3	44	42	40	39	37	36	34	33	32	30	28
−4	46	44	42	41	39	38	36	35	33	31	30
−5	48	46	44	43	41	40	38	37	35	33	31

(Y-Value on the left of the table)

	X	**Y**	**A**	**B**	**C**	**D**	**E**
31.	0	−3	34	38	37	35	36
32.	−4	+2	36	35	33	37	34
33.	+2	−2	31	36	33	38	30
34.	−5	−5	46	19	17	44	48
35.	+1	−3	27	33	36	34	26
36.	−3	+4	28	32	29	31	30
37.	+4	+1	26	39	24	36	25
38.	−1	−5	41	43	37	40	39
39.	+3	+1	27	24	28	25	26
40.	+5	0	4	23	6	25	22

STOP! DO NOT GO ON UNTIL TIME IS UP.

practice test—AFOQT (Form T)

Part 10: Instrument Comprehension

Directions: This part of the test has 25 questions designed to measure your ability to determine the position of an airplane in flight from reading instruments showing its compass heading, its amount of climb or dive, and its degree of bank to right or left.

HOW TO READ THE ARTIFICIAL HORIZON DIAL

In each item, the left-hand dial is labeled ARTIFICIAL HORIZON.

On the artificial horizon, the white area depicts sky, ground is the dark area, and the line between the two is the horizon. The bank scale does include degrees of bank indicators (markings) to the left and right of the pointer (10, 20, 30, 45, 60, and 90 degrees of bank).

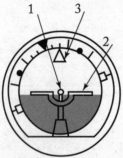

1) Nose on the horizon
2) Wings level
3) No bank

1) Nose slightly above the horizon
2) Right wing down
3) 20 degrees right bank

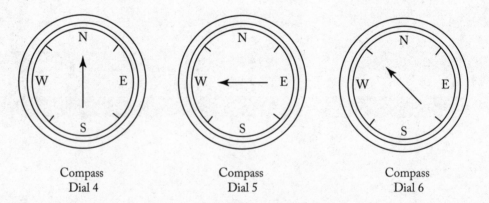

Compass
Dial 4

Compass
Dial 5

Compass
Dial 6

On each item, the right dial is labeled COMPASS. On this dial, the arrow shows the compass direction in which the airplane is headed at the moment. Dial 4 shows it headed north; Dial 5 shows it headed west; and Dial 6 shows it headed northwest.

Each item in this test consists of two dials and four silhouettes of airplanes in flight. Your task is to determine which one of the four airplanes is MOST NEARLY in the position indicated by the two dials. YOU ARE ALWAYS LOOKING NORTH AT THE SAME ALTITUDE AS EACH OF THE PLANES. EAST IS ALWAYS TO YOUR RIGHT AS YOU LOOK AT THE PAGE.

SAMPLE QUESTION EXPLAINED

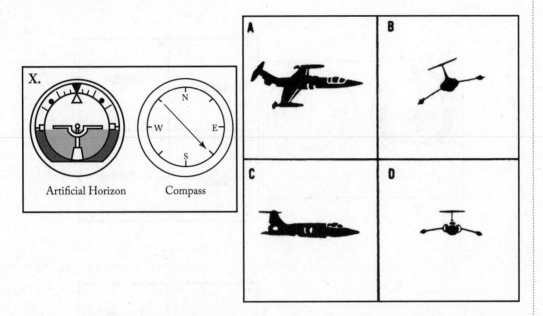

In item X, the dial labeled ARTIFICIAL HORIZON shows that the airplane is NOT banked, and it is neither climbing nor diving. The COMPASS shows that it is headed southeast. The only one of the four airplane silhouettes that meets these specifications is in the box lettered C, so the answer to X is C. Note that B is a rear view, while D is a front view. Note also that A is banked to the right and that B is banked to the left.

Your score on this test will be based on the number of questions you answer correctly. You should try to answer every question. You will not lose points or be penalized for guessing. Do not spend too much time on any one question.

When you begin, be sure to start with question number 1 of Part 10 on your answer sheet.

practice test—AFOQT (Form T)

Part 10: Instrument Comprehension

25 Questions • 5 Minutes

1.

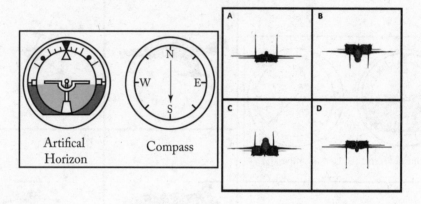

2.

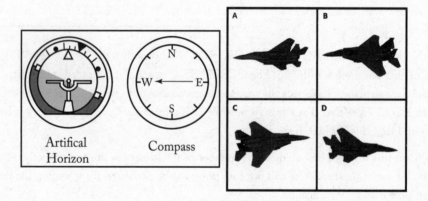

3.

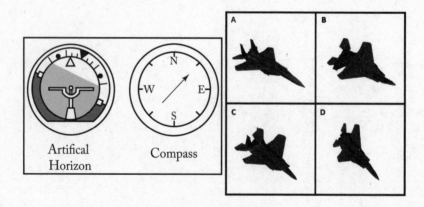

4.

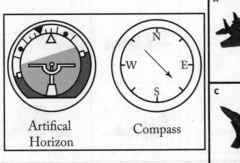

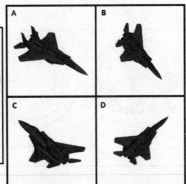

5.

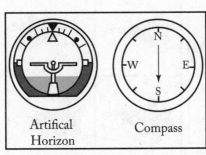

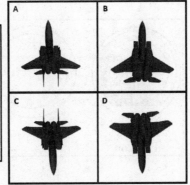

6.

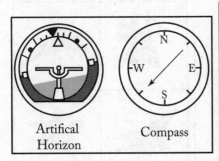

7.

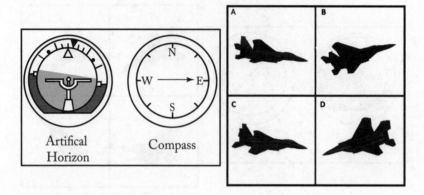

8.

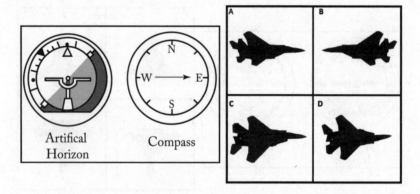

9.

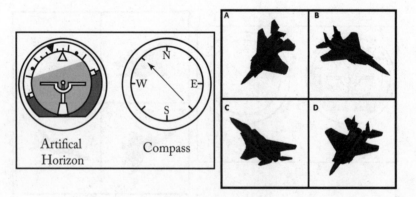

10.

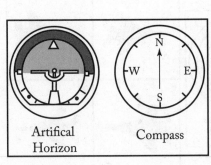 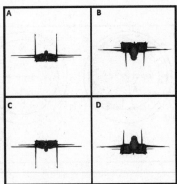

11.

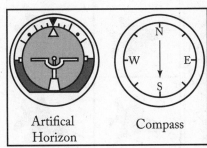 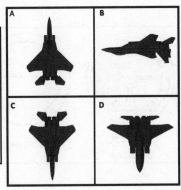

12.

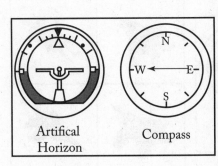 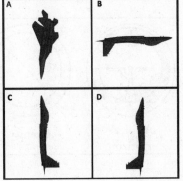

practice test—AFOQT (Form T)

13.

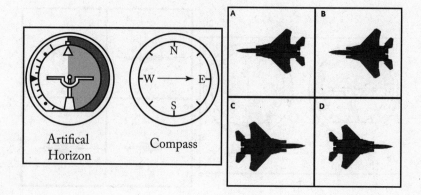

14.

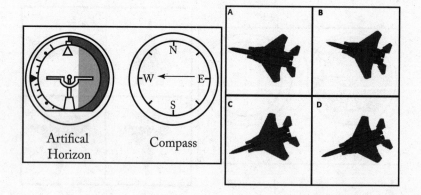

15.

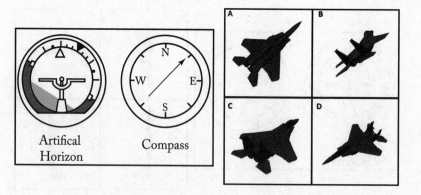

16.

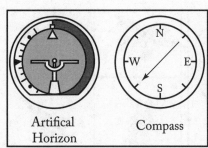 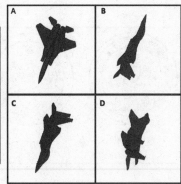

17.

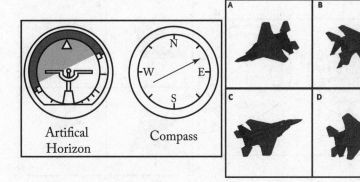

18.

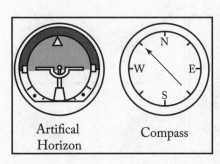 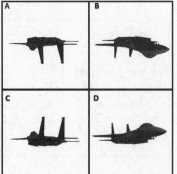

practice test—AFOQT (Form T)

19.

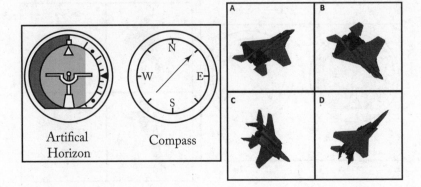

20.

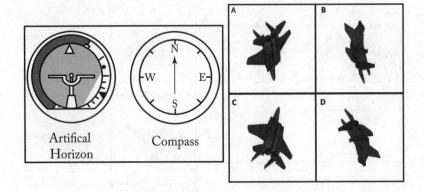

21.

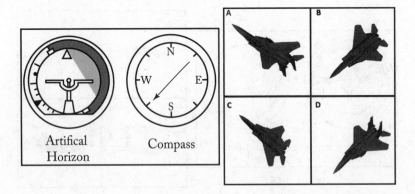

22.

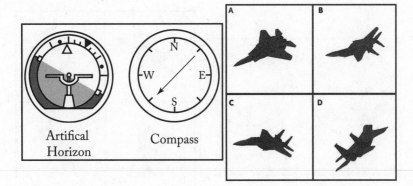

23.

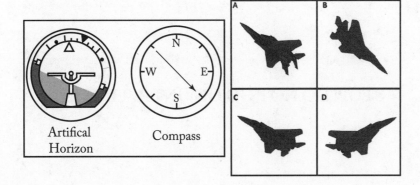

24.

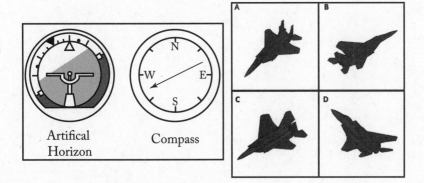

25.

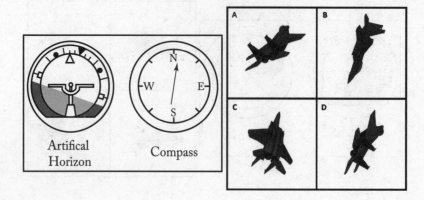

STOP! DO NOT GO ON UNTIL TIME IS UP.

Part 11: Block Counting

Directions: This section contains six (6) diagrams and 30 questions. Given a numbered block, determine how many other blocks the numbered block touches. *Note: Blocks are considered touching only if all or part of their faces touch. Blocks that only touch corners do not count. All of the blocks are the same size and shape.* Then mark the space on your answer sheet that has the same number and letter as your choice. Look at the sample below:

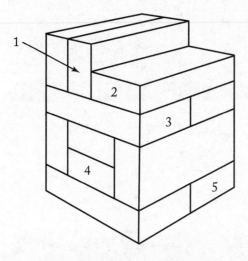

Key					
Block	**A**	**B**	**C**	**D**	**E**
1	1	2	3	4	5
2	3	4	5	6	7
3	5	6	7	8	9
4	2	3	4	5	6
5	2	3	4	5	6

1. **The correct answer is D.** Block 1 touches the other 2 top blocks and the 2 blocks directly below it. The total number of blocks touched by 1 is, therefore, 4.

2. **The correct answer is A.** Block 2 touches blocks 1 and 3, and the unnumbered block to the right of block 3. Since block 2 touches 3 other blocks, the answer is 3.

3. **The correct answer is C.** Now look at sample problem 3. It touches 3 blocks above, 3 blocks below, and 1 block on the right. Therefore, the correct answer is 7.

4. **The correct answer is D.** The total number of blocks touched by block 4 is 5.

5. **The correct answer is C.** Block 5 touches 4 other blocks.

Your score on this test is based on the number of questions you answer correctly. You should try to answer every question. You will not lose points or be penalized for guessing. Do not spend too much time on any one question.

When you begin, be sure to start with question number 1 of Part 11 on your answer sheet.

Part 11: Block Counting

30 Questions • 4.5 Minutes

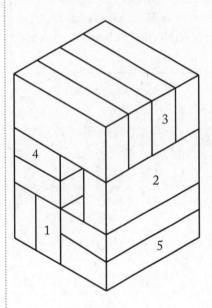

Key					
Block	**A**	**B**	**C**	**D**	**E**
1	1	2	3	4	5
2	3	4	5	6	7
3	5	6	7	8	9
4	2	3	4	5	6
5	2	3	4	5	6

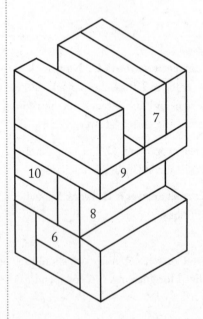

Key					
Block	**A**	**B**	**C**	**D**	**E**
6	3	4	5	6	7
7	1	2	3	4	5
8	3	4	5	6	7
9	2	3	4	5	6
10	3	4	5	6	7

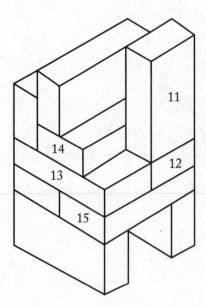

Key					
Block	A	B	C	D	E
11	2	3	4	5	6
12	2	3	4	5	6
13	3	4	5	6	7
14	3	4	5	6	7
15	2	3	4	5	6

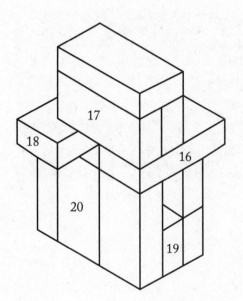

Key					
Block	A	B	C	D	E
16	3	4	5	6	7
17	1	2	3	4	5
18	1	2	3	4	5
19	1	2	3	4	5
20	1	2	3	4	5

practice test—AFOQT (Form T)

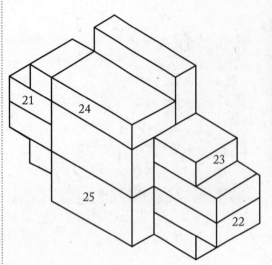

Key					
Block	A	B	C	D	E
21	2	3	4	5	6
22	2	3	4	5	6
23	2	3	4	5	6
24	2	3	4	5	6
25	2	3	4	5	6

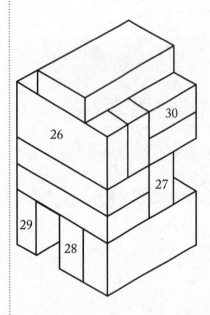

Key					
Block	A	B	C	D	E
26	1	2	3	4	5
27	3	4	5	6	7
28	2	3	4	5	6
29	2	3	4	5	6
30	2	3	4	5	6

STOP! DO NOT GO ON UNTIL TIME IS UP.

Part 12: Aviation Information

Directions: This section contains 20 questions. Then mark the space on your answer sheet that has the same number and letter as your choice. You are to review each question and select the best response given the information provided.

Now look at the two sample questions below:

1. The force necessary to overcome gravitational force to keep the airplane flying is termed

   A. power.

   B. drag.

   C. lift.

   D. thrust.

   E. weight.

   The correct answer is C. To keep the airplane flying, lift must overcome gravitational force.

2. The ailerons are used primarily to

   A. bank the airplane.

   B. control the direction of yaw.

   C. permit a slower landing speed.

   D. permit a steep angle of descent.

   E. control the pitch attitude.

   The correct answer is A. The ailerons, located on the trailing edge of each wing near the outer tip, are used primarily to bank (roll) the airplane around its longitudinal axis. The banking of the wing results in the airplane turning in the direction of the bank.

Your score on this test will be based on the number of questions you answer correctly. You should try to answer every question. You will not lose points or be penalized for guessing. Do not spend too much time on any one question.

When you begin, be sure to start with question number 1 of Part 12 on your answer sheet.

Part 12: Aviation Information

20 Questions • 8 Minutes

Questions 1 and 2 are based on the following diagram.

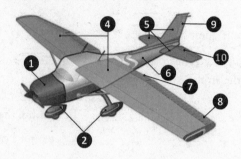

1. Identify the primary component used to move an aircraft about the vertical axis.

    A. 8

    B. 7

    C. 2

    D. 9

    E. 1

2. What is the component listed as number five (5)?

    A. Elevator

    B. Flaps

    C. Empennage

    D. Struts

    E. Rudder

3. What relationship among aerodynamic forces best describes a climb?

    A. Lift, weight, drag, and thrust are equal.

    B. Thrust exceeds drag, and lift and weight are equal.

    C. Lift exceeds drag, and weight exceeds thrust.

    D. Relative wind exceeds drag.

    E. Thrust is equal to drag, and lift exceeds weight.

4. What best describes ground effect?

    A. A cushion of compressed air close to the ground that causes aircraft to float

    B. Caused by low angles of attack and high airspeed close to the ground

    C. Ground disruption of airfoil upwash, downwash, and wingtip vortices decreases drag and increases lift

    D. Friction on an aircraft's tires during landing and takeoff

    E. The weight aerodynamic component opposite to the lift component

5. How does an aircraft make a level (constant altitude) turn in terms of aerodynamic forces?

   A. The vertical and horizontal components of lift both equal weight.

   B. The vertical component of lift is greater than weight.

   C. The horizontal component of lift equals weight, and the vertical component of lift is greater than weight.

   D. The vertical component of lift equals weight, and the horizontal component of lift is less than weight.

   E. The angle of attack is decreased while banking the aircraft.

6. Which of the following best describes aircraft lift?

   A. Differential pressure causing low pressure along the leading edge of the airfoil and high pressure behind the airfoil

   B. Air molecules moving faster under the airfoil and slower above the airfoil creating higher pressure under the airfoil

   C. Produced primarily by thrust

   D. The laminar flow of air molecules generating lower air pressure above the airfoil relative to under it

   E. A reduction in gravity directly related to the speed of the aircraft

7. Using the Airspeed Indicator (ASI) figure, what indicates maximum full flap structural speed and full flap stall speed?

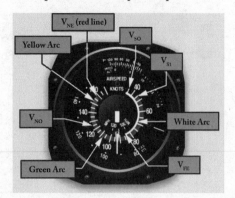

   A. V_{NO}

   B. V_{S1}

   C. V_{NE} (red line)

   D. Yellow arc

   E. White arc

8. According to the Radio Magnetic Indicator (RMI) figure, what directional degree is the aircraft heading?

   A. 262 degrees

   B. 294 degrees

   C. 175 degrees

   D. 086 degrees

   E. 104 degrees

Questions 9–13 are based on the following diagram.

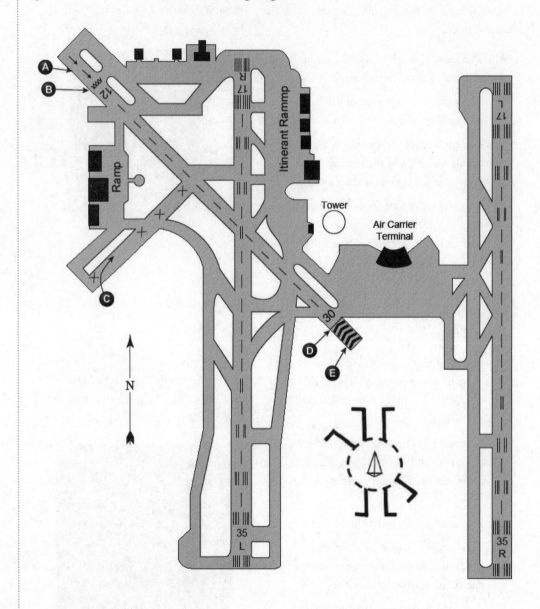

9. What is the indicated traffic pattern for Runway 12, 30, and 35L?

   A. Left-hand pattern for 12, right-hand pattern for 30, and right-hand pattern for 35L

   B. Left-handed pattern for 12, 30, and 35L

   C. Right-hand pattern for 12, left-hand pattern for 30, and left-hand pattern for 35L

   D. Right-hand pattern for 12, left-hand pattern for 30, and right-hand pattern for 35L

   E. Left-handed pattern for 12, 30, and 35L

10. Based on the tetrahedron, what is the most likely active runway?

    A. 35C

    B. 17R

    C. 12

    D. 35R

    E. 17L

11. Which runways are likely NOT precision instrument runways?

    A. 35R and 17L

    B. 17R and 35L

    C. 35L, 35R, 17L, and 17R

    D. 12 and 30

    E. 12, 35L, 17R

12. What does the area labeled as A and B indicate?

    A. Area is not suitable for landing or taxiing.

    B. Displaced threshold is reducing the available landing distance for runway 17.

    C. Displaced threshold is indicating that landing aircraft from runway 30 must not cross.

    D. Static takeoffs are permitted, but rolling takeoffs are not permitted.

    E. Runway 12 is marked for precision approaches.

13. What does area C indicate?

    A. Taxiway for midfield takeoffs on runway 12 and 30 departures

    B. Helicopter landing area

    C. Area closed to all aircraft

    D. Available to taxi but not land

    E. Available to land but not taxi

14. What does a flashing red light from the control tower indicate?

    A. Do not land, or, if on the ground, taxi clear of the active runway.

    B. Give way to other landing aircraft, or, if on the ground, stop your aircraft.

    C. Taxi back to your parking area.

    D. Exercise extreme caution.

    E. You are cleared to land, or, if on the ground, you are cleared to take off.

practice test—AFOQT (Form T)

15. What class of U.S. airspace extends up to and includes flight level 600?

    A. Class A

    B. Class B

    C. Class C

    D. Class D

    E. Class E

16. What is an airspace consisting of defined vertical and lateral limits for the purpose of separating military training activities from nonparticipating IFR traffic?

    A. Prohibited Area

    B. Restricted Area

    C. National Security Areas

    D. Military Operating Area

    E. Security Area

17. What is needed for in-flight icing?

    A. High pressure

    B. Close dew point to temperature differences

    C. Cold fronts

    D. Visible moisture and freezing temperatures

    E. Altitude

18. What is a primary indicator of potential severe windshear (microburst) conditions also associated with virga (evaporating precipitation streaks)?

    A. Cirrostratus clouds

    B. Cirrocumulus clouds

    C. Altocumulus clouds

    D. Cumulus clouds

    E. Cumulonimbus clouds

19. Inflight drowsiness, numbness, tingling in extremities, impaired judgment, and dizziness are symptoms most associated with what aviation physiological condition?

    A. Spatial disorientation

    B. Hypoxia

    C. Motion sickness

    D. Optical illusion

    E. Empty-Field Myopia

20. What does NOT facilitate pilots to timely and accurately assess and manage risk?

    A. Situational awareness

    B. Task management

    C. Risk management

    D. Resource management (on-board and external to the aircraft)

    E. External pressures

STOP! DO NOT GO ON UNTIL TIME IS UP.

AFOQT ANSWER KEYS AND EXPLANATIONS

Part 1: Verbal Analogies

1. D	**6.** A	**11.** D	**16.** C	**21.** A
2. B	**7.** B	**12.** E	**17.** E	**22.** A
3. C	**8.** C	**13.** A	**18.** D	**23.** A
4. D	**9.** C	**14.** E	**19.** C	**24.** B
5. A	**10.** A	**15.** B	**20.** B	**25.** B

1. **The correct answer is D.** A *chapter* is a numbered division of a *book*; a *story* is a numbered floor of a *building*.

2. **The correct answer is B.** A *musician* performs or works on a *stage*; a *physician* heals or works in a *hospital*.

3. **The correct answer is C.** A *carrot* is a type of *vegetable*; *pepper* is a type of *spice*.

4. **The correct answer is D.** *Alpha* is the first Greek alphabet letter or the *beginning* of the Greek alphabet; *Omega* is the last Greek alphabet letter or the *end* of the Greek alphabet.

5. **The correct answer is A.** *Concave* is hollow and curved like a *cavity*; *convex* is bulging and curved like a *mound*.

6. **The correct answer is A.** A *micrometer* is a tool used by a *machinist*; a *trowel* is a tool used by a *mason*.

7. **The correct answer is B.** A *gown* is a type of *garment*; *gasoline* is a type of *fuel*.

8. **The correct answer is C.** A *conductor* leads an *orchestra* but does not play an instrument as part of the group; a *coach* leads a *team* but does not play in the game.

9. **The correct answer is C.** *Hyper-* is a prefix meaning *over*; *hypo-* is a prefix meaning *under*.

10. **The correct answer is A.** *Hypothesis* and *premise* have the same or similar meanings; *explore* and *study* are synonyms.

11. **The correct answer is D.** A *Dachshund* is a breed of *dog*; a *Bengal* is a type of *tiger*.

12. **The correct answer is E.** A *kilometer* is equal to 1,000 *meters*; a *millennium* is equal to 1,000 *years*.

13. **The correct answer is A.** *Trickle* means to flow or fall gently; *gush* means to flow more forcefully than a trickle. *Tepid* means moderately warm; *hot* is a much higher temperature than moderately warm.

14. **The correct answer is E.** An *altimeter* measures *pressure* to provide an indication of altitude in an aircraft. A *spectrometer* measures the *frequency* of various wave forms.

15. **The correct answer is B.** A *node* is a point of component parts in a *network*; a *star* is a connecting point in a *constellation* much like a point on a graph.

16. **The correct answer is C.** A *vector* is a mathematical construct that is used to represent speed and direction, or *velocity*. A *decibel* is a logarithmic unit used to express the intensity of sound.

17. **The correct answer is E.** A *piston* is a component of an *engine*; a *chip* is a component of a *computer*.

18. **The correct answer is D.** A *dozen* contains 12 *units*; a *year* consists of 12 *months*.

19. **The correct answer is C.** A *lamb* is a young *sheep*; a *colt* is a young *horse*

20. **The correct answer is B.** *Pathology* is the study of the progression of *disease*; *geophysics* is the study of the changes in the *Earth* and environment.

21. **The correct answer is A.** *Ignore* and *disregard* have the same or similar meaning; *agree* and *consent* are synonyms.

22. **The correct answer is A.** *Corona* and *nimbus* are words that can both be used to refer to halos or rings of light; *cask* and *barrel* are synonyms.

23. **The correct answer is A.** *Frequently* and *seldom* have opposite meanings; *always* and *never* are antonyms.

24. **The correct answer is B.** A *bus* is a type of *vehicle*; *baseball* is a type of *game*.

25. **The correct answer is B.** *Jubilant* and *apathetic* have opposite meanings; *delighted* and *indifferent* are antonyms.

Part 2: Arithmetic Reasoning

1. D	6. C	11. D	16. B	21. B
2. E	7. D	12. E	17. B	22. C
3. A	8. A	13. C	18. A	23. B
4. E	9. B	14. A	19. E	24. B
5. A	10. B	15. C	20. D	25. D

1. **The correct answer is D.** 4 kilometers = 4,000 meters; $\dfrac{4,000}{15 \text{ laps}} = 200$ meters per lap.

2. **The correct answer is E.** The floor area is 40,000 square feet (200 feet × 200 feet). The floor's maximum safe load is 4,000 tons, or 8,000,000 pounds (4,000 tons × 2,000 pounds). So $\dfrac{8,000,000 \text{ pounds}}{40,000 \text{ square feet}} = 200$ pounds per square feet.

3. **The correct answer is A.** We know the crate weighs 12 pounds and that 12 pounds equals 11 pounds, 16 ounces. The weight of the tool is 9 pounds, 9 ounces. So 11 pounds, 16 ounces minus 9 pounds, 9 ounces equals 2 pounds, 7 ounces.

4. **The correct answer is E.** One million nickels per month equals 12 million nickels each year, and 12,000,000 × 0.05 = $600,000.

5. **The correct answer is A.** The sample size is 50. Four defects were found in the sample. The number of defective articles divided by the sample size $\left(\dfrac{4}{50}\right)$ tells us how much of the sample was defective (0.08, or 8 percent). If 8 percent of the sample was defective, it is probable that the percentage of defective articles in the complete original shipment is also 8 percent.

6. **The correct answer is C.** There are 200 cigarettes in a carton (20 cigarettes × 10 packs), a full carton of 200 cigarettes contains 2,400 mg of tar (12 mg × 200 cigarettes). 2,400 mg equals 2.4 grams.

7. **The correct answer is D.** To stack 36 tons of the item, it takes 108 man-hours (36 × 3). It takes 18 persons to get that much work done in 6 hours $\left(\frac{108}{6} = 18\right)$.

8. **The correct answer is A.** Let x equal the number of envelopes addressed in 1 hour by the slower worker and let $2x$ equal the number of envelopes addressed in 1 hour by the faster worker. Together, they address $3x$ envelopes in an hour.

$$3x \cdot 5 = 750$$
$$15x = 750$$
$$x = 50$$

The slower worker addresses 50 envelopes each hour.

9. **The correct answer is B.** We can assume the room is rectangular and has two long walls and two short walls. To answer this question, we must find the total area of the walls, and then subtract the area taken by the windows and door.

First, let's find the area of one of the long walls: 25 feet × 12 feet = 300 square feet Since there are two long walls, the total area of the long walls is 300 × 2 = 600 square feet.

Next, let's find the area of the shorter walls: 15 feet × 12 feet = 180 square feet. There are two short walls, so the total area of both short walls is 2 × 180, which is 360 square feet. The total wall space, including the windows and door, is 600 square feet + 360 square feet, which equals 960 square feet.

The windows take up 35 square feet each (7 feet × 5 feet), and the door takes up 24 square feet (6 feet × 4 feet). So, the total area that does not need to be painted is: 35 + 35 + 24 = 94 square feet.

The total area of wall space that does need to be painted is 960 − 94, or 866 square feet.

10. **The correct answer is B.** Each stick of margarine is $\frac{1}{4}$ pound. Each stick consists of eight sections or tablespoons. Four sections or tablespoons are $\frac{1}{2}$ of $\frac{1}{4}$ pound, or $\frac{1}{8}$ pound.

11. **The correct answer is D.** $100 × 0.10 = $10.00, and $100 − $10 = $90, the price after the initial 10 percent discount. Then: $90 × 0.15 = $13.50, and $90.00 − $13.50 = $76.50, the price after the additional 15 percent discount.

12. **The correct answer is E.** $1,100,500 × 0.07 = $77,035, and $1,100,500 + $77,035 = $1,177,535, this year's budget. For next year: $1,177,535 · 0.08 = $94,203, and $1,177,535 + $94,203 = $1,271,738, which is closest to $1,271,700 (choice E).

13. **The correct answer is C.** Let x equal the width of rectangle, making the length equal to $4x$. The area of the rectangle is equal to its length times its width, so $324 = x(4x)$. Solve the equation for x to find the width, and then use that measurement to find the length.

$$x(4x) = 324$$
$$4x^2 = 324$$
$$x^2 = 9$$

Since the width is 9 feet, and the length is 4 times the width, the length is 4 × 9, or 36 feet. The dimensions of the rectangle are 9 feet by 36 feet.

14. **The correct answer is A.** The scaled drawing shows $\frac{1}{2}$ inch for every 3 feet of actual floor dimension. Therefore: $\frac{75 \text{ feet}}{3 \text{ feet}} = 25$ feet, and 25 multiplied by $\frac{1}{2}$ equals 12.5 inches; $\frac{132 \text{ feet}}{3 \text{ feet}} = 44$ feet, and 44 multiplied by $\frac{1}{2}$ equals 22 inches.

15. **The correct answer is C.** $\frac{1}{2} \times \frac{1}{2} \times 1$ foot = $\frac{1}{4}$ cubic ft.; $\frac{1}{4}$ of 62.4 = 15.6 pounds.

16. **The correct answer is B.** If 80 percent are either red or green, 20 percent are yellow. The chance of blindly picking a yellow marble is 1 out of 5 (20 percent).

17. **The correct answer is B.** First, find the percentage of recruits 22 years old and younger: 25% +35% =60%. If 60 percent of the recruits were 22 years old and younger, then 40 percent were over 22 years old. $560 \cdot 0.40 = 224$.

18. **The correct answer is A.** Together, one passenger airplane and one freight airplane carry 8 tons (2 + 6 = 8). To carry 160 tons $\left(\frac{160}{8}\right)$, 20 pairs of airplanes are needed. The 20 passenger airplanes carry 2 tons each, so 40 tons of cargo are being shipped on the passenger airplanes.

19. **The correct answer is E.** The square root of 25 = 5. Each side of the square =5". 5" × 2 = 10". 10" × 10" = 100 square inches.

20. **The correct answer is D.** If x equals the capacity of the tank,

$$\frac{1}{8}x + 550 = \frac{1}{2}x$$
$$550 = x - \frac{x}{8}$$
$$550 = 3x = \frac{8}{3}$$
$$550 \cdot \frac{8}{3} = x$$
$$1,467 = x$$

21. **The correct answer is B.** Since 1,200 seconds equal 20 minutes $\left(\frac{1,200 \text{ seconds}}{60 \text{ seconds}}\right)$, and 20 minutes $= \frac{1}{3}$ hour, $\frac{1}{3}$ of 630 miles equals 210 miles.

22. **The correct answer is C.** The interval between 7:00 a.m. and 1:00 p.m. is 6 hours, or $\frac{1}{4}$ of a day, and $\frac{1}{4}$ of 20 minutes equals 5 minutes. Subtracting 5 minutes from a watch reading of 1:00 p.m. equals 12:55 p.m.

23. **The correct answer is B.** The distance is $\frac{1}{40}$ of a mile $\left(\frac{132 \text{ feet}}{5,280 \text{ feet}}\right)$, and 9 seconds equals $\frac{1}{400}$ of an hour $\left(\frac{9}{3,600}\right)$. Traveling $\frac{1}{40}$ mile in $\frac{1}{400}$ hour, the runner moves 1 mile in $\frac{1}{10}$ hour, or 10 miles in 1 hour, or 10 miles per hour.

24. **The correct answer is B.** The "arithmetic mean" is also known as the "average." First add the five salaries together: $18,400 + $19,300 + $18,450 + $18,550 + $17,600 = $92,300. Then divide the total by the number of items being averaged: $92,300 ÷ 5 = $18,460.

25. **The correct answer is D.** If the radius of the wheel is one meter, its diameter is 2 meters. The circumference of the wheel is equal to π (pi = 3.14) multiplied by the diameter (2). The circumference is multiplied by the number of rotations to get the distance traveled.

$$\begin{aligned} \text{circumference} &= (\pi \cdot 2) \cdot 35 \\ &= (3.14 \cdot 2) \cdot 35 \\ &= 6.28 \cdot 35 \\ &= 219.8 \end{aligned}$$

Part 3: Word Knowledge

1. C	6. D	11. C	16. E	21. B
2. A	7. D	12. B	17. A	22. D
3. C	8. C	13. A	18. A	23. D
4. B	9. C	14. B	19. A	24. E
5. B	10. C	15. E	20. D	25. E

1. **The correct answer is C.** To be adamant means to be unwilling to change (an opinion, purpose, or decision), so *inflexible* is the best choice.

2. **The correct answer is A.** An *altercation* is a noisy or angry argument or controversy.

3. **The correct answer is C.** To *assent* means to approve or consent to something.

4. **The correct answer is E.** *Attrition* is the act of wearing down.

5. **The correct answer is B.** *Authentic* means "genuine."

6. **The correct answer is D.** *Conducive* means "helpful."

7. **The correct answer is D.** *Counteract* means "to neutralize."

8. **The correct answer is C.** *Deleterious* means "harmful."

9. **The correct answer is D.** *Dilated* means "enlarged."

10. **The correct answer is C.** *Flexible* means "pliable."

11. **The correct answer is C.** A *fortnight* is two weeks.

12. **The correct answer is B.** *Impartial* means "fair."

13. **The correct answer is A.** *Incidental* means "minor."

14. **The correct answer is B.** *Indolent* means "lazy."

15. **The correct answer is E.** *Notorious* means "well-known" (usually in a negative light).

16. **The correct answer is E.** *Rebuff* means "to snub."

17. **The correct answer is A.** *Spurious* means "false or based on false ideas."

18. **The correct answer is A.** *Succinct* means "concise," or expressed without wasted words.

19. **The correct answer is A.** To be sullen is to be angrily silent.

20. **The correct answer is D.** A symptom is a sign or an indication of a condition.

21. **The correct answer is B.** *Tedious* means "dull."

22. **The correct answer is D.** *Terse* means "pointed," or brief in expression (in a way that may appear unfriendly or rude.)

23. **The correct answer is E.** *Trivial* means "negligible," or of little consequence.

24. **The correct answer is B.** *Verify* means "to confirm."

25. **The correct answer is E.** *Vigilant* means "watchful."

Part 4: Math Knowledge

1. D	**6.** A	**11.** C	**16.** E	**21.** E
2. C	**7.** D	**12.** B	**17.** B	**22.** E
3. D	**8.** D	**13.** B	**18.** D	**23.** D
4. B	**9.** C	**14.** B	**19.** E	**24.** E
5. C	**10.** E	**15.** B	**20.** C	**25.** C

1. **The correct answer is D.** A natural number that has no other factors except 1 and itself is a prime number. Nine is divisible by 1, 3, and 9.

2. **The correct answer is C.** We know that circumference = π × diameter; so

$$C = \pi d$$
$$= \frac{22}{7} \cdot 70$$
$$= 220$$

3. **The correct answer is D.**

$$5x + 3(x - 1) = 29$$
$$5x + 3x - 3 = 29$$
$$8x = 32$$
$$x = 4$$

4. **The correct answer is B.**

$$\frac{7x^2}{2} = \frac{x}{1}$$
$$7x^2 = 2x$$
$$7x^2 - 2x = 0$$
$$x(7x - 2) = 0$$
$$x = 0, \frac{2}{7}$$

5. **The correct answer is C.** Squaring an odd integer results in an odd integer. Adding an odd integer to or subtracting an odd integer from an odd integer results in an even integer. Choices A, B, and D remain odd.

6. **The correct answer is A.**

$$\frac{x - 2}{x^2 - 6x + 8} = \frac{x - 2}{(x - 2)(x - 4)}$$
$$= \frac{1}{x - 4}$$

7. **The correct answer is D.** To divide powers of the same base, subtract the exponent of the denominator from the exponent of the numerator. 10^x divided by 10^y equals 10^{x-y}.

8. **The correct answer is D.** The odd integer power of a negative number is negative; the even integer power of a negative number is positive.

9. **The correct answer is C.** $10,000,000 = 10^6$

10. **The correct answer is E.**

$$\left(\frac{2}{5}\right)^2 = \frac{2}{5} \cdot \frac{2}{5} = \frac{4}{25}$$

11. **The correct answer is C.**

$$3^n = 9$$
$$n = 2$$
so
$$4^{n+1} = 4^{2+1}$$
$$= 4^3$$
$$= 64$$

12. **The correct answer is B.**

$$10^{-2} = \frac{1}{10^2} = \frac{1}{100} = 0.01$$

13. **The correct answer is B.**

$$\sqrt{28} - \sqrt{7} = \sqrt{7 \times 4} - \sqrt{7}$$
$$= 2\sqrt{7} - \sqrt{7}$$
$$= \sqrt{7}$$

14. **The correct answer is B.**

$$h^2 = 5^2 + 12^2$$
$$h^2 = 25 + 144$$
$$h^2 = 169$$
$$\sqrt{169} = 13"$$

15. **The correct answer is B.** A pentagon has 5 sides, and the formula to use is: (number of sides − 2) × 180 = sum of angles. So:

$$(\text{number of sides} - 2) \times 180 = 2 \times 180$$
$$= 3 \times 180$$
$$= 540$$

16. **The correct answer is E.**

$$\frac{3x}{5y} = \frac{1}{2}$$
$$6x = 5y$$
$$\frac{6x}{y} = 5$$
$$\frac{x}{y} = \frac{5}{6}$$

17. **The correct answer is B.** 1 inch ≅ 2,000 feet; 1 inch ≅ 2,000 × 12 inches ≅ 24,000 inches. No other choice, converted into common terms, shows a scale of $\frac{1}{24,000}$.

18. **The correct answer is D.** The coordinates form a right triangle with a horizontal leg of 3 and a vertical leg of 4. The distance between the two points is the hypotenuse of a right triangle.

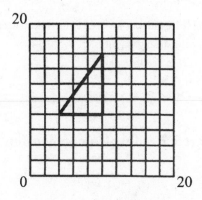

$$H^2 = 3^2 + 4^2$$
$$H^2 = 9 + 16$$
$$H^2 = 25$$
$$H^2 = \sqrt{25}$$
$$= 5$$

19. **The correct answer is E.** The base of the cylinder, (πr^2) times the height, (h) equals the volume of the cylinder. This formula $(\pi r^2 h)$ is not one of the answers listed in the first four choices.

20. **The correct answer is C.** 5 × 3 = 15, which is divisible by both 3 and 5. Perimeters of 9, 12, 18, and 21 are not divisible by 5.

21. **The correct answer is E.**

$$\frac{4!}{3!} = \frac{4 \times 3 \times 2 \times 1}{3 \times 2 \times 1} = 4$$

22. **The correct answer is E.** The cube root of 729 is 9 (because $9^3 = 9 \cdot 9 \cdot 9 = 729$). In turn, 9 is the square of 3 (because $3^2 = 3 \cdot 3 = 9$).

23. The correct answer is D. The logarithm 2.5464 consists of two parts. The 2 is called the characteristic; the 5464 is called the mantissa. A character of 2 indicates three digits to the left of the decimal. For example, the logarithm of 100.00 is 102.00.

24. The correct answer is E. The pattern for the arrangement is shown below:

2, 4, 12, 48, _____

$$2(\times 2) = 4(\times 3) = 12(\times 4) = 48(\times 5) =$$

Multiplying 48 by 5, we find the correct answer to be 240.

25. The correct answer is C. The first and subsequent odd-number items in the series are in regular alphabetical order, skipping one letter each time: A, B, C, D . . . The second and subsequent even-numbered letters in the series are in straight alphabetical: R, S, T . . . Accordingly, the next two letters in the series are U and I.

Part 5: Reading Comprehension

1. C	**6.** D	**11.** E	**16.** A	**21.** E
2. C	**7.** E	**12.** E	**17.** D	**22.** B
3. E	**8.** C	**13.** C	**18.** C	**23.** E
4. D	**9.** A	**14.** A	**19.** D	**24.** A
5. E	**10.** B	**15.** B	**20.** E	**25.** B

1. **The correct answer is C.** The passage begins in identifying DoD budget declines as a byproduct of national economic health, with the following paragraphs identifying SBEs as a significant contributor to that health. A research study (by Dr. Mac McMullen) is mentioned in the final paragraph, with predictive findings of how the financial and nonfinancial national population of SBEs could be improved. The initial DoD budget discussion is tied indirectly with the predictive performance of SBEs.

2. **The correct answer is C.** In the line 68, *performance* refers to the *success* rate of SBEs relative to the enhancement of national prosperity and mitigating defense budget pressures.

3. **The correct answer is E.** Recessions (choice C) are identified as a reason for SBE start-ups, but their failure rate is consistent despite recession events. However, a lack of planning (choice E) is identified as a factor that consistently causes SBEs to become unstable and fail.

4. **The correct answer is D.** The passage discusses the research that indicates the direct relationship between GDP and unemployment levels. When unemployment levels increase, GDP declines. The association between SBE performance and GDP is indirectly associated as having a secondary effect on unemployment rates, so choices A and B are incorrect. The DoD budget declines were attributed to national budgetary fluctuation, not unemployment, so choice C is incorrect. Choice E states the opposite of what is discussed in the passage.

5. **The correct answer is E.** The author would most likely agree that adaptation of project management planning and management techniques can strengthen national prosperity. Research findings indicate that improvements in how SBEs plan and manage can improve national prosperity (defined as GDP), employment, and, indirectly, the DoD budget.

6. **The correct answer is D.** The primary purpose of this passage is to identify methods and models to assess human error in aviation accidents. The recurring theme in the passage relates to human error and the models to assess and correct that error in the aviation environment.

7. **The correct answer is E.** Although a number of models exist to aid in understanding human error, not all of the models are comprehensive in nature or can be used as an investigation framework. The passage states that the Human Factors Analysis and Classification System (HFACS) is the commonly employed framework used by the U.S. military and other organizations in accident investigations.

8. **The correct answer is C.** In this passage, the term *processes* does not refer to manufacturing or production, but to operational procedures across the spectrum of the aviation cycle. Such processes include personnel, training, scheduling, maintenance and operations tasks, and etc.

9. **The correct answer is A.** The author has mentioned that accidents have multiple causes and are not typically solely the result of pilot error. As such, the author would likely disagree with any investigative approach that focuses exclusively on aircrew actions and inactions.

10. **The correct answer is B.** The repeated themes throughout the passage relating to analysis models and human error assessment makes choice B the best answer.

11. **The correct answer is E.** The passage frames the discussion of risk management relative to a poorly executed MTT training project.

12. **The correct answer is E.** Risk is discussed in terms of threats and opportunities, which most closely relate to dangers and prospects (choice E).

13. **The correct answer is C.** Inadequate communication (choice A) is identified as causal to internal MTT issues between squadrons; however, the disparity of training objectives between the MTT and the base receiving the training is not identified as having been caused by communication failures. The primary topic of the passage is risk management and the effect of communicating project threats and opportunities, making choice C the best answer.

answers practice test

14. **The correct answer is A.** Risk management, as a process and tool, is used for proactive organizational decision making of future events. Communication is identified as important to relay and integrate risk management planning across aspects of an organization. Communication is also identified in formulating risk management in the use of unambiguous language in accounting for both project threats and opportunities.

15. **The correct answer is B.** The passage points to a greater chance of project success when an organizational leader uses risk management effectively. The case study involving MTT served as an example of the negative outcomes of a project when risk management is not implemented.

16. **The correct answer is A.** The predominate theme of the passage relates to the evolving threats to the aviation industry, particularly in light of the dramatic transformation of the Air Traffic Control network and its reliance on computer networks and distributed sensors.

17. **The correct answer is D.** The information presented in the passage contradicts the notion that the new Air Traffic Control system is immune to future terror or cyberattacks. Although the space-based nature of sensors, particularly GPS, makes the satellite network more difficult to tamper or physically destroy, the signals broadcast throughout the Earth's atmosphere are still vulnerable to jamming and signal spoofing.

18. **The correct answer is C.** As it appears in the first sentence in paragraph three, the term "networks" refers primarily to "communication" systems because of references to communications and data required for aviation operations. Sentence two of that paragraph also eludes to communications in the form of data for reservations and other flight data required to conduct airline operations.

19. **The correct answer is D.** The author repeatedly notes the evolving nature of threats to the aviation industry over time and the continued focus of terror networks on aviation targets. The author also highlights the growing use of cyberattacks by a variety of perpetrators making the aviation industry a vulnerable economic and terrorism target regardless of the new technology employed.

20. **The correct answer is E.** The recurring focus of threats and discussion of NextGen implementation make choice E the best answer.

21. **The correct answer is E.** A primary theme in the passage is the identification of adult learning principles used to improve training in the mitigation of fratricide events.

22. **The correct answer is B.** Word knowledge can help you understand the context of what happens to a learning curve over time. "Nonlinear" implies that a learning curve changes over time and is not actually a consistent predictive slope typically used in linear analysis.

23. **The correct answer is E.** Institutional bias (choice E) is referred to as a hindrance to learning within the passage.

24. **The correct answer is A.** Operant conditioning is described as a method for enhancing long-term knowledge retention that is incorporated in repeated yet more advanced and complex training scenario phases.

25. **The correct answer is B.** Choice B notes a predominant theme in the passage—that land forces successfully integrated airpower capabilities when not forced upon them, in accordance with adult learning principles.

Part 6: Situational Judgment Test

1. B	**11.** A	**21.** B	**31.** D	**41.** D
2. A	**12.** E	**22.** A	**32.** B	**42.** A
3. B	**13.** C	**23.** B	**33.** E	**43.** D
4. D	**14.** B	**24.** D	**34.** B	**44.** A
5. E	**15.** A	**25.** E	**35.** D	**45.** C
6. B	**16.** C	**26.** D	**36.** A	**46.** B
7. A	**17.** D	**27.** E	**37.** E	**47.** E
8. B	**18.** E	**28.** C	**38.** A	**48.** A
9. B	**19.** B	**29.** E	**39.** D	**49.** E
10. A	**20.** A	**30.** C	**40.** A	**50.** D

1. **The correct answer is B.** The exercise scenario does not meet the monthly training requirement, so the aircrew that did not attend the training session during the month will be delinquent in the requirement for that month. The crews would have to attend a training session prior to the end of the month to avoid delinquency.

2. **The correct answer is A.** The exercise scenario does not meet the monthly training requirement, so fulfilling the senior officer's request would be a serious integrity breach as well as a violation of the training instructions.

3. **The correct answer is B.** The information sent to your personal e-mail account was classified, constituting a security breach that first and foremost must be reported to the security and commanding officers. Doing so represents considerations of both integrity and professionalism.

4. **The correct answer is D.** Using and further distributing the classified evaluation information is a serious breach of security, integrity, and professionalism.

5. **The correct answer is E.** You identified an error that you made, and the professional response is to make the necessary reports to the security and commanding officers and message recipients to prevent further compromise of the data.

6. **The correct answer is B.** Attempting to cover up an identified error shows a complete lack of professionalism and integrity.

7. **The correct answer is A.** Meeting with the junior officer and providing feedback and strategies for success is the mark of a positive leader and mentor. Communication of expectations is also key in helping others be successful and achieve organizational and professional goals.

8. **The correct answer is B.** Taking no interest in your personnel is certainly not good leadership nor does it display resource management in helping quality professionals reach their potential, not only for themselves but also to meet the goals of the organization as well.

9. **The correct answer is B.** Because this incident took place on duty and not off base, the first step is to report the incident to the victim's commanding officer. Standing with your colleague and encouraging her displays professionalism, integrity, leadership, and mentoring.

10. **The correct answer is A.** Encouraging your colleague to remain quiet about the incident only serves to harm her and put others at risk. A confident leader with the highest standards of integrity would not want to foster an environment with a potentially harmful individual in the ranks, as this individual certainly does not display leadership, professionalism, or integrity if the accusations are substantiated.

11. **The correct answer is A.** It is possible that the junior officer you met has service experience of which you are not readily aware. The professional course of action is to seek the facts prior to jumping to conclusions.

12. **The correct answer is E.** The least professional action would be to attempt to discredit this new officer with her peers, subordinates, and senior officers without gathering the facts.

13. **The correct answer is C.** It is possible the commander on duty had a reason for having the door pins retracted prior to your arrival. The most professional course of action is to ask before making assumptions in questioning the professionalism and integrity of other officers, regardless of rank. Communication is the key.

14. **The correct answer is B.** Refusal to perform your duty based on the assumption that others have not performed theirs is not a display of professionalism. This choice also indicates a lack of communication in attempting to ascertain the status of the control center prior to reaching a conclusion.

15. **The correct answer is A.** The only course of action is to provide higher headquarters with the available test data without alteration. Report the senior officer's request to your supervisor in an effort to avoid similar situations in future tests. However, the senior officer's request is a violation of integrity, professionalism, and leadership.

16. **The correct answer is C.** Altering the test data is an integrity violation, and it damages the overall value of the test results. Further, the inaccurate data damages the overall test results and is a waste of organizational resources.

17. **The correct answer is D.** Offering to provide input communicates to your supervisor your willingness to help as well as your understanding of the performance evaluation process. It affords that individual an opportunity to revise the request if perhaps he or she did not understand the proper procedure.

18. **The correct answer is E.** Falsification of documentation, regardless of the fear of repercussion, is a serious breach of integrity, professionalism, and leadership.

19. **The correct answer is B.** As a mentor, pull the officer aside and privately have him correct the uniform discrepancy so he will avoid potential embarrassment and punishment.

20. **The correct answer is A.** Taking no action shows a lack of leadership in the well-being of your personnel, as well as the organization, in enforcing the proper wear of the uniform and military decorations.

21. **The correct answer is B.** Seeking the mentorship and guidance of the commander is a wise choice. However, you must still use your best judgment and develop an accurate evaluation that you can sign with integrity.

22. **The correct answer is A.** Falsification of documentation, regardless of the fear of repercussion, is a serious breach of integrity, professionalism, and leadership.

23. **The correct answer is B.** This is both a resource management concern and one that affects the professionalism of the officer in not wanting to serve with others of the opposite gender. From the level of a junior to mid-level officer, this is not a request that you are able to grant on your own. It is critical to seek guidance from the commanding officer regarding an appropriate course of action.

24. **The correct answer is D.** From the level of a junior to mid-level officer, this is not a request that you are able to grant or deny on your own. Because this is both a resource management concern and one that affects the professionalism of the officer in not wanting to serve with others of the opposite gender, the commanding officer must be informed.

25. **The correct answer is E.** Meeting with the officer in question allows for mentoring to partner his support in improving morale and flight currency problems. The core competency tenant of resource management is also addressed by using a qualified crew to more rapidly aid in advancing the currencies of the other flight crews. Integrity is enforced in having the problem crew take ownership for hoarding flight hours by working directly with the rest of their flight team.

26. **The correct answer is D.** None of the remaining choices are acceptable; however, losing self-integrity in repeating the bad behavior is the worst of the worst.

27. **The correct answer is E.** As a mission critical item, correcting the problem on the stop is a priority in communicating why the procedure is not correct. The scope of the problem requires professional communication with the senior officer; however, indirectly including your boss in the communication informs him that there was a problem and that it is being addressed. Passing the responsibility to someone else does not exhibit skill in problem resolution, which is expected of an officer.

28. **The correct answer is C.** Of the bad options, ignoring the situation would be the least effective action. Apathy is the opposite of proactive leadership.

29. **The correct answer is E.** Leadership is taking responsibility for your officers and enlisted, and that means also taking care of their careers in addition to their training. Resource management is making the time to accept the responsibility of your leadership position. Innovation is addressed in communicating with fellow officers who likely are task-saturated as well yet have already figured out how to write and make time to do performance reports.

30. **The correct answer is C.** The least effective action, and one that goes against a core competency, would be to neglect leadership responsibilities by deprioritizing the report and throwing something together at some point in time.

31. **The correct answer is D.** The part of the scenario where the commander adamantly orders everyone to not cooperate with the investigating team implies that meeting to discuss your concerns with the commander will likely not go well for you. However, integrity and professionalism demand that you ensure the investigation is not obstructed.

32. **The correct answer is B.** Passively not addressing the problem with the investigating team goes against the integrity and professionalism competencies. Even worse would be to proactively comply with the directive. (In this real-life scenario, the obstructionist commander was fired and replaced within 24 hours by the wing commander.)

33. **The correct answer is E.** Partnering with your fellow flight commanders is the professional thing to do. Using what works for you to help them is an innovative way to improve the function of all the flights while helping out your teammates.

34. **The correct answer is B.** All the remaining options are bad courses of action; however, identifying yourself as not being a team player and problem solver violates more of the core competencies.

35. **The correct answer is D.** Finding someone who can take your flight and providing that solution to the operations officer is an example of a proactive problem resolution.

36. **The correct answer is A.** While all the bad choices indicate a lack of integrity, setting yourself up for a sinus block also demonstrates bad resource management. In viewing yourself and your organization as a resource, injuring yourself removes you from the flight schedule for a long duration and creates a chronic scheduling issue instead of an immediate resolvable challenge. Yes, sinus blocks are very painful; however, you would be well enough to take over scheduling duties full time so that the former scheduler could take all your future flights.

37. **The correct answer is E.** Of the options, investing yourself in the organization's performance captures many of the core competencies used to evaluate the situational awareness test. Especially if you are the FNG (*Flying* New Guy), the only way to increase your professional development is by spending time learning what others in the squadron are doing. Helping them when you can also contributes to resource management, in better using your time while helping the organization's performance.

38. **The correct answer is A.** Of the bad options, the choice to leave work early violates more core competencies. Expect to not get promoted or be included as a teammate in your squadron. Good flight positions are reserved for those who seek them and those who demonstrate through their actions that they are a team player.

39. **The correct answer is D.** Leadership, communication, and mentoring are demonstrated through the innovative approach of trying to help the new officer be a better aviator.

40. **The correct answer is A.** Of the bad choices, making assumptions as facts demonstrates poor communication, bad professionalism, and failed mentoring. The other bad choices violate fewer core competencies.

41. **The correct answer is D.** This option maximizes many of the core competencies, including innovation, good demonstrations of resource management, professionalism, and integrity. Even seemingly undesirable positions are great opportunities to show what you can do in solving and managing problems.

42. **The correct answer is A.** Blowing off the assigned duty violates more competencies than other bad choices. Don't expect to be assigned any positions of value in the squadron if you cannot be trusted with this one. SnackO is often an interview position to see how you hold up within this very visual collateral duty. Those who blow it off are often not trusted with most anything else. As a result, their performance reports reflect a lack of flights and missions reserved for the more trusted officers.

43 **The correct answer is D.** This option maximizes many of the core competencies including innovation, good demonstrations of resource management, professionalism, and integrity.

44. **The correct answer is A.** Immediately going up the chain of command may reflect badly on you, showing that you are not a problem solver and demonstrating a lack of professionalism. If it is not a life-threatening event or a safety issue, it is not an emergency and can be addressed in-house (within your team). Professionally, the main focus is on the mission; everything else can be debriefed after as lessons learned.

45. **The correct answer is C.** Since you are in charge of range development, developing and executing a plan that adheres to both Air Force and Army regulations is the most effective option of those offered. It also captures a majority of core competencies used in evaluating the *most* correct response.

46. **The correct answer is B.** Among the bad options, the choice to set up the live weapon range and ignore regulations demonstrates both a lack of integrity and professionalism. Regulations and instructions are designed to optimize performance while preventing damage to equipment, injuries, and death.

47. **The correct answer is E.** As a potential legal matter, the junior officer should be mentored to attain information as to all his options from the military lawyers before meeting with anyone.

48. **The correct answer is A.** Making a formal accusation against a senior officer based on second-hand assumptions would be incredibly unprofessional.

49. **The correct answer is E.** Integrity and professionalism are demonstrated in relaying an accurate assessment. Positioning your aircraft toward the fight while communicating is an innovative use of time management.

50. **The correct answer is D.** Of the bad options, actively relaying inaccurate information to get the mission is a major integrity AND professional problem. Putting the troops in need at risk for personal gain is **never** an acceptable option.

Part 7: Self-Description Inventory

Results of the personality test within the AFOQT are not provided to you; however, they *may* be used as an additional consideration in your selection as an officer candidate, your aviation career field selection, and potentially for future unknown applications. Results and interpretation from the free Penn State University online test (http://www.personal.psu.edu/~j5j/IPIP/), similar to the NEO PI-R test used by the United States Air Force (USAF), are provided directly to you by the associated Penn State department. Review your answers and results relative to information on the NEO PI-R within this guide.

Part 8: Physical Science

1. A	5. A	9. D	13. A	17. A
2. D	6. E	10. A	14. E	18. A
3. C	7. C	11. D	15. E	19. D
4. B	8. B	12. E	16. B	20. B

1. **The correct answer is A.** The magnetic fields in the sun's active regions produce the conditions in which energized particles in the form of solar flares are ejected toward the earth.

2. **The correct answer is D.** The components of the atom that are positively charged are protons.

3. **The correct answer is C.** The differing composition, temperature, and pressure of the earth's outer molten core create convection currents, while the rotation of the planet, because of the Coriolis force, forms whirlpools in the matter. The flowing liquid iron generates the current, producing a magnetic field.

4. **The correct answer is B.** A scientific theory is founded on the analysis of substantial data from repeatable and validated research.

5. **The correct answer is A.** Statistical significance implies reliability of a result. In the case of most statistical tests, the statistical significance indicates that the result occurred randomly.

6. **The correct answer is E.** The troposphere is the layer closest to the surface of the earth. The tropopause (choice C) is between the troposphere and the next highest layer, the stratosphere (choice A). The mesosphere, (choice D) and thermosphere (choice B) are the next two layers, respectively, above the stratosphere.

7. **The correct answer is C.** It takes approximately 7 to 8 minutes for light to travel to the earth from the sun. The time it takes for any matter from a solar flare to reach the earth is far more variable, allowing for time to shelter astronauts in orbit and take other precautions.

8. **The correct answer is B.** Although the ozone protects the surface of the earth from much of the harmful UV radiation, the Earth's magnetosphere provides protection from other radiation hitting the atmosphere. This protection is provided because the solar plasma and ions in solar wind interact with the earth's magnetic fields and are swept around the magnetosphere.

9. **The correct answer is D.** Newton's Third Law of Motion states that every force has an equal and opposite reactive force.

10. **The correct answer is A.** Alpha radiation can be stopped by paper, but beta radiation requires a more substantial barrier. The only selections on the given list sufficient to shield gamma radiation are steel and lead.

11. **The correct answer is D.** According to the National Oceanic and Atmospheric Administration's (NOAA) National Centers for Environment Information, the only gas listed that is not considered a Greenhouse gas is carbon monoxide.

12. **The correct answer is E.** Ice has been detected on three of Jupiter's moons: IO, Europa, and Ganymede.

13. **The correct answer is A.** Nitrogen is the most common gas in the atmosphere at approximately 78 percent. Oxygen makes up 21 percent, and all others compose 1 percent.

14. **The correct answer is E.** A histogram cannot provide data regarding percentiles.

15. **The correct answer is E.** Roll is not an outside force acting on an aircraft in flight. Roll describes the potential motion of the aircraft in flight.

16. **The correct answer is B.** A composite is a material composed of two or more physically and chemically different materials.

17. **The correct answer is A.** A lunar eclipse occurs when the moon passes behind the earth such that the sun's light is blocked by the earth.

18. **The correct answer is A.** Soil erosion leads to soil not retaining nutrients or other materials; therefore, the soil would also not retain pesticides.

19. **The correct answer is D.** At higher altitudes, air pressure is reduced because of greater dispersion of molecules. Refer to the definition of density.

20. **The correct answer is B.** Kinetic energy is energy that is relative to the state of other objects in the immediate proximity.

answers practice test

Part 9: Table Reading

1. C	9. B	17. E	25. A	33. A	
2. B	10. A	18. C	26. A	34. E	
3. E	11. C	19. A	27. D	35. D	
4. C	12. D	20. D	28. B	36. D	
5. A	13. B	21. B	29. E	37. C	
6. B	14. E	22. D	30. C	38. A	
7. E	15. A	23. E	31. E	39. E	
8. D	16. B	24. D	32. B	40. B	

1. The correct answer is C. 32

2. The correct answer is B. 29

3. The correct answer is E. 27

4. The correct answer is C. 35

5. The correct answer is A. 26

6. The correct answer is B. 148

7. The correct answer is E. 131

8. The correct answer is D. 184

9. The correct answer is B. 97

10. The correct answer is A. 224

11. The correct answer is C. 0.03

12. The correct answer is D. 0.04

13. The correct answer is B. 0.07

14. The correct answer is E. 0.05

15. The correct answer is A. 0.04

16. The correct answer is B. 8:21

17. The correct answer is E. 8:16

18. The correct answer is C. 8:53

19. The correct answer is A. 8:27

20. The correct answer is D. 8:30

21. The correct answer is B. 930

22. The correct answer is D. 880

23. The correct answer is E. 445

24. The correct answer is D. 2,810

25. The correct answer is A. 2,050

26. The correct answer is A. 3,200

27. The correct answer is D. 760

28. The correct answer is B. 550

29. The correct answer is E. 2,450

30. The correct answer is C. 1,600

31. The correct answer is E. 36

32. The correct answer is B. 35

33. The correct answer is A. 31

34. The correct answer is E. 48

35. The correct answer is D. 34

36. The correct answer is D. 31

37. The correct answer is C. 24

38. The correct answer is A. 41

39. The correct answer is E. 26

40. The correct answer is B. 23

Part 10: Instrument Comprehension

1. C	6. A	11. C	16. A	21. C
2. B	7. A	12. C	17. B	22. C
3. C	8. C	13. C	18. A	23. D
4. A	9. D	14. A	19. C	24. C
5. B	10. C	15. B	20. D	25. A

1. **The correct answer is C.** Nose on the horizon, no bank, heading south.

2. **The correct answer is B.** Nose on the horizon, 15 degrees left bank, heading west.

3. **The correct answer is C.** Nose below the horizon, 15 degrees left bank, heading northeast.

4. **The correct answer is A.** Nose below the horizon, 15 degrees right bank, heading southeast.

5. **The correct answer is B.** Nose above the horizon, no bank, heading south.

6. **The correct answer is A.** Nose above the horizon, 5 degrees right bank, heading southwest.

7. **The correct answer is A.** Nose slightly below the horizon, 5 degrees left bank, heading East.

8. **The correct answer is C.** Nose on the horizon, 45 degrees right bank, heading east.

9. **The correct answer is D.** Nose below the horizon, 10 degrees right bank, heading northwest.

10. **The correct answer is C.** Nose on the horizon, inverted, heading north.

11. **The correct answer is C.** Nose in an extreme dive, no bank, originating from the north.

12. **The correct answer is C.** Nose in an extreme climb, no bank, originating from the east.

13. **The correct answer is C.** Nose on the horizon, 90 degrees right bank, headed east.

14. **The correct answer is A.** Nose slightly above the horizon, 90 degrees right bank, heading west.

15. **The correct answer is B.** Nose above the horizon, 15 degrees left bank, heading northeast.

16. **The correct answer is A.** Nose in an extreme dive, 90 degrees right bank, heading from the north east to the southwest.

17. **The correct answer is B.** Nose slightly above the horizon, inverted with left wing below horizon, heading east northeast.

18. **The correct answer is A.** Nose on the horizon, inverted, heading northwest.

19. **The correct answer is C.** Nose below the horizon, 90 degrees left bank, heading northeast.

20. **The correct answer is D.** Nose well below the horizon, slightly inverted with greater than 90 degrees left bank, heading north.

21. **The correct answer is C.** Nose above the horizon, slightly inverted with greater than 90 degrees right bank, heading southwest.

22. **The correct answer is C.** Nose on the horizon, 15 degrees left bank, heading southwest.

23. **The correct answer is D.** Nose slightly above the horizon, 10 degrees left bank, heading southeast.

24. **The correct answer is C.** Nose below the horizon, 15 degrees right bank, heading west southwest.

25. **The correct answer is A.** Nose slightly above the horizon, 10 degrees left bank, heading north northeast.

Part 11: Block Counting

1. B	7. B	13. C	19. C	25. D
2. C	8. C	14. C	20. D	26. C
3. C	9. C	15. D	21. B	27. D
4. C	10. B	16. B	22. B	28. B
5. A	11. A	17. D	23. D	29. A
6. C	12. E	18. E	24. C	30. B

1. **The correct answer is B.** 4 total: 2 right, 1 left, 1 above.

2. **The correct answer is C.** 5 total: 1 below, 4 above.

3. **The correct answer is C.** 4 total: 1 right, 1 left, 3 below.

4. **The correct answer is C.** 5 total: 4 above, 1 below.

5. **The correct answer is A.** 2 total: 1 above, 1 left.

6. **The correct answer is C.** 5 total: 1 below, 1 right, 1 left, 2 above.

7. **The correct answer is B.** 2 total: 1 right, 1 below.

8. **The correct answer is C.** 5 total: 2 above, 2 left, 1 below.

9. **The correct answer is C.** 4 total: 1 right, 1 above, 2 below.

10. **The correct answer is B.** 4 total: 2 above, 1 right, 1 below.

11. **The correct answer is A.** 2 total: 1 below, 1 left.

12. **The correct answer is E.** 6 total: 3 above, 1 left, 2 below.

13. **The correct answer is C.** 5 total: 2 above, 2 below, 1 right.

14. **The correct answer is C.** 5 total: 2 below, 1 above, 1 right, 1 left.

15. **The correct answer is D.** 5 total: 2 below, 1 left, 2 above.

16. **The correct answer is B.** 4 total: 2 above, 2 below.

17. **The correct answer is D.** 4 total: 1 above, 1 right, 2 below.

18. **The correct answer is E.** 5 total: 2 above, 3 below.

19. **The correct answer is C.** 3 total: 1 right, 2 left.

20. **The correct answer is D.** 4 total: 1 right, 1 left, 1 above, 1 behind.

21. **The correct answer is B.** 3 total: 1 above, 1 below, 1 in front.

22. **The correct answer is B.** 3 total: 1 above, 1 below, 1 in front.

23. **The correct answer is D.** 5 total: 2 above, 1 in front, 1 left, 1 below.

24. **The correct answer is C.** 4 total: 1 behind, 3 below.

25. **The correct answer is D.** 5 total: 1 above, 4 behind.

26. **The correct answer is C.** 3 total: 1 above, 1 behind, 1 below.

27. **The correct answer is D.** 6 total: 1 above, 2 left, 3 below.

28. **The correct answer is B.** 3 total: 1 right, 2 above.

29. **The correct answer is A.** 2 total: 2 above.

30. **The correct answer is B.** 3 total: 1 below, 1 above, 1 left.

Part 12: Aviation Information

1. B	5. C	9. C	13. C	17. D
2. C	6. D	10. D	14. A	18. E
3. E	7. E	11. D	15. A	19. B
4. C	8. C	12. B	16. D	20. E

1. **The correct answer is B.** The rudder, #7, is used to yaw the aircraft about the vertical axis.

2. **The correct answer is C.** The entire tail end of the aircraft is called the empennage.

3. **The correct answer is E.** Of the four aerodynamic forces acting on an aircraft, lift exceeding weight can result in a bank or climb. Thrust exceeding drag in lieu of lift would also work if relying on the engine for upward propulsion.

4. **The correct answer is C.** The proximity of the surface artificially increases wing performance with a lack of "split" non-performing air around the wing. This is experienced during a landing flair or rotation for takeoff. Departing ground effect when not having minimum required airspeed will result in a loss of lift and a stall.

5. **The correct answer is C.** The lift vector splits into two components of vertical and horizontal during a bank. For a level turn, maintaining altitude is the equalizing of weight relative to the vertical component while increasing the horizontal lift component during a bank (centripetal force).

6. **The correct answer is D.** Air molecules travel the same distance in the same amount of time above and below an airfoil. As a result, the distance between the molecules is greater as they travel a greater distance across the curved upper part of the wing relative to the flat bottom part. The spaced molecules create a low pressure area above the wing, hence lift.

7. **The correct answer is E.** The white arc indicates maximum full flap structural speed and full flap stall speed. Knowing all aspects of this instrument is important for a professional aviator.

8. **The correct answer is C.** The symbol of an aircraft in the center of the RMI (Radio Magnetic Indicator) gauge and the tick marks around the outside are fixed, while the two "needles" (called an automatic direction finder (ADF) and very high frequency (VHF) omni-directional radio range (VOR)) and the magnetic compass card component (called the heading indicator) move. The heading indicator under the fixed tick mark at the top of the gauge indicates 175 degrees and is the aircraft magnetic heading. It is important to note that the RMI is a basic instrument for flight training and it is imperative to know how it functions and to be comfortable in how to use it for situational awareness, navigation (to include point-to-points), and types of approaches.

9. **The correct answer is C.** The lines within the depicted segmented circle are in the same direction and number as runways available. The tick marks at the end of each line depict the pattern direction for each runway. *Note*: Control tower operations are always a priority over segmented circles. For instance, pattern directions may be used to keep aircraft from overflying sensitive areas at pattern altitudes such as a tower or terminal.

10. **The correct answer is D.** The most likely active runway is 35R. The tetrahedron points toward the wind. *Note*: Control tower operations are always a priority over tetrahedron indications.

11. **The correct answer is D.** Non-precision runway markings may be limited to centerlines and runway numbers as depicted with runways 12 and 30. Precision instrument approach runway markings are exhibited on runways 35L/17R and 35R/17L.

12. **The correct answer is B.** Displaced thresholds visually indicate that a part of the runway may be under repair or otherwise not safe for anything but taxing upon.

13. **The correct answer is C.** The X across the runway indicates it is a closed area that is not safe for any use (landing, takeoff, or taxi).

14. **The correct answer is A.** A red light from the control tower indicates that you should not land, and, if you are on the ground, you should taxi clear of the active runway. As a professional aviator, all control tower light gun signals need to be known relative to communicating with aircraft on the ground or in the air.

15. **The correct answer is A.** Class A extends up to and includes flight level 600. As a professional aviator, all airspace class parameters (to include airspeeds, entry operation, equipment restrictions, and day/night cloud clearances) must be known and understood.

16. **The correct answer is D.** All airspace categories (special use, for example) must be known and include how to communicate with agencies controlling and monitoring such airspace. You will likely schedule your own MOA times and coordinate over the radio when entering, using, and departing your MOA.

17. **The correct answer is D.** Anticipating icing conditions, in addition to reading flight weather reports, is critical for pilot candidates. The temperature-dew point spread applies relative to also having freezing temperatures, making choice B not correct.

18. **The correct answer is E.** Microbursts are more common with thunderstorms, and cumulonimbus are clouds associated with thunderstorms. It is important to identify and understand the types of clouds, turbulence, and windshear within your new operational environment.

19. **The correct answer is B.** Hypoxia, low oxygen in your blood, can cause inflight drowsiness, numbness, tingling in your extremities, impaired judgment, and dizziness. You will be exposed to all the options within the question and should have an understanding of each.

20. **The correct answer is E.** Crew resource management (CRM), synonymous for crewed and single pilot aircraft, should be understood to optimize control over your aircraft, your mission, and emergency management. Expect to dry run the management of an emergency procedure daily as a flight student and prior to every mission as a professional aviator.

answers practice test

SUMMING IT UP

- The Air Force Officer Qualifying Test (AFOQT) Form T is the exam used by the U.S. Air Force for all officer candidates, whether or not they apply for a flying position.

- The computer-based Test of Basic Aviation Skills (TBAS) is used as a tool for the selection of U.S. Air Force pilot and RPA pilot candidates. TBAS scores are combined with the candidate's AFOQT Pilot composite scores and flying hours to produce a Pilot Candidate Selection Method (PCSM) score.

- The AFOQT contains 310 test questions and 240 self-description questions. The time required to complete all test sections is approximately 3 hours and 37 minutes. Total testing time (including administration and breaks) is approximately 4 hours and 48 minutes.

- The AFOQT is divided into the following twelve subtests:
  - Verbal Analogies (25 questions, 8 minutes)
  - Arithmetic Reasoning (25 questions, 29 minutes)
  - Word Knowledge (25 questions, 5 minutes)
  - Math Knowledge (25 questions, 22 minutes)
  - Reading Comprehension (25 questions, 38 minutes)
  - Situational Judgment (50 questions, 35 minutes)
  - Self-Description Inventory (240 questions, 45 minutes)
  - Physical Science (20 questions, 10 minutes)
  - Table Reading (40 questions, 7 minutes)
  - Instrument Comprehension (25 questions, 5 minutes)
  - Block Counting (30 questions, 4.5 minutes)
  - Aviation Information (20 questions, 8 minutes)

Aviation Selection Test Battery (ASTB-E)

OVERVIEW

- **ASTB-E Basics**
- **Test Section Descriptions and Strategies**
- **ASTB-E Answer Sheet**
- **ASTB-E Practice Test**
- **ASTB-E Answer Keys and Explanations**
- **Summing It Up**

ASTB-E BASICS

The Aviation Selection Test Battery (ASTB) is created and maintained by the Naval Aerospace Medial Institute (NAMI), a department within the Navy Medicine Operational Training Center (NMOTC) at Naval Air Station (NAS), Pensacola. The ASTB is used by the U.S. Navy, Marine Corps, and Coast Guard to select candidates for pilot and flight officer training programs. Portions of the test are also used by the Navy for selection into Officer Candidate School (OCS). Because your selection—first, as an officer and second, as an aviator—hinges on your ASTB-E score, understanding and appreciating the details of the test is vital to your success when taking it.

The ASTB-E was implemented in December of 2013. The ASTB-E includes sections that focus on technical skills not found in previous versions, including aviation and nautical terminology, aircraft components and function, basic aerodynamic principles, and basic flight rules and regulations. Candidates with aviation and shipboard experience can use their experience to help them succeed on the ASTB-E, but those without experience can improve their scores in these sections by studying.

In addition, the test now incorporates a personality assessment that *may* influence the rest of your military career. The Naval Aviation Trait Facet Inventory (NATFI) is a subtest in the ASTB-E designed to assess personality traits relevant to success as an aviator. Although there are no "right" or "wrong" answers, how you answer the questions can have a lasting impact on your career, so taking this subtest requires extreme caution—you need to understand how the test works and consider what it was designed to measure. This subtest and the others will be described in more detail later in the chapter.

The ASTB-E is composed of seven subtests, each of which is used to measure specific abilities considered essential to a successful aviation career:

1. Math Skills Test (MST)
2. Reading Comprehension Test (RCT)
3. Mechanical Comprehension Test (MCT)
4. Aviation and Nautical Information Test (ANIT)
5. Naval Aviation Trait Facet Inventory (NATFI)
6. Performance Based Measures Battery (PBM)
7. Biographical Inventory with Response Validation (BI-RV)

These subtests are used to define the following six ATSB score component categories:

1. Officer Aptitude Rating (OAR)
2. Academic Qualifications Rating (AQR)
3. Pilot Flight Aptitude Rating (PFAR)
4. Flight Officer Aptitude Rating (FOFAR)
5. Pilot Aviation Fit (PAF)
6. Flight Officer Aviation Fit (FOAF)

Selection for a career program (OCS, SNA, and SNFO), which was discussed in Chapter 2, is scored relative to the component categories and subtests (see Figure 5.1).

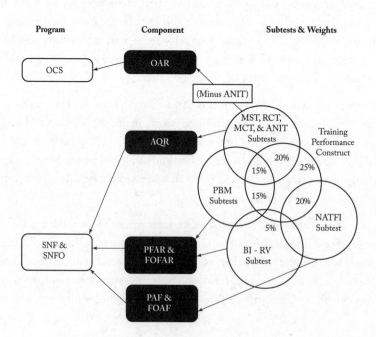

Figure 5.1. Performance weights. Generalization of estimated weighted values and program relationships.

Individuals who want to compete for an aviation career must complete all seven subtests within 90 days of taking the first subtest. Those seeking only a commission who do not want an aviation-related career will take the MST, RCT, and MCT subtests; however, they can later choose to take the remaining four subtests within the 90-day window. An OAR score is compiled based on the three core subtests (MST, RCT, and MCT) and is used as predictor of how well you will do as an officer candidate relative to your peers (see Table 5.1). The composite OAR score will range from 20 to 80 points, where 40 represents the mean of all those having taken the same form of the ASTB-E within a 12-month timeframe. Qualifying scores depend on the number of officer candidate positions and how well you did relative to others wanting those same slots.

Student Naval Aviator (SNA) selection includes a weighted average of AQR and PFAR components and consideration of your PAF score.

- **AQR** is used as a predictor of how well you will do in Aviation Preflight Indoctrination (API) at NAS Pensacola, Florida and ground training aspects of primary flight training at NAS Whiting Field, Florida or NAS Corpus Christi, Texas.

- **API** is required for both Aviator (Pilot) and NFO career tracks.

- **PFAR** is used as a predictor of how well you will do in primary pilot training.

AQR, PFAR, and PAF* use a stanine scoring system (based on a 1 to 9 scale), where 5 represents the mean scores of all your peers within 12 months of your test date. The minimum required SNA (pilot) scores are as follows:

SNA Minimum AQR/PFAR Scores		
Branch	**AQR**	**PFAR**
U.S. Navy	4	5
U.S. Marine Corps	4	6
U.S. Coast Guard	4	5

*PAF minimum scores are derived from the proprietary NATFI subtest and are thus unavailable.

Student Naval Flight Officer (SNFO) selection includes a weighted average of AQR and FOFAR componentsand consideration of your FOAF score.

- **FOFAR** is used as a predictor of how well you will do in primary SNFO training at "main side" NAS Pensacola, Florida.

AQR, FOFAR, and FOAF* stanine scores are used to also evaluate your potential relative to all peers within 12 months of your ASTB-E test date. The minimum SNFO required AQR and FOFAR scores are as follows:

SNFO Minimum AQR/FOFAR Scores		
Branch	**AQR**	**FOFAR**
U.S. Navy	4	5
U.S. Marine Corps	4	6

*FOAF minimum scores are derived from the proprietary NATFI subtest and are thus unavailable.

How the Test Is Administered

Two methods of test administration for the subtests that make up the OAR are available: paper and pencil, and online via a system called APEX. The number of questions and durations vary between the two formats.

Paper: Taking the OAR subtests on paper, you will encounter a fixed number and sequence of questions per subtest. Since any items left unanswered will be scored as incorrect, a good strategy is to eliminate invalid answer choices and make educated guesses on remaining questions if time is about to expire.

Online: The APEX system uses computer-adaptive programing for all of the subtests. Instead of a set number of questions over a set period of time, items in the question bank are ranked relative to their difficultly level. If you correctly answer a question, the next question will be more difficult. If you answer that question incorrectly, the test bank may provide an equally or less difficult question. Depending on how well you do, you may finish the test having answered as few as 20 questions (for the first four subtests); if you answer many questions incorrectly, the test may generate up to the estimated numbers listed in Table 5.1. The computer-adaptive format does not allow you to skip a question and come back to it later. All questions are forced response, meaning that you have to submit an answer to each question in order to move on to the next question. NAMI advises against guessing because incorrect responses are counted against correct responses. That being said, you may need to make some educated guesses to answer the minimum number of questions (see Table 5.1), so pacing yourself to allow time to do so is important. Do *not* randomly guess near the end of the computer-adaptive tests.

Table 5.1

Subtest Composition.

	Paper Version		Online Version		Program		
Subtest	**Questions**	**Minutes**	**Questions**	**Minutes**	**OCS**	**SNA**	**SNFO**
MST	30	40	20–30	up to 40	X	X	X
RCT	20	30	20–30	up to 30	X	X	X
MCT	30	15	20–30	up to 15	X	X	X
ANIT	*Web Only*	n/a	20–30	up to 15		X	X
NATFI	*Web Only*	n/a	88	n/a		X	X
PBM	*Web Only*	n/a	7 sections	n/a		X	X
BI-RV	*Web Only*	n/a	Varies	n/a		X	X

(OAR brace spans MST, RCT, MCT)

Total: 2 to 2 hours and 15 minutes
(1.5 to 2 hours for OAR only)

Note: APEX version uses adaptive question ordering from a question bank.

You **cannot** take the paper format of the OAR as a strategy to then take the subtests on the computer. In fact, you may need to wait a mandatory period of time, after which the paper version will count against your limit of three ASTB-E tests. Only three paper test versions are available, and, while the online format prevents candidates from retaking the ASTB-E before the mandatory waiting period or taking a common version, you are responsible for monitoring these restrictions when retaking a paper version. A mandatory 30-day wait minimum is required before retaking the ASTB-E, and you must wait another 90 days before taking it for a third and final time. You must also ensure that you are not retaking the form of the test you have taken previously. Failure to do so will result in an illegal test for which you will not receive valid test scores but that will count against your three-test limit.

TEST SECTION DESCRIPTIONS AND STRATEGIES

Math Skills Test (MST)

This section is an evaluation of college-level mathematical terms and principles. Skills assessed include basic arithmetic operations, solving for variables, fractions, roots, exponents, and the calculation of angles, areas, and perimeters of geometric shapes. See Chapter 3 for an additional section to practice these skills.

Reading Comprehension Test (RCT)

This subtest is an evaluation of one's ability to read and comprehend technical or academic writing. No knowledge of the subject matter is needed to answer the single question relative to each short passage. The most common question types will ask you either to identify the primary purpose of the passage or to determine if a particular statement is supported by the passage.

Your reading comprehension skills were tested in a broader, more in-depth manner for the SAT® and ACT® exams. This reading comprehension test is focused on rapid comprehension of a short passage and quick analysis to answer a single question. See Chapter 3 for more in-depth practice exercises relating to this skill.

Mechanical Comprehension Test (MCT)

This section tests your knowledge of basic physics, electrical, and mechanical theories. Questions focus on topics such as force, friction, current, fluid, pressure, pulleys, gears, screws, engines, and other machine operations. Physics, basic electronics, and mechanics courses will prepare you well for the questions in this section. If you need a refresher on these subjects, check out Peterson's® *Master the Mechanical Aptitude and Spatial Relations Test.*

Aviation & Nautical Information Test (ANIT)

The ANIT is a knowledge test on aviation and nautical information. The majority of the questions are aviation-related, and some of the nautical information is slanted toward carrier aviation. Aviation categories are aircraft components, aerodynamics, aerodrome operation, instrumentation, flight rules and regulations, and history. Nautical question categories include general carrier terminology, nautical terminology, history, and general terminology common to both aviation and nautical piloting. In addition to the materials provided in this chapter, you can use the U.S. Air Force Officer Qualifying Test (AFOQT) subtest on "Aviation Information" in Chapter 4 as additional preparation for the aviation aspect of the ANIT.

Consider preparation for this subtest as a means to prepare yourself for the rest of your career.

You should own a current copy of the *Federal Aviation Regulations* (FAR) and the *Aeronautical Information Manual* (AIM). Get used to finding information within them as source documents. Any information is an assumption unless you verify it within the FAR, AIM, and service-specific regulations. In addition, you will be doing yourself a disservice by not taking at least both general aviation AND instrument ground school training (offered by some community colleges and for-profit organizations). Pilot training is not just training but an ongoing interview for the rest of your career.

GET THE FACTS

Reference the free FAA online handbooks to augment, review, or expand your understanding of your new profession:

https://www.faa.gov/air_traffic/publications/

Naval Aviation Trait Facet Inventory (NATFI)

The NATFI is a personality test used for officer candidacy and aviation selection and for use in mid-level officer career and command selection. The trend of including personality tests and background surveys includes the USAF's use of the NEO PI-R self-description inventory for similar purposes. The U.S. Army is the only service that currently is not using personality tests for candidate selection or potential career advancement considerations.

Because responses to this test may be a factor for the rest of your career, it is vital that you understand it thoroughly. The NATFI is an ipsative-type personality test adapted for use in the ASTB-E. A forced choice among two questionable (flattering or unflattering) statements is used to generate scores among several personality traits. Traits include aggressiveness, adaptability, work motivation, confidence, warmth, and unrestrained behavior. Candidate selection of one of the two options automates later paired questions to further score each measured trait. Here are examples of three negative paired statements and one positive paired statement:

> **A.** Half the time I do not put things away.
>
> **B.** When people whisper, I think they are talking negatively about me.

> **A.** I will go to any concert as long as it is loud and dangerous.
>
> **B.** I am okay when friends want to have deep conversations, but I don't like all that touchy-feely stuff.

> **A.** My performance goes down when things get tough.
>
> **B.** I am typically late for appointments.

> **A.** I give my all when others count on me.
>
> **B.** I am more productive than other people typically.

Performance Based Measures Battery (PBM)

The PBM was adapted from the U.S. Air Force Education and Training Command's (AETC) Test of Basic Aviation Skills (TBAS) by the Naval Aerospace Medical Research Laboratory (NAMRL) and the Naval Operational Medicine Institute (NOMI). The PBM is administered on the APEX network and uses picture screens along with automated instructions to minimize proctor involvement. In addition to the APEX network, a throttle and joystick are used to interface within seven PBM subtests. The first test measures situational awareness. Tests two through seven are designed to overlap in measuring dexterity and multitasking elements. Multitasking measures are identified as being the greater predictor of success.

The PBM consists of seven subtests, each of which we will describe. Because these tests are administered on computer, practice tests cannot be provided for tests 2 through 7. However, examinees wishing to prepare for the Performance Based Measures Battery may find it useful to practice solving mental rotation problems, as well as practice using flight simulator software with a stick-and-throttle set.

Unmanned Aerial Vehicle (UAV) Test

The Unmanned Aerial Vehicle (UAV) Test is a measure of spatial orientation and reasoning. Two panels of information are presented on the left and right side of the screen (see Figure 5.2). The left side is a **tracker map** indicating a North-oriented chart and a symbol of an aircraft indicating both position and direction of flight. The right side is the **camera view** RELATIVE to the aircraft heading only. There is an aircraft symbol as well as a moveable crosshair. Grey blocks appear around the center. You are instructed to target an object (one of the grey block areas) relative to the aircraft heading by using the joystick to move the crosshairs. For example, in Figure 5.2 you are instructed to image the north parking lot for targeting. Use the left panel (tracker map) to determine aircraft heading. Orient yourself mentally as if you are in the aircraft. When asked to move the crosshairs in a cardinal direction, move them relative to your aircraft's heading. In the example, north is behind your aircraft. Up to eight practice scenarios are followed by up to 48 tasks.

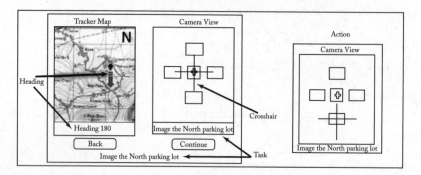

Figure 5.2. UAV test depiction and correct response example.

Practical applications for this skill exceed the operation of UAVs. For instance, imagery from a LITENING pod (used in laser tracking and targeting of moving or stationary objects) will be oriented differently than your relative heading. Spatial orientation complexity is also required when prosecuting Close Air Support (CAS) missions as a terminal attack controller (or forward attack controller) "talks you onto a target" relative to his or her map grid. Use of the LITENING pod (or similar) imagery to refine a talk-on adds yet another layer of spatial orientation complexity. A recommended strategy that will also help later in your career, is to FIRST verify your heading and then orient the area of interest outside of your aircraft as a clock position. The 12 o'clock is off your nose, 3 off your right wing, 6 behind you off your tail, and 9 off your left wing. In reference to the example in Figure 5.2, you are headed south, and the area of interest is north. North is at your 6 o'clock, so you would roll your crosshairs to your 6 o'clock position.

The UAV test is the only subtest for which a practice test is provided in this book. Subtest practice questions in this chapter use a heading indicator instead of the map display in the left panel. Instead of moving crosshairs in the right panel, you select the numbered zone around your aircraft.

Dichotic Listening Test (DLT)

The Dichotic Listening Test (DLT) is an audio test that measures your ability to identify specific left or right ear cues and to acknowledge those cues with specific tasks. You may receive instructions to depress a specific button on the throttle OR joystick whenever you hear an odd/even number (or letter sequence) in the right/left ear. Speed for each response is measured, and incorrect responses count against correct responses. A series of seven letters and/or numbers make up a string, and 40 strings will be played. Expect at least 16 numbers and/or 16 letters among the 40 strings to occur in the correct ear. For example, **"depress the joystick trigger in your right hand whenever you hear an odd number in the left ear. Also, press the thumb button on the left throttle whenever you hear an even number in your right ear."** In the example, if the left throttle button is pressed upon hearing a 6 in the left ear, then a wrong response is recorded and counted against you. (See Figure 5.3)

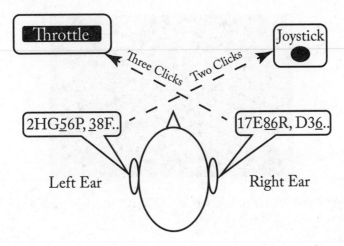

Figure 5.3. Depiction of DLT test. Left and right audio cues trigger depression of specific buttons.

The multitasking skills assessed by the DLT will extend to the management of many radios within your aircraft. For instance, you may designate your VHF-1 radio to your left ear and VHF-2 to your right ear. You may also stack additional radios (UHF, HF) to either ear but at differing volume settings. If you are a multicrewed aircraft, you may have cockpit comms on both ears. Different mental emphasis may correlate to a specific radio during a specific phase of the mission. HF may be tied to the ground controller in relaying a talk-on for a close air support strike, while one of your VHF radios may be your wingman setting up for a weapon release based on your lazing of a target. Radio multitasking techniques vary, but the use of all radios on both ears and at the same volume hampers the ability to filter, organize, prioritize, and relay audio information.

It is important to understand that hearing in each ear is tied to the opposite brain hemisphere. Essentially, the right ear processes audio cues faster because it is associated with the brain's left hemisphere (the area of speech and language processing). Isolated left-ear audio cues are transferred to the brain's right hemisphere (which is unable to fully process speech) and then rerouted to the left hemisphere to be fully processed. Cognitive practice is required to overcome the natural tendency to downplay left-ear cues because of a right-ear bias.

Airplane Tracking Test (ATT)

The Airplane Tracking Test (ATT) measures the ability to track a moving object in two dimensions (vertical and horizontal). An image of a yellow aircraft from the rear perspective is on the main part of the screen, along with red crosshairs, (see Figure 5.4). The ATT test uses the larger right screen panel and the joystick. Ignore the left narrow panel during the ATT. As you move the crosshairs toward the jet, the jet will move away. The jet will behave similar to a magnet moving away from the crosshairs, as if the crosshairs were another magnet with the same polarization. In understanding the behavior, instead of chasing the jet, follow and anticipate the movement. Avoid rapid full-throttle deflections, as the more aggressively you "intercept" the jet, the more aggressively it will respond. Information at the bottom of the screen will let you know if you are locked on and the stage/level you are up to. As the levels increase, the jet reaction increases. This is analogous to the previously mentioned magnetic push becoming greater.

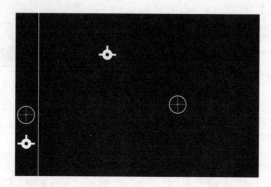

Figure 5.4. ATT and DTT depicted display. ATT uses the right panel and VTT the left.

Vertical Tracking Test (VTT)

The Vertical Tracking Test (VTT) utilizes the narrow left side of the screen and is controlled by the left throttle. Although the throttle serves only as a controller in this test, including a throttle peripheral analogous with those on fixed-wing jets enhances the real-world simulation effect. The VTT functions the same as the ATT, except it is limited to the vertical on the left side of the screen. As with the ATT, to be successful, do not chase the jet using rapid full control deflections. Instead, anticipate the motion as if you were causing the motion, "pushing" it with the same magnetic polarization.

Airplane Tracking and Horizontal Tracking Test (AHTT)

In the Airplane Tracking and Horizontal Tracking Test (AHTT), the main multitasking measure combines both the ATT and VTT simultaneously (see Figure 5.4). Performance is measured on how well you track both jets at the same time. The only way to practice this is through the use of video games. The games will not mimic the target's reactionary response to your tracking; however, you will still go through the motions of putting a target site on an evading target. Although the vertical component of the targeting is not included in the video games, the point is multitasking during targeting. Working in the three dimensions of video-game dogfighting will help somewhat.

Airplane Tracking, Vertical Tracking, and Dichotic Listening Test (AVDLT)

Multitasking increases in the AVDLT by combining the AHTT and DLT. Performance is a measure of speed and accuracy of the DLT and overall tracking performance among both left and right panels.

Emergency Scenario Test (EST)

The Emergency Scenario Test (EST) adds additional multitasking to the AHTT by including three potential emergency scenarios. Fire, engine, and propeller warning light indicators appear at the bottom of the main panel (see Figure 5.5). In addition to a unique audio tone, the indicator will backlight red. Three controls are added to the lower right portion of the screen. You will be required to memorize actions to manipulate the fuel, power, and reset controls. The emergency procedure to perform is different among the three possible emergencies. Fuel and power controls are manipulated using different slider buttons on the throttle. The line in the center of each circle will move up or down to the top red, middle green, and bottom yellow positions. For example, a unique tone associated with an engine fire will accompany a backlit red Fire warning light. The memorized procedure may be to move the Fuel indicator to low (yellow) and Power indicator to low (yellow) and then to hit the Reset button. As a point of relief, the two panel tracking and dichotic listening test enters a duress mode, which suspends the recording of speed and accuracy until the emergency task is performed. Preferential scoring is based, instead, on how fast and accurately you can identify and perform the correct emergency procedure.

The EST assesses multitasking skills during emergencies, evaluating your ability to identify and prioritize the emergency while already task-saturated. For example, an emergency during take-off roll (or any phase of a flight or mission) weighs the consideration of addressing the emergency while still needing to control the aircraft or mission. All parts of the multitask events require compartmentalizing as you would do in a jet. If something does not go well, do not focus on what happened (frustration); instead, file it away and keep going (keeping cool). Similar to when flying a jet, you can debrief yourself when the mission is over and you are back on the ground. Do not let things snowball and detract from doing your best on this multilayered multitasking test.

Figure 5.5. EST depiction. One of three emergency lights at
the bottom turns red and/or includes an audio warning.

Biographical Inventory with Response Validation (BI-RV)

The Biographical Inventory with Response Verification (BI-RV) test consists of 110 questions and is self-paced. This assessment takes between 45 minutes and 2 hours to complete and can be accomplished in more than one attempt. The purpose is to gather biographical and experiential information to help ascertain your ability to complete naval aviation training successfully. This is a key consideration for selection to aviation training. Although the questions relate to your personal experiences, your responses are subject to verification. As such, you must be truthful, as falsifying responses could result in your dismissal from the program even after you have been accepted to training. It is also recommended that you complete this assessment prior to any other section of the ASTB-E. The benefit of having completed the BI-RV in advance of other ASTB-E subtests is that you will gain immediate access to your ASTB-E scores.

The assessment is complex in nature, and the follow-up questions are dependent on your responses to previously answered questions. You will need to complete all of the questions in their entirety to complete the subtest. You may skip sections of the questions and return to them later for completion, but you cannot leave the questions unanswered. The format of the test includes multiple-choice and fill-in-the-blank responses. Although a practice test is not provided in this publication, the following will provide you with potential examples of the types of questions to expect and the information you might be asked to provide. Take advantage of the opportunity to think about these concepts in advance of completing the assessment.

Potential BI-RV Question Types and Formats:

1. How often did you discuss your plans to enter military service with a family member in the last year?

   A. 0 to 1

   B. 2 to 3

   C. 4 to 5

   D. 6 to 7

   E. 8 or more

   For the last question, with which family member did you discuss your plans? (Fill in the blank.)

   _____

2. In the last 2 years, how often did you discuss your plans to enter military service with a teacher, mentor, or coach?

   A. 0 to 1

   B. 2 to 3

   C. 4 to 5

   D. 6 to 7

   E. 8 or more

   For the last question, name the person and their role (teacher, mentor, or coach) with whom you discussed your plans as well as the year. (Fill in the blank.)

   _____

3. How many times have you visited a military recruiter or other military office to discuss your plans to enter military service?

   A. 0 to 1

   B. 2 to 3

   C. 4 to 5

   D. 6 to 7

   E. 8 or more

   For the last question, provide the branch of service, location, and year of the meetings. (Fill in the blank.)

   _____

4. How many individual (non-team) sports did you participate in during your high school career?

   A. 0

   B. 1

   C. 2

   D. 3

   E. 4 or more

   For the last question, provide the sport, level of competition, coach's name, and years of participation. (Fill in the blank.)

   _____

5. How many team sports did you participate in during your high school career?

   A. 0

   B. 1

   C. 2

   D. 3

   E. 4 or more

   For the last question, provide the sport, position played, coach's name, and years of participation. (Fill in the blank.)

   _____

6. Do you participate in organized musical activities?

   A. Jazz or concert band

   B. Marching band

   C. Orchestra or string ensemble

   D. Choir

   E. None of the above

   For the last question, provide the instrument played, band or orchestra conductor's name, and years of participation. (Fill in the blank.)

   _____

7. Do you participate in organized non-sport or non-musical extracurricular activities?

   A. School government

   B. School paper, yearbook, or other publication

   C. Theater or other performance group

   D. Science or technology group

   E. Other

   F. None of the above

   For the last question, provide the name of the activity/group, years of participation, and adult mentor/supervisor. (Fill in the blank.)

   _____

8. Do you volunteer your time to any community or other organizational program?

   A. Community volunteer

   B. Non-profit organization

   C. Religious group

   D. Other

   E. None of the above

   For the last question, provide the name of the organization, years of participation, and supervisor. (Fill in the blank.)

   _____

9. How often have you reached out to current or former military members, such as neighbors or non-immediate family members (grandparent, aunt/uncle, or cousin) to discuss your plans to enter military service?

   A. 0 to 1

   B. 2 to 3

   C. 4 to 5

   D. 6 to 7

   E. 8 or more

   For the last question, provide the branch of service and year. (Fill in the blank.)

   _____

10. At what age did you first meet with a military recruiter to discuss your plans to enter military service?

    A. Under 17

    B. 17 to 18

    C. 19 to 20

    D. 21 to 22

    E. 23 or older

    For the last question, provide thebranch of service, location, and year of the meetings. (Fill in the blank.)

    _____

11. At what age did you start your first paid job?

    A. Under 17

    B. 17 to 18

    C. 19 to 20

    D. 21 to 22

    E. Never been employed

    For the last question, provide the name of the employer, location, year of hire, and supervisor name. (Fill in the blank.)

    _____

ASTB-E ANSWER SHEET

Part 1: Math Skills

1. Ⓐ Ⓑ Ⓒ Ⓓ Ⓔ   7. Ⓐ Ⓑ Ⓒ Ⓓ Ⓔ   13. Ⓐ Ⓑ Ⓒ Ⓓ Ⓔ   19. Ⓐ Ⓑ Ⓒ Ⓓ Ⓔ   25. Ⓐ Ⓑ Ⓒ Ⓓ Ⓔ
2. Ⓐ Ⓑ Ⓒ Ⓓ Ⓔ   8. Ⓐ Ⓑ Ⓒ Ⓓ Ⓔ   14. Ⓐ Ⓑ Ⓒ Ⓓ Ⓔ   20. Ⓐ Ⓑ Ⓒ Ⓓ Ⓔ   26. Ⓐ Ⓑ Ⓒ Ⓓ Ⓔ
3. Ⓐ Ⓑ Ⓒ Ⓓ Ⓔ   9. Ⓐ Ⓑ Ⓒ Ⓓ Ⓔ   15. Ⓐ Ⓑ Ⓒ Ⓓ Ⓔ   21. Ⓐ Ⓑ Ⓒ Ⓓ Ⓔ   27. Ⓐ Ⓑ Ⓒ Ⓓ Ⓔ
4. Ⓐ Ⓑ Ⓒ Ⓓ Ⓔ   10. Ⓐ Ⓑ Ⓒ Ⓓ Ⓔ   16. Ⓐ Ⓑ Ⓒ Ⓓ Ⓔ   22. Ⓐ Ⓑ Ⓒ Ⓓ Ⓔ   28. Ⓐ Ⓑ Ⓒ Ⓓ Ⓔ
5. Ⓐ Ⓑ Ⓒ Ⓓ Ⓔ   11. Ⓐ Ⓑ Ⓒ Ⓓ Ⓔ   17. Ⓐ Ⓑ Ⓒ Ⓓ Ⓔ   23. Ⓐ Ⓑ Ⓒ Ⓓ Ⓔ   29. Ⓐ Ⓑ Ⓒ Ⓓ Ⓔ
6. Ⓐ Ⓑ Ⓒ Ⓓ Ⓔ   12. Ⓐ Ⓑ Ⓒ Ⓓ Ⓔ   18. Ⓐ Ⓑ Ⓒ Ⓓ Ⓔ   24. Ⓐ Ⓑ Ⓒ Ⓓ Ⓔ   30. Ⓐ Ⓑ Ⓒ Ⓓ Ⓔ

Part 2: Reading Comprehension

1. Ⓐ Ⓑ Ⓒ Ⓓ Ⓔ   7. Ⓐ Ⓑ Ⓒ Ⓓ Ⓔ   13. Ⓐ Ⓑ Ⓒ Ⓓ Ⓔ   19. Ⓐ Ⓑ Ⓒ Ⓓ Ⓔ   25. Ⓐ Ⓑ Ⓒ Ⓓ Ⓔ
2. Ⓐ Ⓑ Ⓒ Ⓓ Ⓔ   8. Ⓐ Ⓑ Ⓒ Ⓓ Ⓔ   14. Ⓐ Ⓑ Ⓒ Ⓓ Ⓔ   20. Ⓐ Ⓑ Ⓒ Ⓓ Ⓔ   26. Ⓐ Ⓑ Ⓒ Ⓓ Ⓔ
3. Ⓐ Ⓑ Ⓒ Ⓓ Ⓔ   9. Ⓐ Ⓑ Ⓒ Ⓓ Ⓔ   15. Ⓐ Ⓑ Ⓒ Ⓓ Ⓔ   21. Ⓐ Ⓑ Ⓒ Ⓓ Ⓔ   27. Ⓐ Ⓑ Ⓒ Ⓓ Ⓔ
4. Ⓐ Ⓑ Ⓒ Ⓓ Ⓔ   10. Ⓐ Ⓑ Ⓒ Ⓓ Ⓔ   16. Ⓐ Ⓑ Ⓒ Ⓓ Ⓔ   22. Ⓐ Ⓑ Ⓒ Ⓓ Ⓔ   28. Ⓐ Ⓑ Ⓒ Ⓓ Ⓔ
5. Ⓐ Ⓑ Ⓒ Ⓓ Ⓔ   11. Ⓐ Ⓑ Ⓒ Ⓓ Ⓔ   17. Ⓐ Ⓑ Ⓒ Ⓓ Ⓔ   23. Ⓐ Ⓑ Ⓒ Ⓓ Ⓔ   29. Ⓐ Ⓑ Ⓒ Ⓓ Ⓔ
6. Ⓐ Ⓑ Ⓒ Ⓓ Ⓔ   12. Ⓐ Ⓑ Ⓒ Ⓓ Ⓔ   18. Ⓐ Ⓑ Ⓒ Ⓓ Ⓔ   24. Ⓐ Ⓑ Ⓒ Ⓓ Ⓔ   30. Ⓐ Ⓑ Ⓒ Ⓓ Ⓔ

Part 3: Mechanical Comprehension

1. Ⓐ Ⓑ Ⓒ   7. Ⓐ Ⓑ Ⓒ   13. Ⓐ Ⓑ Ⓒ   19. Ⓐ Ⓑ Ⓒ   25. Ⓐ Ⓑ Ⓒ
2. Ⓐ Ⓑ Ⓒ   8. Ⓐ Ⓑ Ⓒ   14. Ⓐ Ⓑ Ⓒ   20. Ⓐ Ⓑ Ⓒ   26. Ⓐ Ⓑ Ⓒ
3. Ⓐ Ⓑ Ⓒ   9. Ⓐ Ⓑ Ⓒ   15. Ⓐ Ⓑ Ⓒ   21. Ⓐ Ⓑ Ⓒ   27. Ⓐ Ⓑ Ⓒ
4. Ⓐ Ⓑ Ⓒ   10. Ⓐ Ⓑ Ⓒ   16. Ⓐ Ⓑ Ⓒ   22. Ⓐ Ⓑ Ⓒ   28. Ⓐ Ⓑ Ⓒ
5. Ⓐ Ⓑ Ⓒ   11. Ⓐ Ⓑ Ⓒ   17. Ⓐ Ⓑ Ⓒ   23. Ⓐ Ⓑ Ⓒ   29. Ⓐ Ⓑ Ⓒ
6. Ⓐ Ⓑ Ⓒ   12. Ⓐ Ⓑ Ⓒ   18. Ⓐ Ⓑ Ⓒ   24. Ⓐ Ⓑ Ⓒ   30. Ⓐ Ⓑ Ⓒ

Part 4: Aviation & Nautical Information

1. Ⓐ Ⓑ Ⓒ Ⓓ Ⓔ   7. Ⓐ Ⓑ Ⓒ Ⓓ Ⓔ   13. Ⓐ Ⓑ Ⓒ Ⓓ Ⓔ   19. Ⓐ Ⓑ Ⓒ Ⓓ Ⓔ   25. Ⓐ Ⓑ Ⓒ Ⓓ Ⓔ
2. Ⓐ Ⓑ Ⓒ Ⓓ Ⓔ   8. Ⓐ Ⓑ Ⓒ Ⓓ Ⓔ   14. Ⓐ Ⓑ Ⓒ Ⓓ Ⓔ   20. Ⓐ Ⓑ Ⓒ Ⓓ Ⓔ   26. Ⓐ Ⓑ Ⓒ Ⓓ Ⓔ
3. Ⓐ Ⓑ Ⓒ Ⓓ Ⓔ   9. Ⓐ Ⓑ Ⓒ Ⓓ Ⓔ   15. Ⓐ Ⓑ Ⓒ Ⓓ Ⓔ   21. Ⓐ Ⓑ Ⓒ Ⓓ Ⓔ   27. Ⓐ Ⓑ Ⓒ Ⓓ Ⓔ
4. Ⓐ Ⓑ Ⓒ Ⓓ Ⓔ   10. Ⓐ Ⓑ Ⓒ Ⓓ Ⓔ   16. Ⓐ Ⓑ Ⓒ Ⓓ Ⓔ   22. Ⓐ Ⓑ Ⓒ Ⓓ Ⓔ   28. Ⓐ Ⓑ Ⓒ Ⓓ Ⓔ
5. Ⓐ Ⓑ Ⓒ Ⓓ Ⓔ   11. Ⓐ Ⓑ Ⓒ Ⓓ Ⓔ   17. Ⓐ Ⓑ Ⓒ Ⓓ Ⓔ   23. Ⓐ Ⓑ Ⓒ Ⓓ Ⓔ   29. Ⓐ Ⓑ Ⓒ Ⓓ Ⓔ
6. Ⓐ Ⓑ Ⓒ Ⓓ Ⓔ   12. Ⓐ Ⓑ Ⓒ Ⓓ Ⓔ   18. Ⓐ Ⓑ Ⓒ Ⓓ Ⓔ   24. Ⓐ Ⓑ Ⓒ Ⓓ Ⓔ   30. Ⓐ Ⓑ Ⓒ Ⓓ Ⓔ

Part 6: Performance-Based Measures Battery

Part 6.1 Unmanned Aerial Vehicle (UAV) Test

1. Ⓐ Ⓑ Ⓒ Ⓓ Ⓔ   7. Ⓐ Ⓑ Ⓒ Ⓓ Ⓔ   13. Ⓐ Ⓑ Ⓒ Ⓓ Ⓔ   19. Ⓐ Ⓑ Ⓒ Ⓓ Ⓔ   25. Ⓐ Ⓑ Ⓒ Ⓓ Ⓔ

2. Ⓐ Ⓑ Ⓒ Ⓓ Ⓔ   8. Ⓐ Ⓑ Ⓒ Ⓓ Ⓔ   14. Ⓐ Ⓑ Ⓒ Ⓓ Ⓔ   20. Ⓐ Ⓑ Ⓒ Ⓓ Ⓔ   26. Ⓐ Ⓑ Ⓒ Ⓓ Ⓔ

3. Ⓐ Ⓑ Ⓒ Ⓓ Ⓔ   9. Ⓐ Ⓑ Ⓒ Ⓓ Ⓔ   15. Ⓐ Ⓑ Ⓒ Ⓓ Ⓔ   21. Ⓐ Ⓑ Ⓒ Ⓓ Ⓔ   27. Ⓐ Ⓑ Ⓒ Ⓓ Ⓔ

4. Ⓐ Ⓑ Ⓒ Ⓓ Ⓔ   10. Ⓐ Ⓑ Ⓒ Ⓓ Ⓔ   16. Ⓐ Ⓑ Ⓒ Ⓓ Ⓔ   22. Ⓐ Ⓑ Ⓒ Ⓓ Ⓔ   28. Ⓐ Ⓑ Ⓒ Ⓓ Ⓔ

5. Ⓐ Ⓑ Ⓒ Ⓓ Ⓔ   11. Ⓐ Ⓑ Ⓒ Ⓓ Ⓔ   17. Ⓐ Ⓑ Ⓒ Ⓓ Ⓔ   23. Ⓐ Ⓑ Ⓒ Ⓓ Ⓔ   29. Ⓐ Ⓑ Ⓒ Ⓓ Ⓔ

6. Ⓐ Ⓑ Ⓒ Ⓓ Ⓔ   12. Ⓐ Ⓑ Ⓒ Ⓓ Ⓔ   18. Ⓐ Ⓑ Ⓒ Ⓓ Ⓔ   24. Ⓐ Ⓑ Ⓒ Ⓓ Ⓔ   30. Ⓐ Ⓑ Ⓒ Ⓓ Ⓔ

Due to the computer-based nature of the PBM, no practice tests or answers for the remaining subtests (6.2 -6.7) are available.

Part 7: Biographical Inventory with Response Validation (BI-RV)

Answers are respondent dependent. There are no correct or incorrect answers.

ASTB-E PRACTICE TEST

Part 1: Math Skills

30 Questions • 25 Minutes

> **Directions:** The following questions consist of math problem followed by four possible answers. Select which of the four choices is the correct answer to the question.

1. 1,000,000 may be represented as

   A. 10^4
   B. 10^5
   C. 10^6
   D. 10^7

2. If x is less than 0 and y is greater than 0, then

   A. x is greater than y.
   B. $x + y$ is greater than 0.
   C. xy is less than 0.
   D. xy is greater than 0.

3. If $3^{n-2} = 27$, then n equals

   A. 5
   B. 7
   C. 8
   D. 12

4. What is the square root of 4 raised to the fifth power?

   A. 8
   B. 16
   C. 32
   D. 64

5. The third root of 64 is

   A. 2.
   B. 3.
   C. 4.
   D. 8.

6. Successive discounts of 20 percent and 10 percent are equivalent to a single discount of

   A. 28 percent.
   B. 29 percent.
   C. 30 percent.
   D. 31 percent.

7. Angle E is 40° smaller than its complement. What is the number of degrees in angle E?

   A. 25°
   B. 45°
   C. 60°
   D. 90°

8. What is the perimeter of a right triangle whose legs are 3 and 4 feet?

   A. 10 feet
   B. 12 feet
   C. 14 feet
   D. 16 feet

9. Sabrina received grades of 96, 88, and 82 on three tests. What grade must she receive on the next test so that her average for these tests is 90?

   A. 89
   B. 90
   C. 91
   D. 94

10. If the sum of the edges of a cube is 24 inches, what is the volume of the cube?

   A. 4 cubic inches

   B. 8 cubic inches

   C. 16 cubic inches

   D. 64 cubic inches

11. If $a = 4b$ and $8b = 30c$, then $a =$

   A. $6c$

   B. $9c$

   C. $12c$

   D. $15c$

12. A surround sound entertainment system originally priced at $1,000 is first discounted by 20 percent, then later by 10 percent. If a 5 percent sales tax is added to the purchase price, how much would a customer buying the system at the lowest discounted price pay for the system to the nearest dollar?

   A. $720

   B. $750

   C. $756

   D. $800

13. In the figure shown below, what is the measure of angle x?

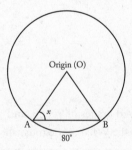

   A. 35°

   B. 45°

   C. 50°

   D. 70°

14. In a 4-hour examination of 420 questions, there are 60 mathematics problems. If twice the amount of time should be allowed for each mathematics problem than for each of the other questions, how many minutes should be spent on the mathematics problems?

   A. 60 minutes

   B. 65 minutes

   C. 70 minutes

   D. 75 minutes

15. A farmer, Cole, who is 6 feet tall, wants to determine the height of his barn. Cole notices that his shadow is 14 feet long. The shadow cast by his barn is 70 feet long. How tall is the barn?

   A. 30 feet

   B. 35 feet

   C. 40 feet

   D. 45 feet

16. If $(x - y)^2 = 60$ and $x^2 + y^2 = 40$, then $xy =$

   A. −40

   B. −20

   C. −12

   D. −10

17. A closed rectangular box with a square base has a height of 3 inches. If the volume of the box is 48 cubic inches, what is the box's surface area in square inches?

   A. 66

   B. 80

   C. 81

   D. 90

18. Two ships are 2,000 miles apart and sailing toward each other. One sails at the rate of 80 miles per day and the other at the rate of 100 miles per day. How far apart will they be at the end of 9 days?

    A. 380 miles

    B. 420 miles

    C. 440 miles

    D. 500 miles

19. The Moellers drove from New York to San Francisco, a distance of 3,000 miles. The first day, they drove $\frac{1}{8}$ of the distance and $\frac{1}{7}$ of the remaining distance on the second day. How many miles did they have remaining to reach their destination?

    A. 2,200 miles

    B. 2,250 miles

    C. 2,400 miles

    D. 2,450 miles

20. A class of 216 recruits consists of three racial and ethnic groups. If $\frac{1}{3}$ are African American, $\frac{1}{4}$ are Hispanic, and the remaining are Caucasian, how many of the recruits are Caucasian?

    A. 94

    B. 90

    C. 75

    D. 68

21. If x^2 varies directly to y, and when $x = 2$, then $y = 10$; what is the value of y when $x = 8$?

    A. 32

    B. 130

    C. 160

    D. 168

22. A Naval detachment has enough rations to feed 15 people for 8 days. If 5 more people join the detachment, for how many fewer days will the rations last?

    A. 1

    B. 2

    C. 3

    D. 4

23. Two trains running on the same track travel at the rates of 40 and 45 mph, respectively. If the slower train starts an hour earlier, how long will it take the faster train to catch up to the slower train?

    A. 5 hours

    B. 6 hours

    C. 7 hours

    D. 8 hours

24. A field can be plowed by 12 machines in 7 hours. If four machines are in need of repair and cannot be used, how many hours will it take to plow the field?

    A. 7.5 hours

    B. 8.5 hours

    C. 9.5 hours

    D. 10.5 hours

25. A cash box contains a certain number of coins, of which 63 are dimes, 33 are nickels, and the rest are quarters. If the probability of selecting a quarter from this bank is $\frac{1}{5}$, how many quarters does the bank contain?

    A. 24

    B. 27

    C. 30

    D. 35

26. If Jonah completes a trip of 240 miles at the rate of 30 mph, at what rate would he have to travel on the return trip in order to average 40 mph for the round trip?

    A. 50 mph

    B. 55 mph

    C. 60 mph

    D. 65 mph

27. An island is defended by a battery of coastal guns placed at the easternmost point of the island, and has a maximum range of 5 nautical miles. A ship is sailing due north at 24 nautical mph along a course that will bring it within 4 nautical miles of the guns. The ship is approaching a position where it will be 5 nautical miles from the guns. Assuming the ship maintains its course and speed, how long will the ship be in range of the gun battery?

    A. 15 minutes

    B. 20 minutes

    C. 25 minutes

    D. 30 minutes

28. A tank with a volume of 500 gallons can be filled by one pipe in 25 minutes and drained by another pipe in 50 minutes. How long would it take to fill the tank if both pipe valves are in the open position?

    A. 50 minutes

    B. 52 minutes

    C. 55 minutes

    D. 56 minutes

29. A bridge crosses a river that is 1,400 feet wide. One bank of the river holds $\frac{1}{5}$ of the bridge while the other holds $\frac{1}{10}$ of the bridge. How long is the bridge?

    A. 1,700 feet

    B. 1,820 feet

    C. 2,000 feet

    D. 2,100 feet

30. How much pure acid must be added to 10 ounces of 50 percent acid solution in order to produce a 75 percent acid solution?

    A. 5 ounces

    B. 6 ounces

    C. 7 ounces

    D. 8 ounces

Part 2: Reading Comprehension Test (RCT)

30 Questions • 25 Minutes

> **Directions:** Each item consists of a passage, which you should assume to be true, followed by four possible answer choices. For each item, select the choice that can be inferred only from the passage itself. Some or all of the choices following each passage may be true and reasonable, but only one of them can be derived solely from the information in the passage.

1. "In a pole-vaulting competition, the judge decides on the minimum height to be jumped. The vaulter may attempt to jump any height above the minimum. Using flexible fiberglass poles, vaulters have jumped as high as 18 feet, 8¼ inches."

   This passage means most nearly that

   A. pole vaulters may attempt to jump any height in competition.

   B. pole vaulters must jump higher than 18 feet, 8¼ inches to win.

   C. pole vaulters must jump higher than the height set by the judge.

   D. pole vaulters must use fiberglass poles.

2. "Only about one-tenth of an iceberg is visible above water. Eight to nine times as much ice is hidden below the waterline. In the Antarctic Ocean, near the South Pole, there are icebergs that rise as high as 300 feet above the water."

   The passage best supports the statement that icebergs in the Antarctic Ocean

   A. are usually 300 feet high.

   B. can be as much as 3,000 feet high.

   C. are difficult to spot.

   D. are hazards to navigation.

3. "You can tell a frog from a toad by its skin. In general, a frog's skin is moist, smooth, and shiny, but a toad's skin is dry, dull, and rough, or covered with warts. Frogs are also better at jumping than toads are."

   The passage best supports the statement that you can recognize a toad by its

   A. great jumping ability.

   B. smooth, shiny skin.

   C. lack of warts.

   D. dry, rough skin.

4. "Thomas Edison was responsible for more than 1,000 inventions in his 84-year lifespan. Among the most famous of his inventions are the phonograph, the electric light bulb, motion picture film, the electric generator, and the battery."

   This passage means most nearly that Thomas Edison

   A. was the most famous inventor.

   B. was responsible for 84 inventions.

   C. invented many things in his short life.

   D. invented the phonograph and motion picture film.

5. "Amateur sportsmen and sportswomen are those who take part in sports purely for enjoyment, not for financial reward. Professional sportsmen and sportswomen are people who are paid to participate in sports. Most athletes who compete in the Olympic Games are amateurs."

   The passage best supports the statement that an amateur sportsperson might be

   A. an Olympic champion.

   B. a member of the Pittsburgh Steelers.

   C. the holder of the heavyweight boxing crown.

   D. a participant in the World Series.

6. "A year—the time it takes Earth to go exactly once around the sun—is not 365 days. It is actually 365 days, 6 hours, 9 minutes, 9½ seconds—or 365¼ days. Leap years make up for this discrepancy by adding an extra day to the calendar once every four years."

   This passage means most nearly that the purpose of leap years is to

   A. adjust for the fact that it takes 365¼ days for Earth to circle the sun.

   B. make up for time lost in the work year.

   C. occur every four years.

   D. to allow for differences in the length of a year in each time zone.

7. "Scientists are taking a closer look at the recent boom in the use of wood for heating. Wood burning, it seems, releases high-level pollutants. It is believed that burning wood produces a thousand times more CO—carbon monoxide—than natural gas does when it burns."

   The passage best supports the statement that CO is

   A. natural gas.

   B. wood.

   C. carbon monoxide.

   D. heat.

8. "The average American family makes a move every ten years. This means that family history becomes scattered. In some cases, a person searching for his or her family's past must hire a professional researcher to track down ancestors."

   This passage means most nearly that every few years,

   A. somebody tries to trace his or her family's history.

   B. the average American family moves.

   C. family history becomes scattered.

   D. professional researchers are hired to track down ancestors.

9. "When gas is leaking, any spark or sudden flame can ignite it. This can create a 'flashback,' which burns off the gas in a quick puff of smoke and flame. But the real danger is a large leak, which can cause an explosion."

   The passage best supports the statement that the real danger from leaking gas is a(n)

   A. flashback.

   B. puff of smoke and flame.

   C. explosion.

   D. spark.

10. "With the exception of Earth, all of the planets in our solar system are named for gods and goddesses in Greek or Roman mythology. This is because other planets were thought to be in heaven, like the gods, and our planet lay beneath, like Earth."

    The passage best supports the statement that all the planets except Earth

    A. were part of Greek and Roman mythology.

    B. were thought to be in heaven.

    C. are part of the same solar system.

    D. were worshipped as gods.

11. "The Supreme Court was established by Article 3 of the Constitution. Since 1869, it has been made up of nine members—the Chief Justice and eight associate justices—who are appointed for life. Supreme Court justices are named by the President and must be confirmed by the Senate."

    This passage means most nearly that the Supreme Court

    A. was established in 1869.

    B. consists of nine judges.

    C. consists of judges appointed by the Senate.

    D. changes with each presidential election.

12. "The sport of automobile racing originated in France in 1894. There are five basic types of competition: (1) the grand prix, a series of races that leads to a world championship; (2) stock car racing, which uses specially equipped standard cars; (3) midget car racing; (4) sports car racing; and (5) drag racing. The best-known U.S. race is the Indianapolis 500, first held in 1911."

The passage best supports the statement that the sport of auto racing

A. started with the Indianapolis 500 in 1911.

B. uses only standard cars, which are specially equipped.

C. holds its championship race in France.

D. includes five different types of competition.

13. "The brain controls both voluntary behavior, such as walking and talking, and most involuntary behavior, such as the beating of the heart and breathing. In higher animals, the brain is also the site of emotions, memory, self-awareness, and thought."

The passage best supports the statement that in higher animals, the brain controls

A. emotion, memory, and thought.

B. voluntary behavior.

C. most involuntary behavior.

D. all of the above.

14. "The speed of a boat is measured in knots. One knot is equal to a speed of one nautical mile per hour. A nautical mile is equal to 6,080 feet, while an ordinary mile is 5,280 feet."

This passage means most nearly that

A. a nautical mile is longer than an ordinary mile.

B. a speed of 2 knots is the same as 2 miles per hour.

C. a knot is the same as a mile.

D. the distance a boat travels is measured in knots.

15. "It is recommended that the net be held by not more than 14 persons nor fewer than 10 persons, although under certain conditions it may become necessary to use fewer persons."

According to this passage, it is

A. best to use between 10 and 14 persons on the net.

B. better to use 10 persons on the net rather than 14.

C. impossible to use a net unless at least 10 persons are available to hold it.

D. sometimes advisable to use more than 14 persons on the net.

16. "The overuse of antibiotics today represents a growing danger, according to many medical authorities. Patients everywhere, stimulated by reports of new wonder drugs, continue to ask their doctors for a shot to relieve a cold, flu, or any other viral infections that occur during the course of a bad winter. But, for the common cold and many other viral infections, antibiotics have no effect."

The passage best supports the statement that

A. the use of antibiotics is becoming a health hazard.

B. antibiotics are of no value in treating many viral infections.

C. patients should ask their doctors for a shot of one of the new wonder drugs to relieve the symptoms of the flu.

D. the treatment of colds and other viral infections by antibiotics will lessen their severity.

17. "In examining the scene of a homicide, one should not only look for the usual, standard traces—fingerprints, footprints, etc.—but also take notice of details that at first glance may not seem to have any connection to the crime."

One may conclude from the above statement that at the scene of a homicide,

A. one cannot tell in advance what will be important.

B. only the usual, standard traces are important.

C. sometimes one should not look for footprints.

D. standard traces are not generally available.

18. "Alertness and attentiveness are essential qualities for success as a telephone operator. The work the operator performs often requires careful attention under conditions of stress."

The passage best supports the statement that a telephone operator

A. always works under stress.

B. cannot be successful unless he or she memorizes many telephone numbers.

C. must be trained before he or she can render good service.

D. must be able to work under difficult conditions.

19. "To prevent industrial accidents, safety devices must be used to guard exposed machinery, the light in the plant must be adequate, and mechanics should be instructed in safety rules that they must follow for their own protection."

The passage best supports the statement that industrial accidents

A. are always avoidable.

B. may be due to ignorance.

C. usually result from inadequate machinery.

D. cannot be entirely overcome.

20. "The leader of an industrial enterprise has two principal functions. He or she must manufacture and distribute a product at a profit, and he or she must keep individuals and groups of individuals working effectively."

The passage best supports the statement that an industrial leader should

    A. increase the distribution of his or her plant's products.

    B. introduce large-scale production methods.

    C. coordinate the activities of employees.

    D. profit by the experience of other leaders.

21. "Genuine coins have an even and distinct corrugated outer edge; the corrugated outer edges of counterfeit coins are usually uneven, crooked, or missing."

According to this statement,

    A. counterfeit coins can rarely be distinguished from genuine coins.

    B. counterfeit coins never lose their corrugated outer edge.

    C. genuine coins never lose their uneven, corrugated outer edge.

    D. the quality of the outer edge of a coin may show that it is counterfeit.

22. "In most U.S. states, no crime is considered to have occurred unless there is a written law forbidding the act, and even though an act may not be exactly in harmony with public policy, such act is not a crime unless it is expressly forbidden by legislative enactment."

Which of the following statements is most nearly in keeping with the above passage?

    A. A crime is committed only with reference to a particular law.

    B. All acts not in harmony with public policy should be expressly forbidden by law.

    C. Legislative enactments frequently forbid actions that are exactly in harmony with public policy.

    D. Nothing contrary to public policy can be done without legislative authority.

23. "Only one measure, but a quite obvious measure, of the merits of the personnel policies of an organization and of the adequacy and fairness of the wages and other conditions of employment prevailing in it, is the rate at which replacements must be made in order to maintain the work force."

This statement means most nearly that

    A. maximum effectiveness in personnel management has been achieved when there is no employee turnover.

    B. organization policies should be based on both social and economic considerations.

    C. rate of employee turnover is one indicator of the effectiveness of personnel management.

    D. wages and working conditions are of prime importance to both union leaders and managers.

24. "Education should not stop when the individual has been prepared to make a livelihood and to live in modern society; living would be mere existence were there no appreciation and enjoyment of the riches of art, literature, and science."

This passage best supports the statement that true education

   A. deals chiefly with art, literature, and science.

   B. disregards practical goals.

   C. should continue throughout the duration of one's life.

   D. teaches a person to focus on the routine problems of life.

25. "Just as the procedure of a collection department must be clear-cut and definite, the steps being taken with the sureness of a skilled chess player, so the various paragraphs of a collection letter must show clear organization, giving evidence of mind that, from the beginning, has had a specific end in view."

The passage means most nearly that a collection letter should always

   A. be carefully planned.

   B. be courteous but brief.

   C. be divided into several long paragraphs.

   D. show a spirit of sportsmanship.

26. "Although manufacturers exercise, through advertising, a high degree of control over consumers' desires, the manufacturer assumes enormous risks in attempting to predict what consumers will want and in producing goods in quantity and distributing them in advance of final selection by the consumers."

The quotation best supports the statement that manufacturers

   A. can predict with great accuracy the success of any product they put on the market.

   B. must depend upon the final selection by consumers for the success of their undertakings.

   C. must distribute goods directly to the consumers.

   D. must eliminate the risk of overproduction by advertising.

27. "In almost every community, fortunately, there are certain people known to be public-spirited; others, however, may be selfish and act only as their private interests seem to require."

This quotation means most nearly that those citizens who disregard others are

   A. community-minded.

   B. fortunate.

   C. not public-spirited.

   D. unknown.

practice test—ASTB-E

28. "Recent entrepreneur interest in, and financial support of the development of reduced cost space transportation systems, has sparked investment in other sectors of the space industry and provided additional opportunities for research."

    This quotation best supports the statement that

    A. entrepreneurs drive research initiatives.

    B. investors take their investment cues from entrepreneur activity.

    C. recent investment trends show a link between entrepreneur and other investor activity in the space industry.

    D. entrepreneurs and investors are directly supporting new opportunities for space research.

29. "Scientific theory is often misconstrued by the public as hypotheses unsupported by data and therefore discounted as not reliable."

    This passage most nearly means that

    A. scientific theory is not understood by the majority of the public.

    B. hypotheses are unrelated to scientific theory and research methodology.

    C. scientific theory is not supported by data and therefore unreliable.

    D. the public is unclear as to the distinction between scientific theory and hypothesis.

30. "The recent legal challenge by law enforcement to compel cellphone manufacturers to provide access to private citizens' data by providing software 'back doors' in encryption software renews the debate about the potential conflicting priorities of privacy, data encryption, and national security requirements."

    This quotation best supports the statement that

    A. law enforcement questions the need for private citizens to have encrypted cellphone capability.

    B. there is a debate as to what direct access to encrypted systems should be granted to law enforcement for national security.

    C. cellphone manufacturers are in conflict with national security priorities by providing encrypted systems.

    D. data encryption and privacy presents a clear challenge to national security priorities.

STOP! DO NOT GO ON UNTIL TIME IS UP.

Part 3: Mechanical Comprehension Test (MCT)

30 Questions • 15 Minutes

> **Directions:** This test has 30 questions designed to measure your ability to learn and reason with mechanical terms. Each diagram is followed with a question or an incomplete statement. Study the diagram carefully and select the choice that best answers the question or completes the statement. Then, mark the space on your answer form that has the same number and letter as your choice.

1.

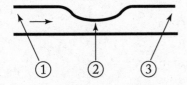

The figure above represents a pipe through which water is flowing in the direction of the arrow. There is a constriction in the pipe at the point indicated by the number 2. Water is being pumped into the pipe at a constant rate of 350 gallons per minute. Of the following, the most accurate statement is that

- **A.** the velocity of the water at point 2 is the same as the velocity of the water at point 3.
- **B.** a greater volume of water is flowing past point 1 in a minute than is flowing past point 2.
- **C.** the volume of water flowing past point 2 in a minute is the same as the volume of water flowing past point 1 in a minute.

2.

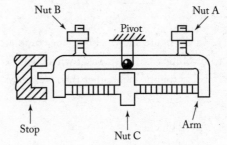

The arm in the figure above is exactly balanced as shown. If nut A is removed entirely, then, in order to rebalance the arm, it will be necessary to move nut

- **A.** C toward the right.
- **B.** C toward the left.
- **C.** B up.

3.

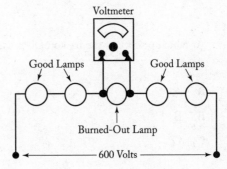

The reading of the voltmeter should be

- **A.** 600
- **B.** 120
- **C.** 0

4.

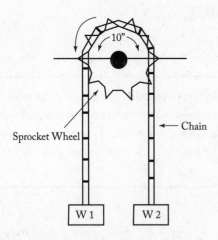

In the figure shown above, one complete revolution of the sprocket wheel will bring weight W2 higher than weight W1 by

A. 24 inches.

B. 36 inches.

C. 48 inches.

5.

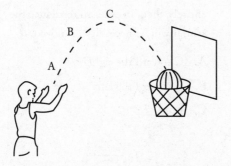

At which point was the basketball moving slowest?

A. A

B. B

C. C

6.

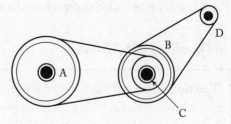

If pulley D is the driver in the arrangement of pulleys shown above, the pulley that turns slowest is

A. A

B. B

C. C

7.

A 150-pound person jumps off a 600-pound raft to a point in the water 10 feet away. Theoretically, the raft would move in the opposite direction a distance of

A. $2\frac{1}{2}$ feet.

B. 3 feet.

C. $3\frac{1}{2}$ feet.

8.

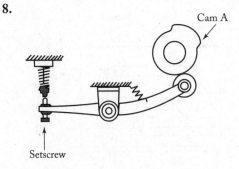

Cam A

Setscrew

If cam A makes 120 complete turns per minute, the setscrew will hit the contact point

A. once each second.

B. twice each second.

C. four times each second.

9.

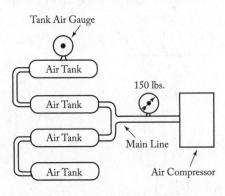

Tank Air Gauge

Air Tank

Air Tank

150 lbs.

Air Tank

Main Line

Air Tank

Air Compressor

As shown in the figure above, four air reservoirs have been filled with air by the air compressor. If the main gauge reads 150 pounds, then the tank air gauge will read

A. 50 pounds.

B. 75 pounds.

C. 150 pounds.

10.

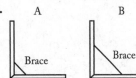

A   B   C

Brace   Brace   Brace

Which of the angles is braced most securely?

A. A

B. B

C. C

11.

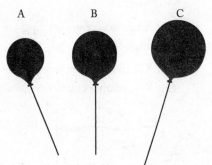

A   B   C

The amount of gas in the balloons is equal. The atmospheric pressure outside the balloons is lowest on which balloon?

A. A

B. B

C. C

12.

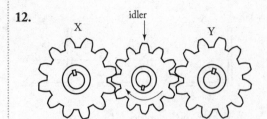

In the figure shown above, X is the driver gear and Y is the driven gear. If the idler gear is rotating clockwise,

A. gear X and gear Y are rotating clockwise.

B. gear X and gear Y are rotating counterclockwise.

C. gear X is rotating clockwise, while gear Y is rotating counterclockwise.

13.

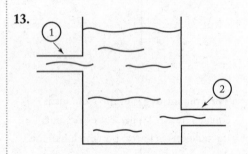

The figure shown above represents a water tank containing water. The number 1 indicates an intake pipe, and 2 indicates a discharge pipe. Which of the following statements is correct?

A. The tank will eventually overflow if water flows through the intake pipe at a slower rate than it flows out through the discharge pipe.

B. The tank will empty completely if the intake pipe is closed and the discharge pipe is allowed to remain open.

C. The water in the tank will remain at a constant level if the rate of intake is equal to the rate of discharge.

14.

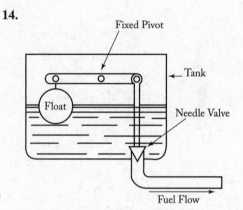

In the figure above, if the float in the tank develops a bad leak, then the

A. flow of fuel will stop.

B. float will stay in the position shown.

C. needle value will remain in the open position.

15.

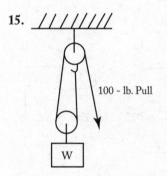

The maximum weight, W, that can be lifted as shown with a pull of 100 pounds is

A. 100 pounds.

B. 200 pounds.

C. 300 pounds.

16.

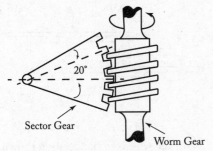

One revolution of the worm gear will turn the sector gear through an angle of

A. 5 degrees.

B. 10 degrees.

C. 15 degrees.

17.

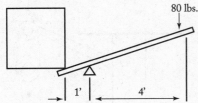

A pry bar is used to move a concrete block. A force of 80 lbs., applied as shown, will produce a tipping force on the edge of the block of

A. 80 lbs.

B. 240 lbs.

C. 320 lbs.

18.

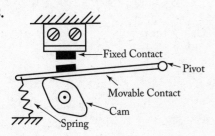

In the figure above, if the contacts come together once every second, the cam is rotating at

A. 30 rpm.

B. 45 rpm.

C. 60 rpm.

19.

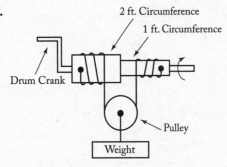

One complete turn of the drum crank in the figure above will move the weight vertically upward a distance of

A. 3 feet.

B. $2\frac{1}{2}$ feet.

C. $1\frac{1}{2}$ feet.

20.

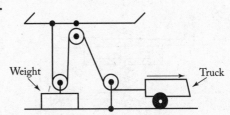

In the figure above, the weight is to be raised by means of the rope attached to the truck. If the truck moves forward 30 feet, then the weight will rise

A. 20 feet.

B. 15 feet.

C. 10 feet.

21.

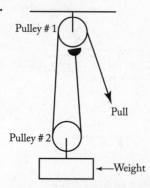

The block and tackle shown has two Pulleys of equal diameter. While the weight is being raised, Pulley 2 will rotate at

A. twice the speed of Pulley 1.

B. the same speed as Pulley 1.

C. one-half the speed of Pulley 1.

22.

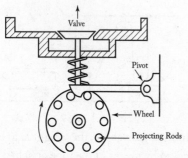

In order to open the valve twice every second, the wheel must rotate at

A. 6 rpm.

B. 9 rpm.

C. 12 rpm.

23.

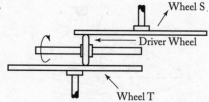

With the wheels in the position shown,

A. Wheel S will rotate at a faster speed than Wheel T.

B. Wheels S and T will rotate at the same speed.

C. Wheel S will rotate at a slower speed than Wheel T.

24.

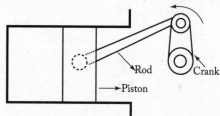

The figure above shows a crank and piston. The piston moves from mid-position to the extreme left and then back to the mid-position if the crank makes a

A. $\frac{1}{4}$ turn.

B. $\frac{1}{2}$ turn.

C. $\frac{3}{4}$ turn.

25.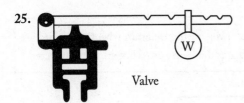

Valve

The figure above shows a lever-type safety valve. It will blow off at a higher pressure if weight W is

A. decreased.

B. moved to the left.

C. moved to the right.

26.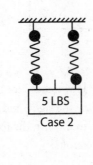

5 LBS
Case 2

5 LBS
Case 1

In the figure above, all four springs are identical. In Case 1, with the springs end to end, the stretch of each spring due to the 5-pound weight is

A. $\frac{1}{2}$ as much as in Case 2.

B. the same as in Case 2.

C. twice as much as in Case 2.

27.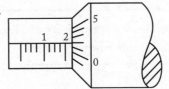

In the figure above, the micrometer reads

A. .2270

B. .2250

C. .2120

28.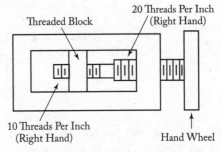

Threaded Block

20 Threads Per Inch
(Right Hand)

10 Threads Per Inch
(Right Hand)

Hand Wheel

In the figure above, the threaded block can slide in the slot but cannot revolve. If the hand wheel is turned 20 revolutions clockwise, the threaded block will move

A. 1 inch to the left.

B. $\frac{1}{2}$ inch to the left.

C. 1 inch to the right.

practice test—ASTB-E

Directions: Answer questions 29 and 30 on the basis of the wiring diagram with three switches and three lamps shown below. (Symbol ⌣ indicates that wires cross but are not connected.)

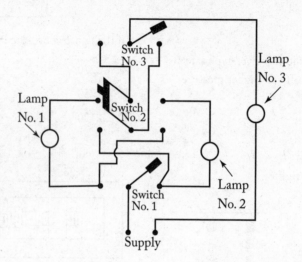

29. If all three switches are closed to the left, the following lamp condition results:

    A. No. 1 and No. 3 light

    B. No. 2 and No. 3 light

    C. Only No. 3 lights

30. If switches No. 1 and No. 2 are closed to the right, and switch No. 3 is closed to the left, the following lamp condition results:

    A. No. 1 and No. 3 light

    B. No. 2 and No. 3 light

    C. Only No. 3 lights

STOP! DO NOT GO ON UNTIL TIME IS UP.

Part 4: Aviation & Nautical Information Test (ANIT)

Directions: Refer to the ANIT discussion in this chapter before taking this subtest. This section contains 30 questions on aviation and nautical knowledge areas. You are to review the questions and select the best response given the information provided. Then mark the space on the answer form that has the same number and letter as your choice.

30 Questions • 15 Minutes

1. What airframe nickname is primarily associated with electronic warfare operations?

   A. Super Stallion

   B. Osprey

   C. Growler

   D. Super Hornet

   E. Viper

2. A right roll using differential ailerons requires what changes?

   A. Rudder moves right to increase drag on the right side and push the nose right

   B. The right aileron moves down to increase that wing's drag, and the left aileron moves up to increase that wing's pressure differential.

   C. The right aileron moves down to increase that wing's pressure differential, and the left aileron moves up to increase that wing's drag.

   D. The left aileron moves down to increase that wing's pressure differential, and the right aileron moves up to increase that wing's drag.

   E. The left aileron moves down to increase that wing's drag, and the right aileron moves up to increase that wing's pressure differential.

3. Using manual elevator trim tabs to reduce backward stick pressure, what must happen?

   A. Flaps are extended.

   B. Nose-up trim is accomplished with elevator trim tab moving up.

   C. Nose-down trim is accomplished with elevator trim tab moving down.

   D. Nose-up trim is accomplished with elevator trim tab moving down.

   E. Nose-down trim is accomplished with elevator trim tab moving up.

4. The angle formed by a wing cord line and relative wind can best be described as

   A. moving the center of pressure (CP) forward with an increase in the angle of attack (AOA).

   B. moving the center of pressure (CP) aft with an increase in the angle of attack (AOA).

   C. moving the center of pressure (CP) aft with a decrease in the angle of attack (AOA).

   D. moving the center of pressure (CP) forward with a decrease in the angle of attack (AOA).

   E. causing increased lift with a negative angle of attack (AOA).

5. Aerodynamic forces acting on an aircraft during a level turn bank are

   A. climb, weight, thrust, and drag.

   B. effective pitch, centrifugal force, thrust, and stall.

   C. vertical lift component, horizontal lift component, weight, thrust, and drag.

   D. vertical lift component, horizontal lift component, gravity, thrust, and drag.

   E. total lift, total weight, vertical thrust component, horizontal thrust component, and centrifugal force.

6. Climbing past 10,000 feet, you set your altimeter to 29.92. At indicated level flight, true altitude changes will

   A. decrease with increases in pressure.

   B. decrease with decreases in pressure.

   C. remain the same despite pressure changes.

   D. increase with increased outside air temperature (OAT).

   E. remain the same despite outside air temperature (OAT) changes.

7. Changing the altimeter to 30.05 from 29.90 is what apparent change in elevation or altitude?

   A. Decrease of 150 feet

   B. Increase of 300 feet

   C. Decrease of 1,500 feet

   D. Decrease of 300 feet

   E. Increase of 150 feet

8. What is V_{s1} on an airspeed indicator (ASI)?

   A. The maximum speed with flaps extended.

   B. A structural cruising speed caution zone, indicated by a yellow band for smooth air only operation.

   C. Maximum structural cruising speed, indicated by a red line.

   D. Minimum steady flight speed, and stalling speed, at the bottom of the green band.

   E. The upper end of the green band, indicating the maximum structural cruise speed in non-smooth air.

9. What is the approximate distance from 40° 00.000 N, 65° 30.5 W and 41° 01.111 N, 65° 30.5 W?

   A. 101 nautical miles (nm) and 111 feet

   B. 1 nautical mile (nm) and 1,111 feet

   C. 61 nautical miles (nm) and 666 feet

   D. 101 nautical miles and 666 feet

   E. Each degree latitude is different distance between the equator and the poles.

Questions 10 and 11 are based on the following figure.

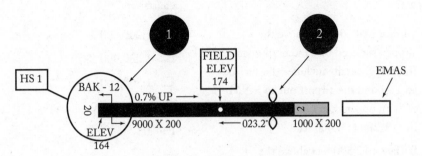

Airfield Diagram

10. In the figure, what do the two ellipse symbols next to either side of the runway 2 indicate?

   A. Landing rollout on runway 20 cannot pass the displaced threshold at the other end of the runway.

   B. PAPI glideslope indicators are available for runway 2.

   C. Landing on runway 2 can be made prior to the displaced threshold.

   D. Obstacles are to either side of the runway.

   E. Landing on runway 2 requires touchdown beyond a displaced threshold.

11. In the figure shown, what needs to be considered for landings on runway 20?

   A. BAC-12 unidirectional arresting gear may be in place.

   B. Runway 20 slopes 0.7 degrees down, so you may have a longer flair.

   C. Landings runway 20 is closed.

   D. BAC-12 bidirectional landing gear may be in place.

   E. Rollout will be uphill 23.2 degrees.

12. What are the parameters for Class D airspace?

   A. Surface to 4,000 feet above the airport, serviced by a radar approach control, generally includes the surface area around the airport out to 5 NM with an upper shelf out to 10 NM from 1,200 to 4,000 feet

   B. Surface to 2,500 feet above the airport and has an operational control tower

   C. Surface to 10,000 feet, horizontal airspace dimensions tailored to the needs and approach patterns of the airport.

   D. Uncontrolled airspace

   E. General airspace 18,000 feet MSL to FL 600

13. What is the maximum indicated airspeed (IAS) below 10,000 feet MSL within Class B airspace?

   A. 200 knots

   B. 250 knots

   C. 300 knots

   D. 350 knots

   E. No airspeed limitation exists for military aircraft.

14. While taxiing, you see a flashing white light from the control tower. What does it mean?

   A. It is not applicable; continue taxing for takeoff.

   B. Exercise extreme caution.

   C. Taxi clear of the runway.

   D. Return to the starting point.

   E. Stop.

15. What is the scale of VFR sectional charts?

   A. 1:200,000

   B. 1:250,000

   C. 1:500,000

   D. 1:1,000,000

   E. 1:1,500,000

16. The outer walls of a ship are called the

   A. bulkhead.

   B. frame.

   C. hull.

   D. keel.

   E. trim.

17. A ship's windlass is designed primarily for

   A. cargo handling.

   B. fueling at sea.

   C. handling anchor chain.

   D. propulsion.

   E. steering.

18. A nautical mile is approximately

   A. 5,280 feet.

   B. 6,076 feet.

   C. 7,076 feet.

   D. 7,400 feet.

   E. 8,000 feet.

19. A yellow jersey and yellow helmet means what on a flight deck?

   A. Catapult and Arresting Gear Officers

   B. Catapult and Arresting Gear Crews or Air Wing Maintenance Personnel

   C. Air Wing Plane Captains or Line Leading Petty Officers

   D. Plane Directors or Aircraft Handling Officers

   E. Liquid Oxygen (LOX) Crews or Plane Inspectors

20. Using the 24-hour basis in navigation, 9:05 p.m. would be written as

   A. 9.05

   B. 905

   C. 0905

   D. 21.05

   E. 2105

21. At sea, the time zones are generally bands of longitude

   A. $7\frac{1}{2}°$ in width.

   B. 15° in width.

   C. 24° in width.

   D. 30° in width.

   E. 45° in width.

22. A ship is at a latitude of 25°N and a longitude of 90°W. It is sailing in the

   A. Adriatic Sea.

   B. Black Sea.

   C. Gulf of Mexico.

   D. Hudson Bay.

   E. Red Sea.

23. A line drawn from a fix in the direction in which a ship is moving is called a

   A. course line.

   B. date line.

   C. line of position.

   D. line of sights.

   E. parallel line.

24. In marine navigation, soundings are used to measure

   A. depth of water.

   B. direction.

   C. Greenwich time.

   D. position of stars.

   E. standard time.

25. As the weight of the load carried by a ship increases,

   A. both the freeboard and draft decrease.

   B. both the freeboard and draft increase.

   C. freeboard increases and draft decreases.

   D. freeboard decreases and draft increases.

   E. None of the above

26. Which of the following is NOT considered to be an "aid to navigation"?

   A. Buoys

   B. Fog signals

   C. Lightships

   D. Loran

   E. Mountain peaks

27. Fog is generally formed when

    A. cold air moves over cold water.

    B. cold air moves over hot water.

    C. colder air moves over warmer water.

    D. warm air moves over warm water.

    E. warmer air moves over colder water.

28. The navigation light associated with "starboard" is colored

    A. green.

    B. red.

    C. white.

    D. yellow.

    E. None of the above

29. An unlighted buoy, used to mark the right side of a channel when facing inland, is called a

    A. bell buoy.

    B. can buoy.

    C. gong buoy.

    D. nun buoy.

    E. spar.

30. Ships or boats are steered by one or more rudders at the stern. The faster the vessel is moving,

    A. the greater the pressure against the rudder and the quicker the turning effect.

    B. the greater the pressure against the rudder and the slower the turning effect.

    C. the less the pressure against the rudder and the quicker the turning effect.

    D. the less the pressure against the rudder and the slower the turning effect.

    E. None of the above

STOP! DO NOT GO ON UNTIL TIME IS UP.

Part 5: Naval Aviation Trait Facet Inventory (NATFI)

No practice section or answers to this section exist. However, before taking the test, be sure that you understand the implications of the test and recommended strategy in this chapter. Although there are no right or wrong answers, consider this subtest as important as any of the others in the ASTB-E.

Part 6: Performance Based Measures Battery (PBM)

Directions: This section is computer-based on the APEX system. Before using items in this practice test, read the associated descriptions in this chapter. There are 7 subtests within the PBM. Items within this practice test are not direct replications of the PBM; instead, tests and recommendations here are designed to help your skill sets in what is being measured during each PBM subtest.

Part 6.1: Unmanned Aerial Vehicle (UAV) Test

Directions: Refer to the UAV discussion in this chapter. The UAV section of the PBM *may* have up to 8 practice scenarios and 48 test trials. FIRST, identify the aircraft heading using the left panel (tracker map). The left map display is replaced, for the purpose of this practice test, with a heading indicator. The direction the arrow points is the aircraft heading. Despite this being different from what you will see on the UAV test, the purpose is the same. NEXT, orient yourself in the right panel (camera view) relative to the aircraft heading. The top of the screen in the right panel is always the "relative" direction that the aircraft is pointed. Instead of rolling crosshairs over to an area about your aircraft in the right panel (required in the actual UAV test), select the option that correlates to zones 1 to 8 in answering the question. Increased speed during the test increases your score, and incorrect actions are counted against correct actions. Speed and accuracy are both assessed.

Sample Questions

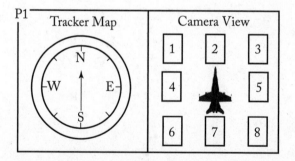

	Questions for Figure P1	**KEY**				
		A	**B**	**C**	**D**	**E**
1	**Target the WEST structure.**	1	2	3	4	5
2	**Image the NORTH structure.**	2	3	4	5	7
3	**Target the EAST parking lot.**	2	3	4	5	6
4	**Image the SOUTH hill.**	2	3	6	7	8
5	**Target the NORTH-WEST field.**	1	2	3	6	8

1. Target the WEST structure.

   A. 2

   B. 3

   C. 4

   D. 5

   The correct answer is D. (4)

2. Image the NORTH structure.

   A. 2.

   B. 3

   C. 4

   D. 5

   E. 7

   The correct answer is A. (2)

3. Target the EAST parking lot.

   A. 2

   B. 3

   C. 4

   D. 5

   E. 6

   The correct answer is D. (5)

4. Image the SOUTH hill.

   A. 2

   B. 3

   C. 6

   D. 7

   E. 8

   The correct answer is D. (7)

5. Target the NORTH-WEST field.

   A. 1

   B. 2

   C. 3

   D. 6

   E. 8

   The correct answer is A. (1)

practice test—ASTB-E

30 Questions (actual test may be up to 48 scenarios) • Time yourself and proceed quickly without sacrificing accuracy.

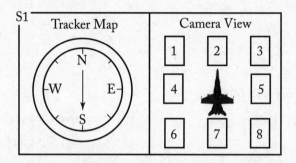

Questions for Figure S1		KEY				
		A	B	C	D	E
1	Target the NORTH structure.	2	4	5	7	8
2	Image the NORTH-WEST building.	1	3	4	6	8
3	Target the EAST parking lot.	2	3	4	5	6
4	Image the SOUTH hill.	2	3	6	7	8
5	Target the SOUTH-WEST field.	1	2	3	6	8

1. Target the NORTH structure.

   A. 2
   B. 4
   C. 5
   D. 7
   E. 8

2. Image the NORTH-WEST building.

   A. 1
   B. 3
   C. 4
   D. 6
   E. 8

3. Target the EAST parking lot.

   A. 2
   B. 3
   C. 4
   D. 5
   E. 6

4. Image the SOUTH hill.

   A. 2
   B. 3
   C. 6
   D. 7
   E. 8

5. Target the SOUTH-WEST field.

    A. 1

    B. 2

    C. 3

    D. 6

    E. 8

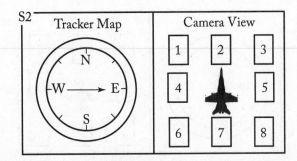

Questions for Figure S2		KEY				
		A	B	C	D	E
6	Target the WEST structure.	2	4	5	7	8
7	Image the SOUTH-WEST building.	1	3	4	6	8
8	Target the EAST vehicle.	2	3	4	5	6
9	Image the SOUTH tower.	2	3	5	7	8
10	Target the NORTH-EAST buildings.	1	2	3	6	8

6. Target the WEST structure.

    A. 2

    B. 4

    C. 5

    D. 7

    E. 8

7. Image the SOUTH-WEST building.

    A. 1

    B. 3

    C. 4

    D. 6

    E. 8

8. Target the EAST vehicle.

    A. 2

    B. 3

    C. 4

    D. 5

    E. 6

9. Image the SOUTH tower.

    A. 2

    B. 3

    C. 5

    D. 7

    E. 8

10. Target the NORTH-EAST buildings.

    A. 1

    B. 2

    C. 3

    D. 6

    E. 8

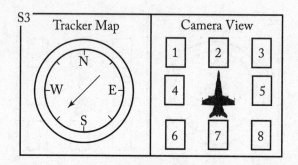

Questions for Figure S3		KEY				
		A	**B**	**C**	**D**	**E**
11	Target the EAST tank column.	2	4	6	7	8
12	Image the SOUTH-EAST Bridges.	1	3	4	6	8
13	Target the WEST group of tanks.	2	3	4	5	6
14	Image the SOUTH-WEST field.	2	3	5	7	8
15	Target the NORTH encampment.	1	2	3	6	8

11. Target the EAST tank column.

    A. 2

    B. 4

    C. 6

    D. 7

    E. 8

13. Target the WEST group of tanks.

    A. 2

    B. 3

    C. 4

    D. 5

    E. 6

12. Image the SOUTH-EAST Bridges.

    A. 1

    B. 3

    C. 4

    D. 6

    E. 8

14. Image the SOUTH-WEST field.

    A. 2

    B. 3

    C. 5

    D. 7

    E. 8

15. Target the NORTH encampment.

   A. 1

   B. 2

   C. 3

   D. 6

   E. 8

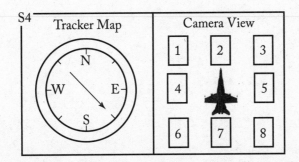

Questions for Figure S4		KEY				
		A	B	C	D	E
16	Target the WEST structure.	2	4	5	7	8
17	Image the SOUTH-WEST building.	1	3	5	6	8
18	Target the SOUTH vehicle.	2	3	4	5	6
19	Image the EAST parked helicopter.	1	3	5	7	8
20	Target the NORTH-EAST vehicle.	1	2	4	6	8

16. Target the WEST structure.

   A. 2

   B. 4

   C. 5

   D. 7

   E. 8

17. Image the SOUTH-WEST building.

   A. 1

   B. 3

   C. 5

   D. 6

   E. 8

18. Target the SOUTH vehicle.

    A. 2

    B. 3

    C. 4

    D. 5

    E. 6

19. Image the EAST parked helicopter.

    A. 1

    B. 3

    C. 5

    D. 7

    E. 8

20. Target the NORTH-EAST vehicle.

    A. 1

    B. 2

    C. 4

    D. 6

    E. 8

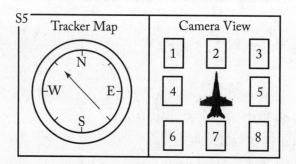

Questions for Figure S5		KEY				
		A	**B**	**C**	**D**	**E**
21	**Target the SOUTH-EAST hills.**	2	4	5	7	8
22	**Image the SOUTH-WEST vehicles.**	1	3	4	6	8
23	**Target the NORTH troops in the open.**	2	3	4	5	6
24	**Target the SOUTH gun emplacement.**	2	3	6	7	8
25	**Target the NORTH-WEST airfield.**	1	2	3	6	8

21. Target the SOUTH-EAST hills.

- **A.** 2
- **B.** 4
- **C.** 5
- **D.** 7
- **E.** 8

22. Image the SOUTH-WEST vehicles.

- **A.** 1
- **B.** 3
- **C.** 4
- **D.** 6
- **E.** 8

23. Target the NORTH troops in the open.

- **A.** 2
- **B.** 3
- **C.** 4
- **D.** 5
- **E.** 6

24. Target the SOUTH gun emplacement.

- **A.** 2
- **B.** 3
- **C.** 6
- **D.** 7
- **E.** 8

25. Target the NORTH-WEST airfield.

- **A.** 1
- **B.** 2
- **C.** 3
- **D.** 6
- **E.** 8

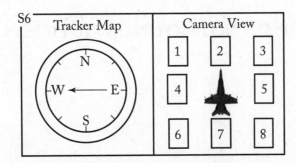

S6

Tracker Map

Camera View

Questions for Figure S6		KEY				
		A	**B**	**C**	**D**	**E**
26	**Image the SOUTH-EAST buildings.**	1	3	6	7	8
27	**Image the SOUTH-WEST roads.**	1	2	3	6	7
28	**Target the NORTH-EAST trucks.**	1	3	6	7	8
29	**Target the SOUTH hills.**	2	4	5	6	7
30	**Target the NORTH-WEST tanks.**	1	3	6	7	8

26. Image the SOUTH-EAST buildings.

    A. 1

    B. 3

    C. 6

    D. 7

    E. 8

27. Image the SOUTH-WEST roads.

    A. 1

    B. 2

    C. 3

    D. 6

    E. 7

28. Target the NORTH-EAST trucks.

    A. 1

    B. 3

    C. 6

    D. 7

    E. 8

29. Target the SOUTH hills.

    A. 2

    B. 4

    C. 5

    D. 6

    E. 7

30. Target the NORTH-WEST tanks.

    A. 1

    B. 3

    C. 6

    D. 7

    E. 8

STOP! DO NOT GO ON UNTIL TIME IS UP.

Part 6.2 to Part 6.7: DLT, ATT, VTT, AHTT, AVDLT, and EST

> **Directions:** No practice tests for these sections are available within this book; however, strategies and recommendations are available within the discussions on these subtests of the Performance-Based Measurement Battery. ExamineesExaminees wishing to prepare for the Performance Based Measures Battery. Candidates preparing for the ASTB-E may find it useful to practice using flight simulator software with a stick-and-throttle set and solving mental rotation problems.

Part 7: Biographical Inventory with Response Validation (BI-RV)

There are no practice questions for this section. See the description and example questions on pages 256–258.

ASTB-E ANSWER KEYS AND EXPLANATIONS

Part 1: Math Skills

Use the answer key to determine the number of questions you answered correctly and to highlight the questions that you should review. For those that you answered incorrectly or were unsure of how you arrived at the correct answer, review the explanations in this section.

1. C	7. A	13. C	19. B	25. A
2. C	8. B	14. A	20. B	26. C
3. A	9. D	15. B	21. C	27. A
4. C	10. B	16. D	22. B	28. A
5. C	11. D	17. B	23. D	29. B
6. A	12. C	18. A	24. D	30. D

1. **The correct answer is C.** The value of the exponent is equal to the number of zeros in the product. In this case, $10 \times 10 \times 10 \times 10 \times 10 \times 10 = 1,000,000$ or 10 to the sixth power.

2. **The correct answer is C.** In this case, x is a negative number and y is a positive number, and, as such, the product is a negative value. Choice B is incorrect as you cannot know if the sum of x and y is greater than 0.

3. **The correct answer is A.** For 3 to some exponential value to equal 27, the exponent must equal 3. Therefore, n must equal 5 or $3n-2 = 27$; $33 = 27$; $n - 2 = 5$.

4. **The correct answer is C.**
$$\left(\sqrt{4}\right)^5 = 2 \times 2 \times 2 \times 2 \times 2$$

5. **The correct answer is C.** $\sqrt[3]{64} = 4 \times 4 \times 4$

6. **The correct answer is A.** The first discount of 20% takes the price to 80% of the original. The second discount of 10% reduces the price by another 8%. The total reduction in price is 28%. For example, assume the original price of the item is $100. A 20% discount reduces the price to $80. The additional 10% discount reduces the price by $8 to $72. From the original price, the $28 reduction divided by $100 is a 28% discount.

7. **The correct answer is A.** Complementary angles are two angles that add up to 90 degrees total. As such, one angle is 40 degrees smaller than its complement. The equation is then $x + (x + 40) = 90$ degrees; $2x + 40 = 90$; $2x = 50$; $x = 25$.

8. **The correct answer is B.** First, solve for the hypotenuse of the right triangle using the Pythagorean theorem, $3^2 + 4^2 = z^2$; $z^2 = 9 + 16 = 25$; $z = \sqrt{25}$; $z = 5$. Solve for the perimeter by adding all of the sides, $3 + 4 + 5 = 12$.

9. **The correct answer is D.** Solve for the missing examination score by setting up the equation for the examination mean (average): $\dfrac{(96 + 88 + 82 + x)}{4} = 90$. Solve for x: $\dfrac{(266 + x)}{4} = 90$; $266 + x = 360$; $x = 94$.

10. **The correct answer is B.** A cube has equal side dimensions and 12 total edges. As such, divide the volume by the number of edges and then cube the result.
Solution: $\dfrac{24}{12} = 2$; $2^3 = 8$ cubic inches.

11. **The correct answer is D.** Use basic substitution to solve for c. Solution: $a = 4b$ and $8b = 30c$; if $b = \dfrac{a}{4}$, substitute in the next equation:

$$8\left(\frac{a}{4}\right) = 30c$$
$$2a = 30c$$
$$a = 15c$$

12. **The correct answer is C.** The initial 20% discount of the surround sound system brings the price down to $800. The second discount reduces the price by another 10% or $80 to $720. The 5% sales tax is based on the final discounted price of $720 and adds $36 for a total of $756. The problem can also be calculated similarly to the previous answer to Question 6, by calculating a 28% discount and then adding the 5%. A tip for rapid calculation: calculate the 72% discount and then multiply by 1.05 to obtain the final price of the item.

13. **The correct answer is C.** Angle AOB is the same as the arc, 80 degrees. All triangles have 180 degrees total, so subtract 80 degrees to obtain the remaining angle measures, which equals 100 degrees. The two sides of the triangle, AO and OB are the same length because they are also the radii of the circle. Therefore, the angles OAB (x) and OBA must be equal and are calculated by dividing the remaining 100 degrees by 2 to obtain 50 degrees.

14. **The correct answer is A.** The total examination time equals 240 minutes (4 hours × 60 minutes). There are 60 mathematics questions and 360 other questions. The variable x represents the time to solve the mathematics problems, and $\dfrac{x}{2}$ represents the time to solve the remaining problems on the examination. To solve for x, $60x + 360\left(\dfrac{x}{2}\right) = 240$ minutes; $60x + 180x = 240$; $240x = 240$; $x = 1$ minute or a total of 60 minutes for all of the mathematics problems.

15. **The correct answer is B.** The key to solving this problem is to use the distances of the shadows to determine the angle and the height of the barn (see the two figures below). The height of the farmer and length of his shadow are known. From this, calculate angle x from the figure below using the following equation: $\tan(x) = $ opposite/adjacent; $\tan(x) = \dfrac{6 \text{ ft.}}{14 \text{ ft.}}$; $x = \tan^{-1}\left(\dfrac{6}{14}\right)$; $x = 23.2°$. Using this angle and the shadow length cast by the barn, use the following to determine the height of the barn: $\tan(23.2) = \left(\dfrac{\text{height of barn}}{70 \text{ ft.}}\right)$; $70 \times \tan(23.2)$; height of barn = 30 ft.

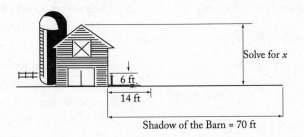

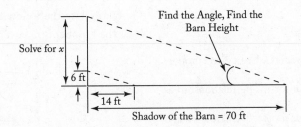

16. The correct answer is D. Use substitution to determine the value of xy. Expand $(x - y)^2 = 60$: $x^2 - xy - xy + y^2 = 60$; $x^2 - 2xy + y^2 = 60$. Substitute 40 for $x^2 + y^2$ in the expanded equation: $40 - 2xy = 60$. Solve:

$$-2xy = 60 - 40$$
$$xy = \frac{20}{-2}$$
$$xy = -10$$

17. The correct answer is B. The rectangular box has a base that is square and the height is 3 inches in length. So the equation for the volume would be $3x^2 = 48$ or $3 \times$ length $\times$ width which are equal. Solve for x:

$$x^2 = \frac{48}{3}$$
$$x = 4$$

To solve for the surface area, there are two square sizes with an area of $4 \times 4 = 16$ each and four connecting sides with dimensions $4 \times 3 = 12$ each. The total surface area is $2(16) + 4(12) = 80$.

18. The correct answer is A. Two ships are travelling directly toward each other over a 9-day period. The first ship travels 80 miles per day for a total of 80 miles/day × 9 days = 720 miles. The other ship travels 100 miles per day for a total of 100 miles/day × 9 days = 900 miles. The ships started 2,000 miles apart and are headed toward each other. Subtract both travelled distances from the 2,000 mile total for 2,000 − 720 − 900 = 380.

19. The correct answer is B. Use the following equation to solve the problem:

$$3{,}000 - 3{,}000\left(\frac{1}{8}\right) - \left(\frac{1}{7}\right)\left(3{,}000 \times \frac{7}{8}\right) = 2{,}250.$$

The initial $3{,}000 \times \frac{1}{8}$ equals the first 375 miles traveled. This reduces the distance remaining to 2,625 miles or $3{,}000 \times \frac{7}{8}$ of the distance. That distance must then be multiplied by $\frac{1}{7}$ to determine the distance traveled the second day and subtracted from the remaining distance.

20. The correct answer is B. The group of 216 recruits are classified into three groups. As such, the equation $216\left(\dfrac{1}{3}\right) + 216\left(\dfrac{1}{4}\right) + x = 216$ can be used to determine the specific ratios. Solving for x, $72 + 54 + x = 216$; $x = 216 - 126$; $x = 90$.

21. The correct answer is C. Use a direct proportion ratio to solve for y. The relationship as stated is $\dfrac{x^2}{y}$. Solve for y: $\dfrac{x^2}{y}$ where $x = 2$ and $y = 10$ is $\dfrac{4}{10}$ and $x = 8$ and y is unknown is $\dfrac{64}{y}$:

$$\frac{4}{10} = \frac{64}{y}$$
$$4y = 640$$
$$y = 120$$

22. The correct answer is B. Use x to depict the number of ration days for 20 personnel. Solve for x: $15(8) = 20x$; $120 = 20x$; $x = 6$ ration days for 20 people. Subtract the 6 days from the initial 8 to determine how many fewer days the rations will last.

23. The correct answer is D. The slower train will gain a 40 mile lead in the first hour. To determine how long the other train needs to catch up, divide the distance by the speed difference of 5 mph: $\dfrac{40 \text{ miles}}{5 \text{ mph}} = 8 \text{ hours}$.

24. The correct answer is D. Use x to depict the number of hours to plow with only 8 operational machines. Originally there were 12 machines that did the job in 7 hours or 12×7 hours. Compare (12 machines)(7 hours) = (8 machines)x; $8x = 84$; $x = \dfrac{84}{8}$; $x = 10.5$ hours.

25. The correct answer is A. Use x to depict the number of quarters in the coin bank. There is a 1 in 5 chance that the coin pulled from the bank is a quarter. The number of quarters is equal to 1/5 or x in the numerator of the equation. The value $x + 63 + 33$ represents the total number of coins in the bank and is placed in the denominator as the equivalent to the total of the ratio. Use the following ratio to solve for the number of quarters:

$$\frac{1}{5} = \frac{x}{(x + 63 + 33)}$$
$$\frac{1}{5} = \frac{x}{(x + 96)}$$
$$x + 96 = 5x$$
$$4x = 96$$
$$x = 24$$

26. The correct answer is C. If Jonah drives 30 mph for 240 miles, his travel time is 8 hours for that portion of the trip. If Jonah wants to improve his overall travel time and achieve a round trip average of 40 mph, he only has 240 miles in which to make up the time. To average 40 mph for 480 miles in which he has already travelled 240 miles in 8 hours, the remaining travel time would take 4 hours based on the following equation: $40 \text{ mph} = \dfrac{480}{x \text{ hours}}$; $40x = 480$; $x = 12$ hours, 8 of which have been used. So to calculate the speed needed to meet the average, $\dfrac{240}{4 \text{ hours}} = 60 \text{ miles}$ per hour.

27. **The correct answer is A.** See the diagram below depicting the scenario described in the problem. The key is to use the gun range data (radius) and ship distance to the gun battery to determine the angle and travel distance. The problem is very similar to that in Question 15. Use the following equation to determine the angle: $\cos(\text{angle}) = \dfrac{4 \text{ nm}}{5 \text{ nm}}$; angle $= \cos^{-1} \dfrac{4}{5}$ angle $= 36.9$. Use the following to determine the distance traveled and multiply by 2: $\sin(36.9) = \dfrac{x}{5}$; $x = 5\sin(36.9)$; $x = 3$. The distance travelled is 6 total nautical miles multiplied by the speed of 24 nautical miles per hour puts the ship range at 15 minutes.

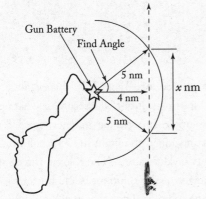

28. **The correct answer is A.** If the tank has a volume of 500 gallons and the pipe filling the tank takes 25 minutes, then the fill rate is $\dfrac{500 \text{ gallons}}{25 \text{ minutes}} = \dfrac{20 \text{ gallons}}{\text{minute}}$. The pipe that drains the tank does so at a rate of $\dfrac{500 \text{ gallons}}{50 \text{ minutes}} = \dfrac{100 \text{ gallons}}{\text{minute}}$. To determine how long it takes to fill the tank when both pipes have valves in the open position, add the fill rate while subtracting the drain rate and then recalculate the fill rate:

$$\frac{20 \text{ gallons}}{\text{minute}} - \frac{10 \text{ gallons}}{\text{minute}} = \frac{10 \text{ gallons}}{\text{minute}}$$

The fill rate is then

$$\frac{500 \text{ gallons}}{10 \text{ gallons per minute}} = 50 \text{ minutes}.$$

29. **The correct answer is B.** To determine the length of the bridge (x), add the width of the river and the segments of the bridge on each shore. Use the following equation:

$$x = 1,400 + \frac{1}{5}(1,400) + \frac{1}{10}(1,400)$$
$$x = 1,400 + \frac{3}{10}(1,400)$$
$$x = 1,400 + 420$$
$$x = 1,820 \text{ ft.}$$

30. The correct answer is D. There are two ways to visualize the calculation for this problem. The first is shown in Table 1. In Table 2, fill in the information from the problem noting that x depicts the unknown amount of pure acid that will be added to transform the solution from 55% to 75%. In the 10 ounces of 55% solution, there are 55 parts pure acid. To obtain the 75% solution, the x ounces will be added to the current 10 ounces to obtain a solution of 75(10 + x) ounces of pure acid. Solve for x: $100x + 550 = 75(10 + x)$; $100x + 550 = 750 + 75x$; $25x = 200$; $x = \dfrac{200}{25}$; $x = 8$ ounces.

Table 1

	Number of Ounces	Parts Pure Acid	Number of Ounces of Pure Acid
Pure Acid	x	100	$100x$
55% Acid Solution	10	55	550
75% Acid Solution	$10 + x$	75	$75(10 + x)$

The second solution is very similar with the values entered into Table 2. In this example, the first column is a little different in that the row is the starting solution, the second is what needs to be added, and the last is the desired resulting solution. In a similar manner above, x will depict the number of ounces of pure acid that must be added to obtain the 75% solution. So the value in column two, row four is the sum of the two values above. The column three values are presented as decimal values of the acid percentages of the solutions. Column four is the actual number of ounces of pure acid contained in the solution. The value in column four, row four should be the product of the values in row four, columns two and three. Solve for x: $7.5 + 0.75x = 5.5 + x$; $2.0 + 0.75x = x$; $2.0 = 0.25x$; $x = \dfrac{2.0}{0.25}$; $x = 8$ ounces.

Table 2

	Number of Ounces	Parts Pure Acid	Number of Ounces of Pure Acid
Starting Solution	10	0.55	5.5
Add	x	1.00	x
Final Solution	$10 + x$	0.75	$7.5 + 0.75x$

Part 2: Reading Comprehension Test (RCT)

Use the answer key to determine the number of questions you answered correctly and to highlight the questions that you should review. For those that you answered incorrectly or were unsure of how you arrived at the correct answer, review the explanations in this section.

1. C	**7.** C	**13.** D	**19.** B	**25.** A
2. B	**8.** B	**14.** A	**20.** C	**26.** B
3. D	**9.** C	**15.** A	**21.** D	**27.** C
4. D	**10.** B	**16.** B	**22.** A	**28.** C
5. A	**11.** B	**17.** A	**23.** C	**29.** D
6. A	**12.** D	**18.** D	**24.** C	**30.** B

1. **The correct answer is C.** The judge decides on the minimum height to be jumped, so pole vaulters must jump higher than the height set by the judge.

2. **The correct answer is B.** Because some icebergs in the Antarctic Ocean rise as high as 300 feet above the water, and because only one-tenth of an iceberg is visible above the waterline, some icebergs in the Antarctic Ocean are as high as 3,000 feet.

3. **The correct answer is D.** A toad's skin is dry, dull, and rough or covered with warts.

4. **The correct answer is D.** The phonograph and motion picture film are listed among Thomas Edison's inventions. Although Edison may be in the running as the most famous inventor, such a statement is not supported by the paragraph, so choice A is incorrect. Choice B is incorrect because the passage specifically states that he was responsible for more than 1,000 inventions. Edison lived 84 years; his was not a short life, so choice C is incorrect.

5. **The correct answer is A.** Because the other three answer choices involve monetary gain for the athlete, choice A can be the only correct answer.

6. **The correct answer is A.** This is a restatement of the paragraph. The other answer choices are not relevant to the paragraph.

7. **The correct answer is C.** The answer, carbon monoxide, is stated in the last sentence of the passage.

8. **The correct answer is B.** Although all four answer choices are somewhat supported by the passage, the one that *best* supports it is the statement that the average American family moves every few years.

9. **The correct answer is C.** The correct answer, explosion, is found in the last sentence of the passage: "But the real danger is a large leak, which can cause an explosion."

10. **The correct answer is B.** This answer choice restates the last sentence of the passage: "This is because other planets were thought to be in heaven, like the gods, and our planet lay beneath, like the Earth."

11. **The correct answer is B.** The other three answer choices are incorrect statements. The year 1869 refers to the establishment of the current nine-member court, making choice A incorrect. Justices are appointed by the President, making choice C incorrect. Justices serve for life, making choice D incorrect.

12. **The correct answer is D.** Most of the passage is devoted to describing the five different types of competition.

13. **The correct answer is D.** The word *also* in the last sentence is the key to the fact that in higher animals the brain controls voluntary behavior, involuntary behavior, emotions, memory, and thought.

14. **The correct answer is A.** Because 6,080 feet is greater than 5,280 feet, choice A is correct.

15. **The correct answer is A.** The recommendation to use neither more than 14 persons nor fewer than 10 persons means that it is best to use between 10 and 14 persons on the net, even if fewer can be used.

16. **The correct answer is B.** Although the paragraph starts by mentioning that there is a growing danger in the overuse of antibiotics, it does not expand on that theme. The passage focuses mainly on the ineffectiveness of antibiotics against viral infections. Because most of the paragraph is devoted to the second theme, choice B is the best answer.

17. **The correct answer is A.** Choices B, C, and D are not valid options. To take notice of details that at first glance may not seem to have any connection to the crime implies that one cannot tell in advance what will be important.

18. **The correct answer is D.** The passage states that the work of the operator often requires careful attention under stress. This means that the operator must be able to work under difficult conditions. The passage does not state that the work must *always* be performed under stress.

19. **The correct answer is B.** The answer to this question is implied in the statement that "mechanics be instructed in safety rules that they must follow for their own protection." If the mechanics must be instructed, then we can infer that accidents may occur if they have not been instructed (that is, if they are ignorant of the rules).

20. **The correct answer is C.** Keeping individuals and groups of individuals working effectively is coordinating the activities of employees. This answer choice is stated in the passage. The other choices require more interpretation. Introduction of large-scale production methods and increasing distribution of products may very well increase profits, but not necessarily.

21. **The correct answer is D.** There is nothing in the passage to support answer choices A, B, or C; only choice D summarizes the data given in the passage.

22. **The correct answer is A.** There is nothing in the passage to support answer choices B, C, or D. Choice A is supported by the excerpt "no crime is considered to occur unless there is a written law forbidding the act" at the beginning of the sentence.

23. **The correct answer is C.** There is nothing in the passage to support answer choices A, B, or D. Choice C is supported by this section: "Only one measure . . . is the rate at which replacements must be made in order to maintain the work force."

24. **The correct answer is C.** There is nothing in the passage to support answer choices A, B, or D. Choice C summarizes the ideas expressed in the quotation.

25. **The correct answer is A.** There is nothing in the passage to support answer choices B, C, or D. Choice A is clearly implied from the ideas expressed in the passage.

26. **The correct answer is B.** There is nothing in the quotation to support choices A, C, or D. Choice B is supported by ". . . the manufacturer assumes enormous risks in attempting to predict what consumers will want and in providing goods in quantity and distributing them in advance of final selection by the consumers."

27. **The correct answer is C.** According to the quotation, citizens who are selfish and act only as their private interests seem to require are not public spirited. Those who disregard others are concerned principally with their own selfish interests. Choice C is therefore the correct answer.

28. **The correct answer is C.** The passage conveys a correlation, not a definitive cause and effect, of entrepreneur investment in new space transportation systems. As such, the statement that entrepreneurs are driving research initiatives, choice A, is incorrect. Investors might look to the trends of entrepreneurs in financial choices, but this is not specifically supported by the passage, making choice B incorrect. The passage does not clearly specify that entrepreneurs or investors are directly supporting space research, making choice D incorrect.

29. **The correct answer is D.** The intent of the passage is to convey that some in the public are not aware of the distinction between the definition and role of hypotheses and scientific theory in research methods. Hypotheses are developed based on the research questions asked by researchers and scientists, and they drive data collection. Once data is collected and analyzed, theories are developed to describe the data and relationships. As such, scientific theory is founded in data, while hypotheses are a starting point for that process, making choices B and C incorrect. Choice A is incorrect because the passage does not support the statement that the "majority of the public" does not understand scientific theory.

30. **The correct answer is B.** The passage refers to the legal challenge by the Federal Bureau of Investigation (FBI) to compel Apple Inc. to decrypt the cell phone data of a suspected terrorist in 2016. Choice A is not supported by the passage, as the quote does not directly specify that law enforcement is questioning the need for the private sector to use encryption for data. Choice C is not supported by the passage, as the quote does not indicate that cell phone manufacturers are in direct conflict with national security objectives. Although encryption may be challenging for law enforcement to crack, it is not a direct threat to national security, making choice D incorrect.

answers practice test

Part 3: Mechanical Comprehension Test (MCT)

1. C	**7.** A	**13.** C	**19.** C	**25.** C
2. A	**8.** B	**14.** C	**20.** B	**26.** C
3. A	**9.** C	**15.** B	**21.** A	**27.** A
4. C	**10.** C	**16.** B	**22.** C	**28.** C
5. C	**11.** C	**17.** C	**23.** C	**29.** A
6. A	**12.** B	**18.** A	**24.** B	**30.** B

1. **The correct answer is C.** The volume of water flowing at points 1, 2, and 3 must be the same because of the conservation of mass: mass in = mass out. Also, since no water is added or removed after point 1, there cannot be any change of volume.

2. **The correct answer is A.** If nut A were removed, it would be necessary to move nut C to the right to counterbalance the loss of the weight of nut A.

3. **The correct answer is A.** No electricity flows through a burned-out bulb. However, the voltmeter acts as a bypass around the burned-out bulb and is therefore connected in series. It measures all of the voltage in the circuit. The voltage is 600 volts.

4. **The correct answer is C.** The circumference of the wheel is 24". One complete revolution will raise W2 24" and lower W1 24", a difference of 48".

5. **The correct answer is C.** The vertical component of the momentum of the ball is zero only at position C.

6. **The correct answer is A.** Pulley A has the largest circumference. In the arrangement shown, pulley A turns slowest.

7. **The correct answer is A.** Let x = theoretical distance moved in the opposite direction.

   $10 \times 150 = x \times 600$; $600x = 1,500$;

   $x = \dfrac{1,500}{600} = 2\dfrac{1}{2}$ feet.

8. **The correct answer is B.** Note that with each complete turn of the cam, the setscrew will hit the contact point once.

9. **The correct answer is C.** The pressure is uniform in the system given. If the main line air gauge reads 150 pounds, the tank air gauge will also read 150 pounds.

10. **The correct answer is C.** As brace C has the greatest area support, it is the most secure.

11. **The correct answer is C.** The greater the pressure outside the balloon, the less expansion within the balloon; the less pressure, the greater the expansion.

12. **The correct answer is B.** When two external gears mesh, they rotate in opposite directions. To avoid this, an idler gear is put between the driver gear and the driven gear.

13. **The correct answer is C.** The tank would overflow only if water flows through the intake pipe at a faster, not slower, rate. The water in the tank would remain at a constant level if rate of intake is equal to rate of discharge. The tank cannot empty completely, as the discharge pipe is not located at the tank's bottom.

14. **The correct answer is C.** If the float in the tank develops a bad leak, it will fill with water and submerge. This will elevate the needle valve, causing it to remain in an open position.

15. **The correct answer is B.** The number of parts of the rope going to and from the movable block indicates a mechanical advantage of 2. Accordingly, a 100-lb. pull can lift, theoretically, a 200-lb. weight.

16. **The correct answer is B.** Note that 2 revolutions of the worm gear will turn the sector gear 20 degrees. Accordingly, one revolution of the worm gear will turn the sector gear through an angle of 10 degrees.

17. **The correct answer is C.** Let x = tipping force produced on the edge of the block. $80 \times 4 = 1 \times x$; $x = 320$ lbs.

18. **The correct answer is A.** Note that with each complete turn of the cam, the contacts come together twice. If the contacts come together 60 times a minute, the cam must be rotating at 30 rpm.

19. **The correct answer is C.** One complete turn of the drum crank will raise the rope 2' on the 2' portion of the drum and 1' on the 1' portion of the drum. The net result is vertical movement upward a distance of $1\frac{1}{2}$.

20. **The correct answer is B.** The theoretical mechanical advantage (TMA) of the pulley system is 2.

$$\text{TMA} = \frac{d_e}{d_R}$$
$$2 = \frac{30}{d_R} = 2d_R = 30$$
$$d_R = \frac{30}{2} = 15 \text{ feet}$$

21. **The correct answer is A.** Pulley 2 is a fixed pulley; Pulley 1 is a movable one. Both are of equal diameter. If the rope is pulled a distance equal to the circumference of pulley 2 (one full turn), pulley 1 would move up only half that distance, making only a half turn.

22. **The correct answer is C.** Twice per second = 120 times a minute. With 10 projection rods on the wheel, the wheel must rotate at 12 rpm (120/10 = 12) to make 120 rod contacts per minute.

23. **The correct answer is C.** Both wheels S and T have the same diameter. However, the driver wheel makes contact with Wheel T close to its center and makes contact with Wheel S very near its edge. Accordingly, Wheel T will rotate at a much faster speed than wheel S.

24. **The correct answer is B.** A $\frac{1}{4}$ turn is needed to get to the extreme left position and another $\frac{1}{4}$ turn is required to return to the mid-position.
$$\frac{1}{4} + \frac{1}{4} = \frac{1}{2}$$

25. **The correct answer is C.** By increasing the length of the level arm, the effort is increased, enabling the valve to blow off at a higher pressure.

26. **The correct answer is C.** In Case 2, each spring is supporting $2\frac{1}{2}$ pounds ($\frac{1}{2}$ of 5 pounds) and would extend a certain distance. In Case 1, each spring is supporting 5 pounds (the full weight) and would extend twice the distance of that for Case 2.

27. **The correct answer is A.** The reading is obtained as follows:

.2 (on the sleeve scale)
.025 (on the sleeve scale)
$\frac{.002}{.227}$ (on the thimble scale)

28. The correct answer is C. The hand wheel tightens to the left when rotated clockwise since it has a right-handed thread. If the hand wheel is turned 20 revolutions, it moves one inch to the left, pulling the threaded block one inch in the opposite direction (to the right).

29. The correct answer is A. If all three switches are closed to the left, the closed circuit would not include Lamp No. 2.

30. The correct answer is B. If switches No. 1 and No. 2 are closed to the right, and switch No. 3 is closed to the left, the closed circuit would not include Lamp No. 1.

Part 4: Aviation & Nautical Information Test (ANIT)

1. C	7. A	13. B	19. D	25. D
2. D	8. D	14. D	20. E	26. E
3. E	9. C	15. C	21. B	27. E
4. A	10. E	16. C	22. C	28. A
5. C	11. D	17. C	23. A	29. D
6. B	12. B	18. B	24. A	30. A

1. **The correct answer is C.** The F-18G is nicknamed Growler and is a replacement for the EA-6B Prowler. Know all tri-service aircraft designations (prefix status, modified mission, vehicle type, design number, and series letter), and be familiar with (at least) your service platform nicknames.

2. **The correct answer is D.** Lift is increased on the left wing and drag is increased on the right wing. During preflight, manipulating your rudder pedal and stick results in visible and anticipated changes to your control surfaces. Knowing instinctively how they move and how they manipulate your aerodynamic forces is fundamental. Know all structural parts of the aircraft and their function(s). Several question may pertain to aircraft components.

3. **The correct answer is E.** Trim tab direction of motion is the opposite as the desired aircraft up/down nose direction. Trim tab moving up pushes the nose down. Trim tab moving down pushes the nose up. Refer to the referenced FAA Chapter 5 within the description of this subtest in this chapter.

4. **The correct answer is A.** Increases in AOA moves the negative pressure area above the wing forward, resulting in eventual stalls at extreme AOA (characterized by the loss of aft control surfaces, ailerons, before full loss of lift). The feeling of stick shaking is caused by the loss of lift on your ailerons as the negative pressure zone (CP) moves forward and your ailerons hence become less responsive.

5. **The correct answer is C.** During a bank, lift becomes total lift and is split between a vertical and horizontal lift component. For example, in a level turn, the vertical lift component is equal to weight while the horizontal lift component is greater than weight. This is the "pulling" sensation (centrifugal force) as you pull yourself into a banked level turn. It is essential to understand all aspects of the aerodynamic components.

6. **The correct answer is B.** Altimeter settings for an area allow an approximation of true altitude and are affected by variances in pressure and temperature. For example, setting 29.92 as a standard above 10,000 feet results in all aircraft to fluctuate their true altitude relative to common pressure and temperature environmental factors at altitude. When clearing of obstacles listed on charts in AGL while relying on altimeter settings from a nearby weather station, you need to consider that the altimeter setting is only an approximation of your true altitude. This is one of the considerations when regulations establish distance buffers. Also, be sure you know the effects of temperature changes on pressure.

7. **The correct answer is A.** Each 00.01 = 10 feet, each 00.10 = 100 feet, and each 01.00 = 1,000 feet.

8. **The correct answer is D.** It is important to know all aspects of the ASI instrument that include the pitot static system and blockage indications.

9. **The correct answer is C.** Latitudes (N/S) are common units of measure, where 1 degree of latitude = approximately 60 nm, 1 minute (or 01.00) = 1 nm, 1 decimal minute (or 0.10) = approximately 600 feet, 0.01 = 60 feet, and 0.001 = 6 feet. Distances longitude (going E/W) are not uniform in distances due to converging lines of latitude near the poles. Understand map data, different types of charts, different scales associated with those different charts, and how to approximate distances. Remember that your guided munitions use the accuracy of your aircraft's position for initial guidance information and may not have time or the ballistics for an inflight update or correction.

10. **The correct answer is E.** This question requires an understanding of symbology and how it applies to you as a professional aviator. Be familiar with all airfield and taxiway symbols in airport directories and terminal publications. Also, know all symbols and indications for VFR charts. IFR chart symbols knowledge would be useful before flight school as well.

11. **The correct answer is D.** As with Question 10, knowing all symbology is vital. Knowing if an airfield is equipped with arresting gear is important so that you'll know to look out for any applicable notices to airmen (NOTAMs) as well as doing a visual check. You may need to touch down past the gear on that primary training session during your cross-country night flight. If you're not aware of such important symbols, and your backseat instructor doesn't catch your mistake, this may result in a mishap that you certainly don't want to occur.

12. **The correct answer is B.** Know all airspace, special use airspace, and parameters (dimensions, equipment requirements, airspeed limits, and day/night cloud clearances).

13. **The correct answer is B.** Know all ASI limits for differing airspace classes and flight corridors (not to be confused with military low-level routes).

14. **The correct answer is D.** Know all light gun signals relative to aircraft on the ground, in the pattern, and to non-aircraft moving about on the airfield. You will see questions from this throughout your career, and you might as well memorize and understand it now. You may have a radio problem (such as having the volume down or wrong presettings), or a problem may exist with the airport, and they may need you to repark for some reason.

15. **The correct answer is C.** Know the scales (and symbology) for terminal area, sectional, and world aeronautical charts. Be familiar with IFR charts and all symbology before flight school, but do not expect to see them on this test.

16. **The correct answer is C.** The outer walls of a ship form the hull, the main body of the ship below the main outside deck.

17. **The correct answer is C.** A ship's windlass is designed primarily for handling the anchor chain.

18. **The correct answer is B.** A nautical mile is equal to 1,852 meters, just a little more than 6,076 feet.

19. **The correct answer is D.** Know all jersey and helmet color designations. Also know that UI on the helmet indicates "Under Inspection" and signifies a person who is getting qualified for that position. Be familiar with which enlisted designations are also associated with jersey and helmet color combinations.

20. **The correct answer is E.** The 24-hour clock uses four digits. Hours and minutes less than 10 are preceded by a zero. 9:05 p.m. would be written as 2105.

21. **The correct answer is B.** They are generally 15° in width. $\frac{360}{15} = 24$ time zones.

22. **The correct answer is C.** The coordinates given indicate a position in the Gulf of Mexico.

23. **The correct answer is A.** A line drawn from the fix in the direction in which a ship is moving is called a course line, showing direction or course.

24. **The correct answer is A.** Soundings are used to measure depth of water by using a lead line or other means.

25. **The correct answer is D.** Increasing the weight of the load raises the waterline, decreasing the freeboard and increasing the draft.

26. **The correct answer is E.** Objects not established for the sole purpose of assisting a navigator in fixing a position are not considered to be an "aid to navigation."

27. **The correct answer is E.** Fog generally forms at night when warmer air moves over colder water.

28. **The correct answer is A.** Red is for port, green is starboard, white indicates in which direction a vessel is going, and yellow is for special circumstances.

29. **The correct answer is D.** The nun buoy is a conical-shaped buoy used to mark the right-hand side of a channel.

30. **The correct answer is A.** The heading of the ship causes water to push against the side of the rudder, creating a force that swings the stern of the ship to the opposite side. The faster the vessel is moving, the greater the pressure against the rudder and the quicker the turning effect.

Part 5: Naval Aviation Trait Facet Inventory (NATFI)

No practice section or answers to this section exist.

Part 6: Performance Based Measures Battery (PBM)

Part 6.1: Unmanned Aerial Vehicle (UAV) Test

1. D	**7.** E	**13.** B	**19.** A	**25.** B
2. E	**8.** A	**14.** A	**20.** C	**26.** C
3. C	**9.** C	**15.** E	**21.** D	**27.** A
4. A	**10.** D	**16.** E	**22.** C	**28.** E
5. C	**11.** C	**17.** C	**23.** B	**29.** B
6. D	**12.** C	**18.** B	**24.** C	**30.** B

1. **The correct answer is D.** The area of interest is at your 6 o'clock, zone 7.

2. **The correct answer is E.** The area of interest is between your 6 and 3 o'clock, zone 8.

3. **The correct answer is C.** The area of interest is at your 3 o'clock, zone 4.

4. **The correct answer is A.** The area of interest is at your 12 o'clock, zone 2.

5. **The correct answer is C.** The area of interest is between your 12 and 3 o'clock, zone 3

6. **The correct answer is D.** The area of interest is at your 6 o'clock, zone 7.

7. **The correct answer is E.** The area of interest is between your 3 and 6 o'clock, zone 8.

8. **The correct answer is A.** The area of interest is at your 12 o'clock, zone 2

9. **The correct answer is C.** The area of interest is at your 3 o'clock, zone 5.

10. **The correct answer is D.** The area of interest is between your 6 and 9 o'clock, zone 6.

11. **The correct answer is C.** The area of interest is between your 6 and 9 o'clock, zone 6.

12. **The correct answer is C.** The area of interest is at your 9 o'clock, zone 4.

13. **The correct answer is B.** The area of interest is between your 12 and 3 o'clock, zone 3.

14. **The correct answer is A.** The area of interest is at your 12 o'clock, zone 2.

15. **The correct answer is E.** The area of interest is at your 12 and 3 o'clock, zone 8.

16. **The correct answer is E.** The area of interest is between your 6 and 3 o'clock, zone 8.

17. **The correct answer is C.** The area of interest is at your 3 o'clock, zone 5.

18. **The correct answer is B.** The area of interest is between your 12 and 3 o'clock, zone 3.

19. **The correct answer is A.** The area of interest is between your 12 and 9 o'clock, zone 1.

20. **The correct answer is C.** The area of interest is at your 9 o'clock, zone 4.

21. **The correct answer is D.** The area of interest is at your 6 o'clock, zone 7.

22. **The correct answer is C.** The area of interest is as your 9 o'clock, zone 4.

23. **The correct answer is B.** The area of interest is between your 12 and 3 o'clock, zone 3.

24. **The correct answer is C.** The area of interest is between your 6 and 9 o'clock, zone 6.

25. **The correct answer is B.** The area of interest is at your 12 o'clock, zone 2.

26. **The correct answer is C.** The area of interest is between your 6 and 9 o'clock, zone 6.

27. **The correct answer is A.** The area of interest is between your 12 and 9 o'clock, zone 1.

28. **The correct answer is E.** The area of interest is between your 3 and 6 o'clock, zone 8.

29. **The correct answer is B.** The area of interest is at your 9 o'clock, zone 4.

30. **The correct answer is B.** The area of interest is between your 12 and 3 o'clock, zone 3.

Part 6.2: Dichotic Listening Test (DLT)

No practice section or answers to this section exist. Please refer to the discussion on the DLT in this chapter.

Part 6.3 to Part 6.7: ATT, VTT, AHTT, AVDLT, and EST

No practice test or answers to these sections exist. Strategies and recommendations are limited to the discussion for each section within this chapter.

Examinees wishing to prepare for the Performance Based Measures Battery may find it useful to practice solving mental rotation problems, as well as practice using flight simulator software with a stick-and-throttle set.

Part 7: Biographical Inventory with Response Verification (BI-RV)

Answers are respondent dependent. There are no correct or incorrect answers.

SUMMING IT UP

The Aviation Selection Test Battery (ASTB-E) is the exam used by U.S. Navy, Marine Corps, and Coast Guard to select candidates for pilot and flight officer training programs.

- Three sections of the ASTB-E (those that determine an examinee's OAR score) are administered both on paper and via the APEX system, but the balance of the test is administered only on the APEX system. Because the tests administered on the APEX system are computer adaptive, the number of questions and the test duration can vary from 2 to 2 hours and 15 minutes.

- The ASTB-E is divided into the following seven subtests:

    1. Math Skills Test
    2. Reading Comprehension Test
    3. Mechanical Comprehension Test
    4. Aviation & Nautical Information Test (ANIT)
    5. Naval Aviation Trait Facet Inventory (NATFI)

- Performance Based Measures Battery (PBM) The PBM consists of the following subtests:
    ○ Unmanned Aerial Vehicle (UAV) Test
    ○ Dichotic Listening Test (DLT)
    ○ Airplane Tracking Test (ATT)
    ○ Vertical Tracking Test (VTT)
    ○ Airplane Tracking and Horizontal Tracking Test (AHTT)
    ○ Airplane Tracking, Vertical Tracking, and Dichotic Listening Test (AVDLT)
    ○ Emergency Scenario Test (EST)

- Biographic Inventory with Response Validation (BI-RV)

Army Selection Instrument for Flight Training (SIFT)

Chapter 6

OVERVIEW

- **SIFT Basics**
- **Test Section Descriptions and Strategies**
- **SIFT Answer Sheet**
- **SIFT Practice Test**
- **SIFT Answer Keys and Explanations**
- **Summing It Up**

SIFT BASICS

The **Army Selection Instrument for Flight Training (SIFT)** is composed of seven subtests and includes one 15-minute break (see Table 6.1). The SIFT is given only on a networked system administered by an Army ROTC, MEPS, Academy, or post-servicing education center. The SIFT takes between two and three hours to complete, depending on the length of time a candidate spends on the adaptive portions of the test.

Scores from the seven subtests are standardized relative to your peers who have taken the test within a designated period of time (12 months is used for the USAF and USN). Your overall performance across all seven categories is then ranked relative to your peers on a 20- to 80-point scale, where 50 is the average score of all those measured for that period of time. As reported by the Army Recruiting Command, the current minimum SIFT score required for consideration for flight school is 40 (subject to change). However, the minimum eligible score is *not* a competitive score. Unlike other service flight tests that can be retaken to attempt to gain a higher score, the SIFT cannot be retaken once you've earned an eligible score. If you do not attain a minimum passing score the first time, the SIFT can be taken a second time only after a minimum 180-day wait. If you do not attain a minimum qualifying score on your second attempt, you cannot retake the SIFT and do not qualify for the Army's Aviation Program.

Selection for the Army's Aviation Program includes a number of factors, and a competitive score is relative to the number of available flight training positions and how well your scores rank among your peers. Flight school selection begins with the highest-ranked person among the pool of candidates until all available slots are filled. Cutting corners and shooting for the minimum score are not effective approaches to getting selected.

The seven SIFT subtests are differentiated into three differing types of tests: **psychometric** (SD and HF), **standardized** (AAIT, SAT and RCT), and **adaptive** (MST and MCT), as shown in Table 6.1.

Table 6.1

Subtest Composition			
Subtest/Activity	**Questions**	**Minutes**	**Interface/Scoring**
Simple Drawings (SD)	100	2	Psychometric Performance Score
Hidden Figures (HF)	50	5	Psychometric Performance Score
Army Aviation Information Test (AAIT)	40	30	Standardized Raw Score
Break		*15*	
Spatial Apperception Test (SAT)	25	10	Standardized Raw Score
Reading Comprehension Test (RCT)	20	30	Standardized Raw Score
Math Skills Test (MST)	Variable Length (est. 20–40)	Up to 40	Adaptive
Mechanical Comprehension Test (MCT)	Variable Length (est. 20–30)	Up to 15	Adaptive

The two psychometric subtests measure accuracy and speed in generating a **precision score.** The precision score is a composite from your total/raw score (number of questions attempted), work rate/speed score (number attempted versus total number of questions), and a hit rate/accuracy score (number of correct responses divided by the number attempted). While unanswered questions do not count against a candidate's score, a portion of the number of problems answered *incorrectly* is deducted from the score; so while guessing may increase your speed score, it will most likely decrease your accuracy score and lower your overall precision score.

The three subtests that use standardized raw scores (AAIT, SAT, and RCT) are knowledge-based measures. A raw score is simply the number of correct answers given versus the total number of questions on the test. Unlike precision scoring, unanswered questions will negatively impact your score. Using a best-guess strategy and NOT leaving any unanswered questions is a viable technique for these three subtests.

The adaptive subtests (MST and MCT) use a question bank in which questions have been divided into categories such as easy, average, and difficult. Upon submission of your answer, the computer scores your response and the result will determine the difficulty level of the next question. Correct answers will increase the difficulty level toward the maximum difficulty subgroup and keep questions within that pool as long as responses are correct. Incorrect responses will lower the difficulty level of the next question. In addition, based on the number of correct versus incorrect responses, the length of the test (number of questions) is reduced or increased until a certain number of points is reached. The SIFT appears to attribute a set point value to each question and terminates the test once a preset total value is reached. Higher raw scores are associated with a lower number of questions, while lower scores are characterized by more questions. The longer you take to answer a question, the lower the value of a correct response. In contrast with the three raw-scored subtests, complete random guessing is NOT a viable strategy. Use informed guessing as needed, but focus on precise answers. Accuracy is vital but not at the expense of excessive time usage per question. The ONLY viable strategy for adaptive testing is to be comfortable and fluent with the material. To optimize your adaptive test performance, prepare for a subtest as if you are the subject-matter expert and need to teach it to others.

Use these strategies for all SIFT subtest types:

Before test day:

- Pay attention to the practice questions so that you can later focus on the questions and not the format.

- Use a timer during all practice tests to adapt to the added anxiety of a time limit.

- Use all available information to practice for each subtest. For example, Peterson's Publishing has an entire book dedicated to mechanical comprehension, *Master the™ Mechanical Aptitude and Spatial Relations Test*.

On test day:

- Use the sheet of formulas and the scratch paper (provided by the SIFT administrator) and familiarize yourself with which formulas are provided before the test starts.
    - When allowed by the administrator, briefly use the scratch paper to jot down anything that may help you but not at the expense of losing time during one of the subtests.

Your flight missions will require detailed mission planning. Taking the SIFT is no different. Your score, relative to your peers, will be a factor in flight school selection and will affect your option to choose which platform you want to fly and your follow-on assignment. If you are going to invest your time in doing something, take pride in yourself by doing it right the first time.

TEST SECTION DESCRIPTIONS AND STRATEGIES

Simple Drawings (SD)

The Simple Drawings (SD) subtest is a spatial reasoning test of speed and accuracy in comparing shapes. Each question has five shapes labeled A to E, and one of the shapes is not like the others. The shapes will appear in 2D and 3D and, in some instances, the difference will be in the shading of the shapes; however, expect only two shades of light and dark. You will have 2 minutes to answer 100 questions, which breaks down to approximately 0.8 seconds per question. You are scored relative to your accuracy (the number correct versus incorrect) and time (the number answered versus unanswered). Incorrect answers (that is, guessing) will hurt you for this subtest. Two strategies are available to you. The primary technique is to train your eyes to look at all five shapes simultaneously (instead of sequentially) and identify the one that is different. Split seconds count, so your hands need to be positioned on the selection keys (or mouse) so you never need to take your eyes from the screen. With some practice and thought, there is no reason to not max out available points on this subtest. Every point counts! It is possible that your eyes could get fatigued, causing you to question yourself. This is where the secondary technique comes in handy. If the odd shape (or shade) does not jump out, work from left to right. Is the second shape different from the first? Is the third different from the first two? Continue working through the shapes. Remember, 0.8 seconds for each question translates to you actually needing to spend half a second on each, since you also need to electronically record your selection. Questions in the practice subtest will include progressively more difficult options to challenge you. Mastering the practice subtest will help you succeed on the actual subtest. Keep in mind though, that the more often you repeat this subtest, the more you will recognize and anticipate, instead of react to, question strings. Because this is an abstract test, putting time and effort in other areas between practice runs may help reduce practice bias.

Hidden Figures (HF)

The Hidden Figures (HF) subtest is designed to assess your ability to quickly identify shapes in a complex visual environment. These are essential skills for aircrews who may need to scan the environment at rapid speeds to identify landmarks for navigation, hazards, targets, and other features. In the Hidden Figures subtest, there are fifty questions to complete in 5 minutes. There are a total of fifty shapes to locate in fifty unique diagrams; however, these shapes are given to you in blocks of five. For each block of five questions, you will search for one of five shapes presented at the top of the page. Within the five diagrams, you may find each of the shapes once, but some of the shapes may be in more than one diagram. The practice test presented in this book contains challenging diagrams. It is likely that the diagrams on the actual SIFT subtest will not be as difficult due to the time constraints of the test. If you successfully master the practice test, you should perform well on the actual exam.

Army Aviation Information Test (AAIT)

The Army Aviation Information Test (AAIT) assesses your knowledge of aerodynamics and performance (approximately 40 percent of the questions), rotary-wing aircraft components and controls (approximately 40 percent of the questions), and rotary-wing maneuvers and performance (approximately 10 percent of the questions), and a general category (approximately 10 percent of the questions). The general category questions assess your knowledge of center of gravity, navigation, instrumentation, and basic Army aircraft designations (what each part of the designation means); platform purpose, and types of engines on each type of aircraft.

Since its implementation in 2013, the number of questions in the AAIT subtest has doubled from 20 to 40, indicating an increased reliance on this section as a success predictor and a focus area of flight training instructor feedback. The test is generated from a test bank, and the questions assess the categories listed above. It is not good enough to know the answer to the question in this practice subtest; you also need to know the entire body of information from which the question came. In addition to knowing the information, you need to apply it. Ask yourself why something is the way it is and how that applies to you as a professional aviator. If you consider the new knowledge as having a relevant purpose, then you will retain it in your long-term memory more easily. Also, when studying a category, approach it as if you are going to teach it to others. Doing so will increase your practical absorption of the information. Describe the material to your fictitious students as to why something is important for them to know and then all the details about that something. You will be doing this prior to your flights (from memory) in explaining widgets, processes, and maneuvers to your instructor before you go out and demonstrate your application of that knowledge. Getting in the habit of teaching yourself will be a bonus for you later.

To prepare for the AAIT, refer to the equivalent Aviation Information test in the AFOQT (see Chapter 4) and the ASTB-E (see Chapter 5). Be aware that half of the questions in the similar subtest in Chapter 5 relate to surface ship operations and will obviously not apply. In addition, three critical online references are available and do a great job describing everything you need to know. The first is the FAA *Helicopter Flying Handbook*. This is an excellent resource that your tax dollars already paid for.

GET THE FACTS

To learn more about the FAA *Helicopter Flying Handbook*, visit the following website:

**https://www.faa.gov/regulations_policies/handbooks_manuals/aviation/
helicopter_flying_handbook/**

Next is a series of FAA handbooks and manuals on various aviation areas, such as aerodynamics. As with the all-inclusive helicopter handbook, these chapters do an excellent job illustrating and identifying critically important information categories. In addition, this page of resources includes links to the most up-to-date versions of the FAA's *Aeronautical Information Manual* and the *Pilot's Handbook of Aeronautical Knowledge*.

GET THE FACTS

To learn more about the various aviation areas, visit the following website:

http://www.faa.gov/regulations_policies/handbooks_manuals/aviation/

Last, but not least, the *United States Army Fundamentals of Flight Manual* is critical. While the FAA documents will help you grasp the information and ideas behind that information, the *Fundamentals of the Army Flight Manual* is needed to translate how that information applies to you. Eighty percent of the AAIT subtest will come from this manual; however, the information will be difficult to absorb if you do not first use the FAA resources. This book is available at retail bookstores, but you should contact an Army recruiter or training officer to ask about availability of a free electronic version.

Spatial Apperception Test (SAT)

The Spatial Apperception Test (SAT) assesses your ability to understand how the view from a cockpit corresponds to an aircraft's position and to perceive aircraft in three-dimensional space. The test presents a series of images of a coastline from the vantage point of looking forward in an aircraft cockpit. (Although in an actual aircraft you would rely solely on your instruments to validate your position, for this test assume you are strapped in your seat and look forward.) Pictures of the aircraft are assumed to be at the same altitude as the view. Substitute the missing artificial horizon for the general skyline, taking into account that the waterline will be more accurate than the more rugged dark land to sky line. You need to determine your angle of bank within 30 degrees. You also need to determine your heading within 30 degrees. Determine your relative heading in relation to the coastline. Use the AFOQT Form T Instrument Comprehension subtest (see Chapter 4) to challenge your self-orientation in preparation for this different type of orientation. Using a modified recovery from unusual altitude aerobatic technique, use the following flow constantly and every time in both orienting yourself relative to the picture:

1. Identify your general nose attitude relative to the horizon. (e.g., "I am slightly/severely nose high/low.")

2. Identify your bank and remember you need to estimate down to 30 degrees of bank. (e.g., "I am in a left/right bank by 30/60/90 degrees.")

3. Orient your heading relative to the shoreline down to 30 degrees. (e.g., I am headed 30/60/90 in/out towards the sea/land.")

Use the very same flow to identify the right and wrong choices. DO NOT go with the first panel that appears correct. Because the SIFT version includes +/– 30° requirements, you will be deceived if you do not scan all four choices. You will have 24 seconds per question to include physically clicking on the correct choice (25 questions over 10 minutes). There is no reason to not maximize your points on this subtest.

Reading Comprehension Test (RCT)

The Reading Comprehension Test (RCT) is an evaluation of reading level and vocabulary knowledge needed to comprehend technical writing, also known as academic writing. No knowledge of the subject matter is needed to answer the single question relative to each short passage. The common question types include:

- Identification of the primary purpose of the passage
- Determination of whether a particular statement is supported by the passage
- Recollection of the applied meaning of a term or phrase within the passage

This reading comprehension test is focused on rapid comprehension of a short passage and quick analysis to answer a single question. See Chapter 3 for more in-depth practice exercises related to this skill.

Math Skills Test (MST)

The Math Skills Test (MST) is an evaluation of college-level mathematical terms and principles. See Chapters 3, 4, and 5 for additional questions to practice these skills.

Mechanical Comprehension Test (MCT)

The Mechanical Comprehension Test (MCT) tests your knowledge of basic physics, electrical, and mechanical theories. Questions focus on topics such as force, friction, current, fluid, pressure, pulleys, gears, screws, engines, and other machine operations. Physics, basic electronics, and mechanics courses will well prepare you for the questions in this section. For refresher references, see Peterson's *Master the Mechanical Aptitude and Spatial Relations Test*.

Now it's time to take the SIFT practice test.

SIFT ANSWER SHEET

Subtest 1: Simple Drawings (SD)

1. Ⓐ Ⓑ Ⓒ Ⓓ Ⓔ   23. Ⓐ Ⓑ Ⓒ Ⓓ Ⓔ   45. Ⓐ Ⓑ Ⓒ Ⓓ Ⓔ   67. Ⓐ Ⓑ Ⓒ Ⓓ Ⓔ   90. Ⓐ Ⓑ Ⓒ Ⓓ Ⓔ
2. Ⓐ Ⓑ Ⓒ Ⓓ Ⓔ   24. Ⓐ Ⓑ Ⓒ Ⓓ Ⓔ   46. Ⓐ Ⓑ Ⓒ Ⓓ Ⓔ   68. Ⓐ Ⓑ Ⓒ Ⓓ Ⓔ   91. Ⓐ Ⓑ Ⓒ Ⓓ Ⓔ
3. Ⓐ Ⓑ Ⓒ Ⓓ Ⓔ   25. Ⓐ Ⓑ Ⓒ Ⓓ Ⓔ   47. Ⓐ Ⓑ Ⓒ Ⓓ Ⓔ   69. Ⓐ Ⓑ Ⓒ Ⓓ Ⓔ   92. Ⓐ Ⓑ Ⓒ Ⓓ Ⓔ
4. Ⓐ Ⓑ Ⓒ Ⓓ Ⓔ   26. Ⓐ Ⓑ Ⓒ Ⓓ Ⓔ   48. Ⓐ Ⓑ Ⓒ Ⓓ Ⓔ   70. Ⓐ Ⓑ Ⓒ Ⓓ Ⓔ   93. Ⓐ Ⓑ Ⓒ Ⓓ Ⓔ
5. Ⓐ Ⓑ Ⓒ Ⓓ Ⓔ   27. Ⓐ Ⓑ Ⓒ Ⓓ Ⓔ   49. Ⓐ Ⓑ Ⓒ Ⓓ Ⓔ   71. Ⓐ Ⓑ Ⓒ Ⓓ Ⓔ   94. Ⓐ Ⓑ Ⓒ Ⓓ Ⓔ
6. Ⓐ Ⓑ Ⓒ Ⓓ Ⓔ   28. Ⓐ Ⓑ Ⓒ Ⓓ Ⓔ   50. Ⓐ Ⓑ Ⓒ Ⓓ Ⓔ   73. Ⓐ Ⓑ Ⓒ Ⓓ Ⓔ   95. Ⓐ Ⓑ Ⓒ Ⓓ Ⓔ
7. Ⓐ Ⓑ Ⓒ Ⓓ Ⓔ   29. Ⓐ Ⓑ Ⓒ Ⓓ Ⓔ   51. Ⓐ Ⓑ Ⓒ Ⓓ Ⓔ   74. Ⓐ Ⓑ Ⓒ Ⓓ Ⓔ   96. Ⓐ Ⓑ Ⓒ Ⓓ Ⓔ
8. Ⓐ Ⓑ Ⓒ Ⓓ Ⓔ   30. Ⓐ Ⓑ Ⓒ Ⓓ Ⓔ   52. Ⓐ Ⓑ Ⓒ Ⓓ Ⓔ   75. Ⓐ Ⓑ Ⓒ Ⓓ Ⓔ   97. Ⓐ Ⓑ Ⓒ Ⓓ Ⓔ
9. Ⓐ Ⓑ Ⓒ Ⓓ Ⓔ   31. Ⓐ Ⓑ Ⓒ Ⓓ Ⓔ   53. Ⓐ Ⓑ Ⓒ Ⓓ Ⓔ   76. Ⓐ Ⓑ Ⓒ Ⓓ Ⓔ   98. Ⓐ Ⓑ Ⓒ Ⓓ Ⓔ
10. Ⓐ Ⓑ Ⓒ Ⓓ Ⓔ   32. Ⓐ Ⓑ Ⓒ Ⓓ Ⓔ   54. Ⓐ Ⓑ Ⓒ Ⓓ Ⓔ   77. Ⓐ Ⓑ Ⓒ Ⓓ Ⓔ   99. Ⓐ Ⓑ Ⓒ Ⓓ Ⓔ
11. Ⓐ Ⓑ Ⓒ Ⓓ Ⓔ   33. Ⓐ Ⓑ Ⓒ Ⓓ Ⓔ   55. Ⓐ Ⓑ Ⓒ Ⓓ Ⓔ   78. Ⓐ Ⓑ Ⓒ Ⓓ Ⓔ   100. Ⓐ Ⓑ Ⓒ Ⓓ Ⓔ

Subtest 2: Hidden Figures (HF)

1. Ⓐ Ⓑ Ⓒ Ⓓ Ⓔ   11. Ⓐ Ⓑ Ⓒ Ⓓ Ⓔ   21. Ⓐ Ⓑ Ⓒ Ⓓ Ⓔ   31. Ⓐ Ⓑ Ⓒ Ⓓ Ⓔ   41. Ⓐ Ⓑ Ⓒ Ⓓ Ⓔ
2. Ⓐ Ⓑ Ⓒ Ⓓ Ⓔ   12. Ⓐ Ⓑ Ⓒ Ⓓ Ⓔ   22. Ⓐ Ⓑ Ⓒ Ⓓ Ⓔ   32. Ⓐ Ⓑ Ⓒ Ⓓ Ⓔ   42. Ⓐ Ⓑ Ⓒ Ⓓ Ⓔ
3. Ⓐ Ⓑ Ⓒ Ⓓ Ⓔ   13. Ⓐ Ⓑ Ⓒ Ⓓ Ⓔ   23. Ⓐ Ⓑ Ⓒ Ⓓ Ⓔ   33. Ⓐ Ⓑ Ⓒ Ⓓ Ⓔ   43. Ⓐ Ⓑ Ⓒ Ⓓ Ⓔ
4. Ⓐ Ⓑ Ⓒ Ⓓ Ⓔ   14. Ⓐ Ⓑ Ⓒ Ⓓ Ⓔ   24. Ⓐ Ⓑ Ⓒ Ⓓ Ⓔ   34. Ⓐ Ⓑ Ⓒ Ⓓ Ⓔ   44. Ⓐ Ⓑ Ⓒ Ⓓ Ⓔ
5. Ⓐ Ⓑ Ⓒ Ⓓ Ⓔ   15. Ⓐ Ⓑ Ⓒ Ⓓ Ⓔ   25. Ⓐ Ⓑ Ⓒ Ⓓ Ⓔ   35. Ⓐ Ⓑ Ⓒ Ⓓ Ⓔ   45. Ⓐ Ⓑ Ⓒ Ⓓ Ⓔ
6. Ⓐ Ⓑ Ⓒ Ⓓ Ⓔ   16. Ⓐ Ⓑ Ⓒ Ⓓ Ⓔ   26. Ⓐ Ⓑ Ⓒ Ⓓ Ⓔ   36. Ⓐ Ⓑ Ⓒ Ⓓ Ⓔ   46. Ⓐ Ⓑ Ⓒ Ⓓ Ⓔ
7. Ⓐ Ⓑ Ⓒ Ⓓ Ⓔ   17. Ⓐ Ⓑ Ⓒ Ⓓ Ⓔ   27. Ⓐ Ⓑ Ⓒ Ⓓ Ⓔ   37. Ⓐ Ⓑ Ⓒ Ⓓ Ⓔ   47. Ⓐ Ⓑ Ⓒ Ⓓ Ⓔ
8. Ⓐ Ⓑ Ⓒ Ⓓ Ⓔ   18. Ⓐ Ⓑ Ⓒ Ⓓ Ⓔ   28. Ⓐ Ⓑ Ⓒ Ⓓ Ⓔ   38. Ⓐ Ⓑ Ⓒ Ⓓ Ⓔ   48. Ⓐ Ⓑ Ⓒ Ⓓ Ⓔ
9. Ⓐ Ⓑ Ⓒ Ⓓ Ⓔ   19. Ⓐ Ⓑ Ⓒ Ⓓ Ⓔ   29. Ⓐ Ⓑ Ⓒ Ⓓ Ⓔ   39. Ⓐ Ⓑ Ⓒ Ⓓ Ⓔ   49. Ⓐ Ⓑ Ⓒ Ⓓ Ⓔ
10. Ⓐ Ⓑ Ⓒ Ⓓ Ⓔ   20. Ⓐ Ⓑ Ⓒ Ⓓ Ⓔ   30. Ⓐ Ⓑ Ⓒ Ⓓ Ⓔ   40. Ⓐ Ⓑ Ⓒ Ⓓ Ⓔ   50. Ⓐ Ⓑ Ⓒ Ⓓ Ⓔ

Subtest 3: Army Aviation Information Test (AAIT)

1. Ⓐ Ⓑ Ⓒ Ⓓ Ⓔ	9. Ⓐ Ⓑ Ⓒ Ⓓ Ⓔ	17. Ⓐ Ⓑ Ⓒ Ⓓ Ⓔ	25. Ⓐ Ⓑ Ⓒ Ⓓ Ⓔ	33. Ⓐ Ⓑ Ⓒ Ⓓ Ⓔ
2. Ⓐ Ⓑ Ⓒ Ⓓ Ⓔ	10. Ⓐ Ⓑ Ⓒ Ⓓ Ⓔ	18. Ⓐ Ⓑ Ⓒ Ⓓ Ⓔ	26. Ⓐ Ⓑ Ⓒ Ⓓ Ⓔ	34. Ⓐ Ⓑ Ⓒ Ⓓ Ⓔ
3. Ⓐ Ⓑ Ⓒ Ⓓ Ⓔ	11. Ⓐ Ⓑ Ⓒ Ⓓ Ⓔ	19. Ⓐ Ⓑ Ⓒ Ⓓ Ⓔ	27. Ⓐ Ⓑ Ⓒ Ⓓ Ⓔ	35. Ⓐ Ⓑ Ⓒ Ⓓ Ⓔ
4. Ⓐ Ⓑ Ⓒ Ⓓ Ⓔ	12. Ⓐ Ⓑ Ⓒ Ⓓ Ⓔ	20. Ⓐ Ⓑ Ⓒ Ⓓ Ⓔ	28. Ⓐ Ⓑ Ⓒ Ⓓ Ⓔ	36. Ⓐ Ⓑ Ⓒ Ⓓ Ⓔ
5. Ⓐ Ⓑ Ⓒ Ⓓ Ⓔ	13. Ⓐ Ⓑ Ⓒ Ⓓ Ⓔ	21. Ⓐ Ⓑ Ⓒ Ⓓ Ⓔ	29. Ⓐ Ⓑ Ⓒ Ⓓ Ⓔ	37. Ⓐ Ⓑ Ⓒ Ⓓ Ⓔ
6. Ⓐ Ⓑ Ⓒ Ⓓ Ⓔ	14. Ⓐ Ⓑ Ⓒ Ⓓ Ⓔ	22. Ⓐ Ⓑ Ⓒ Ⓓ Ⓔ	30. Ⓐ Ⓑ Ⓒ Ⓓ Ⓔ	38. Ⓐ Ⓑ Ⓒ Ⓓ Ⓔ
7. Ⓐ Ⓑ Ⓒ Ⓓ Ⓔ	15. Ⓐ Ⓑ Ⓒ Ⓓ Ⓔ	23. Ⓐ Ⓑ Ⓒ Ⓓ Ⓔ	31. Ⓐ Ⓑ Ⓒ Ⓓ Ⓔ	39. Ⓐ Ⓑ Ⓒ Ⓓ Ⓔ
8. Ⓐ Ⓑ Ⓒ Ⓓ Ⓔ	16. Ⓐ Ⓑ Ⓒ Ⓓ Ⓔ	24. Ⓐ Ⓑ Ⓒ Ⓓ Ⓔ	32. Ⓐ Ⓑ Ⓒ Ⓓ Ⓔ	40. Ⓐ Ⓑ Ⓒ Ⓓ Ⓔ

Subtest 4: Spatial Apperception Test (SAT)

1. Ⓐ Ⓑ Ⓒ Ⓓ Ⓔ	6. Ⓐ Ⓑ Ⓒ Ⓓ Ⓔ	11. Ⓐ Ⓑ Ⓒ Ⓓ Ⓔ	16. Ⓐ Ⓑ Ⓒ Ⓓ Ⓔ	21. Ⓐ Ⓑ Ⓒ Ⓓ Ⓔ
2. Ⓐ Ⓑ Ⓒ Ⓓ Ⓔ	7. Ⓐ Ⓑ Ⓒ Ⓓ Ⓔ	12. Ⓐ Ⓑ Ⓒ Ⓓ Ⓔ	17. Ⓐ Ⓑ Ⓒ Ⓓ Ⓔ	22. Ⓐ Ⓑ Ⓒ Ⓓ Ⓔ
3. Ⓐ Ⓑ Ⓒ Ⓓ Ⓔ	8. Ⓐ Ⓑ Ⓒ Ⓓ Ⓔ	13. Ⓐ Ⓑ Ⓒ Ⓓ Ⓔ	18. Ⓐ Ⓑ Ⓒ Ⓓ Ⓔ	23. Ⓐ Ⓑ Ⓒ Ⓓ Ⓔ
4. Ⓐ Ⓑ Ⓒ Ⓓ Ⓔ	9. Ⓐ Ⓑ Ⓒ Ⓓ Ⓔ	14. Ⓐ Ⓑ Ⓒ Ⓓ Ⓔ	19. Ⓐ Ⓑ Ⓒ Ⓓ Ⓔ	24. Ⓐ Ⓑ Ⓒ Ⓓ Ⓔ
5. Ⓐ Ⓑ Ⓒ Ⓓ Ⓔ	10. Ⓐ Ⓑ Ⓒ Ⓓ Ⓔ	15. Ⓐ Ⓑ Ⓒ Ⓓ Ⓔ	20. Ⓐ Ⓑ Ⓒ Ⓓ Ⓔ	25. Ⓐ Ⓑ Ⓒ Ⓓ Ⓔ

Subtest 5: Reading Comprehension Test (RCT)

1. Ⓐ Ⓑ Ⓒ Ⓓ Ⓔ	5. Ⓐ Ⓑ Ⓒ Ⓓ Ⓔ	9. Ⓐ Ⓑ Ⓒ Ⓓ Ⓔ	13. Ⓐ Ⓑ Ⓒ Ⓓ Ⓔ	17. Ⓐ Ⓑ Ⓒ Ⓓ Ⓔ
2. Ⓐ Ⓑ Ⓒ Ⓓ Ⓔ	6. Ⓐ Ⓑ Ⓒ Ⓓ Ⓔ	10. Ⓐ Ⓑ Ⓒ Ⓓ Ⓔ	14. Ⓐ Ⓑ Ⓒ Ⓓ Ⓔ	18. Ⓐ Ⓑ Ⓒ Ⓓ Ⓔ
3. Ⓐ Ⓑ Ⓒ Ⓓ Ⓔ	7. Ⓐ Ⓑ Ⓒ Ⓓ Ⓔ	11. Ⓐ Ⓑ Ⓒ Ⓓ Ⓔ	15. Ⓐ Ⓑ Ⓒ Ⓓ Ⓔ	19. Ⓐ Ⓑ Ⓒ Ⓓ Ⓔ
4. Ⓐ Ⓑ Ⓒ Ⓓ Ⓔ	8. Ⓐ Ⓑ Ⓒ Ⓓ Ⓔ	12. Ⓐ Ⓑ Ⓒ Ⓓ Ⓔ	16. Ⓐ Ⓑ Ⓒ Ⓓ Ⓔ	20. Ⓐ Ⓑ Ⓒ Ⓓ Ⓔ

Subtest 6: Math Skills Test (MST)

1. Ⓐ Ⓑ Ⓒ Ⓓ Ⓔ	5. Ⓐ Ⓑ Ⓒ Ⓓ Ⓔ	9. Ⓐ Ⓑ Ⓒ Ⓓ Ⓔ	13. Ⓐ Ⓑ Ⓒ Ⓓ Ⓔ	17. Ⓐ Ⓑ Ⓒ Ⓓ Ⓔ
2. Ⓐ Ⓑ Ⓒ Ⓓ Ⓔ	6. Ⓐ Ⓑ Ⓒ Ⓓ Ⓔ	10. Ⓐ Ⓑ Ⓒ Ⓓ Ⓔ	14. Ⓐ Ⓑ Ⓒ Ⓓ Ⓔ	18. Ⓐ Ⓑ Ⓒ Ⓓ Ⓔ
3. Ⓐ Ⓑ Ⓒ Ⓓ Ⓔ	7. Ⓐ Ⓑ Ⓒ Ⓓ Ⓔ	11. Ⓐ Ⓑ Ⓒ Ⓓ Ⓔ	15. Ⓐ Ⓑ Ⓒ Ⓓ Ⓔ	19. Ⓐ Ⓑ Ⓒ Ⓓ Ⓔ
4. Ⓐ Ⓑ Ⓒ Ⓓ Ⓔ	8. Ⓐ Ⓑ Ⓒ Ⓓ Ⓔ	12. Ⓐ Ⓑ Ⓒ Ⓓ Ⓔ	16. Ⓐ Ⓑ Ⓒ Ⓓ Ⓔ	20. Ⓐ Ⓑ Ⓒ Ⓓ Ⓔ

Subtest 7: Mechanical Comprehension Test (MCT)

1. Ⓐ Ⓑ Ⓒ Ⓓ Ⓔ	5. Ⓐ Ⓑ Ⓒ Ⓓ Ⓔ	9. Ⓐ Ⓑ Ⓒ Ⓓ Ⓔ	13. Ⓐ Ⓑ Ⓒ Ⓓ Ⓔ	17. Ⓐ Ⓑ Ⓒ Ⓓ Ⓔ
2. Ⓐ Ⓑ Ⓒ Ⓓ Ⓔ	6. Ⓐ Ⓑ Ⓒ Ⓓ Ⓔ	10. Ⓐ Ⓑ Ⓒ Ⓓ Ⓔ	14. Ⓐ Ⓑ Ⓒ Ⓓ Ⓔ	18. Ⓐ Ⓑ Ⓒ Ⓓ Ⓔ
3. Ⓐ Ⓑ Ⓒ Ⓓ Ⓔ	7. Ⓐ Ⓑ Ⓒ Ⓓ Ⓔ	11. Ⓐ Ⓑ Ⓒ Ⓓ Ⓔ	15. Ⓐ Ⓑ Ⓒ Ⓓ Ⓔ	19. Ⓐ Ⓑ Ⓒ Ⓓ Ⓔ
4. Ⓐ Ⓑ Ⓒ Ⓓ Ⓔ	8. Ⓐ Ⓑ Ⓒ Ⓓ Ⓔ	12. Ⓐ Ⓑ Ⓒ Ⓓ Ⓔ	16. Ⓐ Ⓑ Ⓒ Ⓓ Ⓔ	20. Ⓐ Ⓑ Ⓒ Ⓓ Ⓔ

SIFT PRACTICE TEST

Subtest 1: Simple Drawings (SD)

100 Questions • 2 Minutes

> **Directions:** Identify the figure that is not the same as the others and select the corresponding letter on the answer sheet.

Example:

1.

| A | B | C | D | E |

2.

| A | B | C | D | E |

1. The correct answer is C.

2. The correct answer is B.

1.

| A | B | C | D | E |

2.

| A | B | C | D | E |

3.

| A | B | C | D | E |

4.

| A | B | C | D | E |

5.

| A | B | C | D | E |

6.

| A | B | C | D | E |

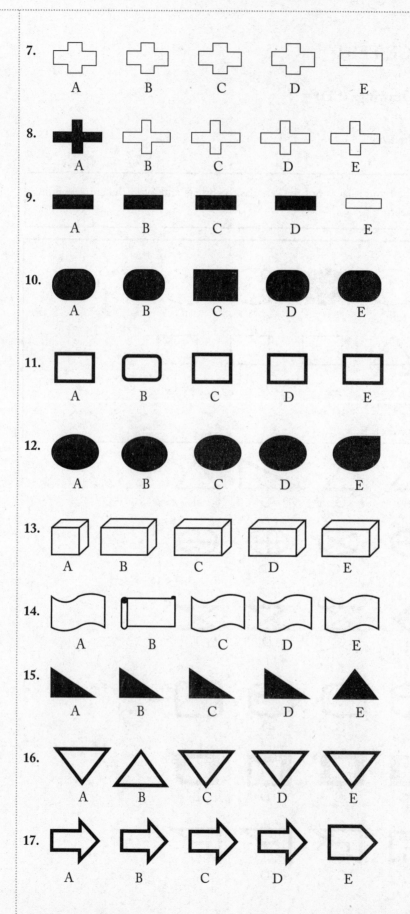

7.

   A   B   C   D   E

8.

   A   B   C   D   E

9.

   A   B   C   D   E

10.

   A   B   C   D   E

11.

   A   B   C   D   E

12.

   A   B   C   D   E

13.

   A   B   C   D   E

14.

   A   B   C   D   E

15.

   A   B   C   D   E

16.

   A   B   C   D   E

17.

   A   B   C   D   E

18.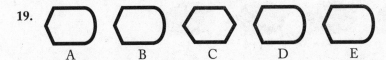

A B C D E

19.

A B C D E

20.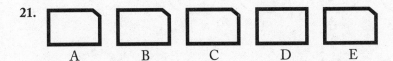

A B C D E

21.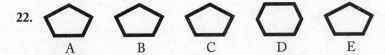

A B C D E

22.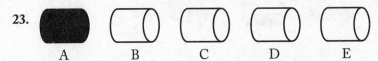

A B C D E

23.

A B C D E

24.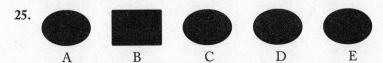

A B C D E

25.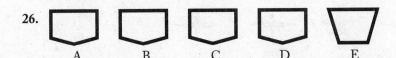

A B C D E

26.

A B C D E

27.

A B C D E

28.

A B C D E

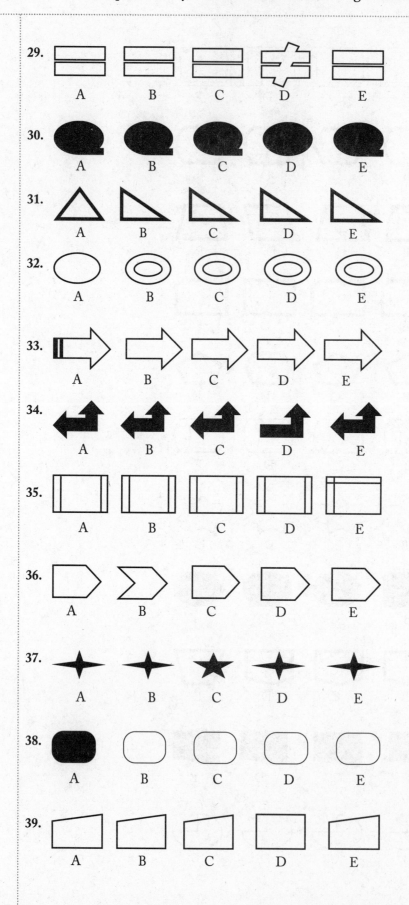

40.

A B C D E

41.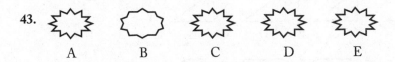

A B C D E

42.

A B C D E

43.

A B C D E

44.

A B C D E

45.

A B C D E

46.

A B C D E

47.

A B C D E

48.

A B C D E

49.

A B C D E

practice test—SIFT

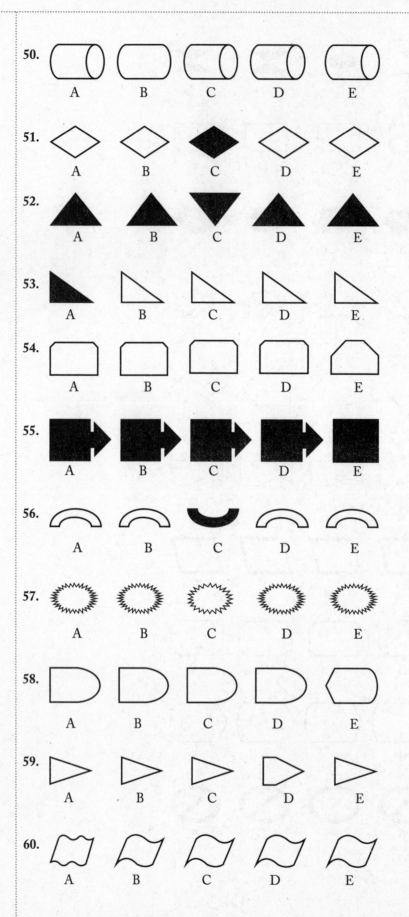

61.

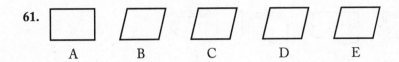

    A   B   C   D   E

62.

    A   B   C   D   E

63.

    A   B   C   D   E

64.

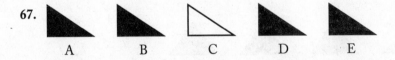

    A   B   C   D   E

65.

    A   B   C   D   E

66.

    A   B   C   D   E

67.

    A   B   C   D   E

68.

    A   B   C   D   E

69.

    A   B   C   D   E

70.

    A   B   C   D   E

71.

    A   B   C   D   E

practice test—SIFT

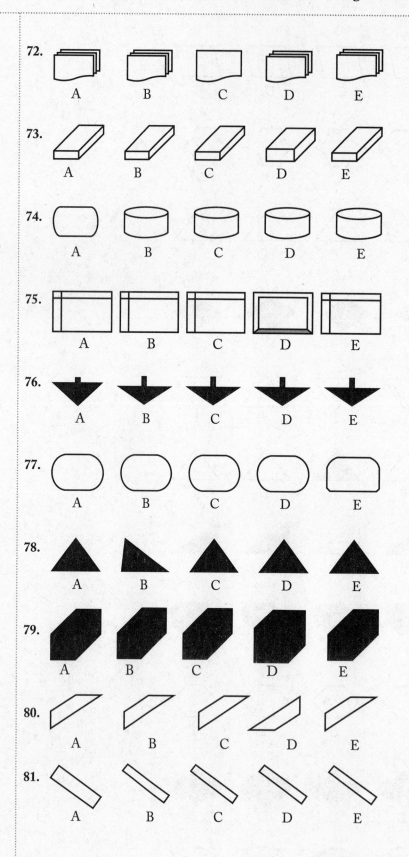

72. A   B   C   D   E

73. A   B   C   D   E

74. A   B   C   D   E

75. A   B   C   D   E

76. A   B   C   D   E

77. A   B   C   D   E

78. A   B   C   D   E

79. A   B   C   D   E

80. A   B   C   D   E

81. A   B   C   D   E

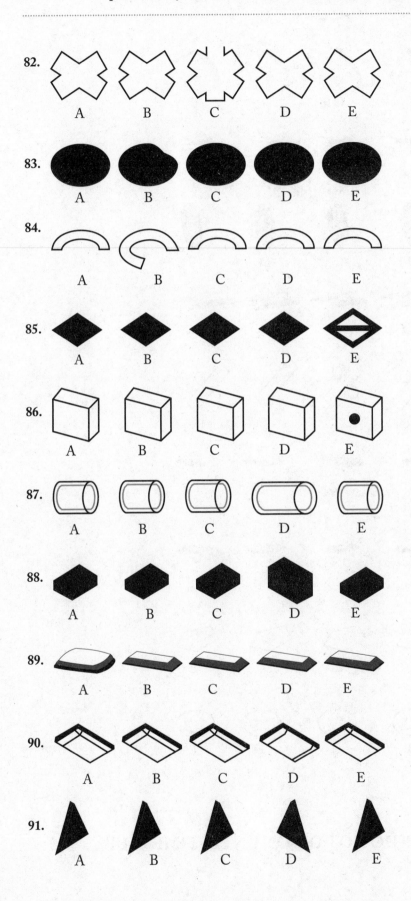

82.   A   B   C   D   E

83.   A   B   C   D   E

84.   A   B   C   D   E

85.   A   B   C   D   E

86.   A   B   C   D   E

87.   A   B   C   D   E

88.   A   B   C   D   E

89.   A   B   C   D   E

90.   A   B   C   D   E

91.   A   B   C   D   E

practice test—SIFT

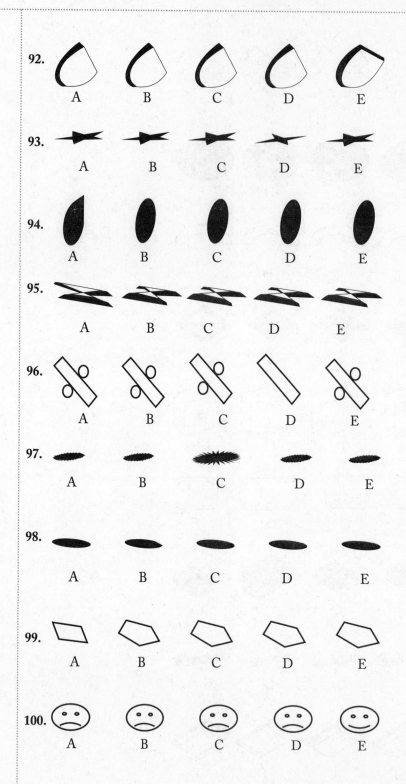

STOP! DO NOT GO ON UNTIL TIME IS UP.

Subtest 2: Hidden Figures (HF)

50 Questions • 5 Minutes

> **Directions:** This subtest contains 50 questions designed to measure your ability to identify a simple shape in a complex drawing. At the top of each page are five figures labeled A, B, C, D, and E. Below are five numbered diagrams. Determine which lettered figure is contained within the diagram and select the corresponding letter on the answer sheet.
>
> Each of the diagrams only contains one of the lettered figures. The correct figure in each drawing will always be the same size and configuration, meaning not rotated or in any other way altered, as it appears at the top of the page.

Example:

The lettered figures are shown below.

Look at diagrams 1 through 3 below. Which of the figures appear in those diagrams?

1.

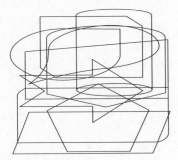

3.

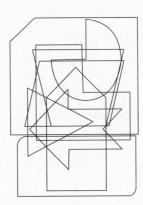

2.

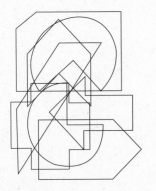

Now look at the same diagrams below. The lettered figures are shaded to indicate the correct response for each question.

1.   The correct answer is C.

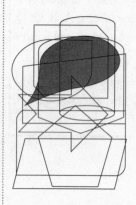

3.   The correct answer is D.

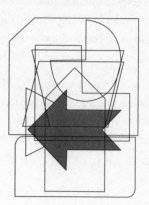

2.   The correct answer is A.

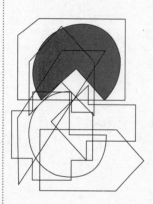

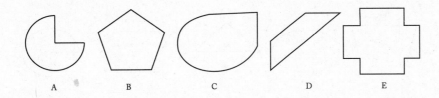

A   B   C   D   E

1.

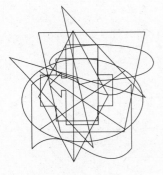

2.

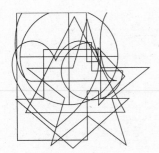

3.

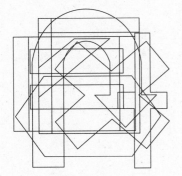

4.

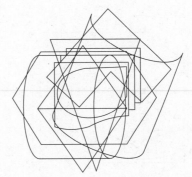

5.

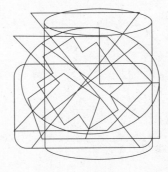

practice test—SIFT

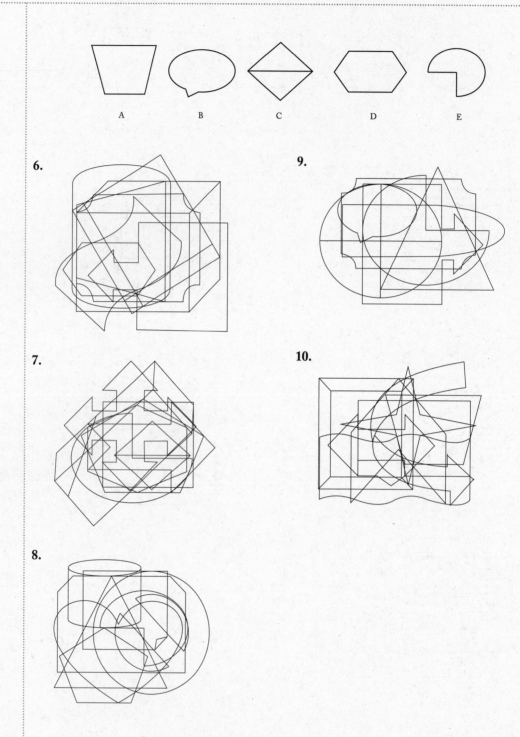

6.

7.

8.

9.

10.

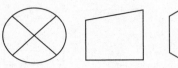

A   B   C   D   E

11.

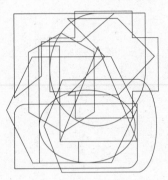

14.

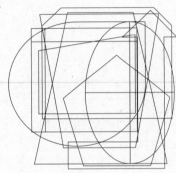

12.

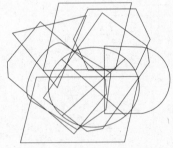

15.

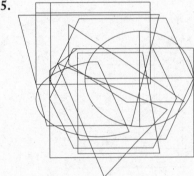

13.

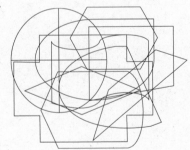

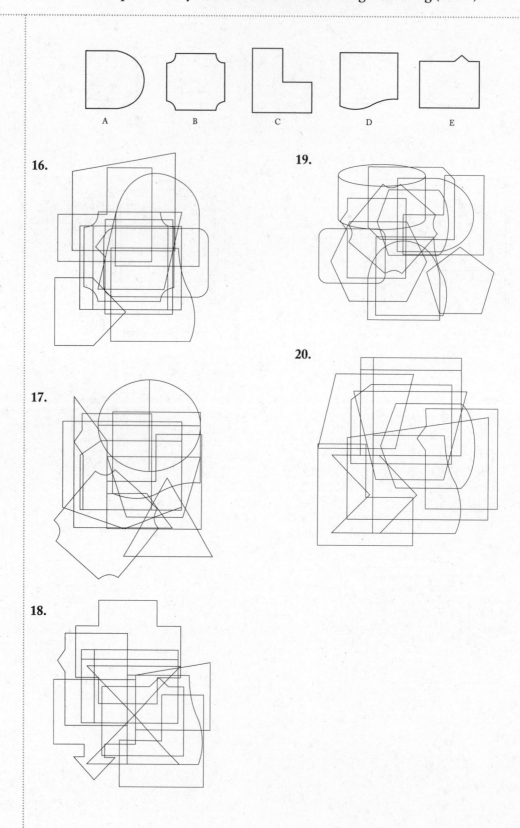

16.

17.

18.

19.

20.

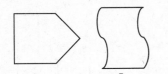

A   B   C   D   E

21.

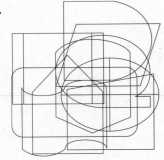

24.

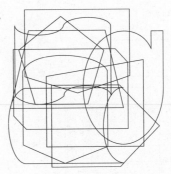

22.

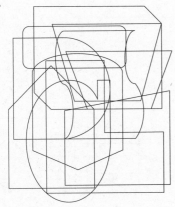

25.

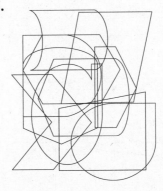

23.

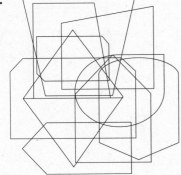

practice test — SIFT

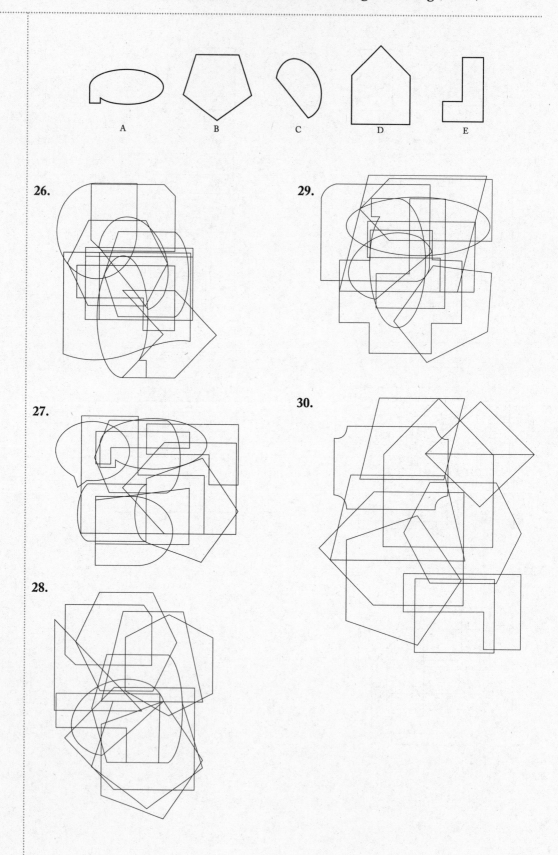

26.

27.

28.

29.

30.

A   B   C   D   E

31.

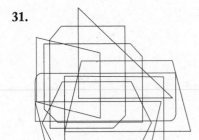

34.

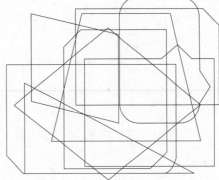

32.

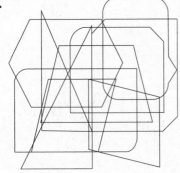

35.

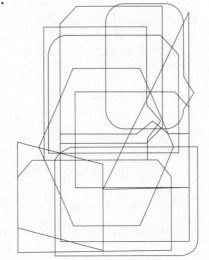

33.

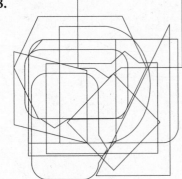

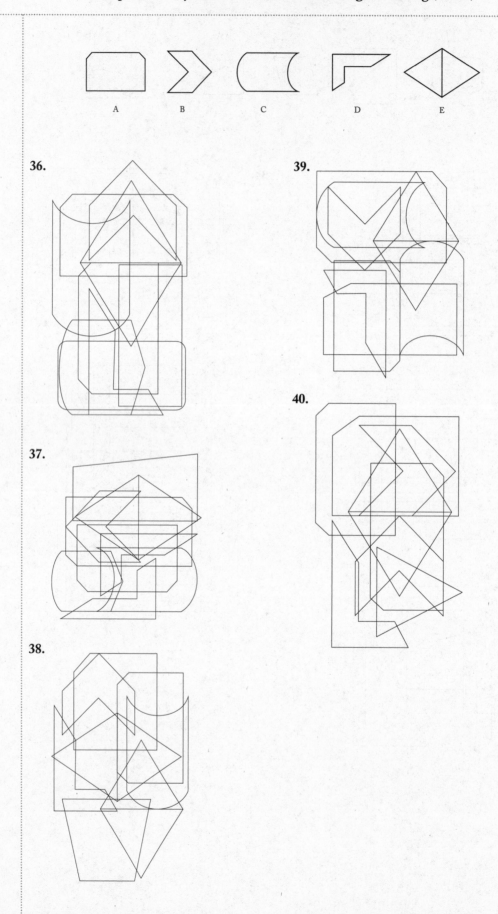

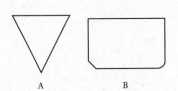

A   B   C   D   E

41.

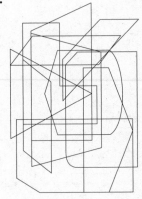

42.

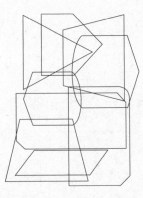

43.

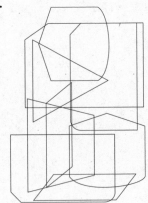

44.

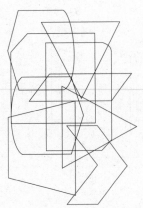

45.

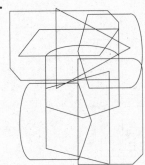

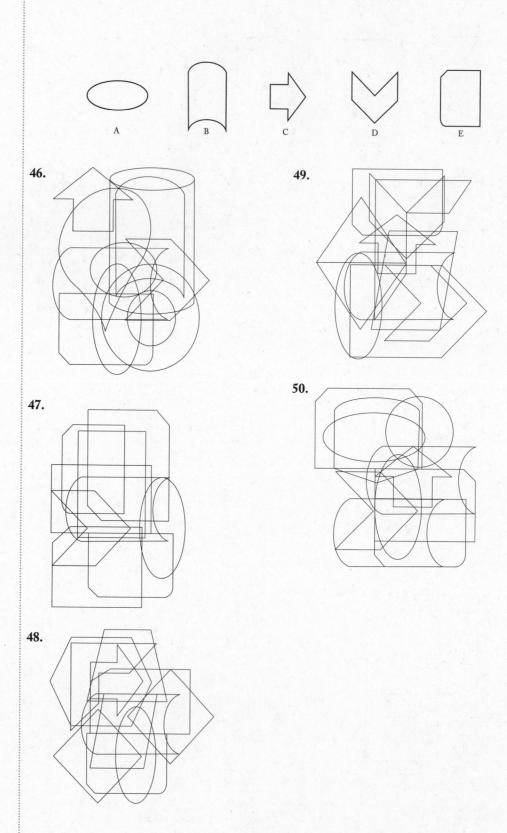

A   B   C   D   E

46.

47.

48.

49.

50.

STOP! DO NOT GO ON UNTIL TIME IS UP.

Subtest 3: Army Aviation Information Test (AAIT)

40 Questions • 30 Minutes

Directions: An incomplete statement is followed by several choices. Decide which one of the choices best completes the statement. Then mark the space on your answer sheet that has the same number and letter as your choice.

Unless otherwise indicated, these questions are based on a helicopter that has the following characteristics:

- An unsupercharged reciprocating engine
- A single main rotor rotating in a counterclockwise direction (looking downward on the rotor)

Example:

You are in a helicopter in straight and level flight with a constant power setting. When the nose of the helicopter is pulled up, the altitude will

- **A.** remain the same.
- **B.** initially increase.
- **C.** initially decrease.
- **D.** initially decrease and then remain the same.
- **E.** None of the above

The correct answer is B. When the nose of the helicopter is pulled up, the altitude will initially increase.

1. A lighted heliport may be identified by

   A. a flashing yellow light.

   B. a blue lighted square landing area.

   C. white and red lights.

   D. a green, yellow, and white rotating beacon.

   E. blue and red alternating flashes.

2. The primary purpose of the tail rotor system is to

   A. assist in making a coordinated turn.

   B. maintain heading during forward flight.

   C. counteract the torque effect of the main rotor.

   D. provide additional thrust and lift.

   E. increase maximum speed.

3. During a hover, a helicopter tends to drift in the direction of tail rotor thrust. This movement is called

    A. flapping.

    B. gyroscopic precession.

    C. transverse flow effect.

    D. translating tendency.

    E. Coriolis force.

4. The upward bending of the rotor blades resulting from the combined forces of lift and centrifugal force is known as

    A. translational lift.

    B. blade flapping.

    C. the Coriolis effect.

    D. dissymmetry of lift.

    E. coning.

5. In a helicopter, the center of gravity (CG) range is usually located

    A. in front of the main rotor mast.

    B. in the rear of the main rotor mast.

    C. directly above the main fuel tank.

    D. directly below the main fuel tank.

    E. a short distance fore and aft of the main rotor mast.

6. The lift differential that exists between the advancing main rotor blade and the retreating main rotor blade is known as

    A. the Coriolis effect.

    B. dissymmetry of lift.

    C. translating tendency.

    D. translational lift.

    E. lift vector.

7. Ground resonance is most likely to develop when

    A. there is a sudden change in blade velocity in the plane of rotation.

    B. a series of shocks causes the rotor system to become unbalanced.

    C. there is a combination of a decrease in the angle of attack on the advancing blade and an increase in the angle of attack on the retreating blade.

    D. initial ground contact is made with a combination of high gross weight and low RPM.

    E. there is a defective clutch or missing or bent fan blades in the helicopter engine.

8. The proper action to initiate a quick stop is to

    A. increase the RPM.

    B. decrease the RPM.

    C. raise the collective pitch.

    D. lower collective pitch and apply forward cyclic.

    E. lower collective pitch and apply aft cyclic.

9. Takeoff from a slope in a helicopter with skid-type landing gear is normally accomplished by

   A. simultaneously applying collective pitch and downslope cyclic control.

   B. bringing the helicopter to a level attitude before completely leaving the ground.

   C. making a downslope running takeoff if the surface is smooth.

   D. rapidly increasing collective pitch and upslope cyclic controls to avoid sliding downslope.

   E. turning the tail upslope, when moving away from the slope, to reduce the danger of the tail rotor striking the surface.

10. The proper procedure for a slope landing in a helicopter with skid-type landing gear is

    A. to use maximum RPM and maximum manifold pressure.

    B. when parallel to the slope, slowly lower the downslope skid to the ground prior to lowering the upslope skid.

    C. if the slope is 10 degrees or less, the landing should be made perpendicular to the slope.

    D. when parallel to the slope, slowly lower the upslope skid to the ground prior to lowering the downslope skid.

    E. if the slope is 10 degrees or less, the landing should be downslope or downhill.

11. Density altitude refers to a theoretical air density that exists under standard conditions at a given altitude. Standard conditions at sea level are

    A. 29.92 inHg (inches of mercury) and 15°C.

    B. 29.92 inHg (inches of mercury) and 20°C.

    C. 29.92 inHg (inches of mercury) and 30°C.

    D. 14.96 inHg (inches of mercury) and 15°C.

    E. 14.96 inHg (inches of mercury) and 30°C.

12. A helicopter pilot should consider using a running takeoff

    A. if the helicopter cannot be lifted vertically.

    B. when a normal climb speed is assured between 10 and 20 feet.

    C. when power is insufficient to hover at a very low altitude.

    D. when the additional airspeed can be quickly converted to altitude.

    E. when gross weight or density altitude prevents a sustained hover at normal hovering altitude.

13. Foot pedals in the helicopter cockpit enable the pilot to

    A. control torque effect.

    B. regulate flight speed.

    C. regulate rate of climb.

    D. regulate rate of descent.

    E. stabilize rotor RPM.

14. If the helicopter is moving forward, the advancing blade will be in the

    A. orward half of the rotor disc.

    B. left half of the rotor disc.

    C. rear half of the rotor disc.

    D. right half of the rotor disc.

    E. It cannot be estimated.

15. The method of control by which the pitch of all main rotor blades is varied equally and simultaneously is the

    A. auxiliary rotor control.

    B. collective pitch control.

    C. cyclic pitch control.

    D. tail rotor control.

    E. throttle control.

16. The combination of factors that will reduce helicopter performance the most is

    A. low altitude, low temperature, and low humidity.

    B. low altitude, high temperature, and low humidity.

    C. low altitude, low temperature, and high humidity.

    D. high altitude, low temperature, and low humidity.

    E. high altitude, high temperature, and high humidity.

17. The most favorable conditions for helicopter performance are the combination of

    A. low-density altitude, light gross weight, and moderate-to-strong winds.

    B. high-density altitude, heavy gross weight, and calm or no wind.

    C. low-density altitude, light gross weight, and calm or no wind.

    D. high-density altitude, light gross weight, and moderate-to-strong winds.

    E. low-density altitude, heavy gross weight, and moderate-to-strong winds.

18. Refer to the figure below. The acute angle A is the angle of

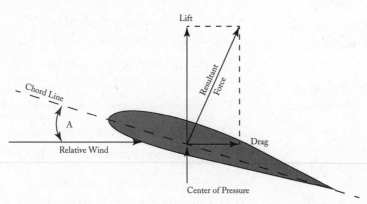

A. dihedral.

B. attack.

C. camber.

D. incidence.

E. pitch.

19. During surface taxiing, the helicopter pilot should use the pedals to maintain heading and the cyclic to maintain

A. ground track.

B. proper RPM.

C. starting.

D. stopping.

E. All of the above

20. The thinner air of higher altitudes causes the airspeed indicator to read "too low." An indicated airspeed of 80 mph at 5,000 feet is actually a true airspeed of approximately

A. 72 mph.

B. 88 mph.

C. 96 mph.

D. 104 mph.

E. 112 mph.

21. How does blade rotation create lift?

    A. Rotary impact pressure reduces gravity under the blades.

    B. Air pressure below the blades is increased.

    C. Low pressure is created at the leading edge of the blades and high pressure at the trailing edge.

    D. Air molecules travel father across the top of the airfoil creating higher air pressure above the blades.

    E. Laminar flow of air molecules generates a low pressure area above the rotating airfoils relative to under.

22. How does raising the collective change the angle of attack (AOA) and center of pressure (CP)?

    A. The relative wind to cord line angle increases, and the CP above the blade moves aft.

    B. The relative wind to cord line angle decreases, and the CP above the blade moves aft.

    C. The relative wind to cord line angle increases, and the CP above the blade moves forward.

    D. The relative wind to cord line angle decreases, and the CP above the blade moves forward.

    E. The air is beat into submission.

23. Without changing your altimeter, your true altitude in flight will

    A. remain the same with changes in outside air temperature (OAT).

    B. increase with increases in outside air temperature (OAT).

    C. increase with decreases in pressure.

    D. decrease with increases in pressure.

    E. increase with increases in pressure.

24. Changing an altimeter from 29.85 to 30.00 is what apparent change in elevation or altitude?

    A. 300 feet increase

    B. 300 feet decrease

    C. 150 feet increase

    D. 150 feet decrease

    E. 1,500 feet increase

25. Ground effect is best described as

    A. compressed air close to the ground that creates a cushion upon which aircraft float.

    B. induced lift cause by decreases in drag due to ground disruption of airfoil upwash, downwash, and blade tip vortices.

    C. an increase in induced drag.

    D. increased with high surface winds.

    E. decreased by smooth surfaces.

26. Assuming no-wind, describe the aerodynamic forces required for stationary hover.

    A. The vertical component of lift equals weight and the horizontal component of lift exceeds drag.

    B. Thrust and lift act in the same vertical direction and are both equal to a combined weight and drag.

    C. Thrust and lift are greater than weight and drag.

    D. Weight and drag are greater than thrust and lift.

    E. Relative wind exceeds drag and lift equals weight.

27. What is NOT a Newton law of motion?

    A. A body at rest will remain at rest and a body in motion will remain in motion.

    B. Acceleration is a change in magnitude or direction of the velocity vector with respect to time.

    C. For every action, there is an equal and opposite reaction.

    D. The force required to produce a change in motion is directly proportional to its mass and rate of change in velocity.

    E. While the amount of total energy within a closed system does not change, the form of the energy may be altered.

28. What airfoil terminology defines the downward flow of air?

    A. Relative wind

    B. Angle of incidence

    C. Center of pressure

    D. Aerodynamic center

    E. Induced flow

29. What changes rotational pitch of the rotor blades?

    A. Collective pitch

    B. Cyclic pitch control

    C. Correlator/governor

    D. Throttle control

    E. Antitorque pedals

30. What is the function of foot pedals in a helicopter?

    A. To move the aircraft about the vertical axis

    B. To move the aircraft about the longitudinal axis

    C. To move the aircraft about the lateral axis

    D. To change the pitch angle of all main rotor blades

    E. To change the pitch angle of the main rotor disc

practice test—SIFT

31. What is an airspeed indicator (ASI) indication of a clogged static port?

    A. ASI is not affected by a clogged static port only the pitot system.

    B. ASI will indicate faster than actual speeds on climbs and slower on descents.

    C. ASI will indicate slower than actual speeds on climbs and faster on descents.

    D. ASI will indicate a faster than actual speed above the altitude that the blockage occurred.

    E. ASI will indicate a slower than actual speed below the altitude that the blockage occurred.

32. During a forward autorotation, the inner 25 percent of blade region is referred to as the

    A. driven region.

    B. blade region.

    C. driving region.

    D. point of equilibrium.

    E. stall region.

33. Which of the following is NOT a factor for weight and balance calculations?

    A. Gross weight

    B. Arm

    C. Moment

    D. CG

    E. Angular momentum

34. Tactical terrain flight at night up to a level of 25-feet-tall trees and obstacles is called what?

    A. Nap-of-the-earth (NOE) flight

    B. Low-level flight

    C. Unaided night flight

    D. Contour flight

    E. Terrain avoidance flight

35. Which of the following is NOT a consideration when using NVGs?

    A. Depth perception is distorted.

    B. Color discrimination is absent due to monochromatic images.

    C. Viewing area is limited, requiring movement of the head and they eyes.

    D. Scanning needs to be slow or spatial disorientation may be induced.

    E. Objects with poor reflective surfaces such as wires and suspension lines are easier to see.

36. What is a Fenestron?

    A. An anti-torque rotor that uses forced air through slots and rotating nozzle

    B. A fan-in-tail type of anti-torque rotor

    C. A type of transmission for the main rotor system

    D. A technique to increase lift by reducing drag during an autorotation

    E. A phenomenon also called Coanda effect

37. What is NOT an effect of ice build-up on your airfoil?

   A. Increase in stall speed

   B. Increased drag

   C. Increased weight

   D. Decrease in lift

   E. Decreased AOA

38. What chart uses a 1:500,000 scale?

   A. World Aeronautical Charts

   B. VFR Terminal Area Charts

   C. Sectional Aeronautical Charts

   D. IFR Enroute High Altitude Charts

   E. IFR/VFR Low Altitude Planning Chart

39. What happens when you push forward on cyclic pitch in a two-bladed rotor system?

   A. Gyroscopic precession exposed to differing blade AOA occurs opposite from stick deflection.

   B. The blade with the increased AOA tends to deflect down.

   C. The blade with the decreased AOA tends to deflect up.

   D. The differing blade has an increased AOA at 90 degrees from stick deflection.

   E. Gyroscopic precession exposed to differing blade AOA occurs 90 degrees from stick deflection.

40. What control surfaces are manipulated to initiate a left roll in a fixed wing aircraft?

   A. Left aileron moves down, right aileron moves up

   B. Left aileron moves up, right aileron moves down

   C. Rudder moves left

   D. Rudder moves righin at

   E. Elevator move down

STOP! DO NOT GO ON UNTIL TIME IS UP.

practice test—SIFT

Subtest 4: Spatial Apperception Test (SAT)

25 Questions • 10 Minutes

Directions: You will have 5 minutes to read these instructions; read them carefully. The two pictures below show an aerial view and a picture of a plane from which the view might have been seen. Note that the view is out at sea and that the horizon appears to be tilted. Note also that the plane is shown flying out to sea and that it is banked. You can determine the position of a plane by the view that the pilot has when he or she looks directly ahead through the windshield of the cockpit.

Each problem in this test consists of six pictures: an aerial view at the upper left and five pictured choices below labeled A, B, C, D, and E. Each pictured choice shows a plane in flight. The picture at the upper left shows the view that the pilot would have looking straight ahead from the cockpit of one of the five pictured planes. Determine which of the five lettered sketches most nearly represents the position or attitude of the plane and the direction of flight from which the view would have been seen. Choose the correct letter answer on your answer sheet.

Try the following two sample problems.

1.

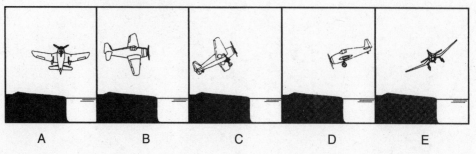

A   B   C   D   E

The correct answer is B. The plane is shown in the position from which the pilot would have seen through the windshield of the cockpit—the view shown in the upper left aerial view. The plane is shown on a level flight, banking right, and flying out to sea.

2.

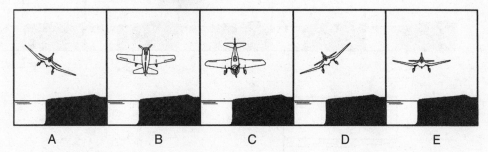

The correct answer is D. The plane is shown on a level flight, banking left, and flying up the coastline.

You will have 10 minutes to answer the 25 questions on the test.

practice test—SIFT

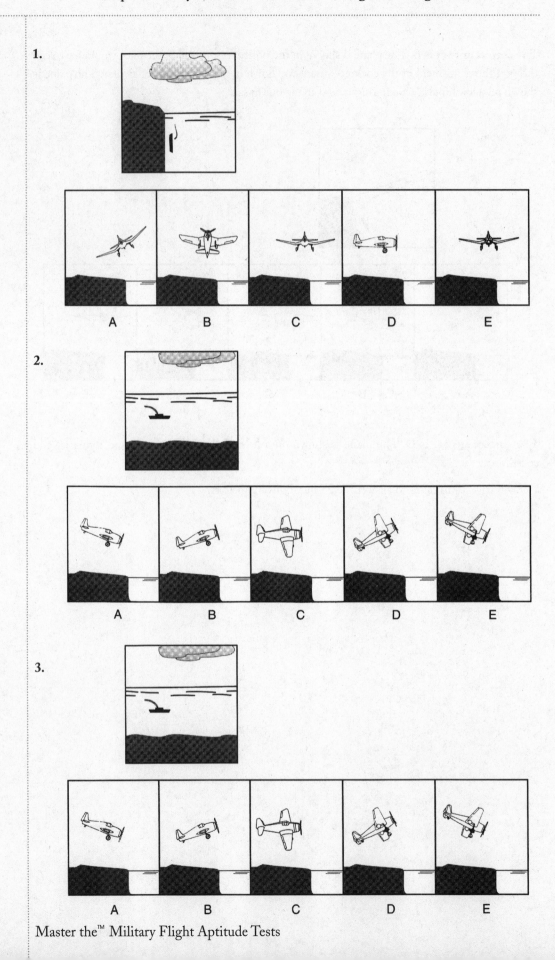

4.

5.

6.

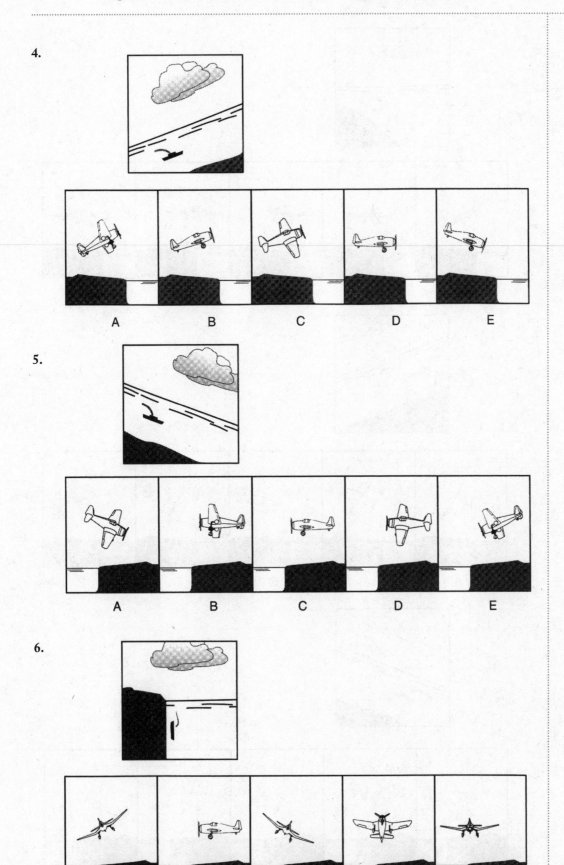

7.

8.

9.

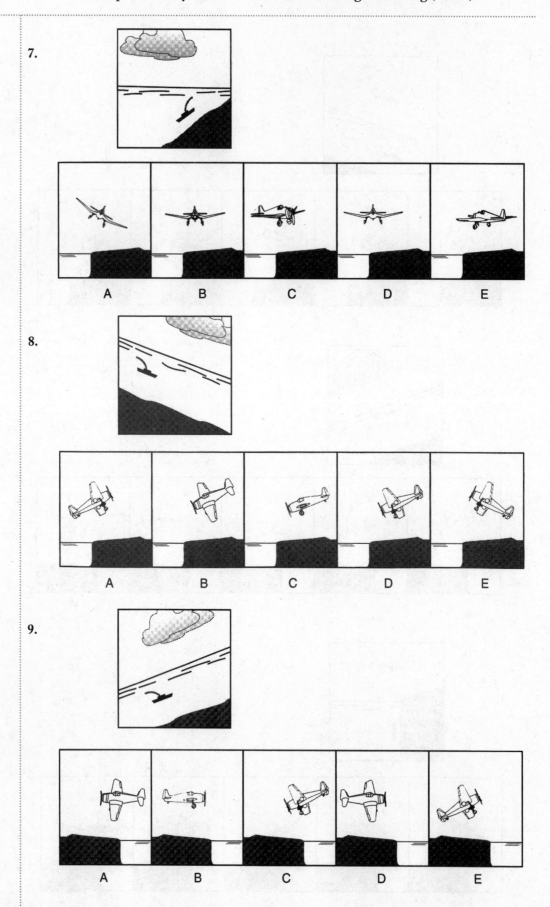

10.

11.

12.

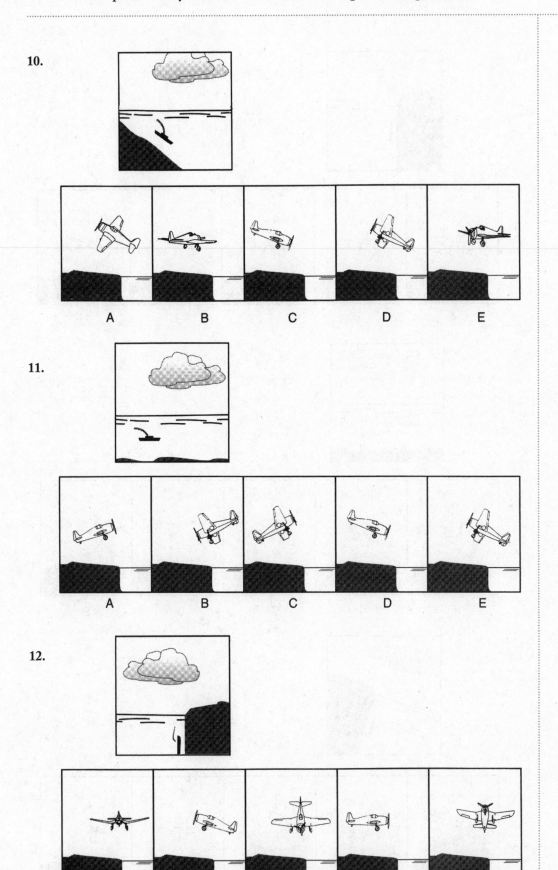

13.

14.

15.

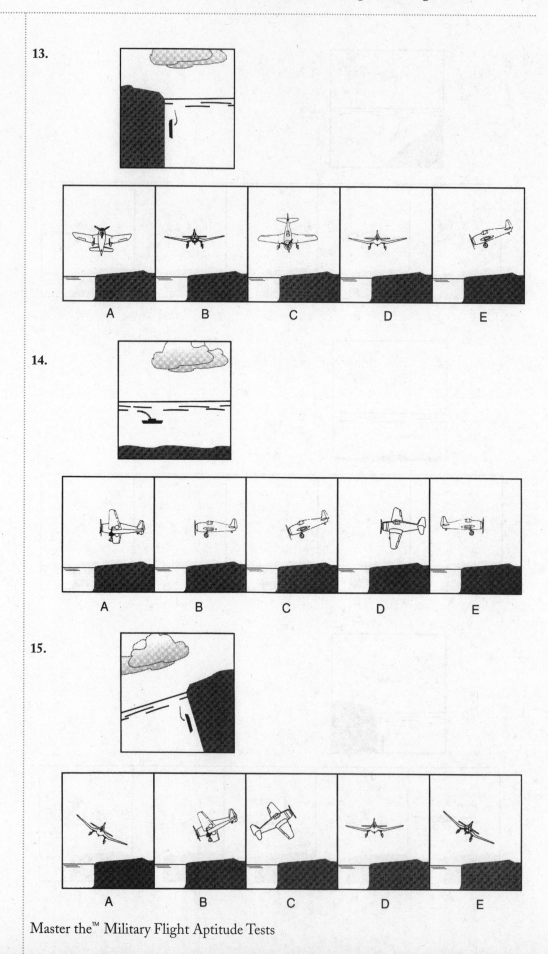

16.

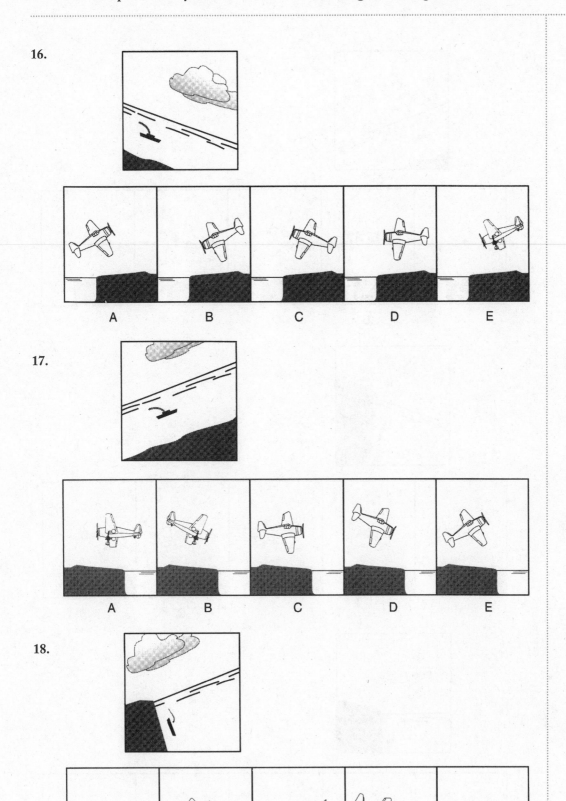

17.

18.

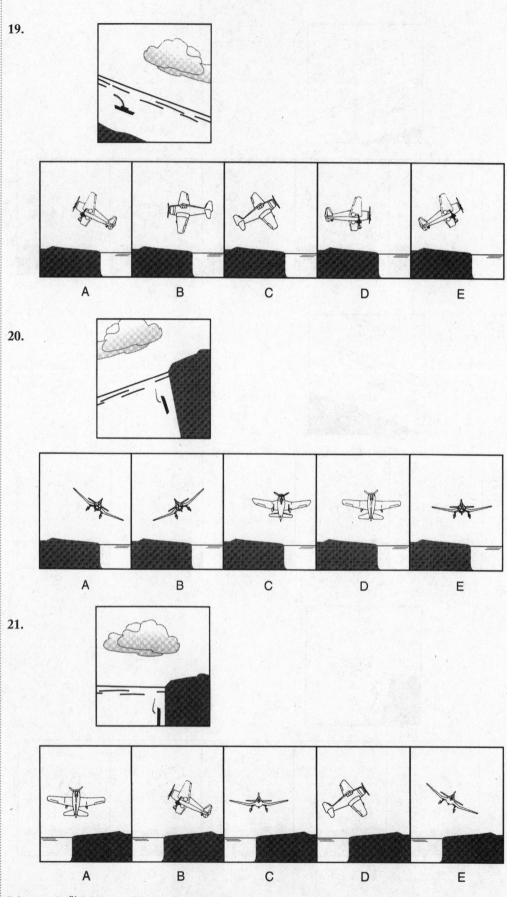

22.

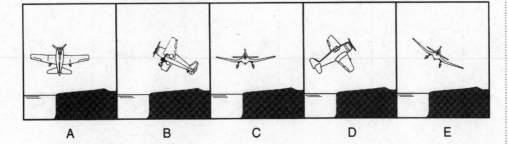

A   B   C   D   E

23.

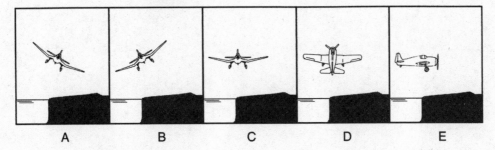

A   B   C   D   E

24.

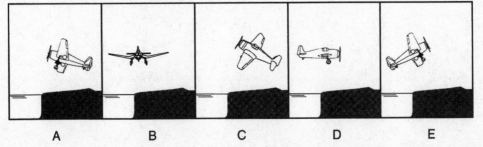

A   B   C   D   E

25.

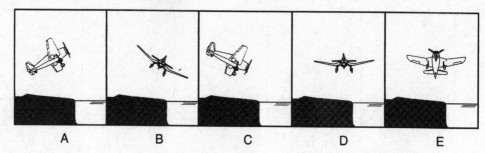

STOP! DO NOT GO ON UNTIL TIME IS UP.

Subtest 5: Reading Comprehension Test (RCT)

20 Questions • 30 Minutes

> **Directions:** Each item consists of a passage which you should assume to be true, followed by five possible answer choices. For each item, select the choice that can be inferred *only* from the passage itself. Some or all of choices following each passage may be true and reasonable, but only one item can be derived solely from the information in the passage.

1. "Professional competence is more than a display of book knowledge or of the results of military schooling. It requires the display of qualities of character which reflect inner strength and justified confidence in one's self." — General Maxwell Taylor

   According to this passage,

   A. job competence should be displayed through ego and arrogance.

   B. professional competence is a careful balance of education, experience, and self-assurance.

   C. one should promote one's professional competence through higher education, additional training, and outward superiority.

   D. individuals in the organization with the most education, training, and rank are those with the most professional competence.

   E. competence is reflective of overall knowledge and pride in the duties assigned.

2. The Global Positioning System (GPS) was originally designed to support military operations by providing accurate timing and to position data so that users could calculate location and velocity. This system consists of three segments: the space segment, the control segment, and the user segment. The U.S. Air Force develops, maintains, and operates the space and control segments. In the space segment, a network of 24–27 orbiting satellites broadcasts two signals to the earth that are collected and used by GPS receivers to determine location and other information. The signal broadcast by each satellite relays the location of the satellite, a spacecraft (satellite) identification code, and data describing the courses of all of the satellites in the constellation. Using the signal data from four or more satellites, a receiver calculates its current position and velocity. Because the network can support unlimited users, GPS has evolved to support countless civilian applications as well as military operations around the globe.

   According to this passage,

   A. a GPS receiver must collect data from all 24 satellites to calculate position and velocity.

   B. GPS was designed to support military and civilian applications.

   C. GPS can only support limited users around the globe.

   D. the U.S. Air Force operates and maintains the GPS satellite network.

   E. the U.S. Air Force determines which civilian applications can be supported by GPS.

3. The U.S. Air Force A-10 Warthog has long been the Close Air Support (CAS) aircraft of choice of the Army to support ground forces in combat. However, the aircraft is aging, and the Air Force has repeatedly sought to retire the airframe and replace the mission with a multirole aircraft, in spite of the desires of Congress and Army leaders. The challenge is that single, multirole aircraft has to be designed to "trade-off" mission capabilities and the result is less than an optimal design for any of the mission requirements. The fear is that the resulting "multirole" platform will not perform as well for CAS missions as the current A-10, leaving Army and Congressional leadership concerned for troop security in combat. However, the Air Force is facing pressure from the same Congressional leaders to cut the budget.

   According to the passage, what is the most important factor in the decision to retain or retire the A-10?

   A. Retention of the CAS capability afforded by the current A-10 aircraft

   B. Ensuring the Air Force focuses on appropriate budget priorities in support of Joint Operations

   C. Certifying the next generation multi-role aircraft is designed to maximize CAS functionality

   D. The role of Congress and Army in pushing priorities for the Air Force budget

   E. Determining how the Air Force will pay for either option of replacing or retaining the A-10

4. Although the U.S. Army initially flew the air mail in 1918 as a proof of concept, the U.S. Post Office took over air mail operations and later contracted air mail services to the airlines starting in 1925. The transfer of the air mail operations from the U.S. Post Office to the emerging airlines was due to the high cost of the government operations, high accident rates among Postal Service pilots, and pressure from the Railroad industry that the government was reducing their opportunities to carry the mail by rail. The airlines successfully carried the mail, often at reduced costs and with improved safety than the government in the years up to the 1930s, when accusations of corruption in the award of contracts forced President Roosevelt to cancel the air mail contracts and order the Army to return to airmail operations. This singular decision resulted in immediate disaster as the Army Air Corps pilots were not trained for such duties, and initial operations resulted in five fatalities and six serious injuries in the first week of operations alone.

   The author of this passage would most like agree that

   A. Army Air Corps were incompetent aviators during this time period.

   B. Both Postal Service and Army Air Corps pilots were poor aviators during this time period.

   C. The experience gained by the airlines in carrying the mail made them most qualified to provide such service.

   D. Army Air Corps and U.S. Postal Service should never have flown the air mail in the first place.

   E. Corruption within the government-contracted air mail service resulted in the later deaths of Army Air Corps pilots.

5. It is commonly understood in the United States that the Wright brothers were the first to fly a powered, controlled, and heavier-than-air airplane. The Wrights later patented their Flyer and won and demonstrated later versions of their aircraft to the Army, one of which was purchased after a demonstration. Glenn Curtiss was another pioneer in heavier-than-air aircraft design and is known as the "Father of Naval Aviation" for his work in the development of seaplanes and carrier operations. It was Curtiss who was instrumental in the design of the Curtiss JN-4J and JN-4N (known as the "Jenny") aircraft that were produced during World War I. This aircraft was available following the war as surplus and was key to the development of civilian aviation, to include the precursor to the airlines as they are known today. What is not as well-known is that in spite of the work of the Wrights and Curtiss prior to World War I, the patent disputes instigated by the Wrights against Curtiss likely held back U.S. aircraft development. As such, most U.S. aircraft manufacturers during World War I produced European designs under license.

What is the author indicating in this passage?

A. The U.S. led in naval aviation development compared to European nations during World War I.

B. The Wrights encouraged competition in aircraft design and production leading up to the war.

C. The Wrights led the U.S. in military aviation aircraft contracts and production in World War I.

D. Glenn Curtiss led the U.S. in military aviation aircraft contracts and production in World War I.

E. The state of U.S. aircraft development was behind that of European development during World War I.

practice test—SIFT

6. Following the use of the atomic bomb to encourage the end of World War II and continued nuclear weapons testing by both the United States and the Soviet Union, the Limited Test Ban Treaty was negotiated in an effort to protect the environment, inhabitants of the earth, and other assets. Due to the number of tests and effectiveness of weapons, nuclear weapons tests resulted in the contamination of areas and people far beyond the test sites. One nuclear ground test by the Soviet Union fused 570 km of telephone lines, damaged 1,000 km of buried power lines, and destroyed a power plant. Weapons testing above the Karman Line (approximately 100 km or 62.1 miles above the earth), caused damage to orbiting satellites. As such, various nations including the United States and Soviet Union agreed to the treaty banning such testing within the atmosphere of the earth and in space. Later, this treaty become the foundation for the Outer Space Treaty of 1967 that banned military bases, weapons placement, and weapons testing in outer space.

According to this passage,

   A. the Limited Test Ban Treaty bans nuclear weapons testing, weapons placement, and military bases in space.

   B. the dramatic reach of nuclear weapons effects resulted in the need for a treaty to protect the atmosphere, people, and assets.

   C. the Limited Test Ban Treaty only bans nuclear weapons testing within the earth's atmosphere.

   D. ground-based nuclear tests do not have the dramatic reach of higher altitude weapons tests.

   E. only the United States and Soviet Union agreed to the Limited Test Ban Treaty.

7. The Women Airforce Service Pilots (WASPs) served the military during World War II. These pilots were trained to fly every aircraft in the military inventory and were charged with duties such as ferrying aircraft, towed target drones, and instrument instructors. Throughout the war, these pilots provided invaluable service to the armed forces, freeing their male counterparts for combat duty. Although the WASPs did not fly combat missions, 38 pilots were killed during their service. Until legislation was passed in 1977 to provide each pilot with a discharge certificate, the WASPs were not considered Veterans. Later in 1984, the WASPs received the World War II Victory Medal and in 2009, President Obama signed legislation for the WASPs to receive the Congressional Gold Medal. Even with Veteran status, the Secretary of the Army rescinded the right for WASPs to be buried at Arlington National Cemetery. Legislation has since been passed restoring this right to these Veterans.

For the purposes of this passage, the term *veteran* should be taken to mean

   A. an individual that honorably served the armed forces and is afforded all rights of that status.

   B. an individual that was conscripted to serve in the armed forces during war time.

   C. an individual that entered active duty service, regardless of discharge status.

   D. an individual that served the armed forces in a combat role.

   E. members of the armed service, dependent on their duties and responsibilities.

8. Throughout the past several decades there has been a movement by some political sectors to "privatize" various government services in order to reduce the overall size of government and cut costs. The notion is that when the government provides goods and services, the resulting products are more expensive than if they are provided by the private sector, meaning by either for profit or not for profit organizations. In the case of for profit organizations providing such services, a market or demand must exist for those services and the organization producing the goods and services must be able to do so at a cost that consumers are willing and able to pay while making a profit. This is not always the case with every good or service that the government might require. In some instances, the government has also attempted to transfer existing systems and programs to the private sector to operate and maintain with mixed results for the same reasons. For example, the privatization of the LandSat satellite system was not successful while the current run Medicare system remains one of the most cost-efficient healthcare systems in the United States.

   From this passage, the author is indicating that

   A. privatization of government products and services cannot be successful.

   B. all healthcare systems should be modeled after the Medicare system.

   C. all products and services provided by the government are more expensive than when provided by non-government sources.

   D. consideration must be given to what types of products and services can be privatized in order to achieve success.

   E. privatization is the only means in which to reduce the size of government and overall spending.

9. When the United States first entered the bombing campaign in the European theatre in World War II, the British were successfully putting only 20 percent of aerial bombs within 5 miles of the target during night time bombing operations. General Curtis LeMay, then a Group Commander, decided that such a low target hit rate was not acceptable and would not achieve the goals of strategic bombing. As such, LeMay controversially transitioned U.S. Army Air Corps bombing from nighttime raids to daylight bombing, significantly increasing the risk for bomber crews while also dramatically enhancing the success of targeting. To compensate for the increased threat to the bombers, LeMay instituted new flight formations to maximize the effectiveness of the bomber guns and other defensive capabilities.

   The author would most like agree that

   A. General LeMay was only concerned with the effectiveness of the bombing raids, not the safety of the aircrews.

   B. General LeMay considered the tactics of bomber formations to minimize losses while maximize the effectiveness of the daylight bombing raid strategy.

   C. British and U.S. nighttime bombing campaigns were not at all effective during World War II.

   D. Bomber guns were not effective defensive capabilities for the aircrews during daylight raids.

   E. The decision to transition to a daylight bombing should not have been controversial based on increased bomb on target accuracy.

10. Brigadier General Billy Mitchell rose through the ranks of the Army Air Corps in World War I and in the following years. However, BGen Mitchell was increasingly vocal about perceived U.S. military weaknesses and asserted that naval surface vessels were obsolete. To demonstrate, on two occasions BGen Mitchell staged the sinking of naval vessels using aircraft. It was Mitchell's belief that a strong air corps was needed for national security and that corps should be run by those with aviation experience. Mitchell was known as repeatedly questioning the resolve of leadership maintaining national security and some of his efforts and activities led to increased funding support for aviation. Mitchell also theorized the rise of Japan and a potential attack on the Philippines and Pearl Harbor. In spite of Mitchell's efforts, he was eventually court-martialed for accusing senior military leaders of "almost treasonable administration of our national defense." Instead of accepting a five-year suspension and loss of pay, Mitchell resigned from the Army. Today, BGen Mitchell is known as the "Father of the United States Air Force."

Which of the following statements might the author agree?

A. BGen Mitchell was an aviation and national security visionary who was unjustly court-martialed for his vision.

B. Had military leaders listened to BGen Mitchell's warnings regarding defense and Japan, World War II could have been prevented.

C. BGen Mitchell had strong opinions related to the future structure of the military forces.

D. BGen Mitchell inappropriately questioned the direction of national security preparations and was justly court martialed for his actions.

E. Although court martialed, BGen Mitchell's efforts have gone unrecognized throughout history.

11. On June 18, 1983, Dr. Sally Ride became the first American woman to fly in space. Dr. Ride served on the Space Shuttle *Challenger* mission as mission specialist. However, 20 years prior to this flight, Valentina Tereshkova, a Soviet cosmonaut, was the first woman to ever fly in space during the *Vostok 6* mission launched on June 16, 1963. Svetlana Saviskaya was the next woman to fly in space in 1982 and became the first woman to perform a spacewalk. Although countless women played key roles in the U.S. space program as computer programmers and mathematicians, and an additional 13 women passed the same physical and psychological tests as the first American male astronauts in the 1960s, none were selected for the Astronaut Corps.

The information in this passage indicates that

A. until Dr. Ride was selected for the Astronaut Corps, there were no other qualified women to serve in this role.

B. Dr. Ride was the first woman to ever travel to space.

C. women have generally played a very small role in the American space program overall, not just in the Astronaut Corps.

D. the potential existed for other qualified women to play a more significant role in the American space program prior to Dr. Ride's flight.

E. women were not interested in the American space program or service as astronauts until Dr. Ride's first flight.

12. For several decades, the aerospace industry has been seeking ways in which to reduce the cost to transport goods and people into space. In the last decade, and particularly with the conclusion of the Space Shuttle Program, several entrepreneurs from several different industries (predominantly information technology) have invested in new space launch systems and are achieving significant successes with relatively small investments and moderate support from the government. Should even a fraction of the new ventures be successful beyond the current industry disruption being caused by SpaceX, with its low cost and highly reliable launch vehicle that they are hoping to develop into a fully reusable system, the effect could be dramatic. The hope is that these new options for space access will open new opportunities for space and micro-gravity research, exploration, and tourism.

    The author of this passage would disagree with all of the following statements EXCEPT:

    A. The government is investing large sums of money to reduce the cost to develop new space systems.

    B. Not all of the current space ventures in development must be successful to cause a dramatic disruption in the space industry.

    C. There is little interest in space exploration and research following the conclusion of the Space Shuttle Program.

    D. There is no commercial interest in space exploration or micro-gravity research.

    E. Entrepreneurs from the information technology field have little to offer the aerospace industry.

13. The Internet is a tremendous tool for information and communications. People are becoming ever more reliant on the Internet not just for information, but as a tool to organize and store data, collaborate, and conduct research. The Internet is a wide-open tool with the potential for vast information sharing with the power to circumvent oppressive governments and topple dictators. Access to post and share data has also created challenges when false or misleading information is spread, such as the case with the fraudulent and retracted Wakefield study linking vaccines to autism. This singular study, in which multiple other studies have disproven the original study and experts have pointed to the multitude of flaws in the original study, still has parents questioning the safety of vaccines leading to outbreaks of previously suppressed diseases in the United States.

    The author of this passage would likely agree that

    A. the Internet is a powerful tool to share information, even if some of that information is false or fraudulent.

    B. due to the potential for sharing of potentially harmful information, information on the Internet should be strictly controlled.

    C. people should not get their information from internet sources because the data could be from questionable sources.

    D. the value of the Internet as a tool for commerce and information sharing has been degraded by the publishing of fraudulent information.

    E. regardless of the multiple studies contradicting the Wakefield study, vaccines cause autism.

14. Data or information fusion is a means to process multiple data types from various sources to create actionable information. Such methods have been traditionally inclusive of Department of Defense and intelligence applications. The extension of data fusion with emergency management processes for enhanced proactive decision-making has not been fully explored. Hard sensor use in emergency management (e.g., satellites) has evolved to include government unmanned aerial systems (UAS) but may have potential to include non-governmental or private sector systems. Soft sensors in emergency management processes (people) include the flow of information from government and private sources. Data fusion emergency management extension is a method of integrating government and private sector information sources at varying levels of information automation for enhanced decision making and utilization of limited resources.

For the purposes of this paper, the term *fusion* is a means of

A. energy generation.

B. merging different information systems together to gather data.

C. creating knowledge from multiple sources of data.

D. automating decision-making for government users.

E. integrating emergency management organizations and responses.

15. Many crime scenes can be extremely complex in nature, in terms of quantity and diversity of evidence; the connections between pieces of evidence to the scene(s), victim(s), and perpetrator(s); connections between weapon(s) and wound(s). Further, it may not be initially clear to investigators what occurred at a crime scene, hence, much analysis by a variety of individuals is required to determine the sequence of events and parties involved. In some cases, the analysis and investigation is additionally complicated if all experts cannot visit the crime scene(s) first-hand. Hence, complex crimes and scenes may benefit from the use of advanced virtual reality and collaborative environments in which evidence and analysis can be presented in a realistic form. This reconstruction may be a benefit for prosecutors and defense attorneys to present the various aspects of the crime and evidence to a judge and jury. This type of virtual reality presentation, if accurately assembled and presented, may streamline court proceedings and aid in the overcoming the so-called "CSI Effect" of recent television presentation of forensic analysis. In addition, the communicative and collaborative aspects could aid in the "force multiplication" of a limited number of experts to participate in a larger number of investigations nation- and perhaps world-wide.

The primary purpose of this passage is to:

A. discuss the complex nature of crime scene analysis and promote techniques shown on *CSI*.

B. use virtual reality techniques to produce better *CSI* productions for the public.

C. use virtual reality techniques in place of current forensics methods to solve complex crimes.

D. replace forensics testimony in court rooms with virtual reality presentations of crime scenes.

E. use virtual reality techniques to augment existing forensics analysis, include additional experts in the process, and add in court presentations of crime scene data.

16. As part of a routine medical examination or visit to a healthcare provider, patients are asked to fill out one or more forms related to their current and past medical history as well as the conditions that affect other family members. Depending on the patients' circumstances, this can be a lengthy process. In addition, multiple medical conditions experienced by several related family members can be difficult to recall and report particularly if the patient completing the form is ill or injured. According to the U.S. Surgeon General, Dr. Richard Carmona, "the medical history is one of the most powerful tools we have to assess risk in patients—and knowing your family [health] history can literally save your life, yet it is often underutilized."

    According to this passage,

    A. patients are not aware of the critical nature of medical and family history data to their healthcare.

    B. providing complete and accurate medical and family health history data is a key factor in assess a patient's health risks.

    C. patients are rarely able to provide a complete and accurate medical and family health history when seeking routine treatment.

    D. physicians rarely seek a complete medical history, as they do not see the value in the data.

    E. medical conditions affecting other family members are not relevant to an individual's health and care.

17. Over the past decade, network visualization tools are becoming a prominent method to aid in the analysis of data. Network visualization has the potential to become a powerful tool across a multitude of analysis disciplines. The drawback to this method is there is very little understanding about how these tools and their various components are perceived by the analysts. In addition, it is not clear whether efforts expended to develop advanced displays and interfaces quantitatively improves the analysis of data. Research specific to network visualization techniques could aid tool designers in understanding how color, shapes, line design, organization, and the cognitive characteristics of the user will affect the analysts' assessment of the presented data. Further, these issues must also be studied in relation to how a decision-maker perceives the presented data.

    The primary purpose of this passage is to:

    A. illustrate that network visualization tools are ineffective in enhancing data analysis.

    B. the efforts expended to develop network visualizations tools have yielded no effective techniques for data analysis

    C. although network analysis techniques show promise, the effectiveness of specific techniques in enhancing data analysis are unclear.

    D. additional research into visualization design techniques is required before any additional network visualization tools are implemented.

    E. the efforts expended to develop network visualizations tools are not effective in enhancing decision making.

18. The American Intelligence Community (IC) collects pertinent data about a variety of situations to provide decision makers with the best possible basis for policy and other resolutions. Industry also relies on information gathering to assess competition and foreign trade, encourage cooperation, and to identify investment and new business opportunities. Intelligence in an industrial setting rarely involves covert operations. Instead, it is characterized by researching business and technology journals, attending trade shows, conducting marketing research, and monitoring stocks and dividends. The types of valuable information to other companies are costing methods, new product development, contract agreements, resource availability, and manufacturing capabilities.

In this passage, the term *intelligence* as related to industry most likely refers to

A. paying employees of the target company to reveal sensitive data.

B. data obtained by hacking into a corporation's computer network.

C. information gathered by covert agents inside of an organization.

D. information obtained through open and publicly available sources.

E. sensitive information about target company executives that could be used as leverage.

19. The development of the Office of Strategic Services (OSS) prior to World War II represented an astounding accomplishment. The British already had an effective and reputable intelligence service from which the United States modelled the OSS and built it up within a relatively short period of time. Unfortunately, President Truman dismantled the intelligence service following the end of the war in the Pacific. However, the leaks of information relating to the atomic bomb to the Soviet Union and the escalation of the Cold War persuaded Congress to renew the efforts of the intelligent gathering community. Congress passed the National Security Act of 1947, which among other actions, created the Central Intelligence Agency (CIA).

The primary purpose of this passage is to:

A. document the history of the formation of the Central Intelligence Agency.

B. highlight that the CIA was created by President Truman and Congress following the end of the war in the Pacific.

C. discuss President Truman's decisions related to the OSS and intelligence gathering after the war.

D. show the importance of the intelligence service during World War II and the Cold War.

E. provide a brief history of the foundation of the intelligence community and early evolution.

20. Management of people and resources poses a number of unique challenges. Since the advent of the Industrial Revolution, management is continually studied in order to increase production and sales and to enhance efficiency overall. Within the study of management are a number of sub-disciplines related to human interaction, resource allocation, logistics, marketing, finance, and several others. In addition, communications technology and the arrival of the Information Age has further altered the work environment and management as employees move away from centralized work locations to distributed operations, stationed in different cities, states, and even countries. As a result of the evolving working environment, new management challenges arise.

According to this passage,

A. management is an evolving challenge as technology and the business environment changes.

B. the Information Age has reduced management challenges as personnel are more distributed.

C. management is a stagnant area of study people, resources, the market, and finance do not change.

D. management is essential in industrial, but information applications, because the principles of efficiency differ.

E. an entirely new sub-discipline of management is required to deal with the changes imposed by the Information Age.

STOP! DO NOT GO ON UNTIL TIME IS UP.

Subtest 6: Math Skills Test (MST)

40 Minutes • Variable Number of Questions (20 Practice Questions Below)

1. $x^2 + 3y - 1 = 15$ and $y = -3$, then what is x?

    A. 2

    B. 3

    C. 4

    D. 5

    E. 6

2. What is the product of $(5x - 3)$ and $(x + 4)$?

    A. $6x + 1$

    B. $5x^2 - 12$

    C. $5x^2 - 3x - 1$

    D. $5x^2 - x - 1$

    E. $5x^2 + 17x - 12$

3. The Halls are moving to a new home and want to fence in a space for their dog, Molly. Previously, Molly had a fenced-in area of 2,100 square feet to play. One side of the new lawn is 42 feet long. If the Halls want the same space for Molly and use the 42 feet for one side of a rectangular space, how much fencing will they need to purchase?

    A. 168 ft.²

    B. 180 ft.²

    C. 184 ft.²

    D. 192 ft.²

    E. 196 ft.²

4. Jonah and Sabrina have an outdoor swing set and a 20-foot square tarp. They want to build a "lean-to" using the swing set as one side and the tarp along the top to provide them a shaded play area when it is hot. If they attach the tarp to the top of the swing set and secure the other side directly to the ground, how much shaded area will they have underneath the tarp?

    A. 240 ft.²

    B. 320 ft.²

    C. 360 ft.²

    D. 400 ft.²

    E. 440 ft.²

5. Aaron drove 4 hours to see his sister, Allison. His average speed due to traffic was 45 mph for the first hour, 62 mph for the second hour, 59 mph for the third hour, and 64 mph for the fourth hour. His Honda gets 22 miles per gallon. How many gallons of gas did Aaron use, one way?

    A. 9 gallons

    B. 9.5 gallons

    C. 10 gallons

    D. 10.5 gallons

    E. 11 gallons

6. On the return trip, Allison drove Aaron back and was able to drive a bit faster because there was no traffic. She drove 63 miles the first hour, 68 miles the second hour, 64 miles the third hour, and 35 miles during the last 30 minutes of the trip. What was Allison's average speed during the duration of the trip?

A. 62.3 mph

B. 62.5 mph

C. 63 mph

D. 64.2 mph

E. 65.7 mph

7. A Navy and Marine F/A-18E Super Hornet each leave Miramar Air Station at the same time. The Marine Super Hornet is flying due east at 775 mph and the Navy Super Hornet is flying due west at 625 mph. How long will it take for the two aircraft to be separated by 3,500 miles?

A. 2.00 hours

B. 2.30 hours

C. 2.45 hours

D. 3.00 hours

E. 3.30 hours

8. If $x^2 + 5x - 10 = 14$, what is x?

A. 3

B. 4

C. 5

D. 6

E. 7

9. The measure of one of the angles of a complementary angle is 50 degrees. What is the measure of the other complementary angle?

A. 10 degrees

B. 30 degrees

C. 40 degrees

D. 50 degrees

E. 130 degrees

10. Allison wants to paint her new room. The room measures 12 feet (length) by 10 feet (width) by 9 feet (height) and has two 8 foot by 3 foot doors that will not be painted and a 3 foot by 4 foot window. If she is not painting the ceiling, how my area will she need paint to cover?

A. 516 ft.^{2}

B. 456 ft.^{2}

C. 396 ft.^{2}

D. 384 ft.^{2}

E. 336 ft.^{2}

11. $\left(\sqrt{5} - \sqrt{3}\right)^2$

A. $2 - 2\sqrt{3}$

B. $-2 - 2\sqrt{3}$

C. $8 + 2\sqrt{15}$

D. $8 - 2\sqrt{15}$

E. $8 - 2\sqrt{8}$

12. In a class of 375 students, 28% are taking shop, 36% are taking home economics, and 12% are taking both courses. How many students are not taking either course?

    A. 82

    B. 90

    C. 93

    D. 104

    E. 135

13. A surveillance radar can detect moving objects up to 15 km away. If the radar is able to cover a 40-degree segment of a circle around the radar, how many square miles is the detection field?
    (Use 3.14 for π.)

    A. 10.5 km^2

    B. 78.5 km^2

    C. 96.5 km^2

    D. 157 km^2

    E. 210 km^2

14. Dave wants to purchase a new telescope, but he can only afford to spend $1,000 total. If the current price of the telescope he wants is $1,300 and sales tax is 5%, how much will the telescope have to be discounted for him not to exceed his budget?

    A. 70%

    B. 72%

    C. 73%

    D. 75%

    E. 80%

15. A patrol aircraft has a maximum range of 600 miles without refueling. If the aircraft departs the airfield and is tasked to make a maximum range circular orbit around the field and return, what is the maximum radius of that orbit? (Use 3.14 for π.)

    A. 72 miles

    B. 75 miles

    C. 80 miles

    D. 82 miles

    E. 140 miles

16. If you were to roll a 10-sided die once, what is the probability that it will land on an odd number?

    A. 1 out of 2

    B. 1 out of 5

    C. 3 out of 10

    D. 5 out of 10

    E. 6 out of 10

17. Solve the following for x:

    $$\frac{4}{x+5} = \frac{5}{x+7}$$

    A. –1

    B. 0

    C. 1

    D. 2

    E. 3

18. Simplify the following expression, assuming all variables represent nonzero real numbers:

    $(-3x)^7(-3x)^4$

    A. $(-3x)^{11}$

    B. $(-3x)^{28}$

    C. $9x^{11}$

    D. $9x^{28}$

    E. $(3x)^{11}$

19. Perform the indicated operation.

    $(5x^3 + 3x - 2x^2) + (4x^2 - 2x^3 + 7x)$

    A. $9x^3 + x + 5x^2$

    B. $9x^3 + 5x + 5x^2$

    C. $x^3 + x + 5x^2$

    D. $3x^3 + x + 9x^2$

    E. $3x^3 + 2x^2 + 10x$

20. Simplify the following expression, assuming all variables represent nonzero real numbers:

    $$\frac{8x^9 - 6x^5 + 10x^4}{2x^3}$$

    A. $\dfrac{4x^6 - 3x^2 + 5x}{x}$

    B. $\dfrac{4x^7 - 3x^3 + 5x^2}{x}$

    C. $\dfrac{2x^6 - 3x^2 + 5x}{x}$

    D. $\dfrac{2x^6 - 6x^2 + 5x^2}{x}$

    E. $\dfrac{4x^7 - 3x^2 + 5x}{x}$

STOP! DO NOT GO ON UNTIL TIME IS UP.

practice test—SIFT

Subtest 7: Mechanical Comprehension Test (MCT)

20 Questions • 10 Minutes

> **Directions:** Decide which mechanical principle is illustrated in each picture. Pick the best answer. There is only one correct answer.

Now look at the sample question below.

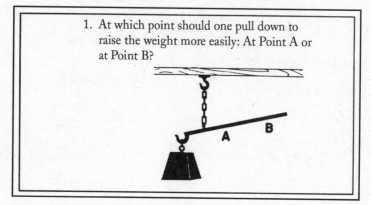

1. At which point should one pull down to raise the weight more easily: At Point A or at Point B?

Pulling down at B gives a longer lever arm, which results in raising the weight more easily. **The correct answer is B.**

20 Questions • 10 Minutes

1. In the figure shown below, one complete revolution of the windlass drum will move the weight up

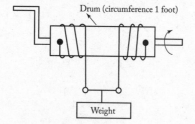

Drum (circumference 1 foot)

Weight

   A. 6 inches.

   B. 12 inches.

2. The figure below shows a cam and a valve. For each cam revolution, the vertical valve rise equals distance

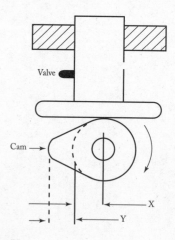

Valve

Cam →

X

Y

   A. Y

   B. X

3. In the diagram below, crank arm C revolves at a constant speed of 400 RPM and drives the lever AB. When lever AB is moving the fastest, arm C will be in which positions?

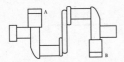

   A. 1 and 3

   B. 2 and 4

4. What is the function of A and B in the crankshaft shown in the drawing below?

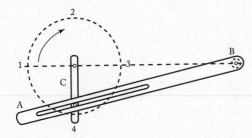

   A. They strengthen the crankshaft by increasing its weight.

   B. They are necessary to maintain the proper balance of the crankshaft.

5. The figure below shows a governor on a rotating shaft. As the shaft speeds up, the governor balls will

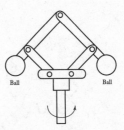

   A. move down.

   B. move upward.

6. The figure below shows a brass and an iron strip continuously riveted together. High temperatures would probably

   A. have no effect at all.

   B. bend the strips.

practice test—SIFT

7. Study the gear wheels in the figure below, and then determine which of the following statements is true.

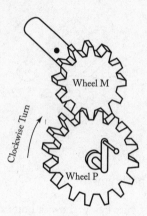

A. It will take less time for a tooth of wheel P to make a full turn than it will take a tooth of wheel M.

B. It will take more time for a tooth of wheel P to make a full turn than it will for a tooth of wheel M.

8. Which hydraulic press requires the least force to lift the weight?

A. A

B. B

9. In the figure below, which upright supports the greater part of the load?

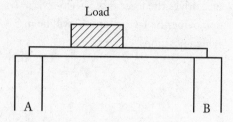

A. Upright A

B. Upright B

10. The figure below shows a crank and piston. The piston moves from mid-position to the extreme right if the crank

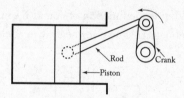

A. makes a $\frac{3}{4}$ turn.

B. makes one turn.

11. When the 100-pound weight is being slowly hoisted up by the pulley, as shown in the figure below, the downward pull on the ceiling to which the pulley is attached is

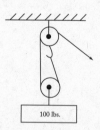

A. 100 pounds.

B. 150 pounds.

12. When the driver wheel is moved from location X to location Y, the driven wheel will

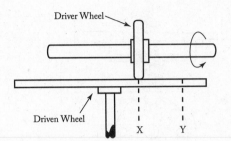

Driver Wheel

Driven Wheel

X　Y

A. turn slower.

B. turn faster.

13. If the ball and spring mechanism are balanced in the position shown above, the ball will move upward if the nut is

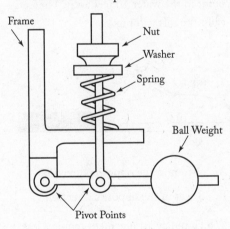

Frame

Nut

Washer

Spring

Ball Weight

Pivot Points

A. loosened.

B. tightened.

14. Neglecting friction, what is the mechanical advantage in using the single fixed pulley shown below?

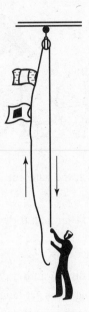

A. 1

B. 2

15. Four gears are shown in the figure below. If gear 1 turns as shown, then the gears turning in the same direction are

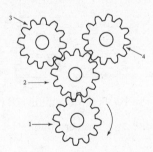

3

2

4

1

A. 2 and 3

B. 3 and 4

16. If both cyclists pedal at the same rate on the same surface, the cyclist in front will

   A. travel at the same speed as the cyclist behind.

   B. move faster than the cyclist behind.

17. If water is flowing into the tank at the rate of 120 gallons per hour and flowing out of the tank at a constant rate of one gallon per minute, the water level in the tank will

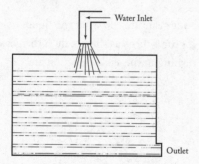

   A. rise 1 gallon per minute.

   B. rise 2 gallons per minute.

18. In order to open the valve in the figure below once every second, the wheel must rotate at

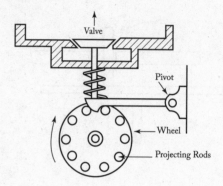

   A. 6 rpm.

   B. 10 rpm.

19. In the figure below, a 150-pound individual jumps off a 500-pound raft to a point in the water 10 feet away. Theoretically, the raft will move

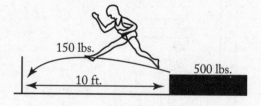

   A. 1 foot in the opposite direction.

   B. 3 feet in the opposite direction.

20. Which pulley arrangement requires less force at F in order to lift the weight?

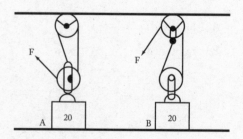

   A. A

   B. B

STOP! DO NOT GO ON UNTIL TIME IS UP.

SIFT ANSWER KEYS AND EXPLANATIONS

Subtest 1: Simple Drawings (SD)

1. D	21. D	41. A	61. A	81. A
2. C	22. D	42. D	62. B	82. C
3. B	23. A	43. B	63. B	83. B
4. E	24. B	44. E	64. A	84. B
5. D	25. B	45. A	65. D	85. E
6. B	26. E	46. A	66. C	86. E
7. E	27. C	47. B	67. C	87. D
8. A	28. A	48. A	68. E	88. D
9. E	29. D	49. C	69. A	89. A
10. C	30. D	50. B	70. C	90. D
11. B	31. A	51. C	71. C	91. D
12. E	32. A	52. C	72. C	92. E
13. A	33. A	53. A	73. D	93. D
14. B	34. D	54. E	74. A	94. A
15. E	35. E	55. E	75. D	95. A
16. B	36. B	56. C	76. A	96. D
17. E	37. C	57. C	77. E	97. C
18. A	38. A	58. E	78. B	98. B
19. C	39. D	59. D	79. D	99. A
20. D	40. C	60. A	80. D	100. E

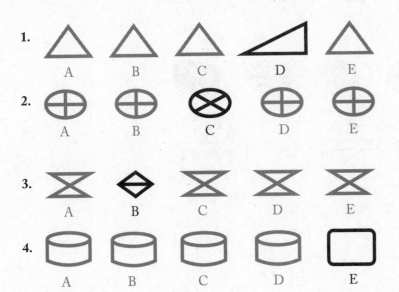

answers practice test

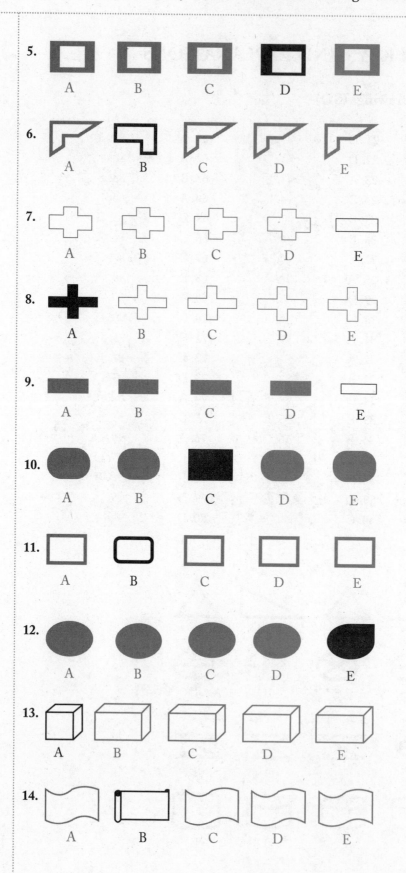

15.
   A   B   C   D   E

16.
   A   B   C   D   E

17.
   A   B   C   D   E

18.
   A   B   C   D   E

19.
   A   B   C   D   E

20.
   A   B   C   D   E

21.
   A   B   C   D   E

22.
   A   B   C   D   E

23.
   A   B   C   D   E

24.
   A   B   C   D   E

answers practice test

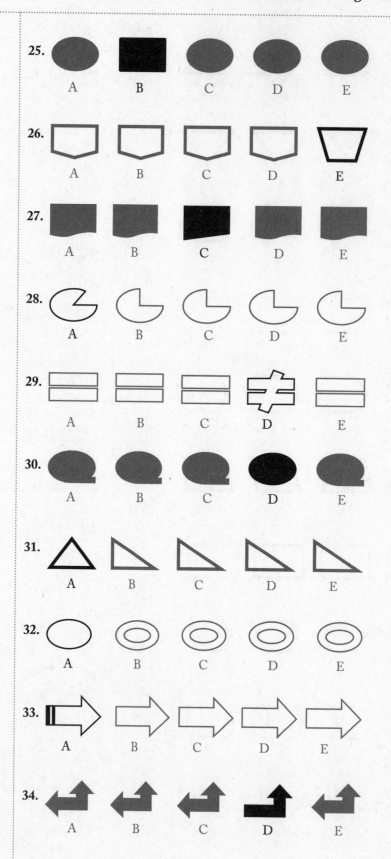

35.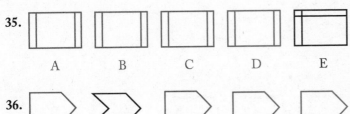

  A   B   C   D   E

36.

  A   B   C   D   E

37.

  A   B   C   D   E

38.

  A   B   C   D   E

39.

  A   B   C   D   E

40.

  A   B   C   D   E

41.

  A   B   C   D   E

42.

  A   B   C   D   E

43.

  A   B   C   D   E

44.

  A   B   C   D   E

answers practice test

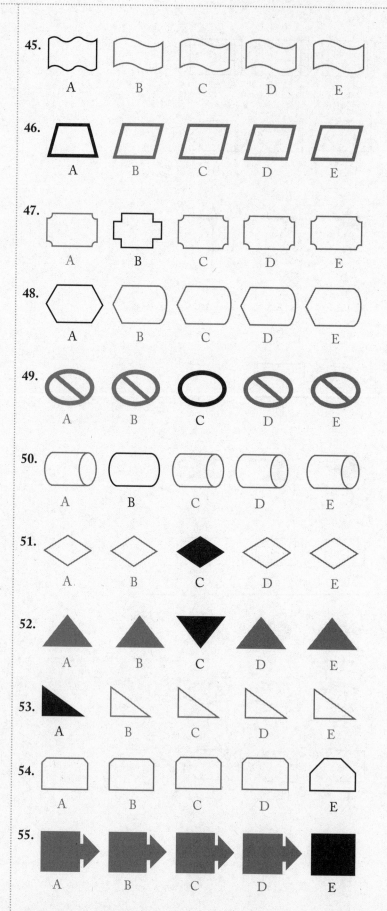

56.

A   B   C   D   E

57.

A   B   C   D   E

58.

A   B   C   D   E

59.

A   B   C   D   E

60.

A   B   C   D   E

61.

A   B   C   D   E

62.

A   B   C   D   E

63.

A   B   C   D   E

64.

A   B   C   D   E

65.

A   B   C   D   E

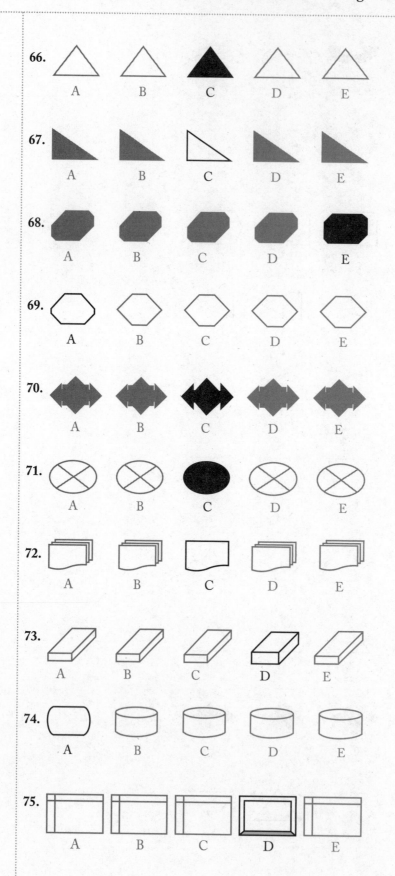

76.

A   B   C   D   E

77.

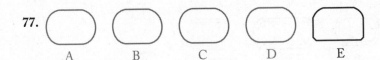

A   B   C   D   E

78.

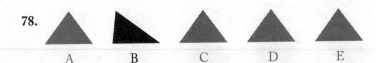

A   B   C   D   E

79.

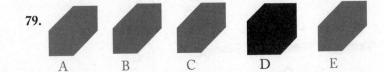

A   B   C   D   E

80.

A   B   C   D   E

81.

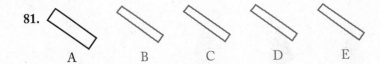

A   B   C   D   E

82.

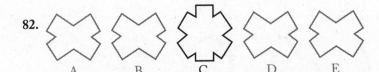

A   B   C   D   E

83.

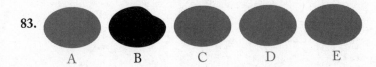

A   B   C   D   E

84.

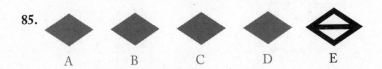

A   B   C   D   E

85.

A   B   C   D   E

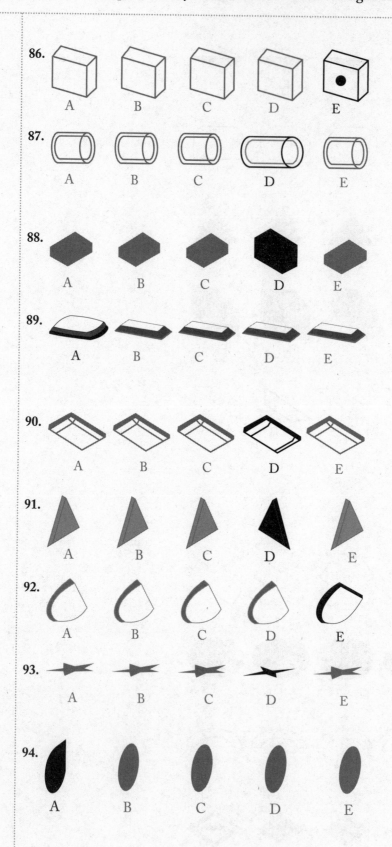

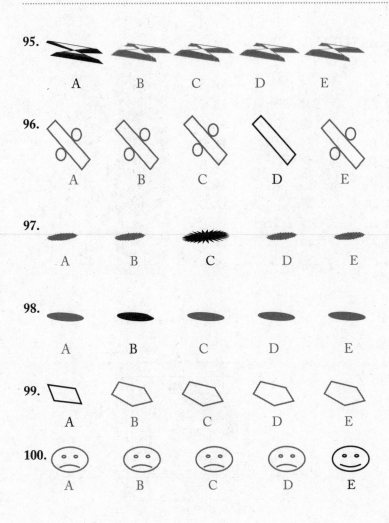

95. A   B   C   D   E

96. A   B   C   D   E

97. A   B   C   D   E

98. A   B   C   D   E

99. A   B   C   D   E

100. A   B   C   D   E

Subtest 2: Hidden Figures (HF)

1. A	**11.** C	**21.** E	**31.** E	**41.** D
2. E	**12.** A	**22.** B	**32.** C	**42.** E
3. D	**13.** D	**23.** D	**33.** A	**43.** B
4. C	**14.** B	**24.** A	**34.** D	**44.** A
5. B	**15.** E	**25.** C	**35.** B	**45.** C
6. D	**16.** B	**26.** C	**36.** A	**46.** B
7. C	**17.** D	**27.** A	**37.** D	**47.** E
8. A	**18.** E	**28.** B	**38.** E	**48.** C
9. B	**19.** A	**29.** E	**39.** C	**49.** D
10. E	**20.** C	**30.** D	**40.** B	**50.** A

1. **The correct answer is A.**

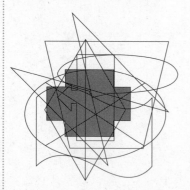

3. **The correct answer is D.**

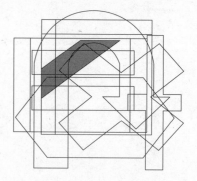

2. **The correct answer is E.**

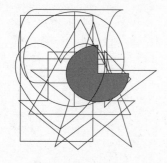

4. **The correct answer is C.**

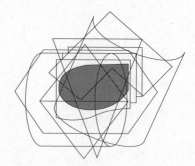

5. **The correct answer is B.**

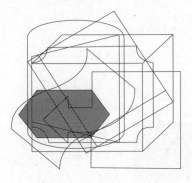

6. **The correct answer is D.**

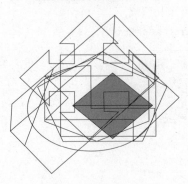

7. **The correct answer is C.**

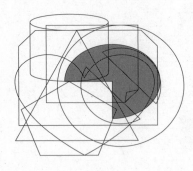

8. **The correct answer is A.**

9. **The correct answer is B.**

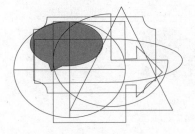

10. **The correct answer is E.**

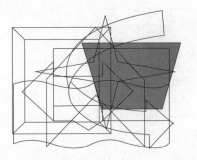

11. **The correct answer is C.**

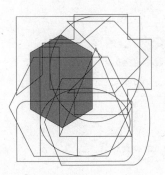

12. **The correct answer is A.**

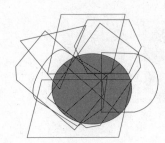

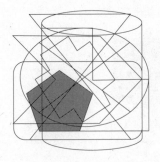

answers practice test

13. The correct answer is D.

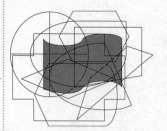

14. The correct answer is B.

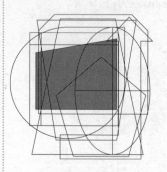

15. The correct answer is E.

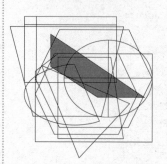

16. The correct answer is B.

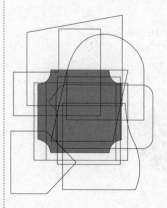

17. The correct answer is D.

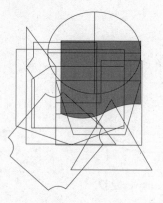

18. The correct answer is E.

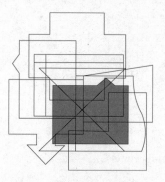

19. The correct answer is A.

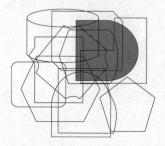

20. The correct answer is C.

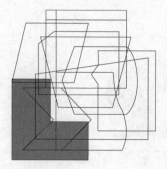

21. The correct answer is E.

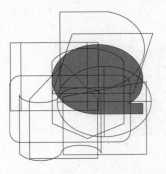

22. The correct answer is B.

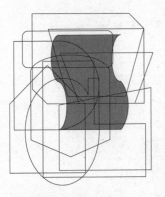

23. The correct answer is D.

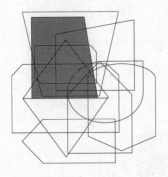

24. The correct answer is A.

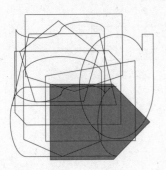

25. The correct answer is C.

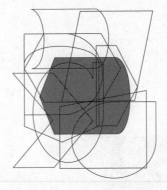

26. The correct answer is C.

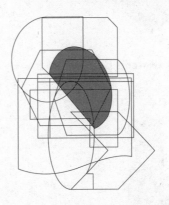

27. The correct answer is A.

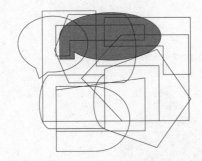

answers practice test

28. The correct answer is B.

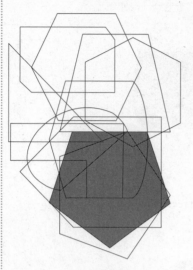

29. The correct answer is E.

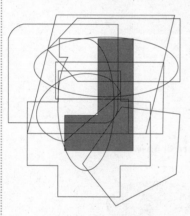

30. The correct answer is D.

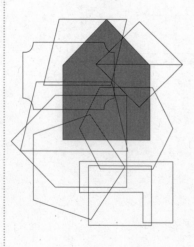

31. The correct answer is E.

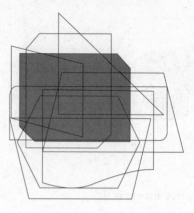

32. The correct answer is C.

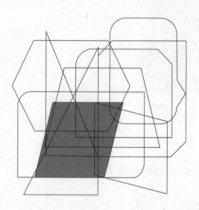

33. The correct answer is A.

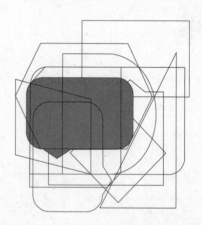

34. The correct answer is D.

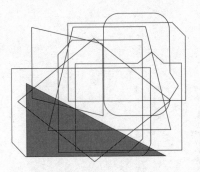

35. The correct answer is B.

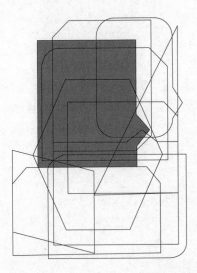

36. The correct answer is A.

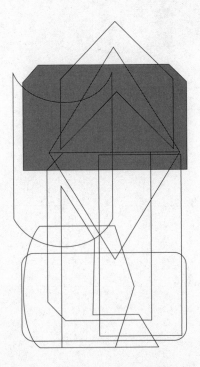

37. The correct answer is D.

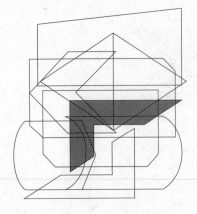

38. The correct answer is E.

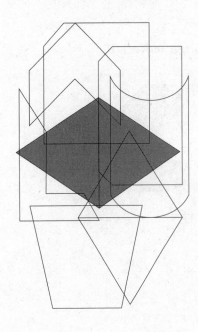

answers practice test

39. The correct answer is C.

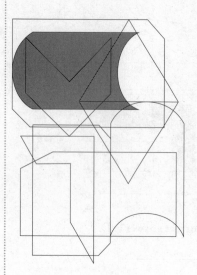

40. The correct answer is B.

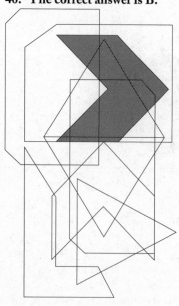

41. The correct answer is D.

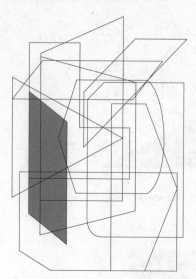

42. The correct answer is E.

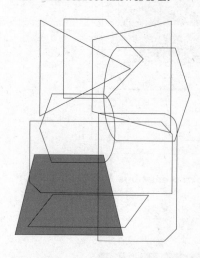

43. The correct answer is B.

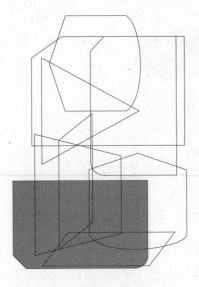

44. The correct answer is A.

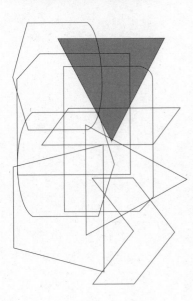

45. The correct answer is C.

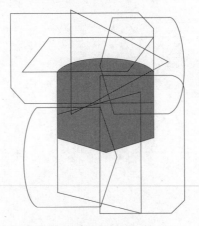

46. The correct answer is B.

47. The correct answer is E.

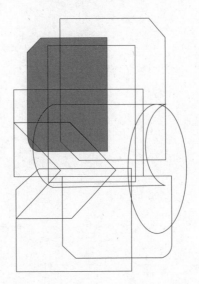

48. The correct answer is C.

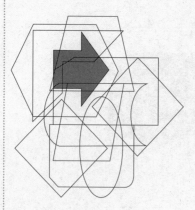

50. The correct answer is A.

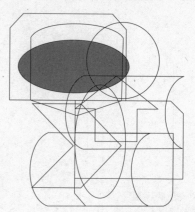

49. The correct answer is D.

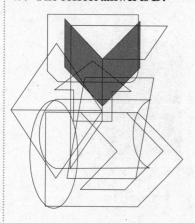

Subtest 3: Army Aviation Info Test (AAIT)

1. D	9. B	17. A	25. B	33. E
2. C	10. D	18. B	26. B	34. A
3. D	11. A	19. A	27. E	35. E
4. E	12. E	20. B	28. E	36. A
5. E	13. A	21. E	29. B	37. E
6. B	14. D	22. C	30. A	38. C
7. B	15. B	23. E	31. C	39. E
8. E	16. E	24. C	32. E	40. A

1. **The correct answer is D.** The color combination of green, yellow, and white flashed by beacons indicates a lighted heliport.

2. **The correct answer is C.** The auxiliary or tail rotor is the anti-torque rotor that produces thrust in the direction opposite to the torque reaction developed by the main rotor.

3. **The correct answer is D.** The entire helicopter has a tendency to move in the direction of tail rotor thrust when hovering. This movement is generally referred to as translating tendency or drift.

4. **The correct answer is E.** The upward bending of the rotor blades caused by the combined forces of lift and centrifugal force is called coning.

5. **The correct answer is E.** The exact location and length of the CG range is specified for each helicopter, but it usually extends a short distance fore and aft of the main rotor mast.

6. **The correct answer is B.** Dissymmetry of lift is created by horizontal flight or by wind during hovering flight. It is the difference in lift (unequal lift) across the rotor disc resulting from the difference in the velocity of air over the advancing blade half of the disc area and retreating blade half of the disc area.

7. **The correct answer is B.** Ground resonance may develop when a series of shocks causes the rotor head to become unbalanced. When one landing gear of the helicopter strikes the surface first, a shock is transmitted through the fuselage to the rotor. When one of the other landing gears strikes, the unbalance can be aggravated and become even greater. This establishes a resonance, which sets up a pendulum-like oscillation of the fuselage—a severe wobbling or shaking.

8. **The correct answer is E.** Rapid deceleration or quick stop is initiated by applying aft cyclic to reduce forward speed and lowering the collective pitch to counteract climbing.

9. **The correct answer is B.** For slope takeoff, first obtain takeoff RPM and move the cyclic stick so that the rotor rotation is parallel to the true horizon rather than the slope. Apply up-collective pitch and apply pedal to maintain heading. As the downslope skid rises and the helicopter approaches a level altitude, move the cyclic stick back to the neutral position and take the helicopter straight up to a hover before moving away from the slope. The tail should not be turned upslope because of the danger of the tail rotor striking the surface.

10. **The correct answer is D.** The helicopter should be landed on a cross-slope rather than on either an upslope or downslope. As the upslope skid touches the ground, the pilot should apply the cyclic stick in the direction of the slope. This will hold the skid against the slope while the downslope skid continues to be let down with the collective pitch.

11. **The correct answer is A.** Standard conditions at sea level are Atmospheric pressure: 29.92 inHg (inches of mercury) and Temperature: 59°F (15°C).

12. **The correct answer is E.** A running take-off is used when conditions of load and/or density altitude prevent a sustained hover at normal hovering altitude. It is often referred to as a high-altitude takeoff. A running takeoff may be accomplished safely only if surface area of sufficient length and smoothness is available and if no barriers exist in the flight-path to interfere with a shallow climb.

13. **The correct answer is A.** Foot pedals in the cockpit permit the pilot to increase or decrease tail-rotor thrust as needed to neutralize torque effect.

14. **The correct answer is D.** With a single main rotor rotating in a counterclockwise direction, the advancing blade will be in the right half of the rotor disc during forward flight.

15. **The correct answer is B.** The collective pitch control lever changes the pitch angle of the main rotor blades simultaneously and equally.

16. **The correct answer is E.** High altitude, high temperature, and high moisture content contribute to a high density altitude condition that lessens helicopter performance.

17. **The correct answer is A.** The most favorable conditions for helicopter performance are the combination of a low-density altitude, light gross weight, and moderate-to-strong winds. The most adverse conditions are the combination of a high-density altitude, heavy gross weight, and calm or no wind.

18. **The correct answer is B.** The acute angle between the chord line of an airfoil and the relative wind is called the angle of attack.

19. **The correct answer is A.** The collective pitch controls starting, stopping, and rate of speed. Pedals are used to maintain heading, and the cyclic is used to maintain ground track.

20. **The correct answer is B.** True airspeed may be roughly computed by adding to the indicated airspeed, 2 percent of the indicated airspeed for each 1,000 feet of altitude above sea level.

21. **The correct answer is E.** Blade rotation induces relative wind. Air molecules travel the same distance in the same amount of time above and below an airfoil (blade). As a result, the distance between the molecules is greater as they travel a greater distance across the curved upper part of the blade relative to the flat bottom part. The spaced molecules create a low pressure area above the airfoil, hence lift.

22. **The correct answer is C.** Increases in blade AOA moves the negative pressure area (center of pressure or CP) above the airfoil forward, decreasing lift and increasing drag.

23. **The correct answer is E.** Two good aviation axioms are: "Going from A high to A low, look out below" and "From hot to cold, look out below." Increases in temperature and/or pressure increase true altitude.

24. **The correct answer is C.** Each 00.01 = 10 feet, each 00.10 = 100 feet, and each 01.00 = 1,000 feet.

25. **The correct answer is B.** The proximity of the surface artificially increases airfoil performance with a lack of "spilt" non-performing air around the wing. The area of ground effect is approximately one rotor diameter distance above the surface.

26. **The correct answer is B.** Without controlling for wind, the four aerodynamic components align vertically with lift and thrust opposite drag and weight.

27. **The correct answer is E.** Bernoulli's Principle deals with fluid pressure and velocity. This is the basis of lift described in question 21.

28. **The correct answer is E.** Expect at least one terminology question. Be familiar with the options in this question. CP is also described in question 22.

29. **The correct answer is B.** The cyclic pitch control changes the rotational pitch of rotor blades, allowing a helicopter to fly forward, backward, left, and right. The collective pitch control (choice A) enables a helicopter to climb and descend. The corrrelator and governor (choice C) make adjustments to keep the rotor and engine rpm constant. The throttle (choice D) controls the power of the engine. Anti-torque pedals (choice E), also called the tail rotor control, control the direction in which the nose of the helicopter points.

30. **The correct answer is A.** Foot pedals are used to move the aircraft about the vertical axis. The cyclic controls movement about both the longitudinal and lateral axes (choices B and C) by changing the pitch angle of the main rotor disk (choice E). The collective pitch control changes the pitch angle of the main rotor blades (choice D). Know all flight controls relative to aerodynamic forces.

31. **The correct answer is C.** A blocked static system will still give you ASI indications but they will be off. Trapped static pressure, like your inner ear, will expand the diaphragm upon climbs and contract on descents and will create anticipated inaccuracies on the ASI. Also note that the altimeter and VSI will freeze at the blocked altitude. Also understand clogged pitot tubes and pitot drain tube indications. As professional aviators, identifying a problem and anticipating the effect is a must.

32. **The correct answer is E.** The inner 25 percent of blade region during a forward autorotation is referred to as the stall region. Understand all aspects of the autorotation and how to do them. Expect one question on emergencies.

33. **The correct answer is E.** Know all weight balance terminology and how to calculate them. Take into account lateral balance considerations. You will need to master complex CG situations later in flight school so you might as well master the basics now at zero ground speed. Expect one CG question on the SIFT.

34. **The correct answer is A.** Expect one question on night operations. Know the altitudes associated with the low level, contour, and NOE.

35. **The correct answer is E.** Low-reflective objects, including suspension wires and power lines, are very difficult to see using NVGs. As in daytime, it is important to anticipate the location of all those massive suspension lines about charted towers as well as where to expect power lines.

36. **The correct answer is A.** A Fenestron is an anti-torque rotor that uses forced air through slots and rotating nozzle. This type of rotor is used to protect the rotor from objects.

37. **The correct answer is E.** Also know icing conditions as well as temperature to dew point spread in freezing temperatures.

38. **The correct answer is C.** Sectional Aeronautical Charts use a 1:500,000 scale. You should be familiar with all low-altitude VFR and IFR type charts. Also, know the symbols on each type of chart.

39. **The correct answer is E.** Cyclic pitch increases one blade's AOA, while decreasing another's. Acting the same as the properties of a gyro, the imbalance occurs 90 degrees from the direction where the force is applied (the side of the orbital plan that pivots in the direction of the cyclic). Moving forward places the plane of the imbalance at your three o'clock for the forward moving blade and nine o'clock for the aft moving blade. Maximum upward defection is at your six o'clock, and maximum downward deflection is at your 12 o'clock. Gyroscopic precision allows you to move forward, aft, and laterally.

40. **The correct answer is A.** To initiate a left roll in a fixed wing aircraft, the pilot moves the left aileron down and the right aileron up The Army does have fixed wing aircraft, to include unmanned systems. Expect one question on fixed wing flight. Reference the equivalent Air Force and Navy/Marine/Coast Guard sections.

Subtest 4: Spatial Apperception Test (SAT)

1. C	**6.** E	**11.** A	**16.** C	**21.** A
2. A	**7.** E	**12.** E	**17.** D	**22.** D
3. B	**8.** B	**13.** C	**18.** A	**23.** C
4. C	**9.** D	**14.** B	**19.** E	**24.** A
5. D	**10.** B	**15.** A	**20.** B	**25.** B

1. **The correct answer is C.** Straight-and-level; flying up the coastline.

2. **The correct answer is A.** Diving; no bank; flying out to sea.

3. **The correct answer is B.** Climbing; no bank; flying out to sea.

4. **The correct answer is C.** Climbing and banking right; flying out to sea.

5. **The correct answer is D.** Level flight; left bank; flying out to sea.

6. **The correct answer is E.** Straight-and-level; flying down the coastline.

7. **The correct answer is E.** Straight-and-level; heading 45° left of coastline.

8. **The correct answer is B.** Diving; banking left; flying out to sea.

9. **The correct answer is D.** Level flight; right bank; flying out to sea.

10. **The correct answer is B.** Straight-and-level; heading 45° right of coastline.

11. **The correct answer is A.** Climbing; no bank; flying out to sea.

12. **The correct answer is E.** Climbing; no bank; flying down the coastline.

13. **The correct answer is C.** Diving; no bank; flying down the coastline.

14. **The correct answer is B.** Straight-and-level; flying out to sea.

15. **The correct answer is A.** Level flight; right bank; flying up the coastline.

16. **The correct answer is C.** Climbing and banking left; flying out to sea.

17. **The correct answer is D.** Diving and banking right; flying out to sea.

18. **The correct answer is A.** Level flight; right bank; flying up the coastline.

19. **The correct answer is E.** Climbing and banking left; flying out to sea.

20. **The correct answer is B.** Level flight; right bank; flying down the coastline.

21. **The correct answer is A.** Climbing; no bank; flying up the coastline.

22. **The correct answer is D.** Diving; no bank; flying out to sea.

23. **The correct answer is C.** Straight-and-level; flying up the coastline.

24. **The correct answer is A.** Climbing and banking right; flying out to sea.

25. **The correct answer is B.** Level flight; left bank; flying down the coastline.

Subtest 5: Reading Comprehension Test (RCT)

1. B	5. E	9. B	13. A	17. C
2. D	6. B	10. C	14. C	18. D
3. A	7. A	11. D	15. E	19. E
4. C	8. D	12. B	16. B	20. A

1. **The correct answer is B.** It can be inferred by the quote that General Taylor believes that professional competence is a careful balance of education, experience, and self-assurance. Choices A and C are incorrect because they promote negative character traits (ego, arrogance, and outward superiority). Choice D is incorrect because education, training, and rank alone are not indicators of professional competence. Choice E is incorrect because knowledge and pride in one's assignment are not sole indicators of competence.

2. **The correct answer is D.** The U.S. Air Force operates and maintains the GPS satellite network. Choice A is incorrect because details about receiver requirements is not addressed in the passage. GPS was designed for military applications originally and later evolved for civilian applications, so choice B is incorrect. The passage states that there is no limit to the users the system can support, so choice C is incorrect. The U.S. Air Force has no authority over civilian applications; it is responsible only for maintaining and operating the satellite constellation, so Choice E is incorrect.

3. **The correct answer is A.** The concern is that another platform will not perform as well for CAS missions as the A-10. Although the passage mentions the Air Force budget, it does not specify how it should directly be spent and who makes the determination, so choices B, D, and E are incorrect. The passage does not indicate the "maximization" of CAS functionality for any new aircraft or platform, only that the capability should be retained, so choice C is incorrect.

4. **The correct answer is C.** The passage mentions the airlines' success and safety when carrying the mail in comparison to that of both the U.S. Post Office and Army Air Corps, so it can be inferred that the author would feel the airlines were more qualified for the task. Choices A and B are incorrect because the passage discusses only accidents, not the qualifications, training, or competence of Army and Postal Service aviators. Choice D is incorrect because the author makes no statement as to whether the Army or Post Office should have initiated or continued airmail service operations. The passage mentions accusations of corruption as a direct link to the deaths of Army Air Corps pilots; such a link cannot be inferred, so choice E is incorrect.

5. **The correct answer is E.** Choice A is incorrect because there is no comparison made between the U.S. and European Naval aviation capabilities. Choice B is incorrect because there is no information provided that the Wrights encouraged competition; in fact, they discouraged it through patent litigation. There is no data provided about the Wrights' or Curtiss' specific contract awards and values to compare to any other manufacturer, so choices C and D are incorrect.

6. **The correct answer is B.** Choice A is incorrect because the Outer Space Treaty, not the Limited Test Ban Treaty, limits weapons placement and military bases in space. Choice C is incorrect because the Limited Test Ban Treaty also bans nuclear weapons testing in space. Choice D is incorrect because the passage highlights a ground test that damaged power and communications lines and a power station. The passage indicates that multiple countries beyond the U.S. and Soviet Union agreed to the Limited Test Ban Treaty, so choice E is incorrect.

7. **The correct answer is A.** The passage is clear in that veterans are those that serve the armed forces. Choice B is incorrect because it indicates that only conscripted or drafted troops and those who serve during war time are veterans. Choice C is incorrect because it indicates that only active duty service members, regardless of the discharge type (honorable, general, dishonorable), are veterans. Choice D is incorrect because it indicates that only those who serve in combat are veterans. Choice E is incorrect because it indicates that only those who serve in certain specific roles are veterans.

8. **The correct answer is D.** Choice A is incorrect because the passage does not definitely state that privatization can never be effective or successful. The author does not argue to transform current private healthcare systems to the Medicare model, so choice B is incorrect. Choice C is incorrect because the passage does not state that all services and products provided by the government are more expensive, and the Medicare example contradicts this statement. The passage does not specify that privatization is the sole means to reduce government spending and overall size; this cannot be inferred, so choice E is incorrect.

9. **The correct answer is B.** Choice A is incorrect because Gen LeMay specifically focused on modifying formations with the sole purpose of providing better defensive capabilities. Choice C is incorrect because the passage does not specify that the bombing campaigns were not at all effective. Choice D is incorrect because the passage indicates that the modified formations exploited the defensive capabilities of the bomber guns. Choice E is incorrect because the safety of the aircrews should have made for some debate in the decision to pursue a daylight bombing strategy.

10. **The correct answer is C.** Choice A is incorrect because BGen Mitchell was not court martialed for his vision, but his criticism of senior leadership. Choice B is incorrect because even if senior military leaders had heeded Mitchell's warnings, there is no guarantee that World War II could have been prevented. Choice D is incorrect because the author makes no judgment as to whether Mitchell's court martial was just or appropriate. Choice E is incorrect because Mitchell is known as the "Father of the United States Air Force"; therefore, his efforts have not gone unnoticed.

11. **The correct answer is D.** The passage states that 13 other women passed the astronaut testing in the 1960s, so choice A is incorrect. Two Soviet female cosmonauts flew to space prior to Dr. Ride, so choice B is incorrect. Examples are provided regarding the roles played by women in the space program prior to Dr. Ride, so choices C and E are incorrect.

12. **The correct answer is B.** The passage states that the government is investing only moderately in these development efforts, so choice A is incorrect. Choices C and D are incorrect because new investment and development efforts have been made since the retirement of the Space Shuttle program. The passage states that IT entrepreneurs have achieved success in the space industry, so choice E is incorrect.

13. **The correct answer is A.** The author does not specify that the Internet should be controlled in any manner, so choice B is incorrect. Choice C is incorrect because the author does not state that all information on the Internet is inaccurate or unreliable. The author has not made any statements comparing inaccurate information to the value of the Internet as a tool for commerce, so choice D is incorrect. Choice E is incorrect because the passage clearly indicates that several studies have been conducted that refute the Wakefield study and its conclusion that vaccines cause autism.

14. **The correct answer is C.** Choice A is incorrect because the passage makes no reference to energy production. The passage is referring to the merging of information, not the systems themselves, so choice B is incorrect. Choice D is incorrect because the passage is not referring to automating decision-making, but rather the automation of some aspects of information processing in advance of decision-making. The passage is not referring to merging emergency management organizations or functions, but rather the automation of some aspects of information processing in advance of responses, so choice E is incorrect.

answers practice test

15. **The correct answer is E.** Choices A and B are incorrect; the passage is not promoting the employment of techniques used on the *CSI* television show or the use of virtual reality to enhance the television *CSI* production. Choices C and D are incorrect because the passage clearly specifies the use of virtual reality to enhance, not replace, forensic analysis and court room testimony.

16. **The correct answer is B.** Choice A is incorrect because the passage does not indicate that patients are unaware of the importance of medical history data. The passage indicates that patients might have difficulty recalling and relying information when injured or ill, not during routine treatment appointments, so choice C is incorrect. Choice D is incorrect because the passage does not indicate that physicians do not seek the medical history data from patients. Choice E is incorrect because the quote from the Surgeon General in direct contrast with the statement.

17. **The correct answer is C.** Choices A, B, and E are incorrect because the passage does not state that network visualization tools are ineffective for either data analysis or decision making. Choice D is incorrect because the passage does not specify that no additional visualization tools should be developed until research is conducted to determine effectiveness.

18. **The correct answer is D.** Choices A, B, and C are incorrect because all of the means of data collection involve some level of covert activity, which the passage specifies is "rare" in industrial intelligence. Choice E is incorrect because the passage does not specify the gathering or use of data directly related to organization executives.

19. **The correct answer is E.** Choices A and B are incorrect as the focus of the passage is on the OSS and CIA. Choice C is incorrect because the focus of the paper is not solely on President Truman's decisions related to intelligence organizations and capabilities. Choice D is incorrect because the passage does not specify the effectiveness of the intelligence organizations during World War II or the Cold War.

20. **The correct answer is A.** Choices B and C are incorrect because the passage clearly indicates that management challenges have evolved in the Information Age. Choice D is incorrect because the passage specifies that the study of management is evolving, not stagnant. The passage does not specify a need for a new sub-discipline of management study, so choice E is incorrect.

Subtest 6: Math Skills Test (MST)

1. D	**5.** D	**9.** C	**13.** B	**17.** E
2. E	**6.** E	**10.** E	**14.** C	**18.** A
3. C	**7.** B	**11.** D	**15.** A	**19.** E
4. B	**8.** A	**12.** B	**16.** D	**20.** B

1. **The correct answer is D.** Use substitution to solve for x:

$$x^2 + 3(-3) - 1 = 15$$
$$x^2 - 9 - 1 = 15$$
$$x^2 - 10 = 15$$
$$x^2 = 15 + 10$$
$$x^2 = 25$$
$$x = \sqrt{25}$$
$$x = 5$$

2. **The correct answer is E.** The product is the result of the multiplication of $(5x - 3)$ and $(x + 4)$:

$$(5x - 3)(x + 4) =$$
$$5x^2 + 20x - 3x - 12 =$$
$$5x^2 + 17x - 12$$

3. **The correct answer is C.** Use the formula for the area of a rectangle (xy = area) to determine the unknown side of the new fenced-in play space for Molly: $x(42) = 2,100$; $x = \frac{2,100}{42}$; $x = 50$. Use the formula for the perimeter of a rectangle ($2x + 2y$ = perimeter) to determine the amount of fencing required: $2(42) + 2(50) = 84 + 100 = 184$ ft.

4. **The correct answer is B.** This question is asking you to apply your knowledge of right triangles to determine the length of the side and then calculate the shaded area of the lean-to (see the figures below for a visualization of the problem). First, use the Pythagorean theorem ($x^2 + y^2 = z^2$) to solve for the length for the missing side of the triangle, x:

$$x^2 + (12)^2 = (20)^2$$
$$x^2 + 144 = 400$$
$$x^2 = 400 - 144$$
$$x^2 = 256$$
$$x^2 = \sqrt{256}$$
$$x^2 = 16$$

Use the formula for the area of a rectangle ($xy = $ area) to determine the shaded area:

$16 \times 20 = 320$ ft.^{2}.

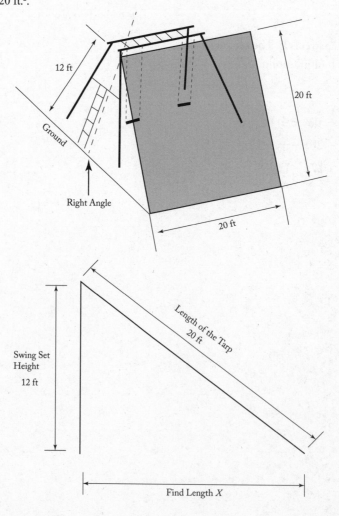

Find the Shaded Area Under the Tarp

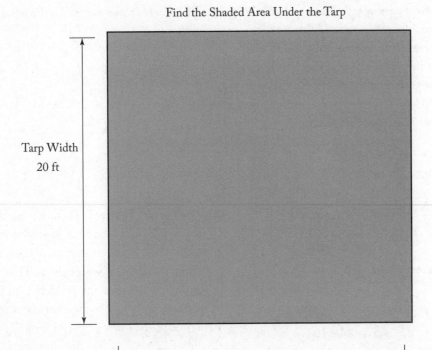

Tarp Width
20 ft

Length *x*

5. **The correct answer is D.** This question is a bit of a trick in that if you do not read the entire question and try to start solving the problem, you will likely do more work than required. The question is asking for the total fuel used, not the average speed over the course of the trip. Speed and time are distractors in this question. You need to focus only on the distance traveled and the miles per gallon of the vehicle. Add the distance and divide by the miles per gallon: (45 miles + 62 miles + 59 miles + 64 miles) ÷ (22 miles/gallon) = 230 miles ÷ (22 miles/ gallon) = 10.5 gallons (rounded).

6. **The correct answer is E.** This problem is asking for the calculation of an average, in this case, speed. Add the four speeds and divide by the time to obtain the average: (63 mph + 68 mph + 64 mph + 35 mph) ÷ (3.5 hours) = 230 mph ÷ 3.5 hours = 65.7 mph.

7. **The correct answer is B.** This problem is a simple multiplication and addition exercise. The aircraft are traveling away from each other at the same time at different speeds. If t represents time to achieve the distance of 3,500 miles, then solve the following equation: $775t + 625t = 3,500$ miles.

$$775t + 625t = 3,500 \text{ miles}$$
$$1,400t = 3,500$$
$$t = \frac{3,500}{1,400}$$
$$t = 2.5 \text{ hours, or } 2.30 \text{ hours}$$

8. **The correct answer is A.** Solve for x:

$$x^2 + 5x - 10 = 14$$
$$x^2 + 5x = 14 + 10$$
$$x^2 + 5x = 24$$
$$x(x + 5) = 24$$

The only possible answer among the choices is $x = 3$.

9. **The correct answer is C.** Complementary angles must equal 90 degrees. Subtract the known 50 degrees from 90 to obtain the answer of 40 degrees.

10. **The correct answer is E.** To solve this problem, find the surface area of the four walls of the room and subtract the two doors and window. The room is 12 feet × 10 feet × 9 feet tall and there are two doors, each 8 feet × 3 feet, and a window, 3 feet × 4 feet. Solve for the surface area of the walls and subtract the unpainted surfaces: $2(12 \times 9) + 2(10 \times 9) - 2(8 \times 3) - (3 \times 4) = 2(108) + 2(90) - 2(24) - 12 = 216 + 180 - 48 - 12 = 336$ ft.^{2}.

11. **The correct answer is D.** Expand to multiply:

$$\left(\sqrt{5} - \sqrt{3}\right)\left(\sqrt{5} - \sqrt{3}\right)$$
$$= \left(\sqrt{5}\right)^2 - \sqrt{5}\sqrt{3} - \sqrt{3}\sqrt{5} + \left(\sqrt{3}\right)^2$$
$$= 5 - 2\sqrt{3}\sqrt{5} + 3$$
$$= 8 - 2\sqrt{3}\sqrt{5}$$
$$= 8 - 2\sqrt{15}$$

12. **The correct answer is B.** The total class size is 375, and a number of students are taking shop, home economics, or both, and some students are taking neither. The fastest method to solve the problem is to first add the percentages of the students enrolled in one or the other course or both: 28% + 36% + 12% = 76%. Multiply the remaining percentage of the student population, 100%–76% = 24%, by the total number of students to get the answer: 0.24(3725) = 90. The alternative is far more time consuming (and not recommended), but it gets the same result. Multiply each group percentage by 375 and subtract the results from the total to reach the same answer: $375 - 0.28(375) - 0.36(375) - 0.12(375) = 375 - 105 - 135 - 45 = 90$.

13. **The correct answer is B.** At first glance, this problem might seem a bit complicated. It is actually a fraction of the circle area problem. Find the area of a circle with a radius of 15 km using the equation πr^2: total area = 3.14(15^2); total area = 3.14(225); total area = 706.5 km^2. The radius of the circle that can be viewed by the radar is 40 degrees, which is one ninth of the total 360 degrees. Divide the total area by 9 to get the area of the radar detection field: $706.5 \div 9 = 78.5$ km^2.

14. **The correct answer is C.** Dave cannot exceed his budget of $1,000 for the telescope. So he needs the price to be discounted to a point at which the tax is also included in the final price. Set up the equation in this manner: $1,000 = 1.05($1,300x). The x signifies the discount Dave needs, and the 1.05 is the 100 percent of the total cost of the telescope plus the 5 percent sales tax. As such:

$$\$1,000 = \$1,365x$$
$$x = \frac{1,000}{1,365}$$
$$x = 0.73, \text{ or } 73\%$$

If you multiply $1,300 by 0.73, the sales price would be $949. With the additional $47.45, the total price for Dave is $996.45, which comes in right under budget.

15. **The correct answer is A.** For this problem, you must solve for the circumference of the circle ($2\pi r$) and account for the radius twice, since the aircraft must fly out to the edge of the circle to start its orbit and return after completing the orbit once. Do not consider the angle of climb to altitude in the calculation. As such, the equation to obtain the solution should be 600 miles = $2r + 2\pi r$. Calculate and round:

$$600 \text{ miles} = 2r + 2(3.14r)$$
$$600 = 2r + 6.28r$$
$$600 = 8.28r$$
$$r = \frac{600}{8.28}$$
$$r = 72 \text{ miles}$$

16. **The correct answer is D.** For a 10-sided die, there are 10 possible outcomes for each roll. Because there are five odd numbers on the die, there is a 5-in-10 chance that the outcome will be an odd number.

17. **The correct answer is E.** Solve the proportion for x in the following manner:

$$5(x + 5) = 4(x + 7)$$
$$5x + 25 = 4x + 28$$
$$5x - 4x = 28 - 25$$
$$x = 3$$

18. **The correct answer is A.** Since the variables are all nonzero and the exponents are outside of the parentheses, indicating that it applies to all of the values within, the solution to this problem is to add the exponents together. No other operations are required.

19. **The correct answer is E.** This question is a bit tricky, as you must carefully note the exponents. First, subtract $2x^3$ from $5x^3$ to get $3x^3$. Next, subtract $2x^2$ from $4x^2$ to get $2x^2$. Then, add $3x$ to $7x$ to get $10x$. The answer is then $3x^3 + 2x^2 + 10x$.

20. **The correct answer is B.** To simplify the equation, start by dividing the numerator by 2 to get $\frac{(4x^9 - 3x^5 + 5x^4)}{x^3}$. Next divide the numerator by x^2, or subtract 2 from each exponent to get $\frac{(4x^7 - 3x^3 + 5x^2)}{x}$.

Subtest 7: Mechanical Comprehension Test (MCT)

1. B	**5.** B	**9.** A	**13.** B	**17.** A
2. A	**6.** B	**10.** A	**14.** A	**18.** A
3. A	**7.** B	**11.** B	**15.** B	**19.** B
4. B	**8.** A	**12.** A	**16.** B	**20.** A

1. **The correct answer is B.** One complete revolution will raise the weight 1 foot or 12 inches.

2. **The correct answer is A.** The distortion of the cam causes the valve to rise when contact is made. The amount of this distortion is the length Y.

3. **The correct answer is A.** The slowest points for lever AB are 2 and 4, where the direction reverses and the velocity momentarily becomes zero. The midpoint, 1 or 3, represents the maximum speed, as it is halfway between these minimum points.

4. **The correct answer is B.** The function of A and B in the crankshaft is to counterbalance the weight for smooth piston motion.

5. **The correct answer is B.** The centrifugal force acts to pull the balls outward. Since the two balls are connected to a yolk around the center bar, this outward motion pulls the balls upward.

6. **The correct answer is B.** The figure shown is a bimetallic strip that works like the wire in a thermostat. High temperatures will cause the metals to heat unevenly. The rivets will keep the strips together, so the only thing that they can do is bend.

7. **The correct answer is B.** Wheel P has 16 teeth; wheel M has 12 teeth. When wheel M makes a full turn, wheel P will still have 4 more teeth to turn. So wheel P is slower and will take more time to turn.

8. **The correct answer is A.** Pressure is defined as $\frac{\text{Force}}{\text{Area}}$. For a given force, 20 lbs., the smaller the area, the greater the pressure produced. The smallest area is at position A, requiring the least force to lift the weight.

9. **The correct answer is A.** Because the load is closer to upright A, it supports more of the load. If the load were directly over A, all of the weight would be supported by A; then upright B could be removed completely.

10. **The correct answer is A.** The piston is now in part of the compression stroke; $\frac{1}{4}$ turn will move it to full compression; $\frac{1}{2}$ more turn will move it to the end of the power stroke. Adding $\frac{1}{4} + \frac{1}{2} = \frac{3}{4}$ turn.

11. **The correct answer is B.** The downward pull of the 100-lb. weight being hoisted plus the 50-lb. effort = 150 lbs.

12. **The correct answer is A.** Imagine the driven wheel as a record. For one rotation of the record, point Y travels much farther than point X. It takes more turns of the driver wheel to turn point Y one complete revolution.

13. **The correct answer is B.** The ball will move up if the arm holding it is pulled up. This will happen when the nut is tightened.

14. **The correct answer is A.** A single fixed pulley is actually a first-class lever with equal arms. The mechanical advantage, neglecting friction, is 1.

15. **The correct answer is B.** Gear 1 turns clockwise; gear 2 turns counterclockwise; gears 3 and 4 turn clockwise.

16. **The correct answer is B.** The formula for circumference of a wheel is $C = 2\pi r$. The wheel radius of the bike in front is larger. One revolution of the larger wheel will cover a greater linear distance along the road in a given period of time.

17. **The correct answer is A.** The water is filling up in the tank at a rate of 120 gallons per hour, or 2 gallons per minute; $\frac{120}{60} = 2$. The tank is also emptying at a rate of 1 gallon per minute. The net flow is increasing by 1 gallon per minute, since

$2\frac{\text{gallons}}{\text{minute}} \text{ input} - 1\frac{\text{gallons}}{\text{minute}} \text{ output} = 1\frac{\text{gallons}}{\text{minute}} \text{ increase.}$

Note: The easiest way to find the answer is to change all measurements to gallons per minute.

18. **The correct answer is A.** Once every second equals 60 times a minute. With 10 projection rods on the wheel, the wheel must rotate at 6 rpm to make 60 rod contacts per minute.

19. **The correct answer is B.** The raft will move in the opposite direction. Let x = theoretical distance moved.

$$10 \times 150 = x \times 500$$
$$500x = 1,500$$
$$x = \frac{1,500}{500} = 3 \text{ feet}$$

20. **The correct answer is A.** The mechanical advantage is calculated by the number of strands supporting the weight. A has 3 strands, B has 2.

SUMMING IT UP

- The Army Selection Instrument for Flight Training (SIFT) is the exam used to determine if a candidate qualifies for the Army's Aviation Program.

- The SIFT is divided into the following seven subtests:

    1. Simple Drawings: 100 questions, 2 minutes

    2. Hidden Figures: 50 questions, 5 minutes

    3. Army Aviation Information Test: 40 questions, 30 minutes

    4. Spatial Apperception Test: 25 questions, 10 minutes

    5. Reading Comprehension Test: 20 questions, 30 minutes

    6. Math Skills Test: variable length (est. 20–40) questions, up to 40 minutes

    7. Mechanical Comprehension Test: variable length (est. 20–40) questions, up to 15 minutes

- The SIFT exam is administered on a networked computer system. The test is comprised of seven subtests, differentiated into three types: **psychometric**, **standardized**, and **adaptive**.

    o The two psychometric subtests (Simple Drawings and Hidden Drawings) measure accuracy and speed in generating a **precision score**. The precision score is a composite from your total/raw score (number of questions attempted), work rate/speed score (number attempted versus total number of questions), and a hit rate/accuracy score (number of correct responses divided by the number attempted).

    o The three subtests that use standardized raw scores (Army Aviation Information Test, Spatial Apperception Test, and Reading Comprehension Test) are knowledge-based measures. A raw score is simply the number of correct answers given versus the total number of questions on the test. Unlike performance scoring, unanswered questions will negatively impact your score.

    o The adaptive subtests (Math Skills Test and Mechanical Comprehension Test) use a question bank in which questions have been divided into categories such as easy, average, and difficult. Upon submission of your answer, the computer scores your response and the result will determine the difficulty level of the next question.

- Total testing time (including administration and breaks) is between 2 and 3 hours, depending on the length of time a candidate spends on the adaptive portions of the test.

NOTES

NOTES

NOTES

NOTES

NOTES

NOTES

NOTES

NOTES

NOTES

NOTES

NOTES

NOTES

NOTES

NOTES

NOTES

NOTES

NOTES

NOTES

NOTES

NOTES